Justice

Justice

RIGHTS AND WRONGS

Nicholas Wolterstorff

PRINCETON UNIVERSITY PRESS

PRINCETON AND OXFORD

Published by Princeton University Press, 41 William Street, Princeton, New Jersey 08540

In the United Kingdom: Princeton University Press, 3 Market Place,
Woodstock, Oxfordshire OX20 1SY

Library of Congress Cataloging-in-Publication Data

Wolterstorff, Nicholas.
Justice : rights and wrongs / Nicholas Wolterstorff.
p.   cm.
Includes bibliographical references and index.
ISBN 978-0-691-12967-9 (hardcover : alk. paper)
1. Christianity and justice. 2. Human rights—Religious
aspects—Christianity. I. Title.
BR115.J8W65 2008   241'.622—dc22   2007019574

British Library Cataloging-in-Publication Data is available

This book has been composed in Baskerville

Printed on acid-free paper. ∞

press.princeton.edu

Printed in the United States of America

5   7   9   10   8   6

CONTENTS

WHY CARE ABOUT A THEORY OF JUSTICE

I came late to thinking about justice, late and fortuitously, or perhaps providentially. It was injustice that impelled me to think about justice, not the imperatives of some theoretical scheme or the duties of some academic position. Injustice in the form of the wronged, which is the form injustice always takes. The victims confronted me; I was not looking for them. I should have noticed them much earlier. The wronged are all about us.

In September of 1976 I attended a conference at the University of Potchefstroom in South Africa. The University of Potchefstroom was then very much a white university, founded and maintained by a branch of the Afrikaners known familiarly as "Doppers." There were Afrikaner scholars present at the conference, and "black" and "colored" scholars from South Africa. There were Dutch scholars who were extremely knowledgeable about what was going on in South Africa and furious with the Afrikaners over the South African policy of apartheid. And there were North Americans like myself who had heard of apartheid but were nowhere near as well-informed as the Dutch.

At first the Afrikaners and the Dutch vented their fury at each other. But as the conference proceeded, the "blacks" and "coloreds" began to speak up, not with the rage of the Dutch but with faces and voices of suffering. They told in slow quiet tones of the many ways in which they were wronged. The Afrikaners responded by saying that it was all for the sake of the future good. Some told of the charity that they and their families had extended to blacks and coloreds: cast-off clothing given to families living in huts in the back yards, Christmas trinkets given to the children, and so forth. They charged that the strategies of resistance and the words of criticism employed by some blacks and coloreds were hurtful and not loving. And they assured their black and colored "brothers," as they called them, that if they just behaved, they would see what a generous people the Afrikaners were at heart. I saw, as never before, the good overwhelming the just, and benevolence and the appeal to love being used as instruments of oppression.

I left South Africa more changed than I knew. Gradually, I realized that I had been confronted with a call to speak up for these wronged and suffering people. At the conference I had come to know some of them, and over the years some, along with a good many others, have become dear friends of mine.

In May of 1978 I attended a conference on the west side of Chicago on Palestinian rights, organized by the Palestine Human Rights Campaign. I had never heard of the organization, I never learned why I had been invited to the conference, and not even in retrospect have I understood what it was in me that led me to attend.

The conference was even more disruptive for me than Potchefstroom had been. I knew that there were Arabs living in Palestine; what I did not know is how intensely they identified themselves as Palestinians and not just as Arabs. Those present at the conference poured out their guts in rhetoric of flaming intensity. They spoke of being driven from their homes in the '48 war, they spoke of their right of return, they spoke of the indignities daily heaped upon them; and they asked why no one heard their cry. Once again I felt that I had been confronted with a call to speak up for this wronged and suffering people, yet without forgetting for a moment all the wrongs inflicted on the Jewish people. Soon I was chairman of the Palestine Human Rights Campaign.

For almost thirty years now I have listened to the Israelis say to the Palestinians what I first heard the Afrikaners say to the blacks and coloreds. We are good people; if you just behave, we will give you most of what you are asking for. Oppressors do all they can to prevent use of the category of justice; they do all they can to cast the situation in terms of better and worse rather than justice and injustice, in terms of good behavior and bad behavior, in terms of benevolence.

I had opposed the Vietnam War, arguing that it was not a just war. Yet the war did not energize me to think about justice in the way these two episodes did. In retrospect, I understand part of why that was. In the case of Vietnam, I had not directly seen the faces or heard the voices of those who were wronged; the injustice of the war remained something of an abstraction to me. Now the faces and the voices of the victims were there before me. That made all the difference: my empathy was evoked.

In the interest of full disclosure I should perhaps explain who is the "I" that discerned injustice in the faces and the voices of the Africans and the Palestinians. I grew up in a tiny village in the farm country of southwest Minnesota, the eldest child of poor immigrant parents. Rather often I saw my parents being treated with the indignity typical of how the well-to-do treat the poor. What I now find remarkable is that my parents never for a moment indicated that they believed they somehow deserved such treatment; rather than internalizing the attitude of their demeaners, they felt bruised, hurt, helplessly angry. They maintained their self-respect, grounded, in their case, in the Calvinist version of Christianity within which they were embedded and into which I was inducted. They were precious in God's sight. All human beings are precious in God's sight. I now realize that a fertile seed bed had been prepared in me for seeing the faces and hearing the voices of victims.

This book is an attempt to speak up for the wronged of the world. I have already done so almost two and a half decades ago in my book *Until Justice and Peace Embrace*. In that book, however, I took for granted a certain account of justice and focused my attention on its application to various situations in our world; in this book, I try to articulate that account.

My description of this book as an attempt to speak up for the wronged of the world will seem preposterous to many readers; he must be talking about some other book, they will think, than this long abstract tome I have in hand. Let me explain. My discussion, like many philosophical discussions, acquired legs of its own; with a blend of fascination and dismay I followed where those legs led me. They did not lead me away from speaking up for the wronged and toward doing something else, although they did lead me into some highly abstract discussions and some probing of old history. There are many explanations of failing to see the faces and hear the voices of those who are wronged, even of those right before one. Sometimes we loathe the victims. Sometimes we are overwhelmed by the fear of what we would have to do if we genuinely saw and heard; so we block out the sight and muffle the sound. And sometimes our frameworks of conviction lead us to discount the significance of what we see and hear. We regard the one before us as a candidate for charity, should we be so inclined; or we insist that his condition is his own fault. We resist acknowledging that the presence of the other before us places a claim on us, issues to us a call to do justice. My speaking up for the wronged of the world takes the form, in this book, of doing what I can to undermine those frameworks of conviction that prevent us from acknowledging that the other comes before us bearing a claim on us, and of offering an alternative framework, one that opens us up to such acknowledgment.

Approach to the Topic

For many centuries now, philosophers and other writers on these matters have distinguished between, on the one hand, what is called *distributive* and *commutative* justice and, on the other hand, *rectifying*, or *corrective*, justice. Rectifying justice consists of the justice that becomes relevant when there have been breakdowns in distributive and commutative justice. My discussion focuses entirely on distributive and commutative justice, or as I shall call them, *primary* justice. No doubt the ideal account of justice would treat both kinds at once, both primary justice and rectifying justice. Only such a unified account can assure us that what is said about primary justice does not require revision in the light of what is needed for an adequate account of rectifying justice, and vice versa. But sufficient for the day will be explaining primary justice.

The account of primary justice that I develop is a theistic account, specifically, a *Christian* theistic account; for I am a Christian believer who holds that God and justice are intimately intertwined. I know full well that there are those who believe that talk of God should be left to theologians and that philosophers should be "methodological atheists." But I have always thought of philosophy in the way I once heard attributed to the esteemed American philosopher Wilfred Sellars: philosophy speaks of how every thing, in the most general sense of "thing," hangs together, in the most general sense of "hangs together." If one believes in God, then not to bring God into the picture, when relevant, is to defect from the philosopher's calling. It would be like a Platonist refraining from mentioning the Forms.

I am aware of the various reasons people have for thinking that philosophers, even if they believe in God, should betray no sign of that in their philosophy. Among the most prominent has been a reason that goes as follows. The calling of the philosopher is to appeal solely to reason; philosophy is an exercise in pure rationality. But belief in God is not rational. To be rational, belief in God would have to be supported by sound arguments that begin from premises that are certain for one and that, for that reason, could enjoy the consensus of the rational among us. But there are no such arguments. Hence to bring God into philosophy is to allow the intrusion of the irrational into the rational.

A good many academics and intellectuals continue to embrace this line of thought. Few philosophers any longer espouse it in public, not because arguments for God's existence have turned up that almost all philosophers find compelling, but because most philosophers no longer find the assumptions made about the rationality of belief compelling. It is not necessary, for one's belief in God to be rational, that one have sound arguments for one's belief starting from premises that are certain for one; one need not have any arguments at all. The movement of so-called Reformed epistemology, to which the present author has been a contributor, has played a prominent role in this change of mentality among philosophers.[1] The point is not that anything goes by way of reli-

---

[1] For those not acquainted with this movement, the best introduction is probably the article "Reason and Belief in God" by Alvin Plantinga, the article "Christian Experience and Christian Belief" by William P. Alston, and the article "Can Belief in God Be Rational If It Has No Foundation?" by the present writer, all in Alvin Plantinga and Nicholas Wolterstorff, eds., *Faith and Rationality: Reason and Belief in God* (Notre Dame: University of Notre Dame Press, 1983).

gious belief. The point is that rationality in belief is a far more subtle matter than it was assumed to be.

My discussion will accordingly be "Anselmian" in a certain way. Anselm opened his *Proslogion* with a prayer to God and continued in the prayer mode for the remainder of the book as he developed his theology. The first thing he asked of God is that God bestow on him a proof of His existence. Thus Anselm assumed the acceptability of engaging in a practice of reflection that presupposes the existence of God without first having proved the existence of God. My discussion differs significantly from Anselm's in that mine is not couched in the form of a prayer, and I do not, in the course of my reflections, offer a proof of God.

I think the movement of Reformed epistemology should be seen as part of a larger revolution taking place within analytic philosophy. Once upon a time, lasting until not long ago, philosophers assumed that philosophy, like religion, had to be rationally grounded in certitudes; they understood the methodology of their discipline as foundationalist. Never mind that rarely if ever did a piece of philosophy measure up to that methodological demand; that was understood to be the demand.

Seldom anymore does the analytic philosopher assume that he is obligated *qua* philosopher to ground rationally what he says in certitudes; analytic philosophy as a whole is on the way to becoming "Anselmian." (Continental philosophy remains more traditional in this regard.) The philosopher, approaching the practice of philosophy from his life in the everyday, finds himself believing many things, both large and small. Perhaps he finds himself believing in physicalism. He then regards the challenge facing him as a philosopher not to be that of discarding all those convictions unless he can rationally ground them in certitudes; the challenge facing him is that of working out the nature and implications of his physicalist convictions in various areas of thought, doing so in such a way as to cope not only with the complications that arise in his own mind but with the objections lodged against his line of thought by others. In principle these objections might prove so powerful that he gives up his physicalism. In place of the old foundationalist picture, the picture of the academic enterprise now being taken for granted by philosophers in the analytic tradition is what I call *dialogic pluralism*. The academic enterprise is a dialogue among persons of differing perspectives. The goal of the enterprise remains to achieve agreement. One does not mount the podium, declare that this is where one stands, and depart to huddle with one's fellow believers. Though agreement is not the condition of the enterprise, it remains the goal. Along the way, we do not merely accept or reject what our philosophical colleagues and predecessors say; we *appropriate* things from what they say for our own purposes. "Yes, there are some mistaken assumptions in his way of setting up the issue; but after one has made allowance for those, there remains a very interesting point." Something like that is how one philosopher engages another. This subtle practice of appropriation is fundamental to the philosophical enterprise. It is fundamental to the dialogue between theists and secularists.

STRUCTURE OF THE DISCUSSION

This book is very different from the one I set out to write. I think of justice as constituted of rights: a society is just insofar as its members enjoy the goods to which they have a right. And I think of rights as ultimately grounded in what respect for the worth of persons and human beings requires. I set out to articulate these ideas.

After I had written a bit, I offered the first chapter as the topic for discussion by a group of graduate students in philosophy, religion, and law at Yale University. The first question was asked by Andrew Dole, one of several graduate students. "Is there only one conception of justice?" Andrew asked. "Yes," I replied without hesitation. "There are different ways of understanding that conception; that's what the big arguments are about. But there is only one conception."

Over the next few days, Andrew's question began to trouble me. Eventually, I concluded that my quick answer was mistaken. There are (at least) two conceptions of primary justice in the Western intellectual tradition, struggling for dominance; I call them the conception of primary justice as inherent rights and the conception of primary justice as right order. Comments made in the literature that I had previously dismissed as confused I now saw to be rather lucid expressions of the conception of justice as right order rather than inept expressions of the conception that I favored, justice as inherent rights.

That recognition plunged me into the middle of a highly charged polemic. Those who favor the conception of justice as right order do not see their conception as simply an alternative way of thinking about justice—take your pick. They argue that the justice as inherent rights conception is of questionable parentage and nefarious in its social effects. It emerged, they say, from seventeenth-century philosophical individualism or, perhaps, before that, from fourteenth-century nominalism. I reluctantly came to the view that I had no choice but to come to grips with this narrative. Eventually, I concluded that the narrative is undoubtedly false. What began to emerge in my mind was a counter-narrative. The conception of justice as inherent rights was not born in the fourteenth or the seventeenth century; this way of thinking about justice goes back into the Hebrew and Christian Scriptures.

This, in turn, cast a different and surprising light on my systematic project. I had thought of myself as engaged in the purely systematic project of articulating an account of justice that included God in the picture. I now began to see that what I was doing was giving expression to the way of thinking about justice that we in the modern West have been bequeathed by our biblical heritage. And that posed to me the question: can that way of thinking about justice survive the erosion of theistic belief? Or better, *how much* of it can survive such erosion? I reflect a bit on this question in my final chapter.

The structure of the book will now come as no surprise. It has three main parts. In Part I, I deal with the contest of narratives. Part II is a transition from narrative to theory; without leaving narrative entirely behind, I begin the development of theory. Part III deals exclusively with theory.

The need for narrative in addition to theory, plus the fact that mine is a theistic account of justice, has forced me to transgress disciplinary boundaries in almost reckless fashion. The book as a whole is philosophical; I offer a philosophical account of justice. But in addition to philosophy of the usual sort, the reader will find theology, biblical interpretation, medieval intellectual history, late-antique intellectual history, and wisps of sociology. I did not march into these various areas out of fashionable devotion to interdisciplinary studies. I found myself dragged into them. My strategy in each case was to identify the best present-day scholars in the field who deal with the questions that concerned me and then use them as guides. I should add that I have not refrained from now and then posing questions to my guides about the direction in which they were leading me.

My discussion became so expansive that, to my regret, there was no room to discuss the relation between love and justice. I will be doing that in a separate volume, *Love and Justice*.[2]

Acknowledgments

My debts are numerous; were I to try to list the individuals who played a role in steering me away from error and confusion, I would certainly forget some. I am indebted to the members of that original discussion group at Yale, to the members of two graduate seminars at Notre Dame

---

[2] Forthcoming. Some of what I have to say on the topic can be found in my essay, "Does Forgiveness Undermine Justice," in Andrew Dole and Andrew Chignell, eds., *God and the Ethics of Belief: New Essays in Philosophy of Religion* (Cambridge: Cambridge University Press, 2005).

in which I presented primitive versions of the manuscript, to a summer seminar sponsored by the Erasmus Institute from Notre Dame in which we discussed the manuscript, to a seminar organized by Michael Perry of the Emory University Law School in which the manuscript was discussed, and to sessions of the Institute for Advanced Studies in Culture at the University of Virginia in which it was discussed.

I must thank the three readers for Princeton University Press; their comments have provoked a much better book than the one they read. And I must single out Terence Cuneo and Chris Eberle for special thanks. Both of them read the entire manuscript in various versions; Chris, especially, has been a wonderfully friendly but querulous interlocutor. The book is vastly better because of his questions. He still disagrees with a good deal of it. But his disagreements over the years have forced me into making it ever more difficult for him to find points of disagreement and ever more difficult for him to defend his disagreement when he finds such points. It is a mark of his talent—not, so I trust, my lack thereof—that he continues to be able to do both.

Justice

INTRODUCTION

WHY HOSTILITY TO JUSTICE AND RIGHTS?

Justice and rights are the most contested part of our moral vocabulary, contested not only, or even mainly, by philosophers, but within society generally. To publish a discourse on justice as rights is to plunge into a hornet's nest of controversy.

Few people oppose talk about responsibility and obligation—therapists who believe that guilt feelings are a bad thing, philosophers who see no acceptable way of accounting for obligation, that is about it. Lots of people pay little attention to their own obligations; few declare themselves opposed to talk about obligations. So too with virtue and love. Though many care little about either, few express opposition to talk about them.

Justice and rights are different. Opposition to rights-talk is common. Some of those opposed are also opposed to talking about justice; they connect the two, rights and justice. Others want to pull them apart. Justice is fine; it is talk about rights that is bad.

Why this hostility? Let us take a brief survey, starting with justice. Large swaths of American Christians believe that in the New Testament love supplanted justice—except for retributive justice. Jesus did not teach, in the second of the two commandments, that we are to treat people justly; he taught that we are to love our neighbors as ourselves. In the now-classic book, *Agape and Eros*, published in the early 1930s, Anders Nygren worked out the idea in detail. After interpreting the love ascribed to God in the New Testament, and enjoined on us with regard to our fellows, as the love of pure impartial benevolence, he declared that what we learn from Jesus' words and deeds is that where such "spontaneous love and generosity are found, the order of justice is obsolete and invalidated."[1]

This attack on justice, coming as it does from within my own religious community, is not one that I can ignore; most secular academics would be inclined to ignore it. I think that is a mistake on their part. Americans continue to be a religious people, dominantly Christian; we must expect consequences for our culture and society as a whole if many among us

---

[1] Translated by Philip S. Watson (London: SPCK, 1953), p. 90.

believe that justice is outmoded. And in any case, similar things are being said by secularists, albeit for different reasons.

In her essay, "The Need for More than Justice,"[2] Annette Baier argues that though justice may still have a place, it has to be supplemented with virtues less cold and calculating. "Care," she says, "is the new buzz-word, . . . a felt concern for the good of others and for community with them. The 'cold jealous virtue of justice' (Hume) is found to be too cold, and it is 'warmer' more communitarian virtues and social ideals that are being called in to supplement it."

Baier explains that the ethics of care is a challenge "to the individualism of the Western tradition, to the fairly entrenched belief in the possibility and desirability of each person pursuing his own good in his own way, constrained only by a minimal formal common good, namely, a working legal apparatus that enforces contracts and protects individuals from undue interference by others" (52). One of the problems with the ethics of justice, she says, is that the rules of justice, at least as understood in a liberal sense, "do little to protect the young or the dying or the starving or any of the relatively powerless against neglect, or to ensure an education that will form persons to be *capable* of conforming to an ethics of care and responsibility" (55).

Others on the contemporary scene are opposed not so much to talk about justice as to talk about rights. The opposition is for a variety of reasons. Some oppose rights-talk because they find so many rights-claims silly that they think it best to purge our vocabulary of all such talk. I agree with the diagnosis but not with the prescribed cure; many rights-claims are silly. The U.N. Declaration on Human Rights declares, in Article 24, that everybody has a right to periodic vacations with pay. Many people do not work for pay. Some, such as children and the handicapped, do not work at all; others work, but not for pay—farmers, housewives, and the like. So how could everybody have a right to a periodic vacation with pay? Claims like this give rights a bad name.[3]

Others are opposed to rights-talk for political reasons. All the great social protest movements of the twentieth century in the West employed

---

[2] In Virginia Held, ed., *Justice and Care: Essential Readings in Feminist Ethics* (Boulder, Colo.; Westview Press, 1995), p. 48. I thank Eleonore Stump for calling this essay to my attention.

[3] The most balanced and reflective discussion of the abuse of rights-talk in the American political arena that I know of is *Rights Talk: The Impoverishment of Political Discourse*, by Mary Ann Glendon (New York: Free Press, 1991). Explaining her approach, Glendon says, "The critique of the American rights dialect presented here rejects the radical attack on the very notion of rights that is sometimes heard on both ends of the political spectrum. It is not an assault on specific rights or on the idea of rights in general, but a plea for reevaluation of certain thoughtless, habitual ways of thinking and speaking about rights" (15).

the language of rights. They employed other language as well; but the language of rights was prominent in their vocabulary because, in general, it proved the most powerful. I have in mind the movements of protest against the position assigned in society to children, to women, to Jews, to African-Americans, to homosexuals; I also have in mind the protests against the Afrikaner regime in South Africa and against the Communist regimes in Hungary and Poland. It was these movements that made common coinage of such phrases as "children's rights," "women's rights," "civil rights," "human rights," and so forth.

One way to defend disagreement with one or another of these social protest movements is to insist that members of the group in question do not have the rights being claimed for them. Children do not have a right to be kept out of the labor force until they are of age, women do not have a right to vote, Jews do not have a right to be treated equally in the academy, South African "blacks" and "coloreds" do not have a right to equal treatment, and so forth. But often defenders of the status quo find the whole discourse of rights menacing; so they try to change the terms of debate. Instead of talking about rights, let us talk about responsibilities, about the social bonds of friendship and loyalty, about what is necessary for a well-ordered society.

Others, again, are opposed to rights-talk for social reasons. They charge that rights-talk expresses and encourages one of the most pervasive and malignant diseases of modern society: possessive individualism. In using such talk one places oneself at the center of the moral universe, focusing on one's own entitlements to the neglect of one's obligations to others and the cultivation of those other-directed virtues that are indispensable to the flourishing of our lives together. The prevalence of rights-talk obscures from us our responsibilities to each other and to our communities, obscures from us the singular importance of love, care, friendship, and the like. It demotes the giving self and promotes the grasping self, demotes the humble self and promotes the haughty self. It both encourages and is encouraged by the possessive atomism of the capitalist economy and the liberal polity. It invites us to think of ourselves as sovereign individuals.

Rights-talk is said to be for the purpose of *me* claiming *my possessions*, *you* claiming *your possessions*, *him* claiming *his possessions*. That is what it is for: claiming one's possessions, giving vent to one's possessiveness, each against the other. Possessive individualists are not abusing an innocent language by wresting it to their own evil purposes. They are using it as it was meant to be used. Rights-talk is inherently individualistic and possessive. The theologian Stanley Hauerwas put it like this in one of his essays:

The language of rights tends toward individualistic accounts of society and underwrites a view of human relations as exchanges rather than cooperative endeavors. Contemporary political theory has tended to concentrate on the language of rights, not because we have a vision of the good community, but because we do not. As a result, we have tried to underwrite the view that a good society is one where everyone is to be left alone rather than one that tries to secure the kind of cooperation that gives one a sense of contributing to a worthy human enterprise.[4]

And then there are the objections coming from philosophers and others among the intelligentsia. Talk about rights is nonsense, said Jeremy Bentham; and talk about natural rights is nonsense upon stilts. The way to respond to this charge is obvious: develop an account of rights that makes sense.

PRELIMINARY DESCRIPTION OF RIGHTS

I have already indicated the position that I will occupy and defend against this fusillade of objections. I will defend the importance of justice and the importance of rights, in the context of defending the thesis that justice is ultimately grounded on inherent rights. At the heart of my defense will be an attempt to change how we think about rights.

Rights are normative social relationships; sociality is built into the essence of rights. A right is a right *with regard to* someone. In the limiting case, that "someone" is oneself; one is other to oneself. Usually, the other is somebody else than oneself. Rights are toward the other, with regard to the other. Rights are normative bonds between oneself and the other. And for the most part, those normative bonds of oneself to the other are not generated by any exercise of will on one's part. The bond is there already, antecedent to one's will, binding oneself and the other together. The other comes into my presence already standing in this normative bond to me.

This normative bond is in the form of the other bearing a legitimate claim on me as to how I treat her, a legitimate claim to my doing certain things to her and refraining from doing other things. If I fail to do the former things, I violate the bond; if I do not refrain from doing the latter things, I also violate the bond. I do not break the normative bond; that still holds. She continues to have that legitimate claim on me as to how I treat her.

---

[4] "On the Right to be Tribal," *Christian Scholar's Review* 16, no. 3 (March 1987): 238–39.

The legitimate claim against me by the other is a claim to my enhancing her well-being in certain ways. The action or inaction on my part to which the other has a right against me is an action or inaction that would be a good in her life. A common apothegm in present-day political liberalism is that "the right has priority over the good." In the order of concepts, it is the other way around: the good is prior to the right. One's rights are rights to goods in one's life. The converse does not hold: there are many things that are or would be goods in one's life to which one does not have a right. I think it would be a great good in my life if I had a Rembrandt painting hanging in my living room. Sad to say, I do not have a right to that good. It is because the good is conceptually prior to the right that the second part of my discussion is devoted to the goods to which we have rights, and the third part to having a right to some good.

I will argue that it is on account of her worth that the other comes into my presence bearing legitimate claims against me as to how I treat her. The rights of the other against me are actions and restraints from action that due respect for her worth requires of me. To fail to treat her as she has a right to my treating her is to demean her, to treat her as if she had less worth than she does. To spy on her for prurient reasons, to insult her, to torture her, to bad-mouth her, is to demean her.

And to demean her is to wrong her. If I fail to treat her in the way she has a right to my treating her, I am guilty; but she is wronged. My moral condition is that of being guilty; her moral condition is that of having been wronged.

Lastly, rights are boundary-markers for our pursuit of life-goods. I am never to enhance the good in someone's life, my own or another's, or that of many others, at the cost of wronging someone or other, depriving her of that to which she has a right. I am never to pursue life-goods at the cost of demeaning someone. Rights have been described, and correctly so, in my judgment, as *trumps*. It may be that a wide range of life-goods can be achieved by pursuing some course of action; but if in pursuing that course of action one deprives someone of some good to which they have a right, thereby wronging them, one is not to do that. That good trumps the other goods.

The language of rights is for talking about these matters. It is for talking about these normative social bonds. It is for talking about the fact that sometimes by not enhancing the well-being of the other I fail to give her due respect. It is for talking about that curious and sometimes perplexing interaction, within the realm of the good, between the worth of the other person and the worth of goods in the life of the other.

The normative social bonds of rights are foundational to human community. I do not only mean that *honoring* these bonds is foundational to human community—though certainly it is. Rights themselves are foundational to human community. I have argued elsewhere that speech is a normative social engagement; causality is not sufficient for explaining how it is that by making certain sounds or inscribing certain marks, one makes an assertion, asks a question, issues a request. I argue that one has to appeal to rights to explain it.[5] But without speech acts such as those, human community is impossible.

How Rights Got a Bad Name

I have been skimming the surface. Everything I have said will be developed and defended in detail in the pages that follow. But a question already jumps out. If this is what rights are, how did they get such a bad name? How did they acquire their bad reputation? Why are so many so hostile for so many different reasons to talking about rights?

It is easy to see why those who oppose social protest movements prefer that the debate not be conducted in terms of rights. The rights of the other place limits on how I treat her. Not even for reasons of great good to be achieved am I permitted to treat her with less than full respect. Those who oppose liberation movements almost always claim that some great good will be maintained and some great evil averted if the status quo is preserved; they do not want to hear about limits on what they are allowed to do to the other in maintaining the status quo. Likewise, those who want to reshape society to fit their social ideals—National Socialists, Communists, and the like—do not want to hear about the limits that rights are, the boundaries that must not be crossed on pain of violating the worth of the other.

That seems clear enough. But if rights are what I claim they are, normative social bonds, why would anybody connect them with possessive individualism? There is a normative social bond between me and the other whereby the other bears legitimate claims on me as to how I treat her. What connection could there possibly be between that and possessive individualism?

The clue lies not in rights themselves but in the honoring and dishonoring of rights and in the claiming of rights. Notice that it is one thing for the other to have a legitimate claim against me; it is another thing for me to *honor* that legitimate claim. Likewise, it is one thing for me to have a legitimate claim against the other; it is another thing for me to *claim* that legitimate claim, to engage in the action of insisting that it be honored. Having a legitimate claim to police protection is one thing;

---

[5] See chapter 3 of my *Divine Discourse* (Cambridge: Cambridge University Press, 1995).

going to a meeting of the city council to insist that the police honor that claim is another.

Now imagine a society inhabited by possessive individualists. What will they do? Each will claim his own rights while neglecting or refusing to honor the rights of others. In no way does this alter the structure of the rights themselves; that structure remains intact and symmetrical. The other comes into my presence bearing claims against me; I come into her presence bearing claims against her. It is the practices of *honoring* and *claiming* rights that have been distorted.

But note that the language of service and responsibility can also be abused, used to express appalling attitudes of domination, on the one hand, and servility, on the other. And while we are on the topic of individualism, let us also note that rights-talk scarcely has a monopoly on the language of choice for the self-preoccupied individualist. We have all known self-preoccupied persons who thought and spoke not at all in terms of rights but entirely in terms of obligation; their souls were filled to overflowing with their own rectitude—or their own guilt. Offensive or sickly self-preoccupation comes in many forms. Sometimes it employs the language of rights, sometimes it employs the language of duty and obligation, sometimes it employs neither.[6]

WHY WE NEED RIGHTS-TALK

I have explained in preliminary fashion what rights are and what it is, within reality, that rights-talk brings to speech. But why is it important that rights be brought to speech? The critics point to the abuses of rights-talk. I concede the abuses. But rather than concluding that we should abolish rights-talk so as to eliminate the abuses, I hold that we should heal rights-talk *of* the abuses. Something of enormous worth would be lost if we could no longer bring rights, and the violation of rights, to speech. The critics focus entirely on the abuses of rights-talk; they do not ask what would be lost if we threw it all out.

What would be lost is our ability to bring to speech one of the two fundamental dimensions of the moral order: the recipient-dimension, the patient-dimension. To the moral status of each of us there are two dimensions, that of moral agent and that of moral patient or recipient. When we speak of duty, obligation, guilt, benevolence, virtue, rational

---

[6] In the idiolect of some philosophers (e.g., John Rawls in *A Theory of Justice*), the word "duty" is reserved for normative constraints generated by some human action, whereas "obligation" is reserved for normative constraints not so generated. I will speak in accord with ordinary English, and treat the two terms as synonyms.

agency, and the like, we focus on the agent-dimension; when we speak of rights and of being wronged, we focus on the recipient-dimension. To eliminate rights-talk would be to make impossible the coming to speech of the recipient-dimension of the moral order.

It may be said, in reply, that rights are the same thing as duties in different words. Suppose one singles out from the agent-dimension generally the part that pertains to obligation and sets to the side those parts that pertain to virtue, love, and the like; what I am calling the recipient-dimension is nothing more, the critic insists, than the obligation part of the agent-dimension, differently described. Everything that can be said in the language of rights can be said in the language of obligation; same facts, different words. Nobody supposes that south and north are fundamentally distinct dimensions of space. I am to the south of you if and only if you are to the north of me; same thing, different words. Nothing is lost if we toss out rights-talk—as long as we keep duty-talk.

In the next chapter I appeal to what I call *the principle of correlatives*: if Y belongs to the sort of entity that can have rights, then X has a right against Y to Y's doing A if and only if Y has an obligation toward X to do A. I hold that this is a necessary truth. But it is not an analytic truth, that is, a proposition true by virtue of the meanings of words and the law of non-contradiction. It is synthetic—to use language that Kant made familiar. It is not because the first clause says the same thing as the second clause that the principle of correlatives is true.

I think the best way to see that we are dealing here with two distinct dimensions of the moral order, connected by necessary truths, rather than one dimension differently described, is to look at duties and rights from the dark sides—from the sides of being guilty and of being wronged. One is guilty if one has failed to do what one was obligated to do; one is wronged if one has not been treated as one had a right to be treated. I think we all have the intuition that your being guilty and my being wronged are not the same thing in different words.

Perhaps the following observation will strengthen this intuition. Suppose that in treating me a certain way you have violated your obligation toward me and that, correlatively, I have been deprived of my right against you to your not treating me that way. You are guilty and I am wronged. Now suppose you are absolved of your guilt. Perhaps you go to a priest, confess your sin, and he absolves you. I am not convinced that absolution for guilt is a possibility; but suppose it is. What then is *my* moral condition? Does your being absolved of your guilt mean that I am now automatically relieved of having been wronged? Of course not. I am in exactly the same moral condition that I was in before the absolution took place. Absolution—if there is such a thing—deals with guilt, not with being wronged.[7] It is repentance by one party and forgiveness by the other that deals with being wronged, though in a way very different from absolution. This will become important in chapter 4.

When one thinks of what one is doing in terms of obligations, one focuses on the bearing of one's actions on one's own moral condition: one is upright or guilty. When one thinks of what one is doing in terms of rights, one focuses on the bearing of one's action on the recipient: her rights are honored or she is wronged. If one thinks exclusively in terms of obligations, and if, furthermore, one thinks of guilt as guilt for violating the moral law rather than guilt for wronging the other, then the person who has been wronged falls entirely out of view.[8]

The language of duty and guilt enables the battered wife to point to the effect of her spouse's actions on his moral condition; he is now guilty. The language of rights and of being wronged enables her to point to the effect of her spouse's action on her own moral condition; she has been wronged, deprived of her right to better treatment, treated as if she were of little worth. He is not only guilty of having acted out of accord with the moral law; he is guilty of having wronged *her*—perhaps even by trying to make her feel guilty when it is he who is guilty.

The language of duty and guilt enables the oppressed to point to the effect of the oppressor's actions on the moral condition of the oppressors; the oppressors are guilty. The language of rights and of being wronged enables the oppressed to bring their own moral condition into the picture: they have been deprived of their right to better treatment, treated as if they were of little worth. The oppressors are guilty of having wronged them. The reason the language of rights has proved so powerful in social protest movements is that it brings the victims and their moral condition into the light of day.

In September 1985 a remarkable pamphlet called *The Kairos Document* was issued by over 150 theologians and church leaders in South Africa.

---

[7] Matthew H. Kramer, in his essay "Rights without Trimmings" (in Matthew H. Kramer, N. E. Simmonds, and Hillel Steiner, *A Debate over Rights: Philosophical Enquiries* [Oxford: Clarendon Press, 1998]), claims to be following W. H. Hohfeld in declaring that, among the various things that are called "rights," *claim-rights* are those for whom the Principle of Correlatives holds by definition of "a right." On this interpretation, instantiations of the Principle of Correlatives would be analytic truths. In chapter 11 I argue that this is a misinterpretation of Hohfeld. Of course, one could introduce such a concept and call it a concept of *rights*; but that would not be the same as our concept of a claim-right.

[8] The recent "Restorative Justice" movement should be mentioned here. The criminal justice system, as it normally functions in the United States, charges the accused with having committed a crime against the state; if he is convicted, the state then punishes him. The Restorative Justice movement tries to bring the breach of moral relationship between the accused and the victim back into the picture, both in the trial stage and in the subsequent punishment and rehabilitation stage.

In what they say about "Church Theology," in a section of the pamphlet called "Justice," the authors point to the difference between the two dimensions of the moral order that I have been calling attention to. They state why those in power prefer to attend only to the agent-dimension and why it is important to bring the recipient-dimension into the light. The pamphlet was written before the overthrow of the white minority regime in South Africa.

> It would be quite wrong to give the impression that "Church Theology" in South Africa is not particularly concerned about the need for justice. There have been some very strong and very sincere demands for justice. But the question we need to ask here, the very serious theological question is: What kind of justice? An examination of Church statements and pronouncements gives the distinct impression that the justice that is envisaged is the *justice of reform,* that is to say, a justice that is determined by the oppressor, by the white minority and that is offered to the people as a kind of concession. . . . The general idea appears to be that one must simply appeal to the conscience and goodwill of those who are responsible for injustice in our land.
>
> The problem that we are dealing with here in South Africa is not merely a problem of personal guilt. . . . We cannot just sit back and wait for the oppressor to see the light so that the oppressed can put out their hands and beg for the crumbs of some small reforms. That in itself would be degrading and oppressive.

The Contemporary Polemic against Justice as Rights

There's a polemic making the rounds nowadays against the way of thinking about justice that I will articulate in the pages that follow—not now a polemic against justice nor a polemic against rights, but a polemic against justice as grounded ultimately on inherent rights. I have explained, in preliminary fashion, how I think of rights. Let me now add that I think of a social order as just insofar as its members enjoy the goods to which they have rights. Some of those rights are conferred on those who otherwise would not have them by actions on the part of human beings—the issuing of legislation, the performance of speech acts, and so forth. Some are not so conferred. The latter are natural rights. Natural rights are in good measure inherent to those who have them. That is to say, they have these rights not because the rights have been conferred on beings of their sort by God or by some socially transcendent norm extrinsic to themselves; they have them on account of the worth of beings of their sort. I hold that all rights are ultimately so grounded. I call this way of thinking about justice *justice as inherent rights.*

The polemic I have in mind against this way of thinking about justice is not merely negative; it offers an alternative way of thinking about justice—*justice as right order.* Natural law for the right ordering of society is what ultimately grounds justice, so it is said, not the inherent rights of members of society.

The polemic against justice as inherent rights by those who favor justice as right order is conducted almost entirely by means of a narrative, and a social critique based on the narrative.[9] Once upon a time, so it is said, everybody who thought about justice thought of it in terms of right order. Individualistic modes of thought then gave birth to the idea of inherent natural rights. As such modes of thought became more common, the old way of thinking about justice gradually lost its appeal and was displaced by the conception of justice as grounded on inherent rights. Individualism is in the DNA of both the idea of inherent natural rights and the conception of justice as inherent rights. There is an intrinsic connection between, on the one hand, the idea of inherent natural rights and the conception of justice as inherent rights and, on the other hand, the possessive individualism of modern society. Earlier we noted that the language of rights is susceptible to being bent to the purposes of the possessive individualist. The claim here is that the connection between the language of inherent natural rights and possessive individualism is not contingent, as I have represented it as being, but essential.

It is said that both for correctly understanding justice and for the health of society we must recover that older, more venerable way of thinking that was displaced by the justice as inherent rights conception. We must rid our thought of the idea that there are inherent natural rights and think of justice as right order. A good brief statement of the contrast between these two ways of thinking, along with an allusion to the narrative, is this passage from an essay by Joan Lockwood O'Donovan:

> A close analysis of the history of the concept of subjective rights in the light of earlier theological-political conceptualization reveals a progressive antagonism between the older Christian tradition of political right and the newer voluntarist, individualist, and subjectivist orientation. The contrasting logic of the two orientations may be conveyed quite simply: where in the older patristic and medieval tradition, God's right established a matrix of divine, natural, and

---

[9] An influential telling of the story is Leo Strauss's *Natural Right and History* (Chicago: University of Chicago Press, 1953). The story, as Strauss tells it, is of what he calls "the classic theory of natural right" losing ground to what he calls "the modern theory of natural right[s]."

human laws or objective obligations that constituted the ordering justice of political community, in the newer tradition God's right established discrete rights, possessed by individuals originally and by communities derivatively, that determined civil order and justice.[10]

In the essay from which this passage comes, O'Donovan elaborates the evaluation to which she here alludes. The introduction and use of the concept of subjective rights in general, and of *inherent natural* and *human* subjective rights in particular, has been a calamity of the first order. The concept of inherent natural rights was born in late medieval nominalism and was an indispensable component in the individualistic mentality of the Enlightenment; it is intrinsically connected to the egocentric possessive individualism that haunts modern society. Patently incompatible though it is with sound Christian theology, "the question that has yet to be satisfactorily answered . . . is why Christian thinkers have been and are willing" to buy into it. Why have they been "willing to adopt a child of such questionable parentage as the concept of human rights" and the conception of justice to which this concept belongs? Her hope, says O'Donovan, is that the historical analysis offered in her essay will at least have "sharpened" the question.[11] Before we do anything else, we must address this narrative.

But why must we address this narrative? Why not follow the time-honored tradition of analytic philosophy and confine oneself to systematic issues? Why not ignore social critique and narratives about origins and proceed immediately to the construction of theory, in the course thereof addressing whatever may be the systematic points at issue between these two ways of thinking? Even the little I have already said about rights, namely, that they are normative social relationships, is enough to cast doubt on the history and the social analysis. No need to play the intellectual historian. Let the narrative wither away.

It is tempting. But it will not do. The power of the polemic against the conception of justice as inherent rights by right order theorists lies almost entirely in the story they tell about the origins and social affinities of theories of the former sort. It does not lie in the power of their systematic argumentation; they have offered surprisingly little of that. The systematic account of justice and of rights that I will develop does indeed show that possessive individualism cannot be in the DNA of the conception of justice as inherent rights; those who think otherwise have to be making a mistake somewhere. But not to identify the mistake is to leave those

---

[10] Joan Lockwood O'Donovan, "The Concept of Rights in Christian Moral Discourse," in Michael Cromartie, ed., *A Preserving Grace: Protestants, Catholics, and Natural Law* (Grand Rapids: Eerdmans, 1997), p. 145.

[11] Ibid., p. 155.

who have been persuaded by the narrative in possession of an unsettling question: if there is no intrinsic connection between the conception of justice as inherent rights and possessive individualism, why did that conception emerge from individualistic ways of thinking? And why, as individualistic modes of thought spread, did the older way of thinking of justice as right order give way to the newer way of thinking of justice as based on inherent rights? Until those questions are addressed and undermined, the case for thinking of justice as based on inherent rights will be incomplete.

We have no choice but to engage in the archeology of rights, showing where and why the familiar narrative is mistaken and offering a counternarrative.

IS THERE A THIRD CONCEPTION OF JUSTICE?

Though I judge that the story about origins told by devotees of the right order conception is seriously mistaken, and the conception itself systematically untenable, I nonetheless hold that they have made an important contribution to reflections on justice by forcefully calling our attention to the fact that, in the thought of the West, there are two fundamentally different ways of thinking about justice. Distinguishing those two ways is indispensable for understanding our intellectual heritage; discerning their structure and implications is indispensable for our own systematic reflections on justice. I depart from adherents of the right order conception in their historical claims about origins; I affirm their historical claim that in the thought of the West there are two fundamentally distinct ways of thinking about justice, both vying for attention and allegiance.

My delineation, in the next chapter, of these two ways of thinking about justice will evoke questions from opposite directions. Some will press the question of whether these two ways are really distinct. Others will press the question of whether there are not additional ways of thinking about justice. My discussion in the next chapter will constitute my answer to the first question. Let me say a word here about the second.

The most obvious candidate for a third way of thinking about justice is justice as equality. Justice as equality has entered deep into the thought and art of the West: justice is a blindfolded woman holding a balanced pair of scales. Aquinas says in one place that "justice by its name implies equality" (*S.th.* II-II, q. 58, art. 2, *resp*). Later he makes the same point a bit more elaborately: "even as the object of justice is something equal in external things, so too the object of injustice is something unequal" (q.

59, art. 2, *resp.*).[12] Aquinas's formula comes, of course, from Aristotle's famous discussion of justice in the *Nicomachean Ethics*: "The just is equal, as all men suppose it to be, even apart from argument" (1131a 13). Many writers—Hume, for example—assume without question that Aristotle was right about this: justice is equality.

I have no stake in there being just two fundamentally distinct ways of thinking about justice. As I explained, my reason for discussing the justice as right order conception is that those who favor this conception have launched a vigorous attack against the conception I favor. But I doubt that justice as equality is a way of thinking about justice that is fundamental in the way that justice as right order and justice as inherent rights are fundamental.

Aristotle is describing for us what he regards as the general pattern of justice, its general contour: justice is always equality of a certain sort. His conception is unlike the two I will be dealing with in that it makes no attempt at grounding justice ontologically. Thus one could marry justice as equality to ontological Platonism. Ultimately, what makes a society just, one could say, is that it conforms to the Form the Just Itself; and the general character of conformity to the Just Itself is equality of a certain sort in commutative, distributive, and retributive engagements. Alternatively, someone committed to a Rawlsian approach could argue against Rawls's two principles of justice and in favor of Aristotelian equality.

I hold that equality does not capture the contour of justice; Aristotle was mistaken about this. Justice is sometimes present when equality of treatment is absent, and equality is sometimes present when justice is absent. Because nothing in what I have to say will depend on whether I am right about this, let me state my reasons for this conclusion very briefly.

In claiming that justice is determined by equality of treatment, be it arithmetical or proportional equality, Aristotle is assuming that justice always involves drawing comparisons between or among persons with respect to treatment. That seems clearly not true. One way of assigning grades in a class is "on the curve"; a certain proportion are to get A's, a certain proportion B's, and so forth. Assigning grades in that way requires making comparisons. And to determine whether a given student has been treated justly, one has to look at what the other students have done and the grades they have received. But one can also assign grades by determining each case on its own merits, in which case one does not make comparisons of treatment. Does this work merit an A? Then justice requires that one give it an A. It makes no difference what the other students have done and how they are being treated. It does not even

---

[12] See also *S. th.* II-II, q. 57, art. 1, *resp.*

make any difference whether there are other students. One can grade the student in a one-member class justly or unjustly. Justice does not require equality of treatment among two or more recipients.

But neither does equality of treatment ensure justice. Imagine the following grading situation. A mathematics professor has instituted a system of grading on the curve according to which 20 percent of the class are to get A's on any test that is given, 20 percent B's, the same for C's, the same for D's, and the remainder are to get F's. He now gives a very difficult examination containing 100 problems. To his astonishment, 20 percent of the class get all the problems right, 20 percent miss just one, another 20 percent miss just two, another 20 percent miss just three, and all the rest miss just four. He announces the grades; and there is a howl of outrage from all but those who missed no problems. This is unjust, they say. Why? The Aristotelian principle of proportional equality has been followed to perfection: the greater the merit, the greater the gain, the less the merit, the greater the loss. Yes. But though differences in treatment perfectly map differences in merit, it is unjust to give a failing grade to someone who missed only four out of a hundred difficult problems.[13]

WHY NO DISCUSSION OF RAWLS'S THEORY?

A few paragraphs back I mentioned John Rawls. Such is the fame of John Rawls's *Theory of Justice* that almost everyone who picks up this book will want to know what I have to say about Rawls. Apart from incidental comments, I do not have anything to say about Rawls. The reason for my silence is straightforward. Though Rawls's theory of justice is an inherent natural rights theory, he does nothing at all to develop an account of such rights. He simply assumes their existence. My interlocutors will be those who do not just appeal to such rights but have something to say about them.

The claim that Rawls's theory of justice is an inherent natural rights theory will take many readers aback. Rawls's presentation of his theory certainly does not give that appearance. Michael Zuckert, in his essay "Big Government and Rights: Locke, Rawls, and Liberalism," states very nicely what the structure of Rawls's theory appears to be: "our rights derive from justice." For Locke, "rights first, then justice"; for Rawls, "jus-

---

[13] These points, about the relation of justice to equality, are developed more fully in Joel Feinberg, "Noncomparative Justice," *Philosophical Review* 83, issue 3 (July 1974). Oliver O'Donovan also argues against justice as equality in chapter 3, "Justice and Equality," in his *The Ways of Judgment* (Grand Rapids: Wm. B. Eerdmans, 2005).

tice first, then rights."[14] But in a well-known article of almost three decades ago, Ronald Dworkin argued that when one looks beneath the surface, one finds inherent natural rights at the basis of the theory.

Fundamental to Rawls's theory is the principle of equal respect for all members of the social order (or for all members who can engage in the relevant "bargaining"). The question is, what is the basis for this principle of equal respect? Dworkin's conclusion is that "justice as fairness rests on the assumption of a natural right of all men and women to equality of concern and respect, a right they possess not by virtue of birth or characteristic or merit or excellence but simply as human beings with the capacity to make plans and give justice."[15]

Dworkin's argument is almost entirely deductive: given other things Rawls says, this has to be his view. But there are passages in *Theory of Justice* that confirm Dworkin's interpretation—though it has to be said that Rawls was evidently very reluctant to bring his appeal to inherent natural rights (and duties) to the surface, which is why most readers miss it. The most explicit passage in the main body of the text is this:

> Some writers have distinguished between equality as it is invoked in connection with the distribution of certain goods, some of which will almost certainly give higher status or prestige to those who are more favored, and equality as it applies to the respect which is owed to persons irrespective of their social position. Equality of the first kind is defined by the second principle of justice which regulates the structure of organizations and distributive shares so that social cooperation is both efficient and fair. But equality of the second kind is fundamental. It is defined by the first principle of justice and by such natural duties as that of mutual respect; it is owed to human beings as moral persons. The natural basis of equality explains its deeper significance.[16]

An even more revealing passage occurs in a footnote—which itself is an indication of how reluctant Rawls was to make explicit the natural rights basis of his theory:

> This fact [that "the capacity for moral personality is a sufficient condition for being entitled to equal justice"] can be used to interpret the concept of natural rights. For one thing, it explains why it is

---

[14] Chapter 12 in *Launching Liberalism: On Lockean Political Philosophy* (Lawrence: University Press of Kansas, 2002), p. 317.

[15] "Justice and Rights," in Ronald Dworkin, *Taking Rights Seriously* (Cambridge: Harvard University Press, 1977), p. 182.

[16] John Rawls, *A Theory of Justice*, rev. ed. (Cambridge: Harvard University Press, 1999), p. 447.

appropriate to call by this name the rights that justice protects. These claims depend solely on certain natural attributes the presence of which can be ascertained by natural reason pursuing common sense methods of inquiry. The existence of these attributes and the claims based upon them is established independently from social conventions and legal norms. The propriety of the term "natural" is that it suggests the contrast between the rights identified by the theory of justice and the rights defined by law and custom. But more than this, the concept of natural rights includes the idea that these rights are assigned in the first instance to persons, and that they are given a special weight. Claims easily overridden for other values are not natural rights. Now the rights protected by the first principle have both of these features in view of the priority rules. Thus justice as fairness has the characteristic marks of a natural rights theory. Not only does it ground fundamental rights on natural attributes and distinguish their bases from social norms, but it assigns rights to persons by principles of equal justice. (442–43).[17]

The most innovative feature of Rawls's approach is that, rather than declaring a society to be just insofar as the inherent natural rights of its members are honored, and then giving an account of those rights, he claims to be able to develop a theory of social justice by appealing to just one such right, the right of rational moral agents to be treated with equal respect. In so doing he is assuming that principles of distribution that fully honor that right will secure the non-violation of every other inherent natural right. Whether this extraordinarily bold assumption is correct is the deepest issue in Rawlsian theory, though rarely discussed. It is an issue that need not detain us.

---

[17] This footnote was called to my attention by Edward Song. I should note that Rawls's position in his later *Political Liberalism* is explicitly and deliberately not a natural rights position.

PART I

The Archeology of Rights

Chapter One

TWO CONCEPTIONS OF JUSTICE

I MENTIONED IN THE INTRODUCTION that there is a polemic making the rounds nowadays against the way of thinking about justice that I will be working with in the pages that follow. I think of justice as grounded ultimately on inherent rights. The polemic I have in mind is conducted by those who think about justice in terms of right order. They conduct their polemic almost entirely by offering a narrative concerning the supposedly disreputable origins of the conception of justice as inherent rights. My project in Part I of the book is to contest that narrative and offer a counter-narrative.[1] This requires first getting clear on what exactly these two ways of thinking about justice come to. That is our project in this chapter; the contest of narratives begins in the next.

Not only do we have to go beyond the rough characterization of the two conceptions that I have given thus far; we have to go beyond the characterization of their own view that the right order theorists give. So intent have they been on polemicizing against the inherent rights conception that they have neglected the systematic development of their own conception. What I present will have to be, at some points, a "rational reconstruction" of their thought.

ANOTHER PRELIMINARY EXPLANATION OF RIGHTS

As preparation for delineating the two conceptions, let me offer an explanation of rights somewhat different from the explanation offered in the Introduction; this explanation is also still preliminary. My focus is on moral rights, though much of what I have to say is true of other sorts of rights as well—legal rights, for example.

---

[1] In his *Whose Justice? Which Rationality?* (Notre Dame: University of Notre Dame Press, 1988), Alasdair MacIntyre also speaks about "different and incompatible conceptions of justice" (ix) and of "conflicting conceptions of justice" (1). He argues, for example, that in the ancient Greeks there was a conflict between the justice of excellence and the justice of effectiveness. What MacIntyre has in mind by conflicting conceptions of justice is what I will call conflicting *understandings of the contours* of justice—that is, conflicting understandings of which sorts of things are just and which are unjust. The conflict of conceptions that I explore is not a conflict about the contours of justice but a conflict prior to that—a conflict over how we should think about justice.

Justinian's great codification of Roman law, *The Digest*, opens with a famous definition of "justice" that came from the third-century Roman jurist Ulpian.[2] Justice (*iustitia*), said Ulpian, is a steady and enduring will to render to each their *ius* (*suum ius cuique tribuere*).[3] There is a question as to how the word "*ius*" in this formula should be translated. Customarily, it is translated as "right": justice is rendering to each their right. However, the Latin "*ius*" was used to cover not only what we call *right* but also what we call *desert*, as in "his just desert."[4] Ulpian's thought is that justice is a steady and enduring will to render to each their right or desert. Whether it was only legal justice that Ulpian had in mind is not clear.

There are many things that could be said about this definition; I have introduced it here in order to make an initial point about rights. In his definition, Ulpian tacitly employed the distinction between *possessing* some *ius* and *being rendered* that *ius*. Someone is a just person in case they have a steady and enduring will to render to each the rights and deserts that are theirs, that they possess. Ulpian uses the possessive "*suum*": <u>*suum ius*</u>, his *ius*. The distinction between *possessing* some *ius* and *being rendered* that *ius* is indispensable; treating a person justly consists of rendering to him a right or desert that he possesses.

Ulpian's eye was on the virtue of justice; my focus will be on the social condition that those who possess the virtue seek to bring about. So for our purposes we need a word that corresponds to Ulpian's term "render-

---

[2] The passage comes from Book I of Ulpian's *Rules* and is to be found in the first section of Book One of Justinian's *Digest*. A recent translation is by Alan Watson, *The Digest of Justinian* (Philadelphia: University of Pennsylvania Press; 1985). Here is Watson's translation of the sentence and the sentence following: "Justice is a steady and enduring will to render unto everyone his right. The basic principles of right are: to live honorably, not to harm any other person, to render to each his own" (no pagination).

[3] Where proper English grammar requires "his or her," and where old-fashioned English grammar would allow "his," I instead use "their." Thus, instead of "render to each his or her *ius*" I say, "render to each their *ius*." I acknowledge that this use of "their," though becoming more common, is still a grammatical barbarism. But in our present linguistic situation I cannot say "his" nor, for the counterpart reason, can I say " her"; and the constant repetition of "his or her" would be tedious.

[4] On page 9 of his *Natural Rights Theories: Their Origin and Development* (Cambridge: Cambridge University Press, 1979), Richard Tuck quotes a passage from the *Institutes* of the Roman jurist Gaius in which the Latin "*ius*" departs in yet a different way from our contemporary English word "right." Gaius is speaking of the *iura* connected with urban estates: "the *jus* of building houses higher and of obstructing the light of neighbouring houses, or not doing so, because it obstructs their light; the *ius* of streams and gutters, that is, of a neighbour taking a stream or gutter overflow through his yard or house; and the *ius* of admitting into one's property someone else's drains." The *jus* of not raising a building beyond a certain height cannot be the right or desert of not raising the building higher; it is the *duty* of not raising the building higher; so also with the neighbor's *ius* of not draining his gutters onto one's property. The meaning of "*ius*" appears to come close to the meaning of our disjunctive: *a right or a desert or a duty.*

ing" but is nonetheless different. Let me speak of someone *enjoying* that to which they possess a right.

Possessing a right does not consist of standing in the relation of *possession* to some member of a peculiar species of entity called "rights." The entire phrase, "possessing a right to," names the relation. "Mary has a right to X" just means that X is rightfully Mary's, that X is Mary's by right, that Mary has right to X. We do speak of "one's rights," thereby inviting the thought that one's rights are rather like one's clothes, one's books, and so on. But this is not so. One's rights consist of those entities to which one stands in the relation of having a right to them.

This observation suggests the question, to what sorts of things can one stand in the relation of *having a right to* them? The answer I articulate and defend is that that to which one has a right is normally a good of some sort—more specifically, a good in one's life or history.[5] If speaking my mind freely is something I have a right to, then speaking my mind freely is a good in my life; if receiving a monthly Social Security payment is something I have a right to, then it is a good in my life. A broken leg is not a candidate for something to which one has a right—except for those unusual cases in which the only way to achieve some good to which one has a right is to have one's leg broken! (I should remind the reader that throughout my discussion I am talking only about primary justice, not retributive.) Exceptions to the generalization offered are to be found among linguistically generated and socially conferred rights. Those who generated or conferred the right to something may have been mistaken in thinking that it was a good.[6] To avoid complicating our discussion unduly, I will usually speak as if it is only to a good that one has a right, taking note of exceptions only when that proves necessary.

The generalization offered, that if something belongs to one by right, then it is a good in one's life or history, is true only if we are talking about the thing per se, as such; when the consequences and accompaniments of that which is the good are brought into the picture, the totality may very well not be among one's goods. Though per se a monthly Social Security payment is a good of mine, I may spend it in such a way that, all things considered, it would be better for me had I not had that income. Or suppose I purchase a ticket for a seat on a certain flight; then the good of a seat on that flight is a right of mine. But it is the seat on the

---

[5] It would appear that I am disagreeing here with the famous analysis of rights by W. N. Hohfeld in *Fundamental Legal Conceptions* (New Haven: Yale University Press, 1919). On Hohfeld's view, the essential logical structure of a right is not a relation of a person or social entity to a good of that person or entity, but the relation of one person to another person with respect to some act. In chapter 6 we will see that these two approaches coalesce.

[6] A second type of exception will be noted at the beginning of chapter 6.

flight *as such* that is the good, not the seat on the flight *all things considered*.[7] If I am bumped because the flight is overbooked and the plane subsequently crashes, then a seat on the flight all things considered was not (would not have been) a good of mine.

The converse of the generalization, that rights are to goods in one's life or history, is not true; many of the things that are or would be goods in one's life and history are not things to which one has a right. My own life would be greatly enhanced, so I believe, were I to have more musical talent than I do have; but to that life-good I do not have a right.

Instead of saying that the virtue of justice consists of the steady and enduring will to render to each his or her right, Ulpian might have said that it consists of rendering to each what is *due* him or her. The two formulae come to the same thing, and both go back into classical antiquity. However, they approach the virtue or social condition from opposite directions. Having a right to some good is the converse of that good being due one. If good G is due person S, then S has a right to G; and if S has a right to G, then G is due S. If what is due me when I am visiting New York City is the good of being free to walk on its streets without being physically assaulted, then I have a right to that good, and conversely.

Primary justice according to Ulpian's formula is present in society insofar as the members of society enjoy the goods to which they have a right. Primary justice according to the alternative formula is present in society when its members enjoy the goods due them. The two formulas come to the same.

A small qualification is necessary. In ordinary English, to say that something is due a person is to suggest that the person does not presently possess or experience that which is due her. What is due a student for doing first-rate work in a college or university course is an "A" on her record (in the American system of grading). If an A for the course has already been inscribed on her record, then one does not say that an A *is* due her but that it *was* due her. For our two formulaes to be strict converses of each other, the word "due" has to be understood in a sense derived from the ordinary sense by removing from it the implication noted. There may be goods that one always enjoys, so that, in the ordinary sense, they are never due one but that are yet such that, were one *not* to enjoy them, one's rights would be violated; the what-is-due-one formula speaks of those as goods due one. Using the ordinary concept, the thing to say would be that justice consists in enjoying those goods that *would be* due one *were one not* enjoying or undergoing them.

---

[7] Or perhaps the right analysis is not that *the seat* is the good in question but, rather, *receiving that which one has purchased.*

Having a right to some good can also be described as being entitled to enjoy it, having a legitimate claim to it. To have a right not to have troops quartered in my house is to be entitled to that good, to have a legitimate claim to it.[8] For the most part, however, I refrain from speaking of what one has a right to as what one has a claim to. I now and then speak of rights as *claim-rights*, for reasons that will become clear later. But speaking of what one has a right to as what one has a claim to leads all too easily to confusion (I courted the confusion in the Introduction). If I am deprived of some good to which I have a right, then the question arises whether I, or someone else on my behalf, may or should perform some act of *claiming* my right. The correct answer, I think, is that often, though not always, it is permissible for me to engage in certain acts of claiming it, and sometimes it is obligatory. If one thinks and speaks of rights generally as those goods in one's life and history to which one has a (legitimate) claim, making these points threatens confusion. *Having a (legitimate) claim* gets confused with *performing some act of claiming*.

It is important to look at rights from the dark side as well as the bright—from the side of being deprived of one's rights as well as from the side of enjoying one's rights. Suppose a person has been deprived of some good to which she has a right. To make things easier for ourselves here, let us suppose that it is a *moral* right of which she has been deprived, not a merely legal right. Being deprived of that to which she has a right constitutes an alteration in her moral condition. She is then *wronged*. When Union Carbide's chemical plant in Bhopal, India, spewed poisonous fumes into the air, it deprived the residents of the valley of a good to which they had a right, namely, the good of having non-noxious air to breathe; thereby the residents were *wronged*.

I have been talking about the sorts of things to which one can have rights; a word should also be said about the sorts of beings that can have rights. I hold that not only individual persons and human beings have rights but also social entities such as groups and organizations. A tribal nation can enjoy, or fail to enjoy, its rights, as can a business organization. For ease of exposition I will often speak as if only persons and human beings possess rights. The reader should remember that this way of speaking is solely for the sake of convenience. In chapter 17 I defend the claim that social entities possess rights and take up the issue of whether animals, plants, works of art, and the like do so as well.

Acts of justice and injustice may have multiple agents. Several people may conspire together to deprive me of my right to walk freely on the streets of Manhattan, with differing degrees of responsibility. Likewise,

[8] As we shall see in chapter 11, the English word "right" is used not only for legitimate claims but also for permissions.

acts of justice and injustice may have multiple patients. If I am deprived
of my right to walk freely on the streets of Manhattan by being knocked
down, with the consequence that I am mentally impaired, then not only
am I wronged but my family is wronged as well.

When I presented Ulpian's formula, I observed that he probably meant
by "*iura*" both rights and deserts. The observant reader will wonder why
subsequently I have talked only about rights and not about deserts. My
reason is as follows. The English term "deserts" has two senses. Sometimes
we use it to refer to what is "due" a person by way of retribution for some
act of wrongdoing on his part; sometimes we use it more broadly to cover
both what a person has a right to and what is "due" a person on account
of his wrongdoing. But these are two very different phenomena. My topic
is exclusively primary justice, not retributive; and I judge that confusion
would be engendered if we used a term that covers both.

That to which one has a right is a life-good; that which is "due" one on
account of one's wrongdoing is a life-evil. Furthermore, though we do
indeed speak of a person's retributive rights, these being the life-evils that
a person has a right to impose on the one who wronged him, retributive
rights are in general permission-rights rather than claim-rights. (The distinction between these two sorts of rights is discussed in chapter 11.) I am
permitted to be angry with the person who wronged me and to see to it
that hard treatment is imposed on him; but it may well be that I am not
obligated to do so—that nobody is wronged if it does not happen.
Though special circumstances may make the exercise of retributive rights
obligatory, that is not in general the case; forgiveness is not a violation of
the moral order. This, at least, is the Christian view of the matter. The view
of pagan antiquity may well have been that punishment of wrongdoers is
obligatory, and that always someone is wronged if punishment for wrongdoing is not forthcoming.[9] I should add that corresponding to the permission-right to impose hard treatment on the one who has wronged one
will often be the claim-right to be free to do so.

PLATO'S VERSION OF JUSTICE AS RIGHT ORDER

I think the best way to proceed is to have before us an example of an
account of justice that is indubitably a right order account, and then
highlight the features that make it an example of that type of account.

---

[9] I discuss these matters in my essay, "Does Forgiveness Undermine Justice?" in Andrew
Dole and Andrew Chignell, eds., *God and the Ethics of Belief* (Cambridge: Cambridge University Press, 2005), pp. 219–47.

The account of justice that Plato develops in the *Republic* will serve this purpose nicely.[10]

The strategy Plato followed for arriving at his account of justice is well known. He first delineated a social order that is, as he put it, "founded and built up on the right lines, [and] is good in the complete sense of the word" (121; 427e); he takes it as "obvious" that such a social order will exhibit justice—along with wisdom, courage, and temperance. Having delineated the right social order, he then singles out that feature of the order that makes it a *just* order.[11]

The central structural feature of the social order Plato delineated is the presence within it of a variety of differentiated social roles—in particular, economic roles, defense roles, and governance roles. These roles have a normative component; to occupy one of these roles is to enter a structure of required ways of treating and of being treated by others. Interspersed with his articulation of this social structure is Plato's development of a theory of human nature according to which each member of society is by nature better fitted to fulfill the demands of certain social roles than of others; in particular, he argues that most people will by nature be quite unsuited for the role of governance. He concludes this part of his argument by contending that a social order will be "built up on the right lines" and "good in the complete sense of the word" just in case members of society are trained for and occupy the social roles for which they are by nature best suited, and insofar as they faithfully execute the requirements attached thereto. In particular, the social order will be the right social order if those who are by nature best suited for governance are trained for and occupy the governance roles and faithfully execute the requirements attached thereto, if those best suited for defense are trained for and occupy the defense roles and faithfully execute the requirements attached thereto, and if those best suited for economic activities are trained for and occupy the economic roles and faithfully execute the requirements attached to those roles. In such a social order, everybody will be doing their "proper work" (139; 441d), performing their "proper function" (140; 441e).

Plato is now in position to take the final step of identifying that feature of the right social order that makes it a just order. As preparation for this identification, Plato identifies those features of the right order that

[10] I will use the F. M. Cornford translation (New York: Oxford University Press, 1945). Page references to Plato are incorporated into my text; I first give the Cornford page, and then the page from the Stephanus edition in which the passage can be found in the original.

[11] "So now at last, son of Ariston, said I [Socrates], your commonwealth is established. The next thing is to bring to bear upon it all the light you can get from any quarter, . . . in the hope that we may see where justice is to be found in it and where injustice" (120; 427d).

account for the presence in the community of the virtues of wisdom, courage, and temperance. The community is wise on account of the wisdom of those who occupy the governance roles; it is courageous on account of the courage of those who occupy the defense roles; and it is temperate on account of the submission of those in the inferior roles of defense and economy to the directives of those in the superior role of governance.

What is left over to account for the justice of the right social order? Well, justice will be what "makes it possible for . . . wisdom, courage, and temperance, to take their place in the commonwealth, and so long as it remains present secures their continuance." (127; 433b–c). And what makes it possible for them to do that is simply that the social order delineated has the features that make for its being the right social order. In short, what makes the right social order a *just* social order is identical with that which makes it *the right* social order. This is the point of the following bit of dialogue between Socrates and Glaucon.

> Really, [Socrates] said, we have been extremely stupid. All this time the thing [we sought] has been under our very noses from the start, and we never saw it. We have been as absurd as a person who hunts for some thing he has all the time got in his hand. Instead of looking at the thing, we have been staring into the distance. No doubt that is why it escaped us.
>
>   What do you mean?
>
>   I believe we have been talking about the thing all this while without ever understanding that we were giving some sort of account of it.
>
>   Do come to the point. I am all ears.
>
>   Listen, then, and judge whether I am right. You remember how, when we first began to establish our commonwealth and several times since, we have laid down, as a universal principle, that everyone ought to perform the one function in the community for which his nature best suited him. Well, I believe that that principle, or some form of it, is justice. (126–27; 432d–433a)

The features of the right social order that make it a just order have been located; the features that make it just are identical with those that make it right. But what accounts for the fact that those features *make it* right and just? That is to say, what accounts for the fact that those features have that *value?* What accounts for the fact that that value is attached to those features? The answer is familiar to all readers of Plato. What makes a social order of that sort right and just is that it measures up to the objective norm for the right and just social order, that objective norm being understood by Plato as one among the Forms. A social order with the features Plato has singled out for attention measures up to the Just Itself; that is what makes it just. And it measures up to the Right Social Order Itself; that is what makes a right social order.

THE GENERAL STRUCTURE OF RIGHT ORDER ACCOUNTS

Let us now step back a bit in order to get a view of the *type* to which Plato's way of thinking about justice belongs: the right order type. Most of humankind have regarded social order as among the greatest of goods and violations of order as the greatest of evils. But not any order is meant. Hitler's Germany was extraordinarily orderly; the trains ran on time. It was a profoundly wrong order, however.

What determines whether a given social order is right? One answer is whether it measures up to the standard for right order. And what is the character and ontological status of that standard? Different answers have been offered. Some argue that the standard is derived, in one way or another, from the actions of human beings. The most common proposal of this sort is that the standard consists of the content of a contract that human beings have made with each other. The alternative is to hold that the standard is *natural*—that is, not brought about by human action. The rightly ordered society is the one that measures up to some socially transcendent standard for right order. Plato's theory was of this sort. A society is rightly ordered insofar as it measures up to the Form for right order.

None of our contemporary right order theorists appeals to Platonic Forms. To the best of my knowledge, all those who hold that the standard for right order is natural (socially transcendent) think of it as a matrix of objective obligations. Recall Joan O'Donovan's description of the standard from the passage quoted in the Introduction: a matrix established by "God's right . . . of divine, natural, and human laws or objective obligations that constituted the ordering justice of political community." The point comes out even more clearly in another passage from the same essay.

> In the older tradition, the central moral political act on the part of ruler and ruled alike was to consent to the demands of justice, to the obligations inhering in communal life according to divine intention and rationally conceived as laws. The ruler commanded, legislated, and issued binding judgments, but these acts were to embody his consent to an order of right and obligation binding his own will. The subject was obligated to obey the ruler's commands, statutes, and judgments, not only because of his rightful au-

thority, but also because these acts conformed to the requirements of justice. (145)

The standard, in short, is objective obligation understood as natural law.[12]

There are possibilities other than the Platonic and the deontological understandings. One could think of the rightly ordered society as the properly formed and properly functioning society, and of the standard as the design plan for such a society. That proper functioning is a different idea from *obligation* is clear from the fact that when a machine or organism malfunctions, it is not, on that account, guilty of violating its obligations.

And now for the conclusion. Justice is present in society, on the right order way of thinking, insofar as the society measures up to whatever is the standard for the rightly ordered society. The Greek tradition inherited by Plato thought of the gods as having established an order for human beings that the Greeks called *dikē*, justice.[13] Injustice is departure from *dikē*, departure from cosmic order. Plato continued that tradition, adapting and developing it in his own way.

Contemporary Right Order Theorists Hold That Natural Rights Is the Issue

In his account of the just society, Plato makes no reference to the rights of members of society. That way of thinking and speaking is simply missing. The right order theorist who follows Plato in this regard would say of a state of affairs that it is right or just that things be thus, that it should be the case that things are thus; but he would not say of a member of the social order that he *has a right* to such-and-such a good. It is right and just that people keep their promises, it should be the case that they do so; and it is right and just that John keep his promise to Ruth. But

---

[12] Cf. the following passage from Leo Strauss: "The premodern natural law doctrines taught the duties of man; if they paid any attention at all to his rights, they conceived of them as essentially derivative from his duties. As has frequently been observed, in the course of the seventeenth and eighteenth centuries a much greater emphasis was put on rights than ever had been done before. One may speak of a shift of emphasis from natural duties to natural rights. But quantitative changes of this character become intelligible only when they are seen against the background of a qualitative and fundamental change, not to say that such quantitative changes always become possible only by virtue of a qualitative and fundamental change. The fundamental change [was] from an orientation by natural duties to an orientation by natural rights." (*Natural Right and History*, p. 182).

[13] See the discussion by Alasdair MacIntyre in chapter 2 of *Whose Justice? Which Rationality?*

Ruth does not *have a right* to John keeping his promise to her. There is objective right; but nobody has rights.

None of our contemporary right order theorists who holds that there is a natural, socially transcendent standard for right order follows Plato in this regard. All hold that in a just society there will be rights conferred on members of the social order by the legislation, the social practices, and the speech acts of human beings. But that, they hold, is the extent of rights; there are no natural rights and, in particular, no natural *human* rights. *Natural right but no natural rights*, to use Oliver O'Donovan's apothegm.[14]

The point is sufficiently important to warrant a citation or two. In *The Desire of the Nations*, Oliver O'Donovan says:

> The language of subjective rights (i.e., rights which adhere to a particular subject) has, of course, a perfectly appropriate and necessary place within a discourse founded on law. One's "right" is the claim on which the law entitles one to demand performance. . . . What is distinctive about the modern conception of rights, however, is that subjective rights are taken to be original, not derived. . . . The right is a primitive endowment of power with which the subject first engages in society, not an enhancement which accrues to the subject from an ordered and politically formed society.[15]

O'Donovan goes on to make clear that, in his view, there is no "primitive endowment of power with which the subject first engages in society."

In a well-known passage in *After Virtue*, where he insisted that belief in natural and human rights is "one with belief in witches and in unicorns," Alasdair MacIntyre claimed that "there is no expression in any ancient or medieval language correctly translated by our expression 'a right' until near the close of the middle ages: the concept lacks any means of expression in Hebrew, Greek, Latin, or Arabic, classical or medieval, before about 1400, let alone in Old English or Japanese even as late as the mid-nineteenth century."[16] MacIntyre concedes that it does not "follow that there are no natural or human rights; it only follows that no one could have known that there were." In a later article, "Are There Any Natural Rights," he elaborates the point.

> It is very clear that what we should currently describe as rights can indeed be exercised, claimed, violated and the violation recognized and penalized without those who do so exercise, claim, violate and

---

[14] *The Desire of the Nations* (Cambridge: Cambridge University Press; 1996), p. 262.

[15] Ibid., pp. 247–48.

[16] Alasdair MacIntyre, *After Virtue: A Study in Moral Theory* (Notre Dame, University of Notre Dame Press, 1981), pp. 66–67.

penalize being able to characterize what they are doing in the idiom of rights. . . . So it does not follow that, where there is no vocabulary to express claims in terms of rights, there can be nothing truly describable as ascribing and claiming rights.[17]

Lest anyone conclude from this that he thinks there are, or might well be, natural rights, MacIntyre immediately goes on to say:

> Not that this makes things any easier for the protagonist of natural rights; for whenever, in times and places not possessing the linguistic idiom of rights, we do nonetheless have good reason for describing transactions in that idiom, it is always in virtue of the existence in that time and place of some particular set of institutional arrangements requiring description in those terms, and the rights in question therefore will always be institutionally conferred, institutionally recognized and institutionally enforced rights; and all such rights of course are *either* rights conferred by positive law or custom *or* rights exercised in practices *or* rights arising from promises. They will not be and cannot be natural rights possessed independently of specific institutional arrangements. (12)

Not only do O'Donovan and MacIntyre deny the existence of natural rights; from the passages quoted, combined with others, it becomes clear that they regard this as one of the fundamental points—if not, indeed, *the* fundamental point—at issue between the two ways of thinking about justice that they see as pitted against each other. Are all rights socially conferred, or are some rights natural, that is, not socially conferred?

Let me give a reason for concluding that this is not in fact the fundamental point at issue. One can be a right order theorist and hold that there are natural rights. But before I get to that, let me clear away a misapprehension about the idea of natural rights that often gets employed in an argument against their existence. It is often said or assumed that to claim that there are natural rights is to imagine distinguishing within human beings between a natural component and a social component, and then to consider what is to be said about the natural component all by itself. And it is said that once one thinks along these lines, then it is all but inevitable that soon one will find oneself thinking of the natural component as an egoistic asocial atom to which sociality and all that it implies—political authority, for example—somehow gets tacked on. In this, so it is said, lies the fundamental error of Enlightenment political theory. The concept of natural rights, says MacIntyre, is "a con-

---

[17] The article was published by Bowdoin College, Brunswick, Maine, as the Charles F. Adams Lecture of February 28, 1983. The passage quoted occurs on p. 12.

ception of individuals both stripped of all social status and yet bearers of rights." "What was originally both in Roman and canon laws *jus*, a norm governing the relationships of individuals within a structure of community, has become *a right*, something possessed by an individual as he or she is alone, prior to any communal relationships."[18]

Those opposed to natural rights argue against this way of thinking that whatever of the natural there may be in human beings is always already socialized. To try to imagine the natural all by itself without the social is to try to imagine what cannot be. One cannot peel the social off the natural. It is the nature of the human being to be social. There are not and could not be any purely natural, asocial human beings. So any rights that anyone has will always be rights that he or she has *as a social being*, never as a purely natural being. There cannot be natural rights.

This is an attack on a straw man. I know of no proponent of natural rights who engages in, or attempts to engage in, the stripping project of which MacIntyre speaks. One's natural rights are not the rights one would have if one were not living in society. One's natural rights are those that have not been socially conferred on one—or those that one would possess even if they had not been socially conferred. In identifying certain of the rights of a member of the social order as *natural* rights, one is not engaged in the impossible project of imagining this entity as a purely natural, asocial being. One is simply taking note of what does and does not account for her having these rights. Natural rights are not the rights of asocial beings but the rights of social beings that have not been socially conferred on them.

Why the Existence of Natural Rights Is Not the Issue

And now for my argument that one can be a right order theorist and concede that there are natural rights. Indeed, if one thinks of the objective standard as a matrix of principles of natural obligation, one must concede that there are natural rights.

Suppose there is such a matrix. The items in the matrix may or may not be the content of law or legislation of some sort. In the Ten Commandments, some of the principles in the matrix have become the content of legislation. "Thou shalt not bear false witness against thy neighbor" declares one of the commandments. The principle of obligation here propounded does not just declare that it is right that a certain state of affairs obtain, namely, the state of affairs of persons not bearing false witness against their neighbors. Of course, it implies the rightness of that

---

[18] "Are There Any Natural Rights," in *After Virtue*, pp. 13 and 14.

state of affairs. But as such, it is a general statement of obligations that attach to the addressees of the command. (Possibly, each of them already had the obligation.) Each of them has the obligation not to bear false witness against his or her neighbor. Such an obligation is regularly called a *subjective* obligation, on the ground that it attaches to a person, a subject—in contrast to the principle of obligation, which, as a principle, does not attach to anyone and can, for that reason, be called *objective*. To think of the standard for right order as a matrix of principles of obligation is to presuppose that there are subjective obligations, along with the possibility of guilt for failure to carry out one's subjective obligations.

Now consider once again a principle mentioned in the preceding chapter, the *principle of correlatives* as I call it:

> If Y belongs to the sort of entity that can have rights, then X has an obligation toward Y to do or refrain from doing A if and only if Y has a right against X to X's doing or refraining from doing A.

For example, John has an obligation toward Mary to refrain from insulting her if and only if Mary has a right against John to John's refraining from insulting her. In chapter 11 I discuss the principle in detail and offer a defense.[19]

Now if a subjective obligation is natural, then the correlative subjective right will also be natural. So if there are natural subjective obligations, there are natural subjective rights. Right order theorists who hold that the standard for right order is a matrix of objective natural obligations presuppose that there are natural subjective obligations. Given the principle of correlatives, they must then also hold that there are natural subjective rights.

It is open to right order theorists of the sort under consideration to try to escape this consequence by denying the principle of correlatives. It would be exceedingly implausible, however, for their denial to take the form of insisting that there are *no* natural subjective duties that have correlative subjective rights. Perhaps they can show that the principle does not hold in the general form in which I have stated it. But if you have a natural subjective obligation toward me to refrain from hitting

---

[19] The need for the condition "if Y is the sort of entity that can have rights" is explained in chapter 17. The principle holds for claim-rights, not for permission-rights. And in a situation in which one does not know all the relevant facts, it holds only if we are thinking of obligation not as what one is culpable for not doing but as what one *would* be culpable for not doing if one knew all the relevant facts; in the terminology that I use, it holds for full-cognition obligation, not for culpability obligation. These issues are discussed in chapter 11. Duties of charity would seem to constitute exceptions to the principle; my discussion in chapter 17 includes an analysis of such duties.

me over the head, then surely I have a correlative subjective right against you to your refraining from hitting me over the head. And if your obligation is natural, my right is likewise natural. Contemporary right order theorists regularly talk as if there could be natural subjective duties without there being natural subjective rights. That cannot be.

Contemporary right order theorists who hold that the standard for right order is a matrix of principles of natural obligations can and should join the inherent rights theorist in affirming Ulpian's formula for justice, modified so that it speaks of the social condition rather than the virtue: a society is just insofar as its members enjoy the goods to which they have a right. Likewise, they can and should join the inherent rights theorist in affirming the existence of natural rights—that is, subjective rights that have not been conferred or generated by the actions of human beings. And they can join and should join in affirming the principle of correlatives for natural duties and rights.

INHERENT RIGHTS IS THE ISSUE

Should we now extend the palm of victory to the inherent rights theorist? Should we conclude that the right order way of thinking about justice has been shown to be untenable—or, more precisely, that that species of right order thinking that holds that the standard for right order consists of a matrix of objective natural obligations has been shown to be untenable? I think not. There remains a fundamental issue under dispute, albeit one that our contemporary right order theorists have not put their finger on. The debate is not over whether or not there are natural rights. It is more theoretical than that—though no less important for being more theoretical. The debate at bottom is over the deep structure of the moral universe: what accounts for what?

Consider my right to a monthly Social Security check from the U.S. government. That right has been conferred on me by legislation. The U.S. Social Security legislation says that all those who are of a certain sort shall be sent a monthly Social Security check. Given that I am of that sort, I have the right that is the correlative to that obligation of the U.S. government: the right against the government to receive that monthly check. I have the right on account of the legislation plus the fact that I am of the sort specified. Were there not that legislation, I would not have that right even though I was of that sort.

The right order theorist implicitly thinks of all rights along these lines. Every right that anybody has is a right conferred on beings of this sort by human agreement, by human speech acts, by human legislation, by some socially transcendent standard that takes the form of divine legislation, by some socially transcendent standard that takes the form of objective obligations that exist apart from divine legislation, or whatever. A person has the rights she does have on account of those rights being conferred on beings of a certain sort and this person being of that sort. Being of that sort is never, by itself, enough. There has to be something that confers the right on persons of that sort. If that which confers the right is a matrix of natural objective obligations, we can flesh out the deep structure just a bit farther: you will have a subjective obligation toward me on account of the fact that one of the principles of objective obligation applies to you; and on account of your having that subjective obligation, I will then have the correlative subjective right against you to your doing whatever you are obligated to do.

Here is the contrast. The inherent rights theorist agrees that many of the rights we possess are possessed on account of something conferring them on us—some human agreement, some piece of human legislation, some piece of divine legislation, whatever. But he holds that, in addition, we possess some rights that are not conferred, some rights that are *inherent*. On account of possessing certain properties, standing in certain relationships, performing certain actions, each of us has a certain worth. The worth supervenes on being of that sort: having those properties, standing in those relationships, performing those actions. And having that worth is sufficient for having the rights. There does not have to be *something else* that *confers* those rights on entities of this sort.

Some of one's rights are such that what accounts for one's having them is not that something or other confers those rights on entities of one's sort but simply that one has a certain worth that comes along with being of that sort. Those rights are not conferred but inherent, inherent to the worth one has. And by virtue of the principle of correlatives, if, on account of your worth, you have a subjective right against me to my treating you a certain way, then I have the correlative subjective obligation toward you to treat you that way.

It is important to note that, for such rights, though the right is inherent in the worth, the worth need not be essential or intrinsic to the person who has it, because the features on which the worth supervenes may not be essential or intrinsic. Suppose that some person possesses the moral worth supervening on having performed some act of supererogatory charity. That would be an example of a worth that is not intrinsic to the person; the person might not have performed that act of charity. In at least some cases, the person who treats another with supererogatory charity has an inherent right to gratitude from the recipient. Inherent rights are non-conferred rights; they may or may not be rights that one could not fail to have.

Just as the contemporary right order theorist need not and should not deny the existence of natural rights in general, only of *inherent* natural rights, so too the inherent rights theorist need not and should not deny the existence of natural (socially transcendent) laws of objective obligation. However, he will see at least some of those laws as having a place in the accounting-structure of the moral universe very different from that which the right order theorist assigns to them. Those natural laws of objective obligation do not account for particular subjective obligations; particular subjective obligations account for the truth of the laws. The particular obligations are ontologically prior to the objective law. I have a subjective right against you to your not torturing me; so you have a subjective obligation toward me not to torture me. Let us suppose that I have that same subjective right against every other human being; then every other human being has that same subjective obligation toward me. And let us suppose that every other human being is like me in this regard. Then there is the following natural law of objective obligation: every human being is obligated not to torture any human being. That natural law of objective obligation is a universal generalization of all those particular natural subjective obligations.

Suppose that on account of the worth we each have it is true that every human being is under obligation not to torture any human being. A theist will then naturally be of the view that God commands all of us not to torture, holds all of us accountable for not torturing. The divine command does not make it wrong; it was already that. What the command brings about is that, if any of us tortures anybody, we do not just wrong the person tortured but we wrong God by disobeying him; God has a right to our obedience. So there are now two reasons for my being obligated not to torture you. I have a subjective obligation not to torture you on account of your having an inherent subjective right against me to my not torturing you; that is one reason. And I have a subjective obligation not to torture you on account of God having commanded that nobody shall torture anybody, that command having conferred on me (generated in me) the subjective obligation to obey God by not torturing you.[20]

A final point is in order. The understanding of natural rights that I have been working with is that natural rights are those not conferred by human action. This understanding is common in the literature; it comes to the surface in some of the passages I have quoted from other writers. On this understanding, divinely conferred rights are natural rights—albeit not *inherent* natural rights. Now it may be that what some right order theorists had in mind, when they spoke of "natural" rights, was not *natu-*

---

[20] The divine command theory is discussed in chapter 12.

ral rights as I have just explained those but *inherent* rights. Here and there one finds hints to this effect. It may be that though the writer explained "natural" rights as those not conferred by human action, what he really had in mind was rights not conferred by *anything*—not by human action, not by divine action, not by laws of objective obligation independent of God, not by anything. It is the claim that there are such rights that he meant to oppose. If so, then what I have presented as a rational reconstruction of his thought is in fact an explication.

Only confusion will result, however, if we fail to distinguish between these two senses of "natural"—natural as not conferred by human action versus natural as not conferred at all. I will use the term "natural" only in the former sense. Rights of the latter sort I will continue to call *inherent* rights. Natural rights come in two sorts: conferred natural rights and inherent natural rights.

Does Aquinas Offer a Mediating Position?

Might Aquinas's views on justice and natural law represent a mediating position between justice as right order and justice as inherent rights?[21] Hovering over my account of the right order position is an internal-external contrast: the standard that determines right order, and hence justice, is *external* to human beings. In the contemporary deontological version of the position, the matrix of natural objective obligations specifies the obligations of human beings of certain sorts in situations of certain sorts—or sometimes of all human beings in all situations. Some human beings are of those sorts and in those situations. The application of the former to the latter, the laws to the human beings, accounts for those human beings having the particular natural subjective obligations that they do have. By virtue of the principle of correlatives, those obligations account, in turn, for the particular natural subjective rights of human beings. That is the picture. I have not ascribed to right order theorists the claim that the standard for right order is *external* to human beings; my presentation of the right order position certainly suggests that, however.

But Aquinas, for one, did not think of what he called "natural law" as external in this way to human beings. God did not create human beings and then, in addition, ordain a matrix of objective obligations for them. It belongs to the nature of the human being to have certain laws for his or her life; a creature for which that was not the case would not be a

---

[21] This possibility was suggested to me by one of the readers for Princeton University Press.

human being. The question is whether this view constitutes a mediating position between justice as right order and justice as inherent rights.

Before I set out to answer that question, let me make a comment about terminology. I noted just above that I am following the common practice of taking a *natural right* to be a right not conferred by any human action, or a right that one would have even if it had not been conferred by some human action. Rights conferred by divine action—by a promise God makes, for example—are natural rights, though not *inherent* natural rights. The counterpart understanding of *natural law* would be law not made by human beings. But that is not what is commonly understood by natural law. No writer would offer the Ten Commandments *qua command-ments* as an example of natural law. Though the content of the command-ments was widely viewed as also contained within natural law, the Ten Commandments *qua commandments* are an example of *positive* law, spe-cifically, *divine* positive law. Positive law, whether human or divine, is not natural law.

I follow the common practice in my usage. I concede that there is danger of confusion when "natural" as an adjective of "rights" is under-stood rather differently from "natural" as an adjective of "law"; but I think the danger of confusion is even greater if we depart from the usage of those who write on these matters. Every now and then I will remind the reader of the difference between these two understandings of "natural."

To say that there is not a consensus view on Aquinas's understanding of natural law is to understate drastically the depth and scope of con-troversy on the matter. Some interpretations—such as that of John Finnis—quite intentionally interpret natural law in Aquinas as not onto-logically grounded in human nature. My principal guide to interpreting Aquinas on this matter will be John Bowlin's *Contingency and Fortune in Aquinas's Ethics.*[22] Bowlin's close reading of the Thomistic text leads him to an interpretation in which natural law is very much grounded in human nature. If Aquinas's position does indeed mediate between jus-tice as right order and justice as inherent rights, it will do so on a Bowlin-like interpretation.

Aquinas's explanation of natural law goes as follows. The universe is ruled by divine providence. Because law, in general, is "a dictate of practi-cal reason emanating from [a] ruler," God's providential rule has the character of *law*. It is outside time; so we can call it *eternal law*.[23]

Any instance of effective law can be regarded from two perspectives, the perspective of the ruler and the perspective of the ruled. To consider

---

[22] Cambridge; Cambridge University Press, 1999.
[23] *S. Th.* I-II 91.1.

it from the perspective of those ruled is to ask what it is within them that accounts for the fact that their actions conform to the law—or to use Aquinas's terminology, accounts for the fact that they "partake" of or "participate" in the law.

In the case of God's eternal law, it would be possible to hold an occasionalist view of how God's providential rule gets effectuated: God directly brings about each and every instance of conformity. That was not Aquinas's view. God's providential rule is "imprinted" on things, this imprint taking the form of their being created with "inclinations to their proper acts and ends."

In the case of human beings, this "imprint" takes a quite extraordinary, "most excellent" form. We too are endowed with inclinations to our proper acts and ends. But in our case, these inclinations do not work deterministically. Instead of our actions being causally determined, we are capable of acting, and to a considerable extent must act, "for an end under the aspect [*ratio*] of good" (*S. Th.* I-II, 94, 2). To so act, we must use our "light of natural reason" to "discern what is good and what is evil," to deliberate over means to ends, and then to make choices. The good and the evil that we attempt to discern are the specifically *human* good and *human* evil. Each kind of thing has its own characteristic good and evil, determined by what constitutes well-being for things of that kind. The good of cats and the good of sunflowers are very different from the good of human beings.

To say that something belongs to *the good* of entities of a certain kind is, for Aquinas, implicitly to make a claim about its role in the appetitive life of entities of that kind; it is to say something about its role as an end, as something sought after, by such entities. It would be a mistake, however, to declare that the good for an entity is whatever it seeks, whatever it desires, whatever ends it inclines toward. For in this world of ours, things are often malformed, they often malfunction; they do not work according to their nature. This is true of human beings with respect to, among other things, their desires and inclinations; often those are disordered, malformed, unnatural. So the relation between the good of an entity and its desires or inclinations has to be put like this: the good of an entity is whatever it desires when functioning *properly*, whatever it *naturally* desires. The well-being of a creature is constituted by the satisfaction of what it naturally or properly desires. The point, as it applies to human beings, is this: because "good has the nature of an end, and evil, the nature of a contrary, hence it is that all those things to which man has a natural inclination are naturally apprehended by reason as being good, and consequently as objects of pursuit, and their contraries as evil, and objects of avoidance" (*S. Th.* I-II, 94, 2).

Our natural reason, with its "inclination to its [own] proper act and end," is thus "an imprint on us" of God's eternal reason. By virtue of our natural reason we have "a share of the eternal reason," we partake of or participate in it. And the directives yielded by that participation constitute what Aquinas calls *natural law.* "Natural law is nothing else than the rational creature's participation of the eternal law." The "participation of the eternal law in the rational creature is called the natural law."[24]

Why call the directives for action yielded by properly functioning human reason *law?* Well, remember that a law is a dictate of practical reason emanating from a ruler. A consequence of the peculiar way in which human beings partake in the divine rule is that we govern ourselves by the use of our reason; we issue directives for our own lives. Think of it like this: "The rational creature . . . partakes of a share of providence by being provident both for itself and for others" (*S. Th.* I-II, 91,2). That is why the directives are called *law.*

Let me note, parenthetically, that apparently only some of the directives issued by rightly functioning practical reason are called *precepts* of natural law by Aquinas. In answering the question of whether there is a human law, Aquinas remarks that "just as, in the speculative reason, from naturally known indemonstrable principles, we draw the conclusions of the various sciences, the knowledge of which is not imparted to us by nature, but acquired by the efforts of reason, so too it is from the precepts of the natural law, as from general and indemonstrable principles, that the human reason needs to proceed to the more particular determination of certain matters" (*S. Th.* I-II, 91, 3). He picks up the thought again in a later article: "the precepts of the natural law are to the practical reason what the first principles of demonstrations are to the speculative reason; because both are self-evident principles" (*S. Th.* I-II, 94, 2). Apparently, it is the directives of right practical reason "imparted to us by nature" and therefore self-evident, rather than "acquired by the efforts of reason," that are the *precepts* of natural law.

The directives of natural law are grounded in our natural, properly formed inclinations. "To the natural law belongs everything to which a man is inclined according to his nature" (*S. Th.* I-II, 94, 3). There is in fact a parallelism between the order of our natural inclinations and the order of natural law's precepts: "According to the order of natural inclinations is the order of the precepts of the natural law" (*S. Th.* I-II, 94,

---

[24] The full passage in which the latter definition occurs is this: the rational creature "has a share of the eternal reason, whereby it has a natural inclination to its proper act and end; and this participation of the eternal law in the rational creature is called the natural law" (*S. Th.* I-II, 91, 2). The main thought in the preceding five paragraphs of text, and all the quotations unless otherwise indicated, are from *S. Th.* I-II, 91,2.

2). Thus natural law, rather than being external to the human being, expresses what human beings are. We are creatures whose participation in God's providential rule takes the form of using our reason to reflect on our natural inclinations and thus, when reason is functioning properly, arriving at directives that coincide with God's eternal law for human life.

So is this Thomistic understanding of natural law a mediating position between the right order conception of justice and the inherent rights conception? That depends not only on how Aquinas understands natural law but also on how he understands justice.

In my Introduction I took note of Aquinas's declaration, several times repeated, that justice "denotes a kind of equality" (*S. Th.* II-II 57, 1; see also II-II 58, 2, and 59, 2). From his discussion it is clear, however, that Aquinas did not regard this as an explanation of what justice is but as a characterization of those situations in which justice is present. For when he asks in Question 58, Article 1, of *Summa Theologiae* II-II, "what is justice," how "justice is fittingly defined," his answer is that justice is "rendering to each his right. . . . A man is said to be just because he respects the rights [*ius*] of others." This, of course, is the Ulpian definition. In the course of his discussion of justice, thus understood, Aquinas indicates that it can also be defined as rendering to each "what is his" or what "is due to him" (*S. Th.* II-II, 58, 11).

And how does Aquinas explain this idea of a good that is due someone, of a good that is someone's by right? I know of no place in which he does explain it.[25] He employs the idea without ever explaining it. Strictly speaking, Aquinas gives no account of justice.

So far as I can see, there were only two options available to him, the same two options that we have been exploring in this chapter. He could have said that someone has a right to some good because failure to render that good to the person would be to treat him as having less worth than he does in fact have; the right is in that way inherent in the person's worth. Or he could have said that some at least of the directives of practical reason specify or imply subjective obligations; and these, given the principle of correlatives, account for rights. In chapter 7 I argue that neither of these positions fits well with Aquinas's eudaimonism.

Our conclusion is this: the fact that Aquinas does not think of natural law as external to the human being, imposed from without, does not result in a position that mediates between justice as right order and justice as inherent rights. Along with everyone else, he has to choose.

---

[25] There is a good and lengthy chapter on Aquinas's treatment of justice in Eleonore Stump's *Aquinas* (London and New York, Routledge, 2003). But Stump does not address the question I am asking.

THE DEBATE REMAINS IMPORTANT

My discussion evokes a pressing question: has not the debate between these two ways of thinking now been sapped of all interest and importance? When the debate was thought to be over the existence or non-existence of natural rights, it seemed interesting and important. Now that has been turned into an arcane debate over what accounts for what in the the deep structure of the moral order, who cares?

I reject the assumption that debates over the deep structure of the moral order are necessarily lacking in interest and importance. Be that as it may, however, I submit that my reconfiguring of the debate leaves the right order theorist no happier with the inherent rights way of thinking than he was before.

Though our contemporary right order theorist can and should concede the existence of natural rights, natural rights have a very different significance for him from what at least some of them have for inherent rights theorists. For the right order theorist, the violation of someone's natural rights is never, in itself and as such, the treating of a human being with less than due respect. It is always instead an indicator of the fact that some natural law of objective obligation has been disobeyed. A partisan of right order may point to the plight of the poor, he may say that their rights are being violated. But pointing to the victims is for him a roundabout way of calling attention to the more fundamental fact that the powerful and the well-to-do are not living up to their obligations. It is not a way of calling attention to the fact that the worth of those human beings who are poor is not being respected. The worth of human beings does not enter into his way of thinking about rights.

Furthermore, one should not be surprised if our contemporary right order theorist continues to oppose talk about natural rights, even if he concedes their existence. Given the power on the contemporary scene of an inherent-rights culture, one must expect that talk of natural rights will be captured by that culture. One can insist that such rights are not inherent; one's voice will not be heard. Best then not to speak even of natural rights. To think of ourselves as bearers of inherent rights is to promote possessive individualism in society, to encourage individualistic modes of thought, and—to mention a point that has been lurking in the background all along—to remove God from the picture. That is the charge. Anything that promotes such destructive thoughts and attitudes should be opposed. It is best not to mention natural rights, lest one's readers assume that they are inherent.

Chapter Two

A CONTEST OF NARRATIVES

THE POLEMIC BY those who favor the right order conception of justice over the inherent rights conception gets most of its power from the story they tell about the origins of the latter conception. Having delineated these two conceptions of justice in the preceding chapter, we are ready now to tackle the narrative.

Actually, it is not just one narrative that the partisans of justice as right order tell but a couple of narratives, with slight variations on each of those. The general contour of all the narratives is the same, however. It is always a story of decline, from the dominance in ancient and early medieval times of the concept of *the right* and the conception of justice as right order to the emergence and eventual dominance in modern times of the concept of *rights* and the conception of justice as grounded in natural rights, with the decline reaching its low point in the international human rights declarations of the 1940s and 1950s.[1] Both of the main narratives identify one great point of crisis, namely, the construction of political theory on the foundation of natural rights by the Enlightenment theorists. One of them identifies an earlier point of crisis as well, the formulation of a doctrine of natural rights by the fourteenth-century nominalist William of Ockham, in his defense of his fellow Franciscans against attacks by the Pope.

More than anything else, it is these declinist narratives that are responsible for stirring up skepticism concerning the existence of natural and inherent rights among those philosophers, theologians, political theorists, and other intellectuals who otherwise share the conviction of the inherent rights theorist that justice is ultimately grounded in something that transcends the social. What good can come from a way of thinking about justice and rights whose parentage is late-medieval nominalism or Enlightenment political theory?

Some will suspect that a genetic fallacy is being committed when the move is made from a declinist story about the origin and employment of the concept of natural rights to the conclusion that the concept should

---

[1] I will tell the story as it has been told by those who believe it, namely, in terms of *natural* rights rather inherent rights.

be discarded as unacceptable and inapplicable.[2] I think not; later I explain why. But in any case, we cannot fully understand the charges made against natural rights, nor comprehend why so many find those charges compelling, without placing them within the context of the declinist narrative.

OCKHAM'S DEFENSE OF THE FRANCISCANS AGAINST THE POPE

The dispute between the Franciscans and the papacy developed as follows.[3] After the death of Francis, disputes arose within the Order about the precise nature of the Franciscan vow of poverty. In the bull that he issued on September 28, 1230, *Quo elongati,* Pope Gregory IX declared that the Franciscans could have use of the things they needed but should not own anything, either individually or communally. Disputes continued. So on August 14, 1279, Pope Nicholas III issued a bull, *Exiit qui seminat,* in which he defined Franciscan poverty in precise legal terms. "In temporal things we have to consider," he said, "especially property, possession, usufruct, right of use and simple factual use,"[4] adding that "the life of mortals requires the last as a necessity, but it can do without the others."[5] The Pope declared that the Franciscans had given up right

---

[2] Robert P. George is among those who suspects—or charges—the commission of this genetic fallacy. In response to Joan Lockwood O'Donovan's telling of the narrative, he says that "surely no mere historical connection is sufficient to establish that those who reject possessive individualism cannot now deploy the language of rights without thereby importing into their thought features of that philosophy that mark it as antithetical to the value of community and other important human goods. Here, I would suggest, only a logical (or, at a minimum, a very strong psychological) connection will suffice." Robert P. George, "A Response," in Michael Cromartie, ed., *A Preserving Grace* (Grand Rapids, Mich.: Eerdmans, 1997), p. 157.

[3] I base my telling on two main sources: Part Two of Brian Tierney, *The Idea of Natural Rights: Studies on Natural Rights, Natural Law and Church Law 1150–1625* (Atlanta, Ga.: Scholars Press, 1997), and John Moorman, *A History of the Franciscan Order: From Its Origins to the Year 1517* (Oxford: Clarendon Press, 1968). There is also some helpful information in chapter 2 of Anabel S. Brett, *Liberty, Right and Nature: Individual Rights in Later Scholastic Thought* (Cambridge: Cambridge University Press, 1997).

[4] *Proprietas, possessio, ususfructus, ius utendi, simplex usus facti.*

[5] Nicholas is virtually quoting here from Bonaventure's *Defense of the Mendicants* (*Apologia pauperum*) of around ten years earlier. In sec. 11 Bonaventure says: "there are four possible relations to temporal goods: property, possession, usufruct, and simple use. The life of mortals may be sustained without the first three, but the last is a necessity. There can, then, be no profession of renunciation of temporal things which extends to their use." Quoted from the translation in O. O'Donovan and J. L. O'Donovan, *From Irenaeus to Grotius: A Sourcebook in Christian Political Thought 100–1625* (Grand Rapids, Mich.: Eerdmans, 1999), p. 318.

of use (*usus juris*) but had retained factual use (*usus facti*). He added that the Franciscan way of life was also the way of Christ and the apostles; they too had no rights of use or possession, only simple factual use.

In late 1322, Pope John XXII initiated a furor. He had been having trouble with the Franciscans over the issue of poverty ever since 1317. In the spring of 1322 he assembled a number of people to discuss the issue and give him advice. They continued their work through the summer, and on December 8, 1322, John issued a bull, *Ad conditorem*, in which he challenged the teaching of the bull of Nicholas III while ostensibly doing no more than interpreting it. His argumentation was ingenious. The simple factual use of things, which Nicholas assigned to the Franciscans, had to be understood as a *licit* use, and a licit use of something is a *rightful* use of it. To use something without a right to use it would be to act against justice. So the simple factual use of the Franciscans implies the right of using. Now when it comes to things that perish in the using—food, for example,—it is absurd to suppose that one can separate a right of using from a right of owning. Only the owner of something can licitly destroy it, as one does with bread when one swallows it. So the Franciscans, whatever they might say, have not really renounced all ownership and all right of use, retaining only "simple factual use." John then tightened the screws by declaring that henceforth the church would no longer own the things that the friars used. Ownership would be turned over to the Franciscan order; like it or not, they were now proprietors.

John's bull evoked intensely hostile reactions from the Franciscans. But John was not one to back away from a quarrel. So on November 12 of the next year, 1323, he issued another bull, *Cum inter nonnullos*, in which he argued that Christ and the apostles had rights of ownership and not merely of use, adding that "henceforth it would be heretical to maintain that Jesus Christ and the apostles did not 'have' anything, individually or in common, or that they had no 'right of using' the things that they actually did have or no right of selling, giving, or exchanging them" (Tierney, *Idea of Natural Rights*, 96). Whereas John's previous bull had turned the Franciscans into owners of property, now he was implying that they were heretics, because at the heart of the Franciscan case for poverty had always been the claim that they were following the way of perfection practiced by Christ and the apostles. On November 16, 1329, John issued yet another bull, *Quia vir reprobus*, in which he developed further the argument that Christ and the apostles held property.

A number of Franciscans, William of Ockham prominent among them, undertook to answer the Pope's arguments. The core of Ockham's reply went as follows. When Nicholas III spoke of the right of using (*ius utendi*) that the Franciscans, following Christ and the apostles, had renounced, he has to be interpreted as meaning the *positive* right of using, because Nicholas explicitly held that the Franciscans had *retained* a natural right of using in cases of extreme need. "Every right of using is either a natural right or a positive right," said Ockham. Nicholas "did not take right of using for a natural right. Therefore he took right of using for a positive right" (quoted in Tierney, *Idea of Natural Rights*, 121). Now John XXII claimed to be doing no more than interpreting what Nicholas had said about the nature of apostolic and Franciscan poverty. So let it be accepted that when John spoke of the right of using (and of possession), he too had the positive right in mind.

Two things follow. In the first place, in claiming that Christ and the apostles had rights of both ownership and use, John must have meant that they were legal owners and users of property—surely a heretical claim. And as to Franciscan poverty, John must also have meant that the Franciscans were the legal owners and users of property. But that was plainly mistaken. Until the Pope forced property on them, the Franciscans had no legal ownership of property; they had renounced it all. What they had not renounced is the *natural* right of using what was given them. This natural right they cannot renounce: "It is licit to renounce property and the power of appropriating but no one may renounce the natural right of using" (quoted in ibid., 164). In sum, the Franciscans, "have no positive right, but they do have a right, namely a natural right" (quoted in ibid., 122).[6]

VILLEY'S NARRATIVE

Ockham's defense of his fellow Franciscans seems acute but harmless. In his answer to the Pope, Ockham employed the concept of a natural right. What was wrong with that? What should he have done instead?

To understand why a good many right order theorists view Ockham's argument as the initial crisis in our Western understanding of justice, we must move beyond the events surrounding Ockham to the story they tell about the events leading up to Ockham, and beyond chronicle to interpretation. When we do that, we encounter the gray eminence be-

---

[6] Bonaventure had anticipated Ockham's position in his *Defense of the Mendicants* of around 1269. After distinguishing four kinds of community of goods—those "derived from the right of natural necessity," those "derived from the right of brotherly love," those "derived from the right of worldly civil society," and those "derived from the right of ecclesiastical endowment"—he argued that the Franciscans had renounced the latter two but not the first two. The first cannot be renounced, because it "derives from the right that naturally belongs to man as God's image and noblest creature." The second "absolutely may not be renounced. It derives from a right poured into us by God." Quotations from the translation in O'Donovan and O'Donovan, *From Irenaeus to Grotius*, p. 317.

hind this version of the declinist narrative, the French legal theorist and philosopher Michel Villey, who from the mid-1940s to the mid-1980s published a voluminous, imposing, and extremely influential body of writings on the history of the concept of subjective rights from Roman antiquity up through the late medieval period.

Villey's narrative came in two main parts.[7] First, he tried to dispose of the idea that the Latin jurists were already working with the concept of rights when they spoke of *ius*. They spoke, for example, of *ius utendi et fruendi*; that would seem to be the right of use and enjoyment. And they spoke of *ius altius tollendi*; that would seem to be the right of building higher. But not so, argued Villey. For they also spoke of *ius non extollendi*, corresponding to *ius altius tollendi*; and it makes no sense to think of that as the right of *not* building higher.

So what then did they mean by *ius*? Often they meant by it, so Villey contended, simply *right* or *the right*, as when we say, "It is right that the victim of a burglary recover his property" or "The right thing for the burglar to do is restore the property." But they also spoke of *iura*, in the plural. To understand this latter usage one has to recall, says Villey, their distinction between *res corporales* and *res incorporales*, that is, between corporeal realities and incorporeal realities. *Iura* were understood by them as incorporeal realities attached to corporeal realities. For example, a piece of property was understood as having *iura* attached to it, those consisting of the legal benefits and burdens that come with the property. Thus *ius*, in this sense, was not a subjective but an *objective* reality; it attaches not to a subject but to an object. Villey was in the habit of taking Ockham's definition of a right, namely, a right is a *potestas licita*, as unquestionably the correct definition. A right is a power attached to a subject. So, given that *iura* were understood as the legal benefits and burdens attached to objective reality, the Latin jurists cannot have been speaking of rights when they spoke of *iura*.

Ulpian's formula, *suum ius cuique tribuens*, would seem to be an insuperable obstacle to this line of thought; here *ius* is something that belongs to persons, not objects. But Villey was not to be deterred. Stoicism, and its near-relative, Platonism, was the philosophical context of Roman juristic thought; and the Stoics, like Plato, thought of justice in terms of right order. So what Ulpian must have had in mind by a person's *ius*, said Villey, is simply that person's share in the goods distributed by a right social order.

<hr>

[7] I am especially indebted here to Part One of Tierney, *Idea of Natural Rights*, and to pp. 51–57 of Charles J. Reid Jr., "The Canonistic Contribution to the Western Rights Tradition: An Historical Inquiry," in *Boston College Law Review* 33 no. 1 (December 1991): 37–92.

The second part of Villey's narrative was the medieval part. Here two deep convictions shaped his telling. First, he firmly embraced the standard neo-Thomist picture of medieval philosophy as reaching its apogee in Aquinas and plunging downhill from there, with Ockham being especially culpable for initiating the nominalistic and atomistic lines of thought that led to the calamities of the Reformation, Descartes, and the Enlightenment. Villey's own contribution to this inherited picture was his development of the thesis that it was Ockham who first developed a full-blown theory of subjective rights in general and of *natural* subjective rights in particular, and that Ockham's nominalism played a crucial role in the formation of his theory. "The cradle of subjective right was the Franciscan Order," said Villey; "William of Ockham, founder of nominalism, an individualist philosophy . . . enemy of the pope and convicted of heresy according to many, may be called the father of subjective rights" (quoted in Tierney, *Idea of Natural Rights*, 27–28). Second, Villey construed what happened in Ockham as the displacement of the traditional conception of justice as objective right order with the newfangled conception of justice as subjective rights.

The details of Villey's narrative about Ockham's medieval predecessors varied considerably from essay to essay, as indeed did his narrative about the Roman jurists. One theme remained constant, however, and it is this persistent theme that is important for our purposes here. Villey claimed that the concept of a subjective right played no systematic role in theoretical writings, either ancient or medieval, before Ockham and his fellow Franciscans. The concept may have had some currency in literary and informal writings, and in casual comments by theorists; but the conception of justice that was systematically employed by medieval theorists was a blend of justice as objective right order with justice as law, *lex*, the former on the way to being transmuted into the latter. Ockham was the first to develop a *systematic theory* of subjective rights. It is for that reason that he can be called "the father of subjective rights."

Villey highlighted three important features of the theoretical context, as he understood it, of Ockham's articulation of the concept. First, Ockham articulated the concept of subjective rights in the context of arguing for the existence of *natural* subjective rights. "Subjective rights from their origin and still today are conceived of as natural rights," says Villey (quoted in ibid., 20).

Second, Ockham defined "*ius*" as *a licit power.* "The right of using," said Ockham, "is the licit power of using" (*ius utendi est potestas licita utendi*). In thus defining "*ius*," Ockham gave birth to our modern concept of a subjective right as "a quality of the subject, something that *subjacet*, that underlies or is inherent in a person. It is a quality of the subject, a faculty, a liberty, an ability to act. In a word, 'subjective right is a *power* of the subject' " (ibid., 28). Villey leaves no doubt as to what he thinks of this development: "The concept of *right* is resolutely twisted to the meaning of *power*" (quoted in ibid., 29).

Third, it was Ockham's philosophical nominalism, with its rejection of universals and its insistence on the importance of the particular, that made it both possible and necessary for him to articulate the concept of a subjective right and to employ it systematically in his theoretical writings. Tierney summarizes Villey's claim thus: "The modern idea of subjective rights . . . is rooted in the nominalist philosophy of the fourteenth century, and it first saw the light of day in the work of William of Ockham. Ockham inaugurated a 'semantic revolution' when he transformed the traditional idea of objective natural right into a new theory of subjective natural rights. His work marked a 'Copernican moment' in the history of the science of law" (14).[8] "It is the whole philosophy professed by Ockham that is the mother of subjective right" (Villey, quoted in ibid., 30).[9]

Employment by the Enlightenment Theorists of the Idea of Natural Rights

Those right order theorists who see Ockham's employment of the concept of natural rights as the first great crisis in our Western understanding of justice see the second great crisis as the employment of the concept by Hobbes, Locke, and their cohorts in developing the foundations of political liberalism. Other right order theorists, Leo Strauss prominent among them, skip over the medieval thinkers who come after Aquinas and regard the early Enlightenment figures as the inventors of the concept of natural rights, that being for them, then, the first rather than the second great crisis.[10]

---

[8] Tierney goes on to say the following: "Villey's argument has been widely and uncritically accepted. Nowadays Ockham is often regarded as the originator of modern rights theories, at least among scholars who seek an origin for them before the seventeenth century" (14).

[9] Here is one of Tierney's descriptions of the general structure of Villey's argument: "Villey has devised a sort of Manichean universe. There is an Aristotelian thought-world, full of light and sweet reason, and an Ockhamist thought-world, where all is darkness and blind will. The good theory of objective right can flourish only in the first thought-world, the bad theory of subjective rights only in the second. When clear-cut affirmations of individual rights are found in texts before Ockham they have to be dismissed as exceptions or aberrations or mere misunderstandings of vulgar persons who were too ignorant to attach precise meanings to the terms they used in day-to-day discourse" (30–31).

[10] I have borrowed the term "crisis" from Leo Strauss, who speaks of "the crisis of modern natural right."

There is no disagreement among the tellers of these two different stories as to how the Enlightenment figures used the concept. Members of society were regarded as bearers of natural rights, with the principal task of the state being to respect those rights in the course of securing them against infringement by other members of society. The "freedom rights" of individuals set limits to state action and to the actions of one's fellows; the "benefit rights" of individuals constitute entitlements to state action and to the actions of one's fellows.

This story, about the employment of the concept of natural rights by political thinkers of the Enlightenment, could be fleshed out a great deal beyond the extremely brief sketch just given. But because the story as told by the right order theorists seems to me essentially correct, and because the texts of Hobbes, Locke, Rousseau, and the like remain a living part of our cultural heritage (as those of Ockham and the medieval papacy do not), let me move beyond chronicle to interpretation. Why does the right order theorist regard the employment of the concept of natural rights by the Enlightenment political theorists as a crisis in our understanding of justice?

Though here too the answers given vary somewhat in their details, they converge in their general thrust. Joan Lockwood O'Donovan formulates the point of convergence crisply: "the modern liberal concept of right belongs to the socially atomistic and disintegrative philosophy of 'possessive individualism.' "[11] In an article well known in legal circles, "Obligation: A Jewish Jurisprudence of the Social Order," Robert Cover, himself Jewish and an esteemed professor at Yale Law School until his untimely death, after remarking that in the Jewish understanding of law the concept of responsibility or obligation is basic, whereas the concept of rights has only a subsidiary role, puts the standard interpretation a bit more elaborately: "The story behind the term 'rights' is the story of social contract. The myth postulates free and independent if highly vulnerable beings who voluntarily trade a portion of their autonomy for a measure of collective security. . . . [T]he first and fundamental unit is the individual and 'rights' locate him as an individual separate and apart from every other individual" (66).[12]

Oliver O'Donovan, in *Desire of the Nations*,[13] highlights a slightly different aspect of the seventeenth- and eighteenth-century developments. When the Enlightenment theorists asked how political authority might emerge from an already extant society, they were conceiving society ab-

---

[11] Joan Lockwood O'Donovan, "Natural Law and Perfect Community: Contributions of Christian Platonism to Political Theory," *Modern Theology* 14, no. 1 (January 1998): 20.

[12] In 5 *Journal of Law and Religion*, 65 (1987).

[13] Cambridge: Cambridge University Press, 1999.

stractly, as an "acephalous organism," says O'Donovan; that is, they were conceiving society as without the exercise of political authority therein. In fact there has never been, and never can be, such a society (246–47).

WHY THE NARRATIVE DOES NOT COMMIT THE GENETIC FALLACY

The main thesis of the declinist narratives about the ideas of subjective rights in general and natural subjective rights in particular is now before us. These ideas, so it is said, are the offspring of philosophical individualism, either that of the nominalism of the late medieval period or that of the political philosophy of the Enlightenment.

Now add to this narrative the claim that it is naïve to suppose that one could just pluck the idea out of such a context and drop it into another. Either one drags along significant elements of the original context and tries to force those elements into the new context, thereby producing incoherence, or one winds up with a different idea masquerading under the same name. The reason the right order theorist is not straightforwardly committing the genetic fallacy in offering one or another of the narratives as a ground for abolishing the concept of natural rights is that she is taking for granted a doctrine of the embeddedness of concepts in the ideological contexts of their origin and prior employment. Once again, Joan Lockwood O'Donovan makes the point better than anyone else:

> The theoretical elaborations of the concept of rights from the fifteenth to the eighteenth centuries, but especially in its classical and Enlightenment heydays, have invested it with lasting intellectual content. For contemporary moral and political theorizing this content is in varying degrees inescapable, being woven into the fabric of politics in this century—the fabric of democratic, pluralistic, technological liberalism. Christian political thought (both Catholic and Protestant) that is not wholly satisfied with this fabric recognizes the need to divest the concept of rights of its offensive theoretical material. But when it attempts to separate some conceptual threads from the fabric, the result inevitably falls short: either too much of the fabric adheres to the threads, or the threads lose their coherence.[14]

---

[14] "The Concept of Rights in Christian Moral Discourse," in Cromartie, *A Preserving Grace*, p. 146. Cf. Richard Tuck, in *Natural Rights Theories*, p. 2: "Because the meaning of a term such as *a right* is theory-dependent, . . . we have to be sure about what role the term played in the various theories about politics which engage our attention." "The elucidation

BEGINNING THE COUNTER-NARRATIVE

How shall we respond? One way to respond would be to develop and then appraise the claim made, or assumed, concerning the intrinsic embeddedness in theoretical and ideological contexts of the concept of subjective rights in general and of natural subjective rights in particular. Surely, many concepts have been successfully employed in contexts very different from those of their birth or previous employment. Why should this not be the case for the concept of subjective rights in general and of natural subjective rights in particular? What makes them different? But let me take a different tack.[15]

In the late 1980s and 1990s there emerged a new body of scholarship that effectively demolished the declinist narratives by proposing and decisively substantiating an alternative narrative concerning the origin of the concept of subjective rights in general and of natural subjective rights in particular. The main authors of the medieval component of this new narrative were specialists in those medieval discussions of canon law that began with the publication of Gratian's *Decretum* around 1140. The most prominent contributor to this new wave of scholarship is the eminent medieval scholar Brian Tierney, in the book already mentioned, plus a large number of articles. Not far behind is a student of Tierney's, Charles J. Reid Jr., in a long article, "The Canonistic Contribution to the Western Rights Tradition: An Historical Inquiry,"[16] and in his Cornell University doctoral dissertation, "Rights in Thirteenth-Century Canon Law: an Historical Investigation."[17]

The basic thesis of the new wave is simple. After mentioning the two narratives concerning the origins of the Western rights tradition that I have canvassed, Reid remarks:

> The chief difficulty with these two schools of thought, from the standpoint of a working medievalist, is that rights are readily identifiable in the legal systems of thirteenth century Europe. Confining

---

of a complex notion such as a right requires a fairly full account of the possible theories about politics which involve the concept."

[15] In writing this part of the chapter I have been aided enormously by the extensive historical and bibliographical knowledge of John J. Witte Jr., of the Emory Law School. Those who want a concise history of the idea of rights that, for the most part, ignores the polemic that is my concern here and is based on the latest scholarship should see chapter 1, "Rights," of his *God's Joust and God's Justice: Law and Politics in the Western Tradition* (Grand Rapids, Mich.: Eerdmans, 2006).

[16] See note 7 above.

[17] December 1994. Reid's argument is further fleshed out in, "Roots of a Democratic Church Polity in the History of Canon Law: the Case of Elections in the Church," *CLSA Proceedings* 6 (1998): 150–78.

the inquiry to medieval canon law, one encounters recurrent mention of the rights of bishops, metropolitans (archbishops), cardinals, popes, and even perpetual vicars. Monastic exemption was put in terms of rights, patrons exercised the right of patronage, and spouses had the right to demand the conjugal debt. Nor was canon law alone. Other medieval European legal systems, such as English common law, also made recurrent references to rights. ("The Canonistic Contribution," 39)

Villey taught us to be alert to the possibility that contemporary scholars are guilty of "unreflectively transposing a modern rights vocabulary onto resistant sources" (39). Reid concedes that that may have happened in a few cases. But overall the evidence is too massive: the canon lawyers worked with the concept of subjective rights. So obvious is this that the question arises, why did Villey and those who followed in his footsteps overlook this evidence? The answer, says Reid, is that these historians, being

conditioned to expect that the most significant debates over rights will be found in philosophical treatises of scholars like Aquinas, Scotus and Ockham, simply have not sufficiently considered juristic sources. In fact, a close scrutiny of juristic materials reveals a sophisticated understanding of rights already operative in the legal systems of twelfth and thirteenth century Europe. This understanding of rights would become part of the medieval *jus commune*, the common law of Europe, that would in turn inform the polemical works of William of Ockham and the writings of early modern philosophers and theologians—figures as diverse and seminal in their own right as John Locke and John Calvin. (39–40)

Tierney's argument is the same. "Modern histories of natural rights theories usually place the origin of such doctrines in the late medieval or early modern periods; rights theories are commonly associated with the spread of nominalist philosophy or the beginnings of an entrepreneurial economy." But I want to suggest, says Tierney, "that the humanistic jurisprudence of the twelfth century, especially the writings of the medieval Decretists, may provide a better starting point for investigating the origins of natural rights theories than either fourteenth-century nominalism or the nascent capitalism of the early modern world" (43).

Tierney describes the social context of the twelfth century as a society "saturated with a concern for rights. At the very highest level popes asserted rights against emperors and emperors against popes. . . . Medieval people first struggled for survival; then they struggled for rights" (54–55). The canon lawyers played a crucial role in this struggle for rights.

Already by the end of the twelfth century they were distinguishing between *ius* as objective law (*lex*) and *ius* as a subjective right, and speaking
of "the right to elect," "the right of administering," "the right of establishing laws," and so forth (57).

What this implies, contra Villey, is that the conception of justice as
right order was not displaced in the fourteenth century by the conception of justice as subjective rights. If it was in fact the case that *ius* had
once been thought of simply as *right* or *the right*, by the twelfth century
that understanding had already disappeared in favor of *ius* as meaning
either objective law or a subjective right, depending on context.[18]

And not only were the canonists by 1200 regularly distinguishing *ius*
as law from *ius* as rights; by that time many of them were also "coming
to realize that the old language of *ius naturale* could be used to define"
not only *lex naturale* but natural rights—"a 'neutral sphere of personal
choice,' 'a zone of human autonomy' " (Tierney, *Idea of Natural Rights*,
77). By a century later it had become common practice to appeal to such
natural rights as the right to property, the right of consent to government, the right of self-defense, the right to means of sustenance, the
rights of infidels, and marriage rights. Thus we find Godfrey of Fontaine,
writing in the 1280s (some forty years before Ockham wrote about natural rights) saying that "each one is bound by the law of nature to sustain
his life, which cannot be done without exterior goods, therefore also by
the law of nature (*iure naturae*) each has dominion and a certain right
(*ius*) in the common exterior goods of this world which right also cannot
be renounced" (quoted in ibid., 38).[19]

---

[18] Assuming that the conception of *ius* as objective *right* or *the right* was indeed dominant
in the early middle ages, its eclipse by the conception of *ius* as law did not escape Villey's
notice. There has been a duel, he says, between two understandings of objective *ius*, the
classical conception of *ius* as right or proper order and the Judeo-Christian conception of
ius as law (Tierney, *Idea of Natural Rights*, 25), with the latter winning out some time in the
early middle ages. That development was lamentable enough in Villey's view. Error was
compounded when *ius* understood as objective law was in turn displaced, so he claimed,
by *ius* understood as subjective rights.

Leo Strauss interpreted early medieval developments along similar lines. He says that
classical natural right doctrine takes on a "profoundly modified form" when, as the result
of the influence of Christianity, law "becomes independent of the best regime and takes
precedence over it." "It is classic natural right in this profoundly modified form that has
exercised the most powerful influence on Western thought almost since the beginnings of
the Christian era." See Strauss, *Natural Right and History*, 144–45.

[19] A contemporary of Ockham, Marsilius of Padua, not a nominalist but an Aristotelian
of sorts, offers the following articulate formulation of the distinction between *ius* as law
and *ius* as rights in his *Defensor Pacis* of 1324: "In one sense right is the same as law, divine
or human, or what is commanded or prohibited or permitted according to these laws. . . .
'Right' is used in a second sense to refer to every controlled human act, power, or acquired
habit, internal or external, both immanent and transient or crossing over into some exter-

Tierney concludes his discussion of pre-Ockham usage of "*ius*" by looking carefully at the writings of the Franciscan Peter Olivi and the canonist
Johannes Monachus, both writing some twenty years before Ockham. He
concludes:

> When Peter Olivi and Johannes Monachus discussed *ius* as subjec-
> tive right, they were not casually or carelessly borrowing a usage
> from vulgar discourse. Rather each was providing a detailed analysis
> (philosophical or juridical) of a concept whose importance was
> fully apparent to them. When Ockham in turn came to write on
> subjective rights there was no need for him to inaugurate a "seman-
> tic revolution." A rich language already existed in which rights theo-
> ries could be articulated. The doctrine of individual rights was not
> a late medieval aberration from an earlier tradition of objective right
> or of natural moral law. . . . [I]t was a characteristic product of the
> great age of creative jurisprudence that, in the twelfth and thir-
> teenth centuries, established the foundations of the Western legal
> tradition. (42)

Lastly, Tierney observes that when we actually look at how Ockham
conducted his argument against the Pope, we see that he made no use
whatsoever of his nominalism. What he consistently appealed to was not
his metaphysics but the writings of the canon lawyers. The irrelevance of
Ockham's nominalism to his employment of the concept of natural
rights fits with the fact that the devoted Thomist, Hervaeus Natalis, writing ten years before Ockham, had an account of subjective natural rights
fully as developed as Ockham's, as did the Aristotelian Marsilius of
Padua, writing around the same time as Ockham. Nominalists, Thomists,
Aristotelians—it made no difference; all were speaking of natural rights.

So what was Ockham's contribution, if any? Well, notes Tierney, "the
core ideas around which Ockham built his doctrine of natural rights
and natural law are genuine canonistic ones, not Ockhamist innovations
or distortions" (202). And as to Ockham's definition of "*ius*" as *licit power*
(*potestas*), Tierney shows that, far from being a semantic innovation on
Ockham's part, this was already "commonplace in twelfth-century
canonistic discourse" (57).[20] What can be said, however, is that "no

---

nal thing or something pertaining thereto, like its use or usufruct, acquisition, holding,
saving, or exchanging, and so on, whenever these are in conformity with right taken in its
first sense." Quoted from the text in O'Donovan and O'Donovan, *Fran Irenaeus to Grotius*,
pp. 439–40.

[20] And it remained commonplace for quite some time after Ockham. For example, Con-
rad Summenhart, writing about 1500, after remarking that "*ius*" can mean law (*lex*), says
that "in another sense *ius* is taken to be the same as a power as when we say a father has a
right (*ius*) as regards his son, or a king as regards his subjects, and men have a right (*ius*)
in their things and possessions" (quoted in Tierney, *Idea of Natural Rights*, 109).

one before Ockham had discriminated so carefully between *ius positivum* and *ius naturale* when the word *ius* was taken in a subjective sense to mean a right. Moreover, Ockham persistently appealed to this distinction in the course of his argument against the pope. Thus it was that the concept of a natural right—not novel in itself—came to be drawn out of the realm of juristic discourse into the center of a major theological debate" (123).

NEAR SYNONYMS FOR "RIGHTS" IN THE DECRETALISTS

An interesting feature of the medieval discussions of canon law that Charles Reid brings to light is the array of synonyms, or near-synonyms, that the decretalists used for "*ius.*"[21] "On occasion," says Reid, "the decretalists used such words as *facultas, potestas, libertas, auctoritas,* and *iustitia* more or less synonymously with *ius* to signify a subjective right. At points, as when the decretalists spoke of the *ius eligendi* [right of electing] as the *facultas eligendi* or the *potestas eligendi,* they clearly intended an exact correspondence" (110).

On first acquaintance, this pattern of usage seems strange to us—so much so that the thought crosses one's mind that perhaps there is something, after all, to Villey's thesis that the early medieval theorists were not working with our concept of a right. There is no surprise in the fact that "*ius*" and "*iustitia*" were sometimes used interchangeably. And we too speak of certain rights as *liberties,* though I think that, if pressed, we would say that these liberties are *examples* of rights rather than that the term "a liberty" is being used as a synonym of "a right." But to speak of rights as faculties, powers, or authorities seems alien.

Further reflection shows, however, that it is far less alien than initially it appears to be. Recall Ockham's explanation of a *right* as *potestas licita* ("*ius utendi est potestas licita utendi,*" "the right of using is the licit power of using"). Latin has two words that are translated as *power* in English, "*potestas*" and "*potentia.*" "*Potentia*" refers to the sort of power one has in mind when one wonders whether one has the power to move a stone out of the way. "*Potestas,*" by contrast, refers to the sort of power the university president claims to have when he says, "By virtue of the power vested in me by the Board of Trustees and the State of Connecticut, I declare you to be graduates of the class of 2004." He might just as well have said, "By virtue of the authority vested in me, I declare. . . ." And we commonly say that when the president exercises his authority or power, he is acting in his capacity as president—that is, in his *facultas* as president. In short, the medieval usage remains our usage.

[21] *Rights in Thirteenth-Century Canon Law,* 109–36.

Furthermore, it scarcely needs to be argued that power, authority, and capacity, thus understood, are intimately connected to rights; it is little short of perverse for Villey to say that in explaining a right as a licit power, Ockham had "resolutely twisted" the concept of *right* "to the meaning of *power.*" It is a nice question whether having a certain power, authority, or capacity is *identical* with having a certain right or set of rights. But those issues are subtle (I say something about them in chapters 11 and 12). Here the point is just that the pattern of linguistic affinities of our word "a right" is not significantly different from that of the medieval Latin word "*ius*" and that this pattern reflects the intimate connection between rights, on the one hand, and liberties, powers, authorities, and capacities, on the other.[22]

RIGHTS IN THE ROMAN JURISTS

Tierney and Reid, being specialists in medieval canon law, do not contest Villey's claim that "*ius*" was used by the ancient Roman jurists to refer either to *the right*, in the sense of *the objectively right thing*, or to the benefits and burdens attached to some corporeal thing, such as a piece of property. Their argument is that by the twelfth century, the employment of "*ius*" in the senses claimed by Villey to be present in Roman jurisprudence had virtually dropped away and that from Gratian onward, "*ius*" was almost always used either as a synonym for "*lex*" or to refer to subjective *rights*.

Charles Donahue Jr., in a recent article, "*Ius* in the Subjective Sense in Roman Law: Reflections on Villey and Tierney,"[23] takes the argument to the next step and demolishes Villey's analysis of the Roman jurists. Looking only at Justinian's *Digest* and not at any of the other texts of Roman law still available to us, he finds no fewer than 191 cases in which someone is said to "have" *ius* (*ius habere*), and no fewer than 103 cases in which *ius* is said to "belong to" someone (*ius esse alicui*). He offers a

---

[22] An aspect of the picture that I am not able to discuss, important though it is, is the relation between "*dominium*" and "*ius*" in medieval Latin texts. Annabel S. Brett, in *Liberty, Right, and Nature*, remarks, "In the history of subjective right, a great amount of importance has in recent years been attached to certain texts and bodies of texts which posit an equivalence between the Latin terms *dominium* and *ius*. First of all it is said that in this equivalence we have the 'origin' of the modern subjective right in its most radical (and therefore strongest and most significant) form, in which it is preeminently associated with liberty, with property, and with a certain idea of sovereignty. Secondly, this conclusion is extended to the discussion of *ius* in a whole range of *moderni* who are thought to be part of the same theological current" (10). After a close study of the texts, in chapter 1 of her book, Brett concludes that none of these claims can be sustained. "It is anachronistic to talk of the equivalence of *ius* and *dominium* as the beginning of a modern subjective rights theory" (11).

[23] In *A Ennio Cortese*, ed. D. Maffei (Rome, 2001), vol. 1, pp. 506–35.

classification and detailed analysis of a great many of these passages. He observes, in addition, that the use of "*ius*" with a possessive adjective or pronoun (*ius meum, tuum, suum, nostrum, alienum, eius, eorum, alterius,* etc.) is also common in the *Digest*, though he closes his discussion without giving a count of these cases and without analyzing the passages in which this usage occurs.

When one speaks of the *ius* that someone *has* or that *belongs to* her, what else could one mean than a subjective right? So too, when one speaks of his right, her right, their right, our right, and so forth, what else could one mean than subjective rights? Though Villey did not scrutinize this vast array of cases with the care that Donahue displays, we know what he would say: in all these cases, what is being said is that the person has a share in the objective right. But the passages do not say that someone has a *share* in *ius* but that someone *has ius*. And in any case, a share would still be something that *belongs to* a subject. The claim that the ancient Roman jurists did not employ the concept of a subjective right is flatly untenable.[24]

Donahue judges that the Latin jurists did not explicitly form the concept of a *natural* right; that may have been a contribution of the canon lawyers of the twelfth century. But if so, the concept of a subjective right was there already, waiting to be used in new ways by the canon lawyers. Let me quote Donahue's summary of his argument: "The notion of subjective right, which Villey believed did not exist (or barely existed) in Roman law, was, in fact, quite fundamental to Roman law. Because the idea of subjective right was quite fundamental to Roman law, there was nothing particularly original about the canonists' and civilians' use of the idea in the twelfth and thirteenth centuries. What was original was the development of the idea of subjective natural right." He adds that he will not venture to say "how important this idea was before the debates about Franciscan poverty, . . . but it clearly was there in a way in which it was not there in Roman law" (506).[25]

NATURAL RIGHTS IN THE CHURCH FATHERS

Among the texts collected by Gratian in the *Decretum* were texts about the rich and the poor. Here is an example: "No one may call his own what is

---

[24] A full discussion of the extent to which the Roman jurists employed the *concept* of a subjective right would look beyond their use of the term "*ius*" to consider their use of such other terms as "*libertas*," "*dominium*," "*potestas*," and "*facultas*." On this point, see Witte, *God's Joust.*

[25] Donahue finds twenty-five occurrences of "*ius naturale*" in the *Digest*. In one instance it clearly refer to a subjective right; in twenty, it clearly refers to objective right; in four, it is ambiguous.

common, of which if he takes more than he needs, it is obtained by violence. . . . The bread that you hold back belongs to the needy, the clothes
that you store away belong to the naked" (in Tierney, *Idea of Natural Rights*,
70). Eventually, a consensus emerged among the decreatalists around the
view that everyone has a natural right to means of sustenance. As already
noted, we find Godfrey of Fontaine saying, "In the law of nature (*iure
naturae*) each one has a certain right (*ius*) in the common exterior goods
of this world, which right cannot be licitly renounced" (ibid., 75). And
Ockham says that "temporal things belong to others because they are
owed by necessity . . . that is they are owed by right reason. And in this
way the superfluities of the rich belong to the poor" (ibid.). What proved
controversial was not whether everyone has a right to means of sustenance
but what the impoverished may do to claim that right.

Several of the texts in the *Decretum* about the poor that the canon
lawyers interpreted as affirming a natural right to means of sustenance
came from the Church Fathers. Perhaps the Church Fathers did not yet
have the concept of a natural right, perhaps their lexicon did not have a
phrase that can be translated as "natural right"; nonetheless, long before
Ockham and long before the canonists of the twelfth century, they recognized and assumed the existence of what we would call *natural rights*
in things they said.[26] If the assumption that there are natural rights is
incompatible with sound Christian doctrine, then it is a heresy of long
lineage and venerable origin. Let me present what is probably the most
vivid example of the point.

In 388 or 389, in the city of Antioch, the great preacher of the Ortho-
dox Church, John Chrysostom, preached seven sermons on the New Testament parable of Lazarus and the rich man. The first sermon was
preached on January 2 and includes references to the riotous and licen-
tious New Year's celebrations that had taken place the day before. (Nothing new under the sun!) After preaching five sermons in January on the
parable, John said that he would move on to another text so that his
hearers would not become surfeited. He seems to have preached the last
two of the seven sermons later in the same year. Let me quote a somewhat
lengthy passage from the second of these seven sermons.[27]

> " . . . this also is theft, not to share one's possessions." Perhaps this
> statement seems surprising to you, but do not be surprised. I shall
> bring you testimony from the divine Scriptures, saying that not only
> the theft of others' goods but also the failure to share one's own

---

[26] Recall the point made by Alasdair MacIntyre in a passage quoted in the preceding
chapter: a society may ascribe and claim rights even though it lacks the vocabulary of rights.

[27] I am quoting from *St. John Chrysostom: On Wealth and Poverty*, trans. Catharine P. Roth
(Crestwood, N.Y.: St. Vladimir's Press, 1984), pp. 49–55.

goods is theft and swindle and defraudation. What is this testimony? Accusing the Jews by the prophet, God says, "The earth has brought forth her increase, and you have not brought forth your tithes; but the theft of the poor is in your houses." Since you have not given the accustomed offerings, He says, you have stolen the goods of the poor. He says this to show the rich that they hold the goods of the poor even if they have inherited them from their fathers or no matter how they have gathered their wealth. And elsewhere the Scripture says, "Deprive not the poor of his living." To deprive is to take what belongs to another, for it is called deprivation when we take and keep what belongs to others. . . . Just as an official in the imperial treasury, if he neglects to distribute where he is ordered, but spends instead for his own indolence, pays the penalty and is put to death, so also the rich man is a kind of steward of the money which is owed for distribution to the poor. He is directed to distribute it to his fellow servants who are in want. So if he spends more on himself than his need requires, he will pay the harshest penalty hereafter. For his own goods are not his own, but belong to his fellow servants. Therefore let us use our goods sparingly, as belonging to others. . . .

The poor man has but one plea, his want and his standing in need; do not require anything else from him; but even if he is the most wicked of all men and is at a loss for his necessary sustenance, let us free him from hunger. . . . The almsgiver is a harbor for those in necessity; a harbor receives all who have encountered shipwreck; and frees them from danger; whether they are bad or good or whatever they are who are in danger, it escorts them into its own shelter. So you likewise, when you see on earth the man who encountered the shipwreck of poverty, do not judge him, do not seek an account of his life, but free him from his misfortune. . . .

Need alone is this poor man's worthiness; if anyone at all ever comes to us with this recommendation, let us not meddle any further. We do not provide for the manners but for the man. We show mercy on him not because of his virtue but because of his misfortune. . . . I beg you remember this without fail, that not to share our own wealth with the poor is theft from the poor and deprivation of their means of life; we do not possess our own wealth but theirs.

Over and over, with rich and varied words, the same theme is sounded: means of sustenance *belong to* the poor. They do not belong to them on account of some accomplishment on their part; they belong to them on account of their need. They do not belong to them on account of the laws or practices of Antioch; John appeals solely to their needs *qua* human beings. They do not belong to them only in case they are virtuous; need alone is the poor man's worthiness.

John's audience would have included the well-to-do; his words would have reminded them of their obligations. He says that the wealthy must "show mercy." But he does not ground their obligation to the poor in their duties of charity; he does not say that failure of the wealthy to share is a failure of obligatory charity on their part. He grounds the obligation of the wealthy to "show mercy" in the poor man's misfortune. Nor is John talking about some abstract objective right order that is being violated in Antioch. He identifies victims and victimizers: the poor and the rich, respectively. The poor are the victims of theft, swindle, and fraud. They are wronged.

I see no other way to interpret what John is doing with his powerful rhetoric than that he is reminding his audience, rich and poor alike, of the *natural rights* of the poor. Failure of the wealthy to share with the poor is *theft* on the part of the rich; they are in possession of what *belongs* to the poor. It is true that there is no word in the passage that is a synonym of our word "a right." But the recognition of natural rights is unmistakably there: the poor are *wronged* because they do not have what is theirs by natural right, what they have a natural right to.

In speaking thus about the poor, Chrysostom was not idiosyncratic in the world of Christian antiquity. "Not from your own do you bestow upon the poor man, but you make return from what is his," said Ambrose of Milan.[28] And here is Basil of Caesarea:

> That bread which you keep, belongs to the hungry; that coat which you preserve in your wardrobe, to the naked; those shoes which are rotting in your possession, to the shoeless; that gold which you have hidden in the ground, to the needy. Wherefore, as often as you were able to help others, and refused, so often did you do them wrong.[29]

The Historical Case Not Yet Closed on Inherent Rights

The narrative told by our contemporary right order theorists, to the effect that the idea of natural rights was born of philosophical nominalism and individualism, is indisputably false, as is their ancillary claim that the idea loses intelligibility outside such contexts. The evidence against this narrative and this claim is as decisive as evidence in intellectual history ever gets. Ockham did not invent the idea of natural rights, nor did his nominalism have anything to do with his employment of the idea; neither did

---

[28] Charles Avila, *Ownership: Early Christian Teaching* (Maryknoll, N.Y.: Orbis Books, 1983), p. 50.
[29] Ibid., p. 66.

the seventeenth-century theorists of political liberalism invent the idea. The idea of natural rights was already common currency among the canon lawyers of the twelfth century; and the recognition of such rights, if not yet the concept, was present in the Church Fathers. No one will accuse the Church Fathers or the canon lawyers of nominalism or social atomism. The concept of natural rights is among the most ecumenical of concepts. Aristotelians, Thomists, nominalists, Lockeans—all have employed the concept, and this is not to mention the many thinkers of diverse persuasions who employed the concept between Ockham and Locke. Assuming that present-day Western society is indeed afflicted by attitudes of possessive individualism, the cause cannot be the use of rights language.

But though things look bad indeed for the right order theorist, not all is yet lost for him. There is something in our discussion that he can take heart from. In the preceding chapter I argued that though contemporary right order theorists typically see natural rights as the fundamental issue under dispute between themselves and inherent rights theorists, they are mistaken on that point. For they affirm the existence of natural subjective obligations. And given the principle of correlatives for duties and rights, if there are natural subjective obligations, then there are natural subjective rights. The right order theorist is bound to concede the existence of natural rights.

I went on to argue that this concession does not mean that the palm of victory goes to the inherent rights theorist. What it means rather is that the fundamental issue under dispute has been mislocated. Conceding the existence of natural rights leaves open the question of whether natural rights are inherent in the worth of the bearer or conferred on the bearer by some objective norm or standard. Which of these is the deep structure of this part of the moral order? That, so I argued, is the fundamental issue. Tierney and Reid do not address this issue—understandably, because it is not the issue that Villey and his followers raised. The issue is more subtle than the one they address. Being told that someone used the concept of a *natural* right does not tell us anything, one way or the other, about whether he thought of at least some of those natural rights as *inherent* to their bearers. To answer that question, we must know his thoughts concerning what I have called "the deep structure of the moral order."

In short, though the evidence cited by Tierney and Reid devastates the narrative told by right order theorists about the origin of the concept of subjective rights in general and natural subjective rights in particular, it does not show that those who employed the concept of natural rights thought of them as inherent in their bearers; the evidence leaves open the possibility that that innovation, the *crucial* innovation, occurred in late medieval times or in the Enlightenment.

The right order theorist can take yet more heart from our discussion. Some of the authors Tierney and Reid quote quite clearly thought of natural rights as conferred on their bearers by some norm—Godfrey of Fontaine, for example, in a passage quoted earlier: "by the law of nature (*iure naturale*) each one has a certain right (*ius*) in the common exterior goods of this world, which right cannot be licitly renounced."[30] There may have been writers of the time who thought of natural rights as inherent to their bearers; if so, Tierney and Reid happen not to quote them.

The consolation I have just now offered the right order theorist is only temporary, however. The canon lawyers of the twelfth century, so Tierney and Reid have shown us, articulated and employed the concept of a natural subjective right. So where did the lawyers get the idea from, or was it new with them? It was not. As I have already noted, a fair number of texts in Gratian's *Decretum* that the canon lawyers interpreted with the concept of a natural right came from the Church Fathers. The lawyers found the Church Fathers recognizing and affirming the natural rights of the poor, the aliens, and others.

So what led the Church Fathers to the recognition and affirmation of natural rights, or was this new with them? If they got it from anywhere, it would have been from either their classical or their biblical inheritance, possibly both. What I propose to show in the next three chapters is that the recognition of natural inherent rights was present in their biblical inheritance; it was to Scripture that Chrysostom appealed in the passage I quoted. The recognition not only of natural rights but of natural *inherent* rights goes back to the Hebrew Bible and the Christian Scriptures.

If this is correct, then the polemic we have been considering has things exactly upside down. The right order theorist discerns that talk of rights as inherent has become the principal language of secular moralists, who claim it as their own. She accepts this claim of the secularists, hands title to the language over to them, and resolves herself to use only the language of right order. Thereby she alienates her birthright and places it in the hands of those many of whom lack the resources for safeguarding it.

---

[30] I think there is reason to believe that this was also Locke's view: subjective natural rights are grounded in objective divine law. If so, then the story about origins becomes complicated indeed. Leo Strauss is completely oblivious to the possibility that Locke was in this way carrying on a tradition rather than subverting it. Strauss says that "Locke's teaching on property, and therewith his whole political philosophy, are revolutionary not only with regard to the biblical tradition but with regard to the philosophical tradition as well. Through the shift of emphasis from natural duties or obligations to natural rights, the individual, the ego, has become the center and origin of the moral world . . ." (*Natural Right and History*, p. 248).

Chapter Three

JUSTICE IN THE OLD
TESTAMENT/HEBREW BIBLE

In chapter 1 we identified two fundamentally different ways of thinking about justice. I called them *justice as right order* versus *justice as inherent rights*. The story commonly told about the origins of these two ways of thinking is that the former goes back into antiquity—pagan, Christian, or both—whereas the latter derives from the nominalism of the fourteenth century or the individualism of the seventeenth.

In chapter 2 we saw that the concept of natural rights was not an innovation of the fourteenth or seventeenth century; the concept goes back at least to the canon lawyers of the twelfth century. The lawyers used it, among other ways, in their interpretation of certain passages from the Church Fathers collected in Gratian's *Decretum.* Already the Church Fathers assumed the existence of natural rights, though without explicitly conceptualizing them as such.

To affirm or assume the existence of natural rights is not necessarily to think or assume that they are inherent in their bearers. One might hold that they are all conferred, in the sense that we have them on account of the application to us of some norm, that norm perhaps being the content of some command of God. Thus the preceding chapter left open the question of the origins of the idea of *inherent* natural rights. In the three chapters that follow I continue the counter-narrative by showing that inherent natural rights were assumed and recognized by the writers of the Hebrew and Christian Scriptures. I am not competent to judge whether they were also assumed in classical Indian and Chinese culture or in ancient Mesopotamian or Egyptian culture. In Part II I discuss whether they had a place in the eudaimonism that characterized the ethical thought of Greek and Roman antiquity.

Just as the idea of a natural right is distinct from the idea of an inherent right, so too the idea of a human right is distinct from both. A human right is a right such that the only status one needs in order to possess the right, the only credential required, is that of being a human being. Our present-day right order theorists seldom bother to distinguish these three ideas of inherent rights, natural rights, and human rights. But their writings leave no doubt that while they are opposed to inherent rights generally, it is especially the claim that there are inherent *human* rights that draws their ire. For that reason it will be important to consider whether the recognition of human rights is also to be found in Christian Scripture or whether that came later from somewhere else.

Two secondary purposes will be served by this discussion of justice in Christian Scripture, in addition to the primary purpose of continuing our counter-narrative. As I mentioned in the Preface, my own account of justice will be a theistic account, specifically, a Christian theistic account; I think of God and justice as intertwined. Our discussion of justice in Christian Scripture will provide us with some of the context and content needed for the theory of justice as inherent rights that I will develop in the systematic part of our discussion. And second, this discussion of justice in Christian Scripture will be my answer to one of the objections lodged against rights-talk and justice-talk that I mentioned in the Introduction: the objection, coming from Christians, that says that justice has supplanted love in Christian Scripture.

The reader should be aware that my interpretation of justice in Christian Scripture is one among others; there is no consensus interpretation. A good many devotees of justice as right order will be appalled by my claim that the recognition of inherent rights was there already in the biblical writings; they hold that in thinking about justice as they do, they are following in the footsteps of the biblical writers. And then there are those writers who argue that though the Old Testament is about justice, the New Testament is all about the supplanting of justice by love. I hold, to the contrary, that justice is a pervasive and inextricable theme in Christian Scripture as a whole, in the New Testament as well as the Old. When relevant, I will introduce some of these alternative interpretations and explain why I do not find them convincing.

What we learn, as we uncover how and why the writers of these texts thought about justice as they did, is that their way of thinking about justice was intertwined with their way of thinking about God, human beings, the relation of God to human beings, and the proper role of justice in divine and human life. That brings the following questions irresistibly to mind. Suppose that justice as inherent rights is a prominent way of thinking about justice in the West, possibly even the dominant way. Suppose further that that way of thinking had its origins in the Hebrew Bible and the Christian Scriptures. And suppose that that way of thinking was set there within a framework of conviction about God, human beings, the relation of God to human beings, and the proper place of justice in divine and human life. What happens when a person finds himself in the position of no longer believing crucial parts of that framework? Is he then deprived of ground for believing that there are natural rights, inherent rights, human rights, and so forth? And what happens when not just a few people but a large number of people, especially intellectuals, find themselves no longer believing that background framework? What changes must we then expect in how society thinks about justice—not immediately, but eventually? What changes must we expect in how human beings are actually treated? I have something to say about these questions in later chapters.

Three preliminary points need to be made. Among the many ways in which the biblical writings differ from those of philosophers and theologians is that none of them is theoretical. Their genres are highly diverse, in some cases diverse even within a single book: poetry, proverbs, narratives, oracles, legal codes, cultic prescriptions, letters, and so on. But there is no theory. I dare say that in spite of this diversity of genres, most readers nonetheless sense a certain rhetorical unity pervading the great bulk of these writings. For one thing, their principal focus is God, or Yahweh. And second, Walter Brueggemann, the esteemed Old Testament scholar, seems to me right when he suggests, in his *Theology of the Old Testament*, that the dominant overarching character of "Israel's speech about God is that of testimony."[1] The writers are "giving their testimony," as we say, not offering apologetic arguments or developing theory. These writers speak a great deal about what is just and unjust; every now and then they step back a bit to speak about the role of justice in God's life and ours. What they do not do is step up to the meta-level and talk about how to think about justice. They do not articulate a conception of justice. We ourselves have to extract the underlying pattern of their thought from their testimony.

Second, my way of treating the biblical writings will be what is nowadays praised or castigated, depending on the writer, as *pre-modern*. I will not be inquiring into the origins of these writings—when they were written, where they were written, by whom they were written, for whom they were written, for what purpose they were written, from what prior documents they were stitched together. Nor will I be reading these writings

[1] Minneapolis: Fortress Press, 1997, p. 119. Brueggemann goes on to make the following point: "testimony as a metaphor for Israel's utterance about Yahweh is deeply situated in the text itself. Specifically, the disputation speech is a dominant form of witness in Second Isaiah, precisely in the exile when truth is in crisis and evidence is uncertain. Thus I regard testimony not simply as a happy or clever convenience for my exposition, but as an appropriate way to replicate the practice of ancient Israel" (p. 120).

In the discussion that follows in this chapter, I interact critically at several points with Brueggemann's book. So let me declare here at the beginning that I have found Brueggemann's work more helpful for my purposes here than any other that I have come across; my critical comments are to be understood as a tribute.

with suspicion, trying to discern some nefarious purposes that they were used to advance, any more than I will be reading the writings of Feinberg, Dworkin, et al. with suspicion or, indeed, the writings of those who insist on reading the biblical writings with suspicion. My interest is entirely in the way of thinking about justice that we find in these writings as we have them. Furthermore, I will be reading these writings as all belonging to a single, highly complex book, the Christian Bible.[2]

Third, for reasons that will become clear in the next chapter, I confine my discussion in this chapter to the Old Testament. The totality of those books that are, for Christians, the Old Testament, is very nearly identical with the totality that is, for Jews, their Bible (though the organization is different). On a good many matters, interpreting these books as part of the Christian Bible yields results quite different from interpreting them as part of the Hebrew Bible. Not so, I think, for the issues dealt with in this chapter. Hence "Justice in the Hebrew Bible" and "Justice in the Old Testament" are equally good descriptions of our topic.

To dip into the Hebrew Bible/Old Testament after reading Plato's *Republic* is to enter a profoundly different, and markedly darker, moral universe, too dark for many. The talk here is of sin, wrongdoing, guilt, anger, punishment, mercy, forgiveness. And everywhere there are moral victims, persons who have been wronged. In the *Republic* there are no moral victims, though hovering over the entire Platonic corpus is the story of Socrates as victim. Mainly that is true because Plato's theory of justice takes the form of a social structure for utopia. The writers of the Old Testament held out the hope of a messianic age; that is the form utopia took for them. But when they spoke of the messianic age, their language was always highly imagistic—lions lying down with lambs, children playing over the nests of poisonous snakes, that sort of thing. Nowhere do they attempt anything approaching principles for the social structure of the messianic age. And in any case, their main focus is not on the messianic age but on this present age. What they see all about them here is *the wronged*.

O'DONOVAN'S THESIS

Among all the attempts to discern and articulate the structure of what the Old Testament writers have to say about justice, the one that poses

---

[2] Those who want a theory and rationale for treating the various "books" of the Bible as parts of a single book, The Bible, should see my *Divine Discourse* (Cambridge: Cambridge University Press; 1995), and my essay, "The Unity behind the Canon" in C. Helmer and C. Landmesser, *One Scripture or Many* (Oxford: Oxford University Press, 2004), pp. 217–32.

the sharpest challenge to my interpretation is that offered by Oliver O'Donovan in *The Desire of the Nations*.[3] Accordingly, I open my discussion with a critical examination of his central thesis.

The Hebrew word in the Old Testament/Hebrew Bible that is standardly translated into English as *justice* is "*mishpat*." The term is often paired with "*tsedeqa*," standardly translated as *righteousness*; "justice and righteousness." My own sense, for what it is worth, is that when the rhetorical context permits, "*tsedeqa*" is better rendered into present-day English as *the right thing*, or *going right*, or *doing right*—even, now and then, as *rectitude*.[4] The word "righteous" is seldom used any more in ordinary speech. When it is, it suggests a person intensely preoccupied with his own moral character who has few "sins" to his debit; the connotation is of *self*-righteousness. "*Tsedeqa*" has no such connotation. In *Natural Law in Judaism*, David Novak makes the interesting suggestion that the pair "justice and righteousness," "*mishpat and tsedeqa*," can be understood as *correct justice*.[5] Even better might be *true justice*.[6]

After presenting what he understands to be the conception of justice employed in the Old Testament, O'Donovan says that this conception

> is often obscured by the influence of a quite different conception of justice, classical and Aristotelian in inspiration, built on the twin notions of appropriateness and proportionate equality—justice as receiving one's own and being in social equilibrium. *Mishpat* is primarily a judicial *performance*. When "judgment" is present, it is not a state of affairs that obtains but an activity that is duly carried out. When it is absent, it is not imbalance or maldistribution that is complained of but the lapsing of a judicial function that always needs to be exercised. So, for example, when Amos calls for *mishpat* to "roll on like a river," he means precisely that the stream of juridical activity should not be allowed to dry up. Elsewhere (5:16) he has demanded that it should be "set up" like a fixed monument in the town's public place, always to be found there.[7] Very comparably, Isaiah of Jerusalem demands that the citizens of Jerusalem should "seek *mishpat*," explaining this as a commitment to giving judgment in the cause of the fatherless and litigating on behalf of the widow

[3] Cambridge: Cambridge University Press, 1996.

[4] The expression "going straight," said of a reformed criminal, captures precisely what I understand to be the root sense of the term.

[5] Cambridge: Cambridge University Press, 1998, p. 41.

[6] On this use of "true," see my essay, "True Words," in Alan G. Padgett and Patrick R. Keifert, *But Is It All True? The Bible and the Question of Truth* (Grand Rapids, Mich.: Wm. B. Eerdmans, 2006), pp. 34–43.

[7] The passage is translated as follows in the NRSV: "Hate evil and love good, and establish justice in the gate."

(Isa. 1:17);[8] and he promises that Yhwh will "bring back judges" to the city "as in the days of old," because Zion is to be "redeemed by *mishpat*" (1:26f.). (39)[9]

O'Donovan holds that though there is a "secondary sense" of the noun "*mishpat*" in the Old Testament, this secondary sense "has still not lost touch with the context of litigation. *Mishpat,* having been proper to the judge, now becomes proper to the plaintiff: it is his 'claim,' which the judge is bound to attend to" (39).

It seems to be universally agreed by linguists that the etymological root of *mishpat* has to do with the rendering of a juridical judgment; and there can be no doubt that when the Old Testament writers use "*mishpat*" and its grammatical variants, they often have juridical judgments and pleadings in mind. O'Donovan's thesis, in that qualified form ("often have") is undoubtedly correct. Of course, those writers are not unique in this regard; the same is true for us. We too often have juridical procedures in mind when we use "justice" and its grammatical variants—as when we speak of "halls of justice" and "the justice system."

Israel's remembering of its engagement with Yahweh over the years included its remembering of Yahweh as giving it, in the rhetorical mode of commandment, an extensive body of laws for the regulation of its life and as instructing it to establish and maintain a judicial system to deal with violations of that law. Thus in the midst of a lengthy catalog of regulations for Israel's life, in the book of Deuteronomy, we find Moses saying:

> You shall appoint judges and officials throughout your tribes, in all your towns that the Lord your God is giving you, and they shall render just decisions for the people. You must not distort justice; you must not show partiality; and you must not accept bribes, for a bribe blinds the eyes of the wise and subverts the cause of those who are in the right. Justice, and only justice, you shall pursue, so that you may live and occupy the land that the Lord your God is giving you. (16:18–20)

What lay behind the injunction of Amos cited by O'Donovan to "establish justice in the gate" was the conviction of the prophet that this divinely

---

[8] The passage reads thus in the NRSV:

Cease to do evil, / learn to do good; / seek justice, / rescue the oppressed, / defend the orphan, / plead for the widow.

[9] Here is the NRSV rendering:

And I will restore your judges as at the first, / and your counselors as at the beginning. / Afterward you shall be called the city of righteousness, / the faithful city. / Zion shall be redeemed by justice, / and those in her who repent, by righteousness.

enjoined judicial system had either collapsed or was seriously malfunctioning in the Northern Kingdom of Amos's day. Other prophets were of the same view concerning the Southern Kingdom (as, no doubt, was Amos himself). Speaking of the Southern Kingdom, of which he was a native, Micah says that

> The official and the judge ask for a bribe,
> and the powerful dictate what they desire;
>   thus they pervert justice. (7:3)

Isaiah of Jerusalem speaks of

> Those who cause a person to lose a lawsuit,
>   who set a trap for the arbiter in the gate,
> and without grounds deny
>   justice to the one in the right. (29:21)

And Isaiah of Babylon says that

> No one brings suit justly,
>   no one goes to law honestly,
> they rely on empty pleas, they speak lies. (59:4)

But O'Donovan's contention is not merely that "justice" ("*mishpat*") in the Old Testament *often* refers either to a juridical judgment or to the claim of a plaintiff before a judge; his claim is that this is the extent of its reference. I take the core of this claim to be that "justice" in the Old Testament refers to *rectifying* justice and the procedures for achieving it, not to *primary* justice.

Primary and rectifying justice seem sufficiently distinct for there to be a linguistic community in which different words are used for these two phenomena. All by itself that would have little significance, because it might still be the case that our word "justice" would be the right translation of both words. Or if one wanted to be fussy, one could translate the one as "rectifying justice" and the other as "primary justice."

Going beyond words, it also seems possible that there should be a community that recognized primary justice but betrayed no recognition of rectifying justice. Evidence for this possibility is the fact that a good many people in the contemporary world react against the very idea of rectifying justice, insisting that we should not think of the judicial system as called to render justice to victims and offenders but to secure some good or other—the good of reforming the offender, the good of protecting society, whatever. I do not regard this as a tenable view of how we should think of the judicial system; but I do not think one can argue for its untenability by showing that it is inconsistent to grant the existence of primary justice and injustice while thinking of the judicial system along consequentialist lines. More generally, I see no inconsistency in recognizing the existence of primary justice and denying the existence of rectifying justice.

The converse, however, seems to me not a coherent view. One cannot hold that there is rectifying justice and deny the existence of primary justice and injustice; one cannot hold that the aim of the judicial system is to render justice to victims and offenders while at the same time holding that the offenses on which judgment is rendered are not offenses against justice. Whether or not one uses the same word for these two phenomena is, as we saw, a different matter altogether and of no great significance.

The point can be supported by looking once more at O'Donovan. After claiming that *mishpat* is primarily juridical judging, and secondarily juridical pleading, O'Donovan goes on to say that when *mishpat* "is present, it is not a state of affairs that obtains but an activity that is duly carried out." If "*mishpat*" were confined in its use to rectifying justice, that might well be true. But notice O'Donovan's description of the juridical activity. "To judge is to make a distinction between the just and the unjust, or, more precisely, to bring the distinction which already exists between them into the light of public observation" (38). If the judge determines that one party is guilty, he goes on to perform another act, namely, that of issuing a sentence. But judging involves at least what O'Donovan says it does.

The judge brings to light, for the case before him, the distinction between the just and the unjust. What else can this be but a distinction within primary justice? With his eye on the demands of primary justice, the judge brings to light whether or not the accused has violated those demands. He brings to light *the state of affairs* on the matter: is the state of affairs that of the accused having *violated* the demands of primary justice, or is the state of affairs that of the accused *not* having violated those demands? The performance of juridical judgment, as an exercise of rectifying justice, *presupposes* the existence of a state of affairs of primary justice or injustice.

While we are on the point of discussing Israel's understanding of rectifying justice, let me note that though Israel's writers are constantly pointing to perversions of the judicial system as the cause of breakdowns in rectifying justice,[10] they are also well aware of the fact that failures to secure just redress may be due to the laws themselves: upright judges interpreting corrupt laws. No doubt that was Israel's situation in Egypt;

---

[10] Cf. Isaiah 59:4:

> No one brings suit justly, / no one goes to law honestly, / they rely on empty pleas, / conceiving mischief and begetting iniquity.

her enslavement was evidently not in violation of Egyptian law. Consider this passage from Isaiah:

> Ah, you who make iniquitous decrees,
>   who write oppressive statutes,
> to turn aside the needy from justice,
>   and to rob the poor of my people of their right,
> that widows may be your spoil,
>   and that you may make the orphans your prey! (Is. 10:1–2)

The needy are deprived of justice, the poor are robbed of their right, the widows are made spoil, the orphans are preyed on, by *iniquitous* decrees and *oppressive* statutes. There is a body of decrees and statutes and an institutional structure for enforcing them; the problem is not lack of those. Nor is the problem necessarily that the judicial system is perverted; the judges may be upright. The cause of the needy being deprived of *justice* and the poor of *their right* is that the laws are iniquitous and oppressive.

What I have been arguing is that, given O'Donovan's own description of what it is to render juridical judgment—a correct description in my view—there has to be primary justice in addition to rectifying justice. The remaining question is whether "*mishpat*" is ever used to refer to primary justice in the Old Testament or whether it is, as O'Donovan claims, restricted in its use to juridical judgings and pleadings. Once again, it would make little difference if it were so restricted; the linguistic situation would then be that what the term "*mishpat*" referred to presupposed the existence of primary justice even though it was not itself used to refer to that. But are there passages in which "*mishpat*" is unambiguously used to refer to primary justice? There are indeed. Let me offer a sample, beginning with some passages that it is possible though not plausible to interpret O'Donovan's way, and moving on to those that can only be interpreted as speaking of primary justice.

The famous passage from Amos that O'Donovan cites as an illustration of his thesis is open to his interpretation; but it neither requires it nor is that the more plausible interpretation. The prophet has been speaking on behalf of God to the people of Israel generally. Immediately before the passage in question, God says that he finds the cultic activities of the people offensive and unacceptable. Then we get the passage,

> But let justice roll down like waters,
>   and rectitude like an ever-flowing stream.[11]

---

[11] The NRSV has "righteousness" instead of "rectitude."

The first line, taken by itself, could be a reference to juridical proceedings; the prophet might be enjoining his auditors to see to it that there are just laws and a judicial system producing just verdicts. But the parallelism with the second line makes it unlikely that that is what he means. For the rectitude that the prophet enjoins his auditors to make "an everflowing stream" is surely the rectitude of each and every Israelite, not only of judges. That makes it likely that the same is true for the justice of which he is speaking.

It seems even more likely that the justice spoken of in the equally famous passage from Micah is not the justice of juridical proceedings. "O mortal" is the prophet's address to his auditor. What the Lord requires of you is

> to do justice, and to love kindness,
>   and to walk humbly with your God.

Given the address "O mortal," and given the parallelisms between *doing justice,* on the one hand, and *loving kindness* and *walking humbly with God,* on the other, I find it implausible to suppose that "doing justice" is a reference to juridical proceedings—though let it be noted that the passage occurs within the context of an imagined juridical proceeding with the people as accused and God as judge.

Consider a few passages culled from the book of Isaiah. When Isaiah of Jerusalem presents God as saying, about a renewed Jerusalem, that He will

> make justice the line,
>   and [rectitude] the plummet (28:17),

"justice" is not plausibly interpreted as referring to juridical proceedings. So too when Isaiah of Babylon writes,

> I the Lord love justice,
>   I hate robbery and wrongdoing. (61:8)

Robbery is not a judicial act. And when the prophet speaks (42:1–4) in visionary language of the Servant establishing justice, I find it implausible to suppose that he means that the Servant will establish a fair legal system; he means that the Servant will bring about a general social condition in which there is no need for a judicial system to vindicate those who have been treated unjustly:

> Here is my servant, whom I uphold. . . .
> I have put my spirit upon him;
>   he will bring justice to the nations. . . .
> He will faithfully bring forth justice:
> He will not grow faint or be crushed
>   until he has established justice in the earth.

Additional citations to the same point could continue at length. Let me conclude with two from the Psalms.

> Happy are those who observe justice,
>   who [act with rectitude] at all times (106:3),

and

> It is well with those who deal generously and lend,
>   who conduct their affairs with justice. (112:5)

In both cases the psalmist is speaking of private citizens and their conduct, not of those responsible for the judicial system.

My conclusion is that just as we use our word "justice" to speak of both primary and rectifying justice, so Israel used its word "*mishpat*" to speak of both. Israel's writers move seamlessly back and forth between these two applications of the term, as do we. A second conclusion, more important because it goes beyond linguistic usage, is that one cannot even think in terms of rectifying justice unless one recognizes the existence of primary justice and injustice.

WHY THE QUARTET OF THE VULNERABLE?

A striking feature of how the Old Testament writers talk about justice is the frequency with which they connect justice, both primary and rectifying, with the treatment of widows, orphans, resident aliens, and the poor. Alike in the presentation of the original legal code, in the accusations by the prophets of violations of the code, and in the complaints of the psalmist about violations, some or all of the members of this quartet regularly get special attention when justice, *mishpat,* is under discussion.[12]

In Deuteronomy 24:17 Moses enjoins the people, "You shall not deprive a resident alien or an orphan of justice; you shall not take a widow's garment in pledge" (cf. Exodus 22:21–22). In Deuteronomy 27:19 the priests call out, in a ritualized cursing ceremony, "Cursed be anyone who deprives the alien, the orphan, and the widow of justice," to which the people say "Amen." In Isaiah 1:17, Isaiah of Jerusalem says:

> Seek justice,
>   rescue the oppressed,
>   defend the orphan,
>   plead for the widow.

---

[12] In their emphasis on the widows, the orphans, the sojourners, and the poor, Israel's writers were not unique in the ancient Near East. For a good summary, see Enrique Nardoni, *Rise Up, O Judge* (Peabody, Mass.: Hendrickson, 2004).

And in 10:1–2 (a passage already quoted) he excoriates those

> who make iniquitous decrees,
>   who write oppressive statutes,
> to turn aside the needy from justice,
>   and to rob the poor of my people of their right,
> that widows may be your spoil,
>   and that you may make the orphans your prey!

The theme is too pervasive in these writings, and too familiar by now to most readers, to need further elaboration.[13]

The widows, the orphans, the resident aliens, and the impoverished were *the bottom ones, the low ones, the lowly.* That is how Israel's writers spoke of them. Given their position at the bottom of the social hierarchy, they were especially vulnerable to being treated with injustice. They were *downtrodden,* as our older English translations nicely put it. The rich and the powerful put them down, tread on them, trampled them. Rendering justice to them is often described as "lifting them up."[14]

The prophets and the psalmist do not argue the case that alleviating the plight of the lowly is required by justice. They assume it. When they speak of God's justice, when they enjoin their hearers to practice justice, when they complain to God about the absence of justice, they take for granted that justice requires alleviating the plight of the lowly. They save their breath for urging their readers to actually *practice* justice to the quartet of the vulnerable low ones.

It seems safe to infer that they did not have to deal with the contention, common in present-day America, that it is the fault of the poor themselves that they are poor and that, accordingly, they have no right to aid.[15] Apparently, they did not have to deal with the contention that such aid as comes their way is charity, not justice, for which the poor ought to be grateful. Israel's writers sometimes describe help for the lowly as mercy; but the idea was not abroad that it is *only* a matter of mercy, not a matter of justice.

What are we to make of this striking fact, that when justice and injustice are the topic, the quartet of the vulnerable low ones is so often sin-

---

[13] Only a handful of Old Testament passages cite all four members of the quartet of the vulnerable, one of those being Zechariah 7:9–10. What is also interesting about this passage is the clear distinction it makes between rendering true juridical judgments and treating the vulnerable with justice. "Thus says the Lord of hosts: Render true judgments, show kindness and mercy to one another; do not oppress the widow, the orphan, the alien, or the poor."

[14] Psalm 147:6: "The Lord lifts up the downtrodden, he casts the wicked to the ground."

[15] In the Wisdom literature, one now and then comes across the assumption that *some* poverty is the fault of the poor themselves; they are lazy. For example, Proverbs 6:6–11, which begins with the well-known couplet, "Go to the ant, you lazybones; consider its ways and be wise."

gled out for attention, apart from the fact, just noted, that injustice is often the right category to use in describing the source of their plight? Was there, to use a phrase made popular by the Latin American liberation theologians, "a preferential option for the poor" in the original law code of Israel, in the accusations of its prophets, and in the complaints of its song writers?

That depends on what one means by the phrase "preferential option for the poor." Israel did not think that its legal system should be skewed in favor of the poor; its writers were not "bleeding heart liberals." In Leviticus 19:15 Moses says to the people, "You shall not render an unjust judgment; you shall not be partial to the poor or defer to the great: with justice you shall judge your neighbor." In Exodus 23:2 he says that "when you bear witness in a lawsuit, you shall not side with the majority so as to pervert justice; nor shall you be partial to the poor in a lawsuit." And in Deuteronomy 1:16–17 he charges the judges to "give the members of your community a fair hearing, and judge rightly between one person and another, whether citizen or resident alien. You must not be partial in judging: hear out the small and the great alike; you shall not be intimidated by anyone, for the judgment is God's."

May it then be that Israel's writers were radical egalitarians with respect to social power and wealth? Did they regard differentials in social status as inherently unjust? Is that the significance of the repetitive emphasis on justice for the quartet of the vulnerable low ones? I think not. It may well be that in the messianic age, as the writers imagined it, all differentials in social status would disappear. But here in this present age, it is not wrong that there be kings, judges, and priests, and that their positions be treated with due honor.

Here is a third possibility: is the emphasis by Israel's writers on justice for the vulnerable low ones perhaps an indication of their conviction that social and cultural rights are more important than political rights, to use present-day language? Is it an indication, thus, of their view as to the *contours* of justice, that is, of the sorts of things they regarded as just or unjust and of the relative importance they assigned to those different sorts? We have already seen that, in the contour of justice that Israel's writers were working with, the plight of the low ones was often seen as a case of injustice. Can we make the further inference that, in their contour of justice, social and cultural rights were more important than political rights?

Walter Brueggemann appears to draw this inference, or one very close to it. He says, in one passage, that

> the intention of Mosaic justice is to redistribute social goods and social power; thus it is distributive justice. This justice recognizes that social goods and social power are unequally and destructively

distributed in Israel's world (and derivatively in any social context), and that the well-being of the community requires that social goods and power to some extent be given up by those who have too much, for the sake of those who have not enough. (736–37)

And in another passage he says that "Israel understands itself . . . as a community of persons bound in membership to each other, so that each person-as-member is to be treated well enough to be sustained as a full member of the community" (421). Brueggemann recognizes that "both *distributive* justice and *retributive* justice can find warrant in the text of Israel." But he goes on to say that "it seems unambiguous . . . that in Israel's core texts related to the Mosaic revolution, Yahwism is a practice of *distributive* justice" (738).

I doubt that we should infer, from the emphasis by Israel's writers on the injustice wreaked on the vulnerable low ones, that "Yahwism is a practice of *distributive* justice." Not only is some of the injustice to which the writers point commutative rather than distributive; the emphasis on a well-functioning judicial system, and on God as judge of Israel and the nations, is too prominent to warrant placing rectifying justice in the shadows. Rather often what the writers have in view, when speaking of the plight of widows, orphans, aliens, and the impoverished, is the collapse or perversion of the judicial system. A place midway between Brueggemann's emphasis on primary justice in Israel and O'Donovan's on rectifying justice seems to me the right place to be.

Nor were Israel's writers indifferent to the injustice of attacks on person and property. How could they be? Israel was constantly under attack by foreign powers. When Isaiah imagines what it will be like for justice to "dwell in the wilderness" (32:16), he says that

> My people will abide in a peaceful habitation,
>   in secure dwellings, and in quiet resting places. (32:18)

Security is everyone's right. The prophets do not approve burglarizing the wealthy or assaulting the powerful. Yet they do not single out violence against the high and mighty for special attention. They do not regard violent assault on those who have much property and social power by those who have little as more heinous than the reverse. In that regard, their attitude was radically different from that of the rich and powerful in society—be it the society of ancient Israel or the society of present-day America.

All this having been said, it must nonetheless be affirmed that Brueggemann has his finger on something important. Israel's writers must have believed that when we look at the actual condition of widows, orphans, resident aliens, and the poor and compare it with the condition of other social classes, we discover that the former are not only disproportionately vulnerable to injustice but usually disproportionately actual victims of injustice. Injustice is not equally distributed. The low ones enjoy those goods to which they have a right—food, clothing, voice, security, whatever—far less than do the high and mighty ones.

It takes no special insight to understand why Israel's writers believed this. For any society whatsoever, it is likely that those at the bottom are suffering the most grievous injustice. Here is why. Robbery and assault are events, episodes. If the victim of a robbery is a wealthy person, the robbery is an episode in a life that likely has been going quite nicely. By contrast, it is all-too-likely that the *daily condition* of those at the bottom is unjust. Widows are burglarized and assaulted; episodes of injustice also occur in their lives. But in addition, their *situation* is all-too-often unjust— demeaning, impoverished, voiceless.

Now for the final point. Discussions of justice and injustice occur in the context of a variety of different aims and concerns. One's aim might be to set forth the basic social structure of a fully just society. Or one's aim might be to discover the social and psychological causes of one and another kind of injustice in some actual society. Perhaps neither of these theoretical aims would require any particular attention to the plight of the vulnerable low ones in one's society.

But suppose that one's aim is the practical aim of advancing the cause of justice in one's society. Suppose that the context of one's discussion is the struggle against injustice. Then one has to make judgments of priority. One has to decide where lie the greatest injustices and where lies the greatest vulnerability. Other things being equal, one focuses one's attention on those. I suggest that it was because the orientation of Israel's writers was practical rather than theoretical that the quartet of the vulnerable low ones looms so large in their writings. What they say about justice and injustice occurs within the context of an imperative they had heard from Yahweh and that they now announced to their fellows: seek justice, undo the bonds of injustice. Israel's religion was a religion of salvation, not of contemplation—that is what accounts for the mantra of the widows, the orphans, the aliens, and the poor. Not a religion of salvation *from this earthly existence* but a religion of salvation *from injustice* in this earthly existence.

Why the Injunction to Render Justice to the Low Ones?

That this orientation toward salvation or deliverance is what lies behind the mantra becomes clear when we consider the reasons offered for the injunction to render justice to the vulnerable bottom ones. Two distinct

though related reasons are offered. Both appeal to the fact that justice
for the widows, the orphans, the aliens, and the impoverished is high on
God's agenda for Israel; thus both are intrinsically theistic reasons. But
that fact functions somewhat differently in the two reasons.

In Leviticus 19:33 Moses says to the people:

> When an alien resides with you, you shall not oppress the alien. The
> alien who resides with you shall be to you as the citizen among you;
> you shall love the alien as yourself, for you were aliens in the land
> of Egypt.

In Deuteronomy 24:17 he says to the people:

> You shall not deprive a resident alien or an orphan of justice; you
> shall not take a widow's garment in pledge. Remember that you were
> a slave in Egypt and the Lord your God redeemed you from there.
> Therefore I command you to do this.

And in Deuteronomy 24:21 Moses says:

> When you gather the grapes of your vineyard, do not glean what is
> left; it shall be for the alien, the orphan, and the widow. Remember
> that you were a slave in the land of Egypt; therefore I am command-
> ing you to do this.[16]

The idea is that those with social power in Israel are to render justice to
the vulnerable bottom ones *as a public remembrance, as a memorial,* of Yahweh's deliverance of Israel from Egypt. Yahweh delivered Israel from its
condition as enslaved aliens in Egypt; Israel is to render justice to the
poor and lowly among her as a public memorial of her deliverance.[17]

In the texts we have just now considered it is *Moses* who enjoins Israel
to treat those at the bottom with justice and who cites Yahweh's deliverance of Israel as his reason; Israel is to do justice as a memorial of its
deliverance by God from the injustice of slavery. More often—and now
we come to the second of the two reasons offered for the injunction to
do justice—Israel's writers present their injunction to render justice to
the vulnerable bottom ones as giving voice to God's injunction. It is God,
not Moses, who enjoins Israel to treat the quartet of the vulnerable low
ones with justice, usually without any specific reference to Israel's deliverance from Egypt.

---

[16] See also Deut. 15:15.

[17] I discuss in some detail this idea of doing something as a memorial in "The Remembrance of Things (Not) Past," in Thomas Flint, ed., *Christian Philosophy* (Notre Dame: University of Notre Dame Press, 1990).

A great many passages could be cited as examples. Among the most poetic is this one from the second Isaiah,

> Is not this the fast that I choose:
>   to loose the bonds of injustice,
>   to undo the thongs of the yoke,
>   to let the oppressed go free,
>   and to break every yoke?
> Is it not to share your bread with the hungry,
>   and bring the homeless poor into your house;
>   when you see the naked, to cover them,
>   and not to hide yourself from your own kin? (58:6–7)

Why does Yahweh, in passages such as this, enjoin Israel to practice justice? Yahweh does so because the undoing of injustice and the bringing about of justice is Yahweh's own abiding cause; Yahweh's deliverance of Israel from its plight in Egypt was just one example of Yahweh's abiding commitment to justice.

> Yahweh raises the poor from the dust,
>   and lifts the needy from the ash heap,
> to make them sit with princes,
>   with the princes of his people. (Psalm 113:7–8)

Israel is to participate in Yahweh's abiding commitment to justice by imitating Yahweh in pursuing justice. That is the second reason for the injunction to practice justice. Be just even as I am just, says Yahweh. It can even be said that by doing justice, Israel *knows* Yahweh (Jeremiah 22:16).

And why is justice Yahweh's cause? Israel is to participate in Yahweh's cause by imitating and obeying Yahweh in pursuing justice. But why does Yahweh desire justice—not only justice for the bottom ones but justice for all? Because, say Israel's writers, Yahweh loves justice. Yahweh's love of justice is offered as an explanation of the fact that Yahweh acts justly and commands Israel to act justly as well. "I the Lord love justice," we read in Isaiah 61:8; in Psalm 37:28, "The Lord loves justice." In Psalm 99:4, Yahweh is identified as "Mighty King, lover of justice."[18]

One's initial reaction is that this is not very forthcoming. God acts justly and enjoins the doing of justice by his human creatures because God loves justice. Yes; but what does that tell us that we did not already know? Perhaps more than appears on first hearing. This answer dismisses the thought that God's command to do justice is arbitrary. "Yahweh might have enjoined either justice or injustice; for no good reason, Yah-

---

[18] The counterpart, naturally, is that God is displeased by injustice—angered, even: "The Lord saw it, and it displeased him, that there was no justice" (Isaiah 59:15).

weh enjoins justice." Not at all. Yahweh *loves* justice. Yahweh's pursuit of justice and Yahweh's injunction to practice justice are grounded in Yahweh's love.

Of course it is not the abstract entity *justice as such* that God loves. What God loves is the *presence* of justice in society. And God loves the presence of justice in society not because it makes for a society whose excellence God admires, but because God loves the members of society—loves them, too, not with the love of admiration but with the love of benevolent desire. God desires that each and every human being shall flourish, that each and every shall experience what the Old Testament writers call *shalom*. Injustice is perforce the impairment of *shalom*. That is why God loves justice. God desires the flourishing of each and every one of God's human creatures; justice is indispensable to that. Love and justice are not pitted against each other but intertwined.

JUSTICE IN THE OTHER NATIONS

Israel has been doing double duty in our discussion. We been discussing how justice functions in Israel's testimony concerning Yahweh, and we have been discussing the proper role of justice in Israel's life, according to that testimony. We have not strayed beyond Israel's borders in speaking of the proper role of justice in life. Ineluctably the question arises, however: to what extent does the testimony of Israel's writers concerning the proper role of justice in life pertain to what the writers call "the nations"? Was it only Israel that Yahweh held accountable for doing justice, or did Yahweh hold the other nations accountable as well? And if Yahweh did hold the other nations accountable, did Yahweh also require of them that they give priority in their struggle against injustice to alleviating the condition of those at the bottom?

Moses's command to the members of Israel that they render justice to the vulnerable low ones among them as a memorial of their deliverance from Egypt was obviously neither addressed to the surrounding nations nor did it apply to them. Neither did another reason that I have not yet mentioned.

Both in Leviticus and Deuteronomy, Moses, speaking on behalf of God, announces in the preface to his presentation of the legal code that Israel is and ought to be a holy people. In Leviticus he says, "You shall be holy; for I the Lord your God am holy" (19:2). In Deuteronomy he says, slightly more elaborately, "You are a people holy to the Lord your God; it is you the Lord has chosen out of all the peoples on earth to be his people, his treasured possession" (14:2). What then follows in both cases is what, to us, is a bewildering mish-mash of regulations concerning ritual cleanliness, instructions concerning cultic practices, and principles of justice.

The implication is that Israel's writers understood the doing of justice as an essential component of what it was to be a holy people—which explains why the prophets moved so seamlessly back and forth between condemnations of injustice in Israel and condemnations of the violation of cultic and purity regulations.[19] But the other nations were not holy peoples in the way that Israel was a holy people. Hence the reason Yahweh offers to Israel for his injunction to them to do justice, namely, that they are a holy people, does not pertain to the other nations.[20]

The difference between Israel and the surrounding nations goes yet deeper. Not only do the two reasons just cited not pertain to the surrounding nations. Israel's writers were of the view that the surrounding nations had not received from God anything even resembling the Mosaic legislation. No other nation had received the Torah.

> Yahweh declares his word to Jacob,
> his statutes and ordinances to Israel.

---

[19] For example, Amos, in 2:6–8:

> Thus says the Lord: / For three transgressions of Israel, / and for four, I will not revoke the punishment; / because they sell the righteous for silver, / and the needy for a pair of sandals— / they who trample the head of the poor into the dust of the earth, / and push the afflicted out of the way; / father and son go in to the same girl, / so that my holy name is profaned; / they lay themselves down beside every altar / on garments taken in pledge; / and in the house of their God they drink / wine bought with fines they imposed.

Cf. Isaiah 58:13, where the writer urges Israel to "refrain from trampling the sabbath" shortly after the famous passage in which Yahweh says that the fast he chooses "is to loose the bonds of injustice."

[20] I am disagreeing, in a way, with Brueggemann in these comments. On p. 197 of *Theology of the Old Testament* he remarks, "The prophets, for all their great variation, can . . . be understood as taking up the tradition of Mosaic command when Israel has failed in its work of obedience. While the prophetic materials focus extensively on the tradition of justice, we can also identify, at least in Ezekiel, a concern that trouble is coming upon Israel . . . because the priestly requirements for holiness have been violated and Jerusalem has been profaned." Then on p. 421 he says, "While the commands in the tradition concerning listening are many and varied, we may say in sum that *Israel's obligation is to do justice.* Israel is a community put in the world, so the testimony suggests, for the sake of justice." (One finds a similar comment on p. 736.) This elevation of justice vis-à-vis ritual purity and cultic fidelity seems to me not correct. Israel, according to the Mosaic declaration, was not so much "put in the world" as it was "elected"; and it was elected to be a holy people. Holiness was the overarching rubric; justice was an essential part of that, but only a part. And though the prophets were not much concerned with ritual purity (but see the Amos passage quoted above) they were intensely concerned with the essentials of cultic fidelity; the prophetic message is laced through with denunciations of idolatry.

He has not dealt thus with any other nation,
    they do not know his ordinances. (Psalm 147:19–20)[21]

Israel's writers did believe that every now and then Yahweh issued specific commands to particular persons from other nations, usually
through the mouth of a person from Israel; but that was it. The prophets
anticipated that the other nations would eventually become acquainted
with the Torah that God had issued to Israel; Israel would become, in
that way, a light to the nations.[22] But the Torah, though meant as a gift
to all nations, was delivered by Moses to Israel. The writers suggest that
God is in covenant with humankind in general, not just with Israel. But
God's role in that covenant, unlike God's role in the covenant with Israel,
did not include issuing legislation.

Yet in spite of these differences between Israel and the surrounding
nations, Israel's writers clearly did regard the other nations as accountable to God for their injustice; accountability extends beyond the reach
of the Torah. Before Amos turns his fire on Judah and the Northern
Kingdom, he fires broadsides against six of the surrounding nations for
the brutality of their conduct of war. He declares that "evil" will befall
them on account of such behavior, this evil being "sent" (as he puts it in
five of the six cases) by the Lord. What Amos assumes is that they knew
better, or should have known better. Exactly *how* they knew, or should
have known, better, he does not say. We can be confident, however, that
he did not think they knew or should have known better because they
had received published commandments from Yahweh—the Torah.
When he gets to his condemnations of Judah, he says exactly this: they
have rejected "the law of the Lord" and not kept "his statutes."[23]

---

[21] Isaiah of Jerusalem does say that
    The earth lies polluted under its inhabitants; / for they have transgressed
    laws, / violated the statutes, / broken the everlasting covenant. / Therefore a
    curse devours the earth, / and all its inhabitants suffer for their guilt. (24:3–4)

But given that no reference is here made to the laws and statutes as *Yahweh's* laws, it is not
clear that the prophet is speaking about anything other than ordinary lawlessness. His
reference to "the everlasting covenant" is of course different.

[22] Cf. Isaiah 42:6–7; Yahweh is addressing Israel:
    I have given you as a covenant to the people, / a light to the nations, / to open
    the eyes that are blind, / to bring out the prisoners from the dungeon, / from
    the prison those who sit in darkness.

See also Isaiah 51:4:
    Listen to me, my people . . . ; / a teaching will go out from me, / and my justice
    for a light to the peoples.

See also Deuteronomy 4:6.

[23] Gene M. Tucker, who writes the notes for Amos in the HarperCollins *Study Bible* edition of the NRSV (San Francisco: HarperCollins, 1993), says that the reason for Yahweh's

Psalm 82 is especially interesting and important in this regard. A common trope in the literature of the ancient Near East was that of the gods meeting in council. The psalmist imagines such a council taking place. God takes his place in the council and addresses the gods of the nations. First, God issues a complaint against the gods:

> How long will you judge unjustly
> and show partiality to the wicked?

Then, an injunction:

> Give justice to the weak and the orphan;
> maintain the right of the lowly and the destitute.
> Rescue the weak and the needy;
> deliver them from the hand of the wicked.

The gods, instead of following this injunction of God to secure the practice of justice in the nations under their control, have themselves become benighted:

> They have neither knowledge nor understanding,
> they walk around in darkness.

As a consequence, "all the foundations of the earth are shaken." God then issues his judgment on these gods of the nations:

> You are gods,
> children of the most high, all of you;
> nevertheless, you shall die like mortals
> and fall like any prince.

The psalmist concludes in his own voice:

> Rise up, O God, judge the earth;
> for all the nations belong to you.

The point would seem to be, to put it into your and my way of thinking, that while an awareness of the requirements of justice is available to all nations and, more particularly, an awareness of the requirements of jus-

---

judgment on the surrounding nations is their "violations of standards of international conduct" (1359). It is certainly true that the condemnations are *for* violations of standards of international conduct; but in at most one case does Amos actually appeal to an explicitly recognized standard as a reason for his condemnation. About Tyre he says that it "did not remember the covenant of kinship"; possibly this is a reference to an actual treaty. That is the closest Amos comes to giving a reason for his condemnation of a nation. In the case of his condemnation of Edom, however, he may be alluding to a reason when he says that Edom "cast off all pity." If so, this is a very interesting reason indeed, very different from breaking a treaty or violating an internationally recognized code of conduct in warfare.

tice for the vulnerable low ones, false religion impairs that awareness. God's Torah, issued to Israel but meant to be heard by all eventually, is a corrective. The Torah formulates in the mode of commandment the universal requirements of justice.

The last clause just quoted, "for all the nations belong to you," alludes to an assumption in the passage, and an important point in general, that I have not yet taken note of. In *Desire of the Nations*, Oliver O'Donovan forcefully calls attention to the prominence in Israel's testimony of the acclamation, "Yahweh is king." Israel's testimony concerning Yahweh was, among other things, political; Yahweh was her ruler. In turn, prominent in Israel's understanding of Yahweh's authority was that Yahweh was both just in Yahweh's own dealings with Yahweh's subjects and required justice of Yahweh's subjects in their dealings with each other; in particular, Yahweh required of the kings of the earth, who are to mediate Yahweh's rule to the people, that they maintain a judicial system that secures justice to the wronged. Thus we get the following picture of the relation between the divine king and the earthly king in Psalm 72:

> Give the king your justice, O God,
>   and your rectitude to a king's son.
> May he judge your people with rectitude,
>   and your poor with justice.
> May the mountains yield prosperity for the people,
>   and the hills, in rectitude.
> May he defend the cause of the poor of the people,
>   give deliverance to the needy,
>   and crush the oppressor. (Psalm 72:1–4)

For the most part, what Israel had in mind when it acclaimed Yahweh as king was that Yahweh was *their* king. But that clause from Psalm 82—"for all the nations belong to you"—hints at the conviction that Yahweh was king not just of Israel but of all the nations. Every now and then this conviction comes to explicit expression. "The Lord, the Most High, is awesome, a great king over all the earth," says the song writer in Psalm 47:2.

The topic we have just now been discussing would usually be considered under the rubric of *natural law*: did Israel have a doctrine of natural law? That is the rubric under which David Novak discusses it in the book already mentioned, *Natural Law in Judaism*. I have refrained from speaking of *natural law* when expounding the thought of Israel's writers, and will continue to do so. The Hebrew prophets and song writers assume that Yahweh holds even those who have not heard Torah accountable for doing justice. But they never suggest that we should think of this "holding accountable" as taking the form of legislation, on analogy to Torah. Their picture is not that God somewhere, sometime, somehow issued legislation to all humanity, thereby holding them accountable for acting justly, and then, on top of that, issued special legislation to Israel covering the same ground and more. You and I may discuss whether that is how we should flesh out their way of thinking. But if and when we do thus flesh it out, we are going beyond what they actually say or assume.

One approach to the question of whether God holds those who have not received or heard about the Torah accountable to himself for acting justly, is the approach we have just now taken: does God hold the nations surrounding Israel accountable? Another approach is to ask whether God held human beings accountable *before* the deliverance of the Torah. That is Novak's approach, and the approach of the Jewish tradition generally.[24] What Novak shows is that if one looks closely at various of the stories in Genesis, it becomes clear that Yahweh did indeed hold humankind accountable before the issuance of the Torah. The story about Abraham and Sodom, in Genesis 18, is especially illuminating in this regard.

When some men from Abraham's entourage, including his nephew Lot, resolved to go to Sodom, Abraham accompanied them for a while and gave them directions. In the meantime, Yahweh had been hearing a loud outcry against the behavior of Sodom and Gomorrah and had resolved, if the outcry proved well founded, to punish those cities for their sins. For some time already Yahweh had been treating Abraham as an intimate. So he asked himself, "Shall I hide from Abraham what I am about to do . . . ? No, for I have chosen him, that he may charge his children and his household after him to keep the way of the Lord by doing righteousness and justice."

Abraham had learned well God's lessons about justice. When Yahweh revealed his intention to destroy Sodom and Gomorrah, Abraham protested, "Will you indeed sweep away the righteous with the wicked? Suppose there are fifty righteous people within [Sodom]; will you then sweep away the place and not forgive it for the fifty righteous who are in it? Far be it from you to do such a thing, to slay the righteous with the wicked, so that the righteous fare as the wicked! Far be that from you! Shall not the Judge of all the earth do what is just?" Yahweh saw the point and relented, whereupon Abraham began to worry that maybe there were not even fifty righteous people in Sodom and Gomorrah. So he asked Yahweh to suspend judgment on Sodom if there were forty-five righteous people in the city. And so it went, until Abraham and Yahweh were down to ten. "For the sake of ten I will not destroy it," said Yahweh.

---

[24] Though Novak, as I mentioned, discusses these issues under the rubric of *natural law*, his definition of "natural law" makes no reference to legislation. Natural law, he suggests, consists of "those norms of human conduct that are universally valid and discernible by all rational persons" (*Natural Law in Judaism*, p. 1).

The story shows that there was an awareness on the part of Abraham, and perhaps also on the part of the people of Sodom and Gomorrah, that God holds a human being accountable to himself for acting justly—and that justice is required even of Yahweh. Moses and the issuance of the Torah are still in the future.

COUNTER-TESTIMONY

The Yahwism that I have been articulating is very confident and optimistic. God will secure justice in the world; and in this project, those at the bottom of the social hierarchy will have priority. In his *Theology of the Old Testament*, Walter Brueggemann forcefully calls to our attention that in Israel's writings there is also a strong current of what he aptly calls "counter-testimony." Not all members of Israel see evidence of the divine justice of which so many of her writers speak so confidently. So they cry out, complain, accuse Yahweh of absence, forgetfulness, indifference—cry out that their crying out is not heard. They hold God to the justice that God has promised and enjoined.

> How long, O Lord. Will you forget me forever?
> How long will you hide your face from me?
> How long must I bear pain in my soul,
>   and have sorrow in my heart all day long?
> How long shall my enemy be exalted over me?
> Consider and answer me, O Lord, my God! (Psalm 13:1–3)

The justice whose absence they lament is, of course, the justice they heard promised and enjoined by Yahweh; they hold Yahweh to that very same justice. Our purpose throughout has been to uncover Israel's understanding of justice as such—the judgments Israel made as to whether Yahweh acted justly in this case or that have been of interest to us for the light they shed on that understanding. Thus for our purposes there is nothing new in this counter-testimony. But its presence must not be ignored, nor must the presence be ignored of actions attributed without judgment to Yahweh that appear unjust by Israel's own understanding of justice. The counter-testimony is not only outside Israel's texts but within.

RECOGNITION OF RIGHTS IN THE OLD TESTAMENT

We have in hand enough material to ask what we can infer concerning the deep structure of that way of thinking about justice that we find in Israel's writers.

When one attends to the prominence of divine legislation in Israel's life, everything points to the conclusion that we are dealing with a right order way of thinking. By issuing the Torah, God has established a matrix of obligations for the ordering of Israel's life. Insofar as Israel follows those rules of obligation, her life is rightly ordered and justice is present in the land. Departure from the divinely ordained order is injustice.

But when we turn our attention from the legislation to the pervasive presence of social victims in Israel's writings, doubts set in. This is not typical right order talk. Social victims do not have the significance in right order thinking that Israel's writers appear to give them. In right order thinking, victims point away from themselves and their plight to the fact that someone is not living up to his or her obligations. That is where something is not right; the existence of victims is a mere consequence. A right order thinker has his focus wrong if his emphasis is on the *indicators* of obligation-violation rather than on the violations themselves.

But though the presence of social victims across the pages of the Hebrew prophets makes us question whether we are dealing with right order thinking, it does not establish that we are not. So let us dig deeper. Two fundamental themes emerge from our discussion. God holds human beings accountable for doing justice; and God is himself committed to justice, both in the sense that God does justice and in the sense that God works to bring it about that human beings treat each other justly. Underlying these two themes is God's love of justice.

There is a strong tendency in biblical commentators to place Israel's understanding of justice entirely within the context of God's covenant with Israel. God made a covenant with Israel; in fulfilling his side of the covenant, God issued the Torah to Israel, requiring of Israel that it act justly. As we have seen, however, that is not how Israel's writers thought of the matter. God also holds accountable those who do not belong to Israel. Being accountable to God for doing justice is not contingent on being a member of the covenant people.

Let us now reflect for a moment on this theme of God holding humankind accountable for doing justice. Suppose I make known to you that I am holding you accountable for treating some third party with justice. Then I am presupposing that there already is such a thing as treating her with justice and that you know, in the relevant respects, what that is. The new factor added by my holding you accountable, supposing it to be a valid action on my part, is only that you would now be wronging me as well as her should you fail to render justice to her and that, should you wrong her, I would on that account have retributive rights toward you. The normative structure of justice is assumed to be there already.

Apply the example to the case before us. In saying that Yahweh holds humankind accountable for doing justice, Israel's writers were assuming that there already is a normative structure of rights and obligations. Yahweh holds Israel and the surrounding nations accountable for instantiating that antecedent normative structure in their societies. Bribing judges does not become a case of perverting justice because Yahweh commands Israel that it not be done; bribing judges was already that. It is because bribing judges was already a case of injustice that it is among the things proscribed by Yahweh's general command to do justice. Bribing judges is not unjust because God forbids it; God forbids it because it is unjust. Had God's only command been, Do justice, it would still have had content. The same structure is present in Yahweh's command to Israel to avoid unclean animals. An animal does not become unclean because Yahweh commands Israel not to eat it. Animals are antecedently divided into the clean and the unclean; Yahweh then enjoins Israel to avoid the unclean animals. The command does not create the distinction; the command is posterior to the distinction.[25]

We reach the same conclusion if we reflect on the second of the two themes we mentioned, that Yahweh is committed to justice, and on the background reason for these two themes, namely, Yahweh's love of justice. Yahweh is committed to doing and bringing about justice. Now suppose that justice is defined as whatever it is that God holds human beings accountable for doing. Then what could be the force of saying that God does and brings about justice and that God loves justice? Its force would have to be that God does and brings about whatever God holds you and me accountable for doing; and that God loves whatever God holds us accountable for. But this renders incoherent the idea that God holds us accountable for doing justice, and is himself committed to justice *because* he loves justice. If justice were whatever God holds us accountable for, then God's love of justice could not be God's *reason* for holding us accountable for doing justice.

These considerations establish, so it seems to me, that Israel's writers were not conceiving of justice as that which conforms to God's commands or, more generally, as that which God holds us accountable for. Justice is not reduced to whatever it is that God holds us accountable for or whatever it is that God loves in human affairs. The concepts are distinct.

---

[25] I am very much attracted to Mary Douglas's suggestion that in good measure the thought underlying the distinction between clean and unclean animals was that certain species of animals are malformed species and that certain members of well-formed species are malformed members. Snakes were an example of the former; they do not move about in the way that is proper for land-dwelling animals. Malformed species, and malformed

What these considerations do not establish, however, is that Israel's writers were implicitly working with the conception of justice as inherent rights rather than with that of justice as right order. We should hold open the possibility that they were not working with any conception, not even implicitly; maybe our questions about deep structure get no definitive answers when put to Israel's writings. For as I said at the beginning, in these writings there is no theory.

So the justice that God holds us accountable for, that God is committed to, and that God loves: is there any indication of what its deep structure is assumed to be? In particular, is there any indication that its deep structure is assumed to be that of justice as inherent rights?

What are we looking for here? Three things. First, is there any recognition in Israel's writings of the recipient-side of the moral order, or is only the agent-side recognized? That is to say, is there any recognition of rights and of being wronged, or is it only obligation, guilt, virtue, and the like that get attention? Second, is there any recognition of the worth of persons and of human beings? And third, if there is recognition of rights and of the worth of persons and human beings, is there any indication that that worth is seen as grounding how a person or human being has a right to be treated?

Israel's writers did use the language of *rights* and *wronging*—at least in our English translations.[26] But they did so infrequently. So if the case for their recognition of the recipient-side of the moral order depended entirely on their use of rights language, the case would be weak. Or more precisely, the conclusion would have to be that their recognition of the recipient-side was slight and peripheral. In fact I think it was central to their thought. The assumption of Israel's writers that God holds us accountable for doing justice has the consequence that when we fail to do justice, we wrong God. We not only fail in our *obligations* to God. We *wrong* God, deprive God of that to which God has a *right*.

Where do Israel's writers assume that injustice wrongs God? They assume it in what they say about divine forgiveness and divine anger. Israel's writers do not speak often about human beings forgiving each other, but they speak often and emphatically about God forgiving human beings. Here is a small sample.

---

members of species, are unclean. See her famous "The Abominations of Leviticus" in her *Purity and Danger* (New York: Praeger, 1970).

[26] Here are a few examples. In Exodus 22:21 we read, "You shall not wrong or oppress a resident alien"; in Isaiah 10:2 we read about the "right" of the poor; in Isaiah 40:27 we read about Israel's "right" being disregarded; and in Proverbs 31:8–9 we read:

Speak out for those who cannot speak, / for the rights of all the destitute. /
Speak out, judge righteously, / defend the rights of the poor and needy.

To this one should add the frequent reference in Genesis to birthrights.

In one of the revelations on Mt. Sinai, God said to Moses: I the Lord
am

> merciful and gracious,
> slow to anger,
> and abounding in steadfast love and faithfulness,
> keeping steadfast love for the thousandth generation,
> forgiving iniquity and transgression and sin,
> yet by no means clearing the guilty. (Exodus 34:6–7)

In Psalm 103:2–3 the song writer exclaims,

> Bless the Lord, O my soul,
>   and do not forget all his benefits—
> who forgives all your iniquity,
>   who heals all your diseases.

In Psalm 79:9 he cries out,

> Help us, O god of our salvation,
>   for the glory of your name;
> deliver us, and forgive our sins,
>   for your name's sake.

And in Psalm 85: 2 he addresses God:

> You forgave the iniquity of your people;
>   you pardoned all their sins.
> You withdrew all your wrath,
>   you turned from your hot anger.

Speaking of the day when Yahweh will bring about justice, Isaiah says,
"The people who live there will be forgiven their iniquity" (33:24). Micah
exclaims about Yahweh,

> Who is a God like you, pardoning iniquity
>   and passing over the transgression
>   of the remnant of your possession?
> He does not retain his anger forever,
>   because he delights in showing clemency.
> He will again have compassion upon us;
>   He will tread our iniquities under foot. (Micah 7:18–19)

And in the remarkable book of Jonah, the prophet becomes incensed
when it appears that the God whom he has known as "merciful, slow to
anger, abounding in steadfast love, and ready to relent from punishing"
(4:2) is prepared to extend his forgiveness beyond the boundaries of
Israel to Nineveh.

Forgiveness is not something that one can scatter higher and yon upon wrongdoers; I cannot forgive some malefactor in Afghanistan whose only relation to me is that I have read about him in the newspaper. One forgives the person who has wronged one. In being wronged, one acquires certain rights of retribution. To forgive the person who has wronged one is to forgo claiming some or all of those rights.

In speaking of God as forgiving human beings for the injustice they perpetrate, Israel's writers were assuming that God is wronged by injustice. The sign that John Chrysostom was assuming the existence of the natural rights of the poor was his speaking of the shoes of the wealthy person as *belonging to* the poor person who has no shoes. The sign that the Old Testament writers were assuming that God has a right to our doing what he holds us accountable to himself for doing is their speaking of God as *forgiving* us for not doing that.

Now and then this way of thinking of wrongdoing, namely, as the wronging of God, receives articulate expression. The psalmist, addressing God, says

> Against you, you alone, have I sinned,
>   and done what is evil in your sight,
>   so that you are justified in your sentence
>   and blameless when you pass judgment. (Psalm 51:4)[27]

Once we see that Israel assumed injustice to be the wronging of God, depriving God of that to which he has a right, then the anger over humankind's wrongdoing that Israel's writers attribute to God also falls into place. The liberal tradition of Christianity finds it either offensive or embarrassing to think of God as angry; God is love. But as Jeffrey Murphy and Jean Hampton argue with great cogency in their book, *Forgiveness and Mercy*, anger is the emotion one rightly feels when one recognizes that one has been wronged.[28] It follows that full forgiveness requires forgoing claiming that right; it requires the abating of one's anger. And that is how Israel's writers describe God; God's anger will not last forever.

What Israel's writers presuppose, of course, is that God has the right to hold us accountable for doing justice.[29] So now consider these two rights: the right God has to hold us accountable to himself for doing

---

[27] For another example, see Psalm 106:6–7. It is commonly thought that Psalm 51 is a psalm of David after he had been convicted by the prophet Nathan of wrongdoing in the Bathsheba episode. What many commentators note is that David is willing to confess that he has wronged God but appears unwilling to confess that he has wronged Bathsheba and her husband.

[28] Cambridge: Cambridge University Press, 1988.

[29] This is a permission-right rather than a claim-right; the distinction will be explained in chapter 11.

justice, and the right God has against us to our obeying him when he exercises this prior right and does in fact hold us accountable. Surely, God does not have these rights on account of some norm that applies to him! They are not conferred upon God. They belong to God inherently; they come along with what God is and what God does.

Over and over Israel's writers speak and sing of God's excellence: God's majesty, God's glory, God's knowledge, God's power, God's creativity, God's goodness. To cite examples would be otiose. God's right to hold us accountable for doing justice, and God's right to our obedience when God does in fact hold us accountable, are assumed by Israel's writers to be grounded in God's excellence. In that assumption by Israel's writers, that God has rights grounded in God's excellence, is to be discerned a recognition of inherent natural rights.

One last point. Prominent in Israel's praise of God's excellence is praise of God for doing justice. That might in principle be understood, I suppose, as praise of God for himself doing what God holds his human creatures accountable for doing. What makes that understanding impossible is that God's statutes are praised as just. God's statutes cannot be just because they conform to God's statutes.

HUMAN WORTH

Partisans of justice as right order will cry foul. When they said that the idea of natural or inherent rights was born of fourteenth-century nominalism or seventeenth-century individualism, they did not have God's rights in mind; they were thinking of the rights human beings have. Let it be conceded, they will say, that Israel's writers assumed that God has inherent rights. The point remains that they did not assume that *human beings* have inherent rights. The problem with thinking of human beings as having inherent rights can in fact now be stated more sharply: to think of human beings as having inherent rights is to think of human beings as little gods, sovereign individuals!

This once again reformulates the issue. Now the issue is not the recognition of inherent rights as such. Now the issue is the scope of the inherent rights that are recognized. Does the recognition of inherent rights extend to those of human beings, or is it only God who is recognized as having inherent rights?

Rather than complaining that the right order theorist is a moving target and letting it go at that, let us address this new issue. Is there any indication that Israel's writers thought of human beings as having worth—less worth than God, of course, but nonetheless, worth—and that they thought of that worth as grounding rights?

There are indeed such indications. The writer of Psalm 8 can scarcely contain himself when he thinks of human worth. God has placed human beings just a bit lower in the cosmic scale of worth than divine beings (or angels) and "crowned them with glory and honor." God has "given them dominion over the works of [God's] hands." The writer is of course echoing the first chapter of Genesis, where God resolves to create human beings in his image.

Later in Genesis, in a sentence included within the blessing that God pronounces upon Noah and his children, we read,

> Whoever sheds the blood of a human,
>   by a human shall that person's blood be shed;
> for in his own image
>   God made humankind. (Genesis 9:6)[30]

The proscription against murder is grounded not in God's law but in the worth of the human being. All who bear God's image possess, on that account, an inherent right not to be murdered.

It will remain for later writers to follow out the implications of the thought that human beings are created as beings of worth and that, among their rights, are rights grounded in that worth—inherent rights. But the relevant ideas were there already in Israel's writings. John Chrysostom was not exercising his own inventive imagination when he said that means of sustenance belong to the impoverished person simply on account of his being human. He was applying to the situation at hand a theme that he had heard in the Scriptures from which he preached. Once one has said that God has worth, that that worth grounds God's right to worship and obedience, and that human beings likewise have worth, it proves impossible not to continue in this line of thought and hold that human beings have rights on account of their worth. The writer of Genesis took the first step down that road.

---

[30] In chapter 16 I discuss what constitutes the image of God.

Chapter Four

ON DE-JUSTICIZING THE NEW TESTAMENT

IN MY PRESENTATION thus far of what the Christian Scriptures say about justice, I have spoken exclusively of the Old Testament. It is time to turn to the New.

The New Testament is all about justice. Or to express myself a bit more cautiously and precisely: justice, along with its negative, injustice, is one of the main themes in the New Testament—*real* justice and *real* injustice, not some spiritualized counterpart thereof. In this world of ours, persons are wronged, justice is breached. That is the ever-present context of the New Testament writings. Sometimes the writers bring this context to the fore; often they take it for granted. From their location within that context they speak about the coming of justice, about the struggle against injustice, about judgment on breaches of justice, and about forgiveness for such breaches.

What I have just said, if true, will take many readers by surprise. There has long been a powerful strand of thought in the Christian tradition that de-justicizes the New Testament. The New Testament, so it is said, is about love, not about justice. Justice is the theme of the Old Testament; love, the theme of the New. The Christian puts considerations of justice behind her. Love is her motive and guide. Many non-Christians have gone along and accepted that love supplants justice in the New Testament.

Rather than plunging ahead and acting as if this tradition of interpretation did not exist or as if it were beneath our notice, I think it best to postpone for a bit our consideration of justice in the New Testament and present this alternative line of interpretation as forcefully as possible. Best to bring the polemics to the surface rather than to muffle them.

HAUERWAS'S CHALLENGE

Stanley Hauerwas, in a now-infamous passage in the second chapter of *After Christendom,*[1] says that "justice is a bad idea for Christians." What does he mean? Does he mean what his words mean? If so, why does he say this?

---

[1] Nashville: Abingdon Press, 1991.

The chapter opens with the remark that "if there is anything Christians agree about today it is that [their] faith is one that does justice. You cannot be Christian without a concern for the poor, the oppressed, the down-trodden" (45). The reason Christian leaders give for such concern, says Hauerwas, is not that to be Christian is to "have some special compassion for the poor and oppressed but because they have claims against us—that is, rights" (45).

"Raising questions about this enthusiasm for justice and rights among contemporary Christians is about as popular," he continues, "as admitting you secretly admire the Islamic revolution of Iran." Nonetheless, he boldly goes on to argue "that the current emphasis on justice and rights as the primary norms guiding the social witness of Christians is in fact a mistake" (46).

This seems to be a bold, blunt challenge to the interpretation I will be presenting—or is it? I do not discern the "enthusiasm for justice and rights" among contemporary Christians that Hauerwas claims to notice; I find that many of them want nothing to do with the category of justice, except for criminal justice, and even more want nothing to do with the concept of rights. But let that pass. Hauerwas's explanation of why justice is popular among present-day Christians is that it "has to do with the church's attempt to remain a societal actor in societies that [they] feel are slipping away from [their] control. The current emphasis on justice among Christians springs not so much from an effort to locate the Christian contribution to a wider society as it does from Christians' attempt to find a way to be societal actors without that action being colored by Christian presupposition" (58). The result is that in "the interest of working for justice, contemporary Christians allow their imaginations to be captured by the concepts of justice determined by the presupposition of liberal societies" (63). But that "larger social order [does not know] what it is talking about when it calls for justice" (68). Consequently, in working for justice, Christians "lose the critical ability to stand against the limits of our social orders. [They] forget that the first thing as Christians [they] have to hold before any society is not justice but God" (68).

These comments make clear, so it seems to me, that Hauerwas did not mean what his words mean when he said that "justice is a bad idea for Christians." I take his point to be that the *vocabulary* of justice and rights has been so corrupted by its use in the "larger social order" that Christians should refuse to use it; it cannot be redeemed. It "is certainly not my intention," he remarks cryptically in the last paragraph of the chapter, to say that Christians "must give up working for justice in the societies of modernity" (68). Apparently, they should not call it justice, however. That is what I take Hauerwas to be saying; he does not explain the remark.

I accept Hauerwas's challenge that as we look at justice in the New Testament, we not read the texts with alien understandings. But Hauerwas assumes that the language of justice and rights cannot be redeemed from its use by secularists; we are stuck with the disjunction of justice or God. I disagree. Not only can the language be redeemed. It must be redeemed—because, for one thing, to reject the language and conceptuality of justice would be to render the New Testament unintelligible. Pull justice out and nothing much is left. Justice understood in such a way, however, that it is not God *or* justice but God *and* justice—the justice of God and the justice God enjoins.

Most readers of Hauerwas's apothegm that "justice is a bad idea for Christians" will not give it the close and charitable reading I have just given it. They will interpret him as meaning what his words mean, namely, that justice is a bad idea for Christians. If they furthermore *believe* what his words mean, then Hauerwas's remark will have given a strong boost to the spiritualizing pietism that he himself strongly opposes.

Nygren on Nomos, Eros, and Agape

The most radical attack ever launched on the view that the New Testament is about justice was launched by Anders Nygren in his now-classic *Agape and Eros.*[2] It is fashionable nowadays to be dismissive of Nygren: his theology is unacceptable, his exegesis untenable, his intellectual history questionable, and so forth. All true; nonetheless, both the systematic power of his thought and the range of his influence make him worthy of attention.

Nygren's central question was, what is the nature of the love ascribed to God in the New Testament and enjoined on us for our fellows? The question assumes that the two are the same. The New Testament word for this love is *agape.* What is agape?

No one in the history of Christianity ever gave a more sharply focused answer to the question Nygren posed than the one he gave: agape is gratuitous benevolence. Nygren's reason was straightforward. The New Testament presents God's forgiveness of the sinner as the paradigmatic manifestation of God's love, God's agape. Any proposal as to the nature of agape has to be tested by considering whether it fits God's forgiveness of the sinner. God's forgiveness of the sinner is gratuitous benevolence.

This thesis, that agape is gratuitous benevolence, became the dominant opinion among Christian ethicists of the twentieth century. They dismissed Nygren's theology, his exegesis, his history, but not his central

---

[2] Translated by Philip S. Watson (London: SPCK, 1953).

thesis, that the love ascribed to God in the New Testament and enjoined on us for our fellows is gratuitous benevolence.

Nygren did more, however, than give this sharply focused account of New Testament love; had he done nothing more, he would not be relevant to my purposes. With a systematic rigor wondrous to behold he pursued the implications of that answer. If the love that God shows for human beings and enjoins on us for our fellows is agape, what follows? Among other things, what follows, so Nygren argued, is that the person who treats his fellows as God enjoins will never be motivated by justice. Let us follow Nygren's argument for a while.

Nygren saw three "fundamental motifs" locked in a struggle for the heart and mind of the West: the *eros*-motif, which received its finest and purest expression in Plato and the Platonic tradition; the *nomos*-motif, which received its finest and purest expression in the testimony of the Old Testament writers concerning justice; and the *agape*-motif, which received its finest and purest expression in certain of Jesus' parables, in Paul's teaching about God's love, and in Martin Luther's writings. The religion espoused by Jesus and the apostles stands in fundamental opposition both to Hellenism and to the religion of the Old Testament. The New Testament is not a fulfillment of the Old, not even a continuation, but a repudiation in the context of an alternative.[3]

Eros, as Nygren understands it, is that form of love that seeks to enhance the well-being of the agent. Such love is not agape. Sometimes eros takes the form of seeking to enhance the well-being of the other in order to enhance one's own well-being. Eros in that form resembles agape in seeking to enhance the well-being of the other. But it is not agape, not benevolence—certainly not *gratuitous* benevolence. God does not forgive the sinner as a means to enhancing God's own well-being.

Nomos comes together in Nygren's mind with justice; what he says about nomos can almost always be paraphrased as something said about justice. Agape does not act for the sake of securing justice. It is true that to seek justice for the other is to seek to enhance the well-being of the other; but agape does not seek to enhance the well-being of the other

---

[3] Nygren does not conceal the affinities of his thought with that of Marcion, the second-century figure regarded by mainstream Christianity as heretical. No one at the beginning of the post-apostolic period "asserted the Christian idea of love with such force" as Marcion, says Nygren (252). Marcion held that Paul was the only true apostle of Jesus and that the gospel of Luke was the only gospel faithful to Jesus' teaching, though even it requires a bit of editing. The creating and law-giving God of the Old Testament is inferior to the God of love that Jesus taught and Paul preached. The contrast between the two is the contrast between law and gospel, justice and love. Nygren's comment that "there is . . . some justification for regarding the dependence of Christianity on the Old Testament as a disaster," would be enthusiastically seconded by Marcion.

because justice requires it. Looking at God's agapic forgiveness of the sinner once again explains why. God does not forgive the sinner because justice requires it. Justice does not require it; the sinner would not be wronged if God did not forgive him. Our love of the neighbor must be like that, unmotivated by considerations of justice. Agape is justice-blind.

Speaking of Jesus' teaching, Nygren declares that "fellowship with God is not governed by law but by love. God's attitude to men is not characterized by *justitia distributiva*, but by agape, not by retributive righteousness, but by freely giving and forgiving love" (70). "Agape shatters completely the legal conception of the relationship between God and man. That is the reason for the conflict of Jesus with the Pharisees and Paul's campaign against 'the Law.' Agape is the opposite of 'Nomos,' and therefore a denial of the foundation on which the entire Jewish scale of values rested" (200–201).[4]

A puzzle now confronts Nygren. If agape is incompatible both with eros and with nomos (justice), what then accounts for agape? What evokes it? May it be that though agape is not required by the worth of the other, it is nonetheless evoked by recognition of the other's worth as befitting to that worth? No.

> When God's love is shown to the righteous and godly, there is always the risk of our thinking that God loves the man on account of his righteousness and godliness. But this is a denial of Agape. . . . It is only when all thought of the worthiness of the object is abandoned that we can understand what Agape is. God's love allows no limits to be set for it by the character or conduct of man. The distinction between the worthy and the unworthy, the righteous and the sinner, sets no bounds to His love. (77–78)

Granted that God's forgiveness of the sinner is not evoked by the "character or conduct" of the sinner; may it perhaps be evoked by her intrinsic worth *qua* human being? That was Adolf von Harnack's suggestion: God's love of human beings is grounded in "the infinite value of the human soul." The idea has a "destructive effect" on our understanding of divine love, says Nygren.

> The suggestion that man is by nature possessed of such an inalienable value, easily gives rise to the thought that it is this matchless value on which God's love is set. Even though the Divine spark may

---

[4] Cf. p. 250: For Judaism, "love to God is the deepest and most inward expression of man's relation to God which the Old Testament knows. Even so, fellowship between God and man is based on justice and regulated by the Law. Nomos is the controlling idea, and love has its place within the legal framework. Christianity, however, effects a complete revolution." See also pp. 70–71.

seem to have been wholly quenched in a man sunk in sin, it is none the less present in "all who bear a human face." . . . Viewed in this light, God's forgiveness of sins means merely that He disregards the manifold faults and failings of the outward life and looks only at the inward imperishable value which not even sin has been able to destroy. His forgiving love means that He sees and values the pearl of great price, regardless of the defilement that happens at present to cling to it. He overlooks the defects and imperfections and concentrates on the essence of the personality which wins His approbation.

If this interpretation of Divine forgiveness and love were correct, God's love . . . would have an adequate motive in the infinite value inherent in human nature. The forgiveness of sins would then imply merely the recognition of an already existing value. But it is evident enough that this is not the forgiveness of sins as Jesus understands it. (79–80)

In short, agape is completely "indifferent to value," be it acquired merit or intrinsic worth. "When God's love is directed to the sinner, then . . . all thought of valuation is excluded in advance" (ibid.). Agape has "nothing to do with the kind of love that depends on the recognition of a valuable quality in its object" (78).

Not only does God as a matter of fact not love us on account of our worth; Nygren argues that God *could not* love us on account of our worth. For we have no worth antecedent to God's love. The worth we have as human beings is entirely the worth bestowed on us by God's love. Justice recognizes worth; agape creates worth. "God does not love that which is already in itself worthy of love, but on the contrary, that which in itself has no worth acquires worth just by becoming the object of God's love. . . . Agape does not recognise value but creates it. . . . The man who is loved by God has no value in himself; what gives him value is precisely the fact that God loves him. *Agape is a value-creating principle*" (78).

Nygren is not forthcoming on why he denies all worth to human beings other than the worth bestowed on them by God's love. But I think we can surmise how he was thinking. The clue is contained in the following sentence: "When fellowship with God is conceived of as a legal relationship, Divine love must in the last resort be dependent on the worth of its object. But in Christ there is revealed a Divine love which breaks all bounds, refusing to be controlled by the value of its object" (76).[5] Nygren is assuming not only that when one seeks to render justice to someone,

---

[5] Passages such as this make it pretty clear that the conception of justice Nygren was working with was that of justice as grounded in inherent rights. In what way his argument would have to be revised if he were thinking in terms of justice as right order is a nice question.

one seeks to do what the worth of the person requires; he is also assuming, conversely, that all action motivated by the worth of persons is doing what one does because, so one judges, the worth of the person requires it. The possibility that the action might in some way *befit* the worth of the person without being *required* by it does not occur to Nygren.[6]

Given this assumption, if God were confronted by human beings who had worth antecedent to his love of them, God's treating them in certain ways would be required of God by their worth. Not to treat them thus would be to treat them unjustly. It does not follow that, to do what justice requires, God would have to act *for the sake of* justice. In principle it might turn out that God, acting out of gratuitous generosity, always happened to do whatever respect for the antecedent worth of human beings required. Nonetheless, the serpent of requirement would have wriggled its way into the garden of pure agape. There would be actions that were in fact required of God. Even if God did not do what God does *because* it was required of God, God's love would incorporate doing what is required of God.

Agape cannot tolerate even that note of requirement. Not only does God always act out of pure generosity and never out of requirement; there is nothing in what God does that is required of God. Forgiveness is not required. Agape is generosity all the way down. It is my guess that that is how Nygren was thinking.

Our love for our fellows must be like God's love for us. We must love them with a love purified of all eros and of all nomos—purified of all concern with our own well-being and of all concern with the worth of our fellows. Our love is to be eros-free and justice-indifferent. I am not even to love my neighbor for the sake of "God in my neighbour" (215). For then "the neighbour is merely an intermediate object of love, while its ultimate object is God. [Then it] is not man as such, but 'God in man,' that is loved. . . . Agape-love is directed to the neighbour himself, with no further thought in mind and no side-long glances at anything else" (214–15).

So once again, the question: what accounts for agape? Nygren answers:

There is no motive for the love in the loved object itself, and no motive must be found outside the object, in some ulterior purpose, or else the love will not be true and unfeigned, will not be Agape. For unless love for one's neighbour is directed to the neighbour alone, unless it is concerned exclusively with him and has literally

---

[6] Tal Brewer called this point to my attention. A few pages back, I separated Nygren's argument that agape does not aim to do what justice requires from his argument that agape is in no way motivated by recognition of the worth of persons. Nygren was probably not making that separation.

no other end in view—not even that of gaining God's love—then it has no right to the name of neighbourly love. (216)

A possibility Nygren never discusses is that agape is grounded in attachment. Often one's benevolent concern for the well-being of the other is evoked by one's attachment to the other. I do not commit myself to the well-being of my children because I regard enhancing their well-being as a means to enhancing my own, nor do I do so because I regard enhancement of their well-being as required by due respect for their worth; I do so because I am bonded with them, attached to them.

Nygren would reject the suggestion that such love is agape. Benevolence grounded in attachment is preferential benevolence; agape is nonpreferential. It is a point I have not previously mentioned. Agape is benevolence for anyone who is "the neighbor," in Jesus' sense of *neighbor.* One's neighbors include those to whom one has no attachment, even those for whom one feels aversion, revulsion, hostility—those who are one's enemies. Our question, says Nygren, is what could "induce a man to love just simply his neighbour, with no further object in view? What, above all, can induce him to love an enemy" (215)?

All other possibilities having been eliminated, we must conclude that "the only ground for [God's love] is to be found in God Himself. God's love is altogether *spontaneous*" (75). God loves "quite simply because it is His nature to love" (201). The explanation of my agapic love of the neighbor must likewise lie in me.

We must step carefully here. In my case, the explanation cannot be that it is my nature to love; for it is not. Rather, it is God's love infused within me that is the cause of my agapic love for my neighbor. "God is the starting-point and permanent basis of neighbourly love. He is not its *causa finalis,* but its *causa efficiens.* . . . Being Himself Agape, He brings forth Agape. . . . [E]veryone who is loved by [God] and has been gripped and mastered by His love cannot but pass on this love to his neighbour. In this way God's love passes over directly into the Christian's love for his neighbour" (216).

And what, finally, of our love for God? I have been following Nygren in speaking of the love that the New Testament attributes to God and enjoins on us for our fellows. But the New Testament also enjoins love of God on us. How is that to be understood? It cannot be understood as erotic love. God's forgiveness of the sinner is the paradigmatic form of all God's love; and in that love there is no eros, no self-love. But neither can it be understood as agapic love. The person who seeks to promote God's well-being has not understood God. Add that our love for God could never be spontaneous in the way that agape is spontaneous. "What sense would there be in saying that our love for God was 'unmotivated'? Is not our love for God in fact 'motivated' in the very highest degree? Is it not motivated by the Agape He has shown toward us" (93)? But other than erotic love and agapic love, there are no forms of love that Nygren recognizes.

Where other thinkers would have viewed the implication that we cannot love God as a *reductio ad absurdum* of the position developed, Nygren displays the courage of his systematic convictions and maintains that it is best not to speak of *love* of God, better to speak of *faith* in God. Faith "excludes man's spontaneity, inasmuch as it is God's Agape that has 'chosen' him and made him a slave of God. . . . Christian love of God is . . . identical with absolute possession by God. . . . It is the *free*—and in that sense spontaneous—surrender of the heart to God. . . . It flows by inescapable necessity from the fact of his belonging unreservedly to God; and being aware of so belonging, it devotes its whole attention to the carrying out of God's will. It is obedience to God, without any thought of reward" (94–95). Nygren sees himself as confirmed in this position by the fact that the apostle Paul seldom speaks of our love for God, preferring instead to speak of faith in God, *pistis* (124ff.).[7]

We have spoken of God's agapic love for us, and of our surrender to that love in faith whereby God's agapic love for us flows into and through us to become our agapic love for the neighbor. Where, in the scheme, does enhancing one's own well-being fit in? Nowhere. "Agape . . . excludes all self-love. Christianity does not recognise self-love as a legitimate form of love. Christian love moves in two directions, towards God and towards its neighbour; and in self-love it finds its chief adversary, which must be fought and conquered. . . . Agape recognises no kind of self-love as legitimate" (217).

Nygren in Summary

What I find fascinating and valuable in Nygren is the unwavering determination with which he pursues the implications of the conviction that New Testament agape is gratuitous impartial benevolence. Jesus "enters into fellowship with those who are not worthy of it." His doing so is directed, says Nygren, "against every attempt to regulate fellowship with

[7] Nygren acknowledges that John does speak often and freely of our love for God. This, he says, constitutes "an incipient weakening" (153) of the Agape-motif. It contains "perils . . . for the nature and content of the Christian Agape motif"; it harbors the "danger that the unmotivated nature of Divine love may be insufficiently recognised" (153). It is especially in this forthright elevation of Paul and demotion of John that one sees Nygren's pronounced Marcionite tendencies.

God by the principle of justice" (86). Those whom Jesus opposed in word and deed were "the spokesmen for justice in the relation between God and man" (83). "That Jesus should take lost sinners to Himself was bound to appear, not only to the Pharisees, but to anyone brought up and rooted in Jewish legal righteousness, as a violation of the order established by God Himself and guaranteed by His justice" (83). For them it was "a violation, not merely of the human, but above all of the Divine, order of justice, and therefore of God's majesty" (70). " 'Motivated' justice must give place . . . to 'unmotivated' love" (88). What we learn from Jesus' words and deeds is that "where spontaneous love and generosity are found, the order of justice is obsolete and invalidated" (90). Over and over Nygren sounds the theme: agape is incompatible with acting to bring about justice.

WHY NYGREN CANNOT BE RIGHT ABOUT LOVE AND JUSTICE

We do not have to consult the text of the New Testament to see that Nygren's position is untenable. We will be doing that in the next chapter; but Nygren's position is internally contradictory. Agape is justice-blind, says Nygren. And the paradigmatic example of agape is forgiveness of the wrongdoer, in particular, God's forgiveness of human wrongdoers. Those claims are not compatible. Forgiveness has to be justice-alert; it cannot be justice-blind. We get our first glimpse of why de-justicizing the New Testament is impossible.

Two features of God's forgiveness stand out for Nygren. The sinner cannot claim a right to be forgiven; justice to the sinner does not require that God forgive him. But neither does God forgive the sinner so as to enhance God's own well-being. Our forgiveness of our fellows is to be like God's in that it is not done to enhance our own well-being. And by virtue of the very nature of forgiveness it will be like God's in that justice to the recipient does not require it.

There are important features of forgiveness that Nygren ignores, however. Let us explore some of those. Forgiveness can occur only under certain conditions; I can forgive you only if you have wronged me, and only *for* the wrong you have done me. If the good in my life that you failed to bring about is not a good due me from you, then there is nothing for me to forgive you for. I may regret your failure; but I cannot forgive you for it. The concept of forgiveness incorporates the concept of being wronged. It follows that if we never employ the concept of being wronged in our engagements with our fellow human beings, the concept of justice being violated, we cannot understand ourselves as forgiving them.

Might forgiveness occur nonetheless? That is to say, can one forgive someone without *understanding* oneself as forgiving them—in the way, say, that one might kick someone without having the concept of kicking and thus without understanding oneself as kicking him? Start with the question, can one forgive someone without recognizing that he has wronged one? I think not. One's external behavior might be like what it would be had one recognized that the other had wronged one and had one forgiven him; but it would not be forgiving him. Forgiveness can occur only in the objective context of the agent having been wronged and in the conceptual and epistemic context of the agent recognizing that she has been wronged.

Take a further step. The person who has been wronged thereby acquires certain retributive rights. On account of Michael's having wronged her, Mary has rights she did not have before, retributive rights, or a new ground for retributive rights she already had—the right to feel anger or indignation toward Michael, the right to impose hard treatment on him or have it imposed, and so forth.[8] Now suppose Mary recognizes that she has been wronged but not that she thereby has retributive rights. The concept of retributive rights is not part of her conceptual repertoire. The concept of primary rights is, but not that of retributive rights. Can she forgive Michael?

I think not. To forgive the person who has wronged one is to forgo exercising some or all of one's retributive rights. But one can genuinely *forgo* exercising one's retributive rights only if one recognizes that one has them. One's external behavior, once again, might be just as it would be if one forgave. The very same things that the forgiving person refrains from doing might be things that one does not do; one might not impose hard treatment on the person who wronged one. But that is not yet to forgive.

To see the point, it may help to note that there are other situations in which one might not do the things one has a retributive right to do and yet not forgive. The haughty aristocrat who recognizes that he has been wronged but does not exercise his retributive rights because he cannot be bothered with people he thinks are "scum" is not thereby forgiving the person who wronged him.

Nygren never tires of emphasizing that forgiveness, by its very nature, is not a case of doing what justice toward the recipient requires. This is true; nonetheless, the person who has abolished from her mind all

---

[8] As I mentioned earlier, retributive rights are permission-rights rather than claim-rights. They have corresponding claim-rights, however. Corresponding to the retributive permission-right to impose hard treatment on the one who wronged one is the claim-right to *be free* to impose hard treatment.

thought of justice and injustice can neither understand herself as forgiving nor actually forgive. Forgiveness can occur only in the objective context of the agent having a right that has been violated and acquiring retributive rights on that account, and in the conceptual and epistemic context of the agent recognizing that she has been wronged and that she has thereby acquired retributive rights. Justice-blind love cannot forgive.

One cannot preserve the thought and reality of forgiveness while abolishing the thought and reality of justice. If justice were a bad idea for Christians, forgiveness would have to be a bad idea for Christians. But forgiveness is at the heart of the moral vision of Christianity, so justice has to be there too.

A Nygrenist Reply

I can imagine a response by a chastened Nygrenist. Let it be granted that forgiveness requires recognizing rights and the violation of rights. The person blind to justice cannot forgive. What remains the case, however, is that the person who forgives is not *motivated* by what justice requires, because justice does not require forgiveness. Our love of our fellows should be like that. Though certain forms of love of neighbor will have to be justice-alert, forgiveness being a prime example, love of the neighbor must never be justice-*motivated.* Nygren should not have said that "the order of justice is obsolete and invalidated." He should have said that *being motivated* by justice is obsolete and invalidated. The right way to put it is the way he does put it in one place: " 'motivated' justice must give place . . . to 'unmotivated' love." That is what his argument entitles him to say. And that is enough for his purposes. He can still say that love supplants justice in the New Testament—though to make clear what is meant we have to add, *with respect to motivation.*

A full response to this position would require a chapter or essay of its own. Here I can do no more than indicate why I find even this chastened Nygrenism problematic.[9] The concept of agape does not, all by itself, give us an ethic; we have an ethic only if we also have a rule of application for the concept. There was near-consensus in the agapist movement of the twentieth century on the rule of application. "Equal regard" became the standard term for the rule.[10] Using the concept of *neighbor* that Jesus employed, the rule is that we are to seek to enhance the well-being of each and every neighbor for its own sake, and to do so in such a way

---

[9] In my forthcoming *Love and Justice,* I develop in considerable detail what here I merely indicate.

[10] See Outka, *Agape.*

that the well-being of each neighbor is given equal regard to that of every other.

And let it be understood that enhancing the well-being of someone will often require imposing a life-evil of one and another sort on him: a bit of pain in order to get the leg set, a bit of coercion in order to cultivate some virtue, that sort of thing. Agapists sometimes talk as if one ought never to impose any life-evil on anyone, not even for the sake of bringing about a great enhancement in well-being. So far as I can tell, none of them actually believes that.

I think we must expect the application of agapism, thus understood, to perpetrate and abet injustice. Suppose that Michael is abusing Mary in your presence. I would say that Mary then not only has a right against Michael to his not abusing her but a right against you to your trying to stop him. Add now that you are an agapist; the manner of your intervention, if you do intervene, will be determined by your commitment to giving equal regard to the well-being of Michael and Mary. What will you do?

Suppose you wrestle Michael to the ground, and when you have him pinned down, you call the police. That would certainly enhance Mary's well-being. Would it also enhance Michael's? It might. It might make him penitent; and depending on one's understanding of well-being, that might be an enhancement of his well-being that outweighs the pain of the hard treatment. Then again, it might have the opposite effect and you might anticipate that it would. It might make him furious, embittered, and determined not only to continue abusing Mary but to get even with you. So what do you, as an agapist, do in such a case? So far as I can see, you tolerate injustice. You do nothing.

But this is an untenable position. In not coming to Mary's defense, you are violating her right against you to protection. Your agapism implies that this inaction on your part is permissible. It is not. By virtue of the principle of correlatives, if Mary has a right against you to assistance, you have an obligation toward her to render assistance. What that means is that it is not permissible for you not to render her assistance. Given that the agapist will now and then find himself perpetrating and abetting injustice, chastened Nygrenism is as untenable as unchastened Nygrenism.

Chapter Five

JUSTICE IN THE NEW TESTAMENT GOSPELS

WE ARE IN THE MIDDLE of our archeology of the recognition of rights, more particularly, the recognition of inherent natural rights. My thesis is that that recognition goes back to the Old and New Testaments.

The claim by Nygren and others, that justice is supplanted by love in the New Testament, is a frontal challenge to this thesis. If love supplants justice in the New Testament, then of course it supplants recognition of inherent natural rights, and then the story about the recognition of inherent rights will have to be told very differently from how I tell it. The alternative story would begin with the recognition of inherent rights in the Old Testament, then it would leap over the New Testament and pick up again with some of the Church Fathers who, failing to discern the radical thrust of the New Testament, would slide back into Old Testament ways of thinking. That would be the story.

My argument against Nygren thus far has been a priori. If there is forgiveness in the New Testament, there has to be justice in the New Testament. Our project in this chapter is to confront Nygren's thesis about the supplanting of justice in the New Testament with the actual text.

Ideally, we would look at both the gospels and the letters of the New Testament. Of the letters, we would look most carefully at Paul's letter to the Romans. For while Romans, as I interpret it, says more about justice than any other of the New Testament letters, it has also, ironically, served as the *locus classicus* for those who wish to de-justicize the New Testament. For our purposes here, however, it would be overkill to look at both the gospels and the letters.[1] I will look just at the gospels.

Of the gospels, I will pay special attention to Luke-Acts, with side-glances every now and then at the other gospels. I discern no significant disagreement among the gospels on the matters we will be discussing—except for the fact that justice is more prominent in Luke-Acts than it is in the other gospels. That is a reason for focusing on Luke-Acts. Another reason is polemical: Nygren thought that agapism received its purest formulation in Luke's gospel.

---

[1] In my forthcoming book *Love and Justice*, I do discuss at some length the intertwinement of love and justice in Romans.

To meet the challenge posed by Nygren it will not be sufficient to show that justice receives positive mention here and there in Luke-Acts and the other gospels; Nygren would concede as much. We have to show that justice is an ineradicable component in the thought of the gospels. My thesis will be that two of the basic themes we identified in the Old Testament, God as committed to doing and bringing about justice and God as holding us accountable for doing justice, are carried forward into the New Testament, the latter theme being especially prominent in Romans. In the gospels, the former theme is both highlighted and given a decisive new twist: Jesus is identified as inaugurating the reign of justice. That identification becomes the center of a profoundly ironic narrative: the person identified as inaugurating God's reign of justice, namely, Jesus of Nazareth, himself falls victim to a miscarriage of justice. Jesus joins the victims; therein, God joins the victims.

Once we have seen the role of justice in the thought of the New Testament gospels, we will then look back and reflect on how the writers think of justice. Is there any sign of the recognition of inherent rights?

The Translation Issue

Those who approach the New Testament solely through English translations face a serious linguistic obstacle to apprehending what these writings say about justice. In most English translations, the word "justice" occurs relatively infrequently. It is no surprise, then, that most English-speaking people think the New Testament does not say much about justice; the Bibles they read do not say much about justice. English translations are in this way different from translations into Latin, French, Spanish, German, Dutch—and for all I know, most languages.

The basic issue is well known among translators and commentators. Plato's *Republic*, as we all know, is about justice. The Greek noun in Plato's text that is standardly translated as "justice" is "*dikaiosunē*"; the adjective standardly translated as "just" is "*dikaios*." This same *dik*-stem occurs around three hundred times in the New Testament, in a wide variety of grammatical variants.[2]

To the person who comes to English translations of the New Testament fresh from reading and translating classical Greek, it comes as a surprise to discover that though some of those occurrences are translated with grammatical variants on our word "just," the great bulk of *dik*-stem words

---

[2] I thank Sue Rozeboom for providing me with a list of all occurrences of *dik*-stem words in the New Testament, as well as with data from the Septuagint that I will be referring to a bit later.

are translated with grammatical variants on our word "right." The noun, for example, is usually translated as "righteousness," not as "justice." In English we have the word "just" and its grammatical variants coming from the Latin *iustitia*, and the word "right" and its grammatical variants coming from the Old English *recht*. Almost all our translators have decided to translate the great bulk of *dik*-stem words in the New Testament with grammatical variants on the latter—just the opposite of the decision made by most translators of classical Greek.[3]

I will give just two examples of the point. The fourth of the beatitudes of Jesus, as recorded in the fifth chapter of Matthew, reads, in the New Revised Standard Version, "Blessed are those who hunger and thirst for righteousness, for they will be filled." The word translated as "righteousness" is "*dikaiosunē*." And the eighth beatitude, in the same translation, reads "Blessed are those who are persecuted for righteousness' sake, for theirs is the kingdom of heaven." The Greek word translated as "righteousness" is "*dikaiosunē*." Apparently, the translators were not struck by the oddity of someone being persecuted because he is righteous. My own reading of human affairs is that righteous people are either admired or ignored, not persecuted; people who pursue justice are the ones who get in trouble.

It goes almost without saying that the meaning and connotations of "righteousness" are very different in present-day idiomatic English from those of "justice." "Righteousness" names primarily if not exclusively a certain trait of personal character. And as I remarked in chapter 3, the word in present-day idiomatic English carries a negative connotation. In everyday speech one seldom any more describes someone as *righteous*; if one does, the suggestion is that he is *self*-righteous. "Justice," by contrast, refers to an interpersonal situation; justice is present when persons are related to each other in a certain way. There is, indeed, a long tradition of philosophical and theological discussion on the *virtue* of justice. But

---

[3] The only exceptions among contemporary English New Testament translations that I know of are two Catholic translations, the New American Bible and the Jerusalem Bible, both of which appeared in the early 1970s. In these two, most occurrences of *dik*-stem words were translated with variants on "just." In subsequent revisions of the New American Bible, and in the New Jerusalem Bible, these translations have been altered to conform to the pattern described in the text above. I have not been able to discover the rationale for these revisions; I would guess, however, that it has to do with reactions in the United States and England to Catholic liberation theology.

Concerning translations of Plato, on occasion Cornford translates "*dikaiosunē*" as *doing right*. And the fine scholar of classical philosophy Gregory Vlastos remarks in a footnote to an essay on justice that " 'Righteousness,' the quality of acting rightly, would be closer to the sense of *dikaiosyne*" that Aristotle was working with in the *Nichomachean Ethics* ("Justice and Equality," in Jeremy Waldon, ed., *Theories of Rights* [Oxford: Oxford University Press, 1984], p. 41).

that use of the term has almost dropped out of idiomatic English; we do not often speak any more of a person as just. And in any case, the concept of the virtue of justice presupposes the concept of those social relationships that are just.

So when the New Testament writers speak of *dikaiosunē*, are they speaking of righteousness or of justice? Is Jesus blessing those who hunger and thirst for righteousness or those who hunger and thirst for justice?

A thought that comes to mind is that the word changed meaning between Plato and the New Testament. Had Jesus' words been uttered in Plato's time and place, they would have been understood as blessing those who hunger and thirst for the social condition of justice. In Jesus' time and place, they would have been understood as blessing those who hunger and thirst for righteousness—that is, for personal moral rectitude.

Between the Hebrew Bible and the Greek New Testament there came the Septuagint translation of the Hebrew Bible into Greek. This translation was begun in Alexandria sometime in the third century before Christ and continued for a hundred years or more; tradition holds that the initial work was done by seventy scholars—hence the name "Septuagint." One of the challenges facing the Septuagint translators was how to catch, in the Greek of their day, the combination of "*mishpat*" with "*tsedeqa*" that we find so often in the Old Testament, standardly translated into English as *justice* and *righteousness*. The solution they settled on was to translate "*tsedeqa*" as "*dikaiosunē*," and to use a term whose home use was in legal situations, namely, "*krisis*," to translate "*mishpat*." "*Mishpat* and *tsedeqa*" became "*krisis* and *dikaiosunē*." For the most part, this is also how they translated the Hebrew words even when they were not explicitly paired with each other: *mishpat* (justice) becomes *krisis*, *tsedeqa* (righteousness) becomes *dikaiosunē*. The pattern is not entirely consistent, however; every now and then, when *mishpat* is not paired off with *tsedeqa*, it is translated with *dikaiosunē* or some other *dik*-stem word (e.g., I Kings 3:28, Proverbs 17:23, Isaiah 61:8).

I think the conclusion that those of us who are not specialists in Hellenistic Greek should draw from this somewhat bewildering array of data is that, in the linguistic circles of the New Testament writers, *dikaiosunē* did not refer definitively either to the character trait of righteousness (shorn of its negative connotations) or to the social condition of justice, but was ambiguous as between those two. If "*dikaiosunē*" had referred decisively in Hellenistic Greek to righteousness rather than to justice, why would the Septuagint translators sometimes use it to translate "*mishpat*," why would the Catholic translators of the Jerusalem Bible and the New American Bible usually translate it as "justice," and why would all English translators sometimes translate it as "justice"? Conversely, if it referred decisively to justice, why would the Septuagint translators usually not use it to translate "*mishpat*," and why would almost all translators sometimes translate it as "righteousness"? Context will have to determine whether, in a given case, it is best translated as "justice" or as "righteousness"—or as something else instead; and if context does not determine, then it would be best, if possible, to preserve the ambiguity and use some such ambiguous expression as "what is right" or "the right thing."

Let me make one final observation about translation. When one takes in hand a list of all the occurrences of *dik*-stem words in the Greek New Testament, and then opens up almost any English translation of the New Testament and reads in one sitting all the translations of these words, a certain pattern emerges: unless the notion of legal judgment is so prominent in the context as virtually to force a translation in terms of justice, the translators will prefer to speak of righteousness.

Why are they so reluctant to have the New Testament writers speak of primary justice? Why do they prefer that the gospel of Jesus Christ be the good news of the righteousness of God rather than the good news of the justice of God? Why do they prefer that Jesus call his followers to righteousness rather than to justice? I do not know; I will have to leave it to others to answer that question. But in any case, to a person reared on English translations of the New Testament, the thesis that justice is supplanted in the New Testament has a certain initial plausibility.

Whatever the complications concerning the translation of "*dikaiosunē*," everybody agrees that "*krisis*" has to be translated as "justice." Criticizing the Pharisees for punctiliously tithing "mint and rue and herbs of all kinds" while neglecting "justice [*krisis*] and the love of God," Jesus says that "it is these you ought to have practiced, without neglecting the others" (Luke 11:42).

THE NEW TESTAMENT NARRATIVE CONTINUES THE OLD

The cast of characters in the opening of Luke's Gospel belonged to the underclass of Jewish society: Zechariah, a minor priest; two hill-country women, both pregnant, Elizabeth, the elderly wife of Zechariah, and Mary, a young relative of Elizabeth; Simeon, a pious elderly Jerusalemite; Anna, an extremely pious eighty-four-year-old widow; and some shepherds. The name of King Herod is mentioned only to tell us when it all happened. These members of the underclass have found their voice. They all speak of what they expect from Mary's son, who is about to be born or has just been born. What they say comes to more or less the same thing. Mary says that he will bring down the powerful from their thrones and lift up the lowly. Zechariah says that he will rescue his people from their enemies. And so forth. It sounds enormously hopeful for those, like themselves, who are downtrodden, and mighty menacing for those at the top who tread them down. If one reads these exclamations of the underclass in Luke's opening chapters with the Old Testament in mind, it is impossible not to interpret them as expressing the expectation that Mary's son will undo injustice and bring about justice. ·

It might just be that, in the subsequent development of Luke's story, we learn that Mary's son, Jesus, dashed all these grandiose expectations that erupted when he was born or about to be born. In fact it becomes clear that Luke regarded these grandiose expectations as somehow fulfilled, or on the way to being fulfilled.

Luke presents his narrative as the continuation of a story already told. The story already told is the one told in the Old Testament about God's dealings with God's covenant people, Israel. Luke's narrative, picking up where the old left off, is about what it was that God was doing by way of the life, execution, and resurrection of Jesus and by way of the growth of the early church. Richard Hays, whose book, *The Moral Vision of the New Testament*, I have found very helpful,[4] puts it nicely:

> The Gospel of Luke and the Acts of the Apostles are two parts of a single grand literary work in which Luke tells the story of salvation history in a stately and gracious manner. God's mighty act of deliverance through Jesus Christ is narrated as an epic, in such a way that the church might discover its location in human history, particularly within the history of God's dealings with his people Israel. (112)

As will be evident from what has been said, the narrative offered by Luke is far from mere chronicle; Luke interprets the events he narrates and interprets the significance of the person central to his narrative, Jesus, Mary's son. He does so by borrowing heavily from the interpretive categories of the Old Testament—which is what one would expect, given that he regards his narrative as continuing that older narrative. He also employs some categories current in Hellenistic culture of the day, and some categories that emerged in Judaism during the inter-testamental period. But over and over, when trying to say who this strange person Jesus is and what might be the significance of the events surrounding him, he followed the example of Jesus himself and employed the categories of biblical Judaism. Fully aware of how baffling he was to those around him, Jesus interpreted himself with the categories of biblical Judaism, creatively modified.

Hays remarks that "no single christological conception ... systematically governs Luke's presentation of Jesus. In an eclectic fashion, [Luke]

---

[4] San Francisco: HarperCollins, 1996.

has combined a number of christological traditions" (114), weaving them together "into a rope that is larger and more substantial than any of the individual strands" (120). Let me present two of the three Lukan christological conceptions that Hays elucidates, and then add a third of my own. In each of these, justice proves central. To de-justicize the New Testament is to render oneself incapable of understanding who Luke thought Jesus was, and who Jesus in Luke's narration thought himself to be.

JESUS AS THE ONE WHO BRINGS JUSTICE

Jesus is the Spirit-anointed servant who proclaims the coming of justice. Shortly after he began teaching and preaching in public, Jesus attended the synagogue in Nazareth on a Sabbath and was invited to read from Scripture and to comment on what he read. "The scroll of the prophet Isaiah was given to him," says Luke. "He unrolled the scroll and found the place where it was written":

> The Spirit of the Lord is upon me,
> because he has anointed me to bring good news to the poor.
> He has sent me to proclaim release to the captives
> and recovery of sight to the blind,
> to let the oppressed go free,
> to proclaim the year of the Lord's favor.

Jesus then "rolled up the scroll, gave it back to the attendant, and sat down." "The eyes of all in the synagogue were fixed on him," expecting him to offer some comment on the reading. Jesus then said that "today this scripture has been fulfilled in your hearing" (Luke 4:17–21). The congregants, we are told, responded not only with approval but with amazement that Joseph's son would say such things. But when Jesus went on to suggest, using stories from the Old Testament about the prophets Elijah and Elisha, that God's favor was not restricted to Israel, they were "filled with rage."

The same self-identification, albeit a bit more allusive, occurs a few chapters later. When John the Baptist was in prison, dumped there by Herod, he received reports about Jesus from some of his followers. Those reports disturbed him. He had been led to believe that Jesus was the Messiah and that he, John, was the Messiah's forerunner. But Jesus was not doing what John expected the Messiah to do. So John sent two of his disciples to Jesus with the question, "Are you the one who is to come, or are we to wait for another?" They put their question to Jesus right after he had "cured many people of diseases, plagues, and evil spirits, and had

given sight to many who were blind." The answer Jesus gave them alluded
to his earlier self-identification in the synagogue. Go and tell John what
you have seen and heard, that "the blind receive their sight, the lame
walk, the lepers are cleansed, the deaf hear, the dead are raised, and the
poor have good news brought to them" (Luke 7:22). Jesus then declared
blessed "anyone who takes no offense" at him.

Before I comment on the significance of these two self-identifications
by Jesus, let me bring into the picture a closely similar identification that
Matthew offers in his own voice. In Matthew's story, Jesus has already
been teaching and healing for some time when Matthew intrudes into
the story and offers his interpretation of the significance of the events
he has narrated: "This was to fulfill what had been spoken through the
prophet Isaiah":

> Here is my servant, whom I have chosen,
>   my beloved, with whom my soul is well pleased.
> I will put my Spirit upon him,
>   and he will proclaim justice [*krisis*] to the Gentiles. . . .
> He will not break a bruised reed or quench a smoldering wick
>   until he brings justice [*krisis*] to victory.
>   And in his name the Gentiles will hope. (Matt. 12:17–21).[5]

What are we to make of these identifications? The first thing to note is
that in his report of what transpired in the synagogue, Luke adapted
the passage from Isaiah to which Jesus' opening words refer, namely,
61:1–2, by dropping a line and adding a line from another related passage, Isaiah, 58:6–7. The Isaiah 61 passage promises the deliverance and
restoration of God's people by the anointed one and goes as follows:

> The Spirit of the Lord God is upon me,
>   because the Lord has anointed me;
> he has sent me to bring good news to the oppressed,
>   to bind up the brokenhearted,
> to proclaim liberty to the captives,
>   and release to the prisoners;
> to proclaim the year of the Lord's favor,
>   and the day of vengeance of our God. (Isaiah 61:1–2)

---

[5] The passage in Isaiah of which Matthew gives a near-quotation, 42:1–4, goes as follows:
Here is my servant, whom I uphold, / My chosen, in whom my soul delights; / I
have put my spirit upon him; / he will bring forth justice to the nations. / He
will not cry or lift up his voice, / or make it heard in the streets; / a bruised
reed he will not break, / and a dimly burning wick he will not quench; / he will
faithfully bring forth justice. / He will not grow faint or be crushed / Until he
has established justice in the earth.

The related passage from which Luke borrowed a line speaks explicitly of God's demand for justice:

> Is not this the fast that I choose:
> to loose the bonds of injustice,
> to undo the thongs of the yoke,
> to let the oppressed go free,
> and to break every yoke?
> Is it not to share your bread with the hungry,
> and bring the homeless poor into your house;
> when you see the naked, to cover them,
> and not to hide yourself from your own kin. (Isaiah 58:6–7)

The import is unmistakable. Jesus identified himself in the synagogue as God's anointed one, the Messiah, whose vocation it is to proclaim to the poor, the blind, the captives, and the oppressed the good news of the inauguration of "the year of the Lord's favor" when justice-in-shalom will reign. In Hays's words, "By evoking these texts at the beginning of his ministry, Luke's Jesus declares himself as the Messiah who by the power of the Spirit will create a restored Israel in which justice and compassion for the poor will prevail" (116).

Before we move on to the second christological conception, it is worth taking note of some other indications of the fact that Jesus took for granted the prophetic sensibility to injustice—that is, took for granted the fact that the fate of the vulnerable low ones is to be interpreted in terms of justice rather than charity and that they are to have priority in the struggle against injustice. The paradigmatic examples in the Old Testament of the vulnerable low ones were the widows, the orphans, the resident aliens, and the poor. The widows and the poor are as prominent in Luke's narration as they were in the Old Testament witness. But the orphan has been replaced by the prisoner; the prisons of the day were apparently hell-holes peopled in good measure by political prisoners. And the category of the alien undergoes a significant transformation, which I address later.

Referring to the scribes, Jesus says that "they devour widows' houses" (Luke 20:47; cf. Mark 12:40). He tells the ruler who claims to have faithfully kept the Torah and now asks what he must do to inherit eternal life that he must sell all that he owns "and give the money to the poor" (Luke 18:22; cf. Matthew 19:21). In the Beatitudes, as we find them in Luke, Jesus blesses the poor and the hungry (6:20–25). And the parable he tells about Lazarus and the rich man "who was dressed in purple and fine linen and who feasted sumptuously every day" is about the judgment executed on the rich man for allowing Lazarus to lie impoverished at his gate, "covered with sores," longing "to satisfy his hunger with what fell

from the rich man's table" (16:19–31). To these we may add the episode
about John the Baptist recorded in chapter 3 of Luke: when the crowds
ask John what they must do to avoid the judgment of doom that he announces, his answer is that "whoever has two coats must share with anyone who has none; and whoever has food must do likewise" (3:11).

Two episodes from Matthew's Gospel illustrate the same point. In the
well-known story of the "Great Assize" (Matthew 25), the Son of Man says
to those on his right hand, "Come, you that are blessed by my Father,
inherit the kingdom prepared for you from the foundation of the world;
for I was hungry and you gave me food, I was thirsty and you gave me
something to drink, I was a stranger and you welcomed me, I was naked
and you gave me clothing, I was sick and you took care of me, I was in
prison and you visited me" (25:34–36). The just ones (*dikaioi*)[6] are puzzled by this invitation; they do not recall having treated the Lord thus.
The explanation they receive is that "just as you did it to one of the least
of these who are members of my family, you did it to me."

In chapter 26 of his Gospel, Matthew reports the episode of a woman
anointing Jesus with expensive ointment (cf. Mark 14:3ff.). The disciples,
we read, "were angry and said, 'Why this waste? For this ointment could
have been sold for a large sum and the money given to the poor' " (Matthew 26:8–9). Jesus corrects them, not by calling into question their
concern for the poor—he remarks that there will be no shortage of occasions for them to do justice to the poor—but by declaring that in the
situation at hand, there was something of even higher priority than doing
justice to the poor: the woman has anointed the body of Jesus for his
imminent burial.

JESUS AS INNOCENT

A second identification of Jesus to which Hays calls attention—this one
not by Jesus but by others—is that of Jesus as the innocent martyr. Or as
Hays translates the Greek, of Jesus as the "righteous" martyr. Three times
in Luke's Gospel Pilate declares that he has found Jesus innocent: "I find
no basis for accusation against this man" (23:4), I "have not found this
man guilty of any of your charges against him" (23:14), "I have found in
him no ground for the sentence of death" (23: 22). When one of the
criminals executed alongside Jesus mocks him, the other criminal re-
bukes him, "Do you not fear God, since you are under the same sentence
of condemnation? And we indeed have been condemned justly [*dikaios*],
for we are getting what we deserve for our deeds, but this man has done

---

[6] The NRSV has "righteous."

nothing wrong" (23:40–41). At the moment of Jesus' death the centurion, observing what was taking place, "praised God and said, 'Certainly this man was innocent [*dikaios*]' " (23:47).

Luke carries forward this identification of Jesus as innocent martyr into his Acts of the Apostles. In one of Peter's speeches to a crowd in Jerusalem, he reproaches them for having rejected "the Holy and Innocent One" (*ton hagion kai dikaion*) and for asking instead "to have a murderer given to you" (3:14); in the speech that Stephen gives at his martyrdom he similarly accuses his hearers of killing "the Innocent [*dikaios*] One" (7:52);[7] and when the Ethiopian eunuch asks Philip of whom it was that the prophet Isaiah (Isaiah 53:7–8) was speaking when he said that "Like a sheep he was led to the slaughter" and "In his humiliation justice [*krisis*] was denied him," Philip explains that the prophecy has been fulfilled in Jesus (Acts 8:33).

Hays shows in some detail that "the cumulative effect of these passages is to demonstrate that Jesus died in accordance with the Scriptures, as the Righteous [Innocent] One prefigured in Isaiah, the lament psalms, and Wisdom of Solomon" (119). For our purposes here, what is important to note is the obvious fact that the person who refuses to think in terms of justice cannot understand Luke's identification of Jesus as the innocent, the just, the *dikaios* martyr.

JESUS AS KING

A third style of identification carries essentially the same significance. One of the most prominent features in the preaching of Jesus, as recorded in the synoptic gospels, is that he proclaimed the coming of the kingdom of God and urged his hearers to prepare by repenting of their sins. Mark, with characteristic abruptness, opens his narrative of Jesus' public ministry with the words, "Now after John [the Baptist] was arrested, Jesus came to Galilee, proclaiming the good news of God, and saying, 'The time is fulfilled, and the kingdom of God has come near; repent, and believe in the good news' " (1:14–15). Matthew is a bit more expansive. John the Baptist has been proclaiming, "Repent, for the kingdom of heaven has come near" (3:2). When Jesus heard about John's arrest, he returned to Galilee so as to fulfill the messianic prophecy

---

[7] The NRSV translates "*dikaios*" in these two passages as "righteous." That seems to me clearly a mistranslation. Of course Jesus was righteous, or upright. But the point that is relevant when Jesus' execution is spoken of is not that he was of righteous character but that he was innocent of the charges. Furthermore, to translate "*dikaios*" as "righteous" is to obscure the connection with the passages from Luke's gospel that are cited in the preceding paragraph.

found in Isaiah 9:1–2 about the origins of the messiah,[8] and there he began to proclaim, "Repent, for the kingdom of heaven has come near" (4:17). And shortly after the episode in the synagogue, Luke reports Jesus as saying, "I must proclaim the good news of the kingdom of God to the other cities also; for I was sent for this purpose" (4:43; cf. 8:1). Sometimes Luke's Jesus, like the Jesus of Mark and of Matthew, adds a note of imminence: "Yet know this: the kingdom of God has come near" (10:11; cf. 10:9). "In fact, the kingdom of God is among you" (17:21).

The important point for our purposes is that Jesus does not merely proclaim the coming of God's kingdom; he is identified as the *king* of this kingdom. For the most part this identification occurs unemphatically, and never directly by Jesus himself. Jesus confines himself to saying that "all things have been handed over to me by my Father" (Luke 10:22) and, a bit more explicitly, that "all authority in heaven and on earth has been given to me" (Matt 28:17).[9] But on first meeting Jesus, Nathanial declares "You are the Son of God! You are the King of Israel!" (John 1:49). And in chapter 20 of his gospel, Matthew tells the story about the mother of two of Jesus' disciples coming to him with the request that he "declare that these two sons of mine will sit, one at your right hand and one at your left, in your kingdom." Jesus replies that she is under the false impression that it is up to him to determine seating arrangements in the kingdom; it is up to the Father. What the reply assumes is that Jesus will in fact be the king of the kingdom.

The most emphatic identifications of Jesus as king are made, significantly, by Gentiles. In Matthew's infancy narrative, wise men from the East arrive in Jerusalem shortly after the birth of Jesus asking, "Where is the child who has been born king of the Jews?" When King Herod heard this, "he was frightened, and all Jerusalem with him." So Herod assembled the chief priests and scribes and asked them where the messiah was to be born. In Bethlehem, they said, citing as evidence a passage from the prophet Micah (5:2). Matthew's near quotation is this:

> And you, Bethlehem, in the land of Judah,
>   are by no means least among the rulers of Judah,
> for from you shall come a ruler
>   who is to shepherd my people Israel. (2:6)

---

[8] Matthew's citation of Isaiah goes as follows:
   Land of Zebulun, land of Naphtali, / on the road by the sea, across the Jordan, Galilee of the Gentiles— / the people who sat in darkness have seen a great light, / and for those who sat in the region and shadow of death / light has dawned (Matt. 4:15–16).

[9] Jesus does, though, identify himself as Lord (*kurios*; e.g., John 13:14) and regularly allows himself to be so identified. This would have come to very nearly the same thing as king, *basileus*.

Jump now to Jesus' final hours. Jesus has been sent to Pilate with criminal accusations. Pilate, clearly puzzled by the accusations, directed that Jesus be brought to him for interrogation. Pilate opened the interrogation, according to the narration in John's Gospel, by asking Jesus whether he was "the King of the Jews." Jesus responded by asking whether Pilate was asking this on his own initiative or whether others had told Pilate about him. Pilate answers that he himself is not a Jew; it is Jesus' own people who have lodged charges. So "what have you done?" he asks. Jesus replies that his kingdom is not of this world. If it were, "my followers would be fighting to keep me from being handed over to the Jews. But as it is, my kingdom is not from here." Pilate then says, "So you are a king!" Jesus replies, "You said it. For this I was born, and for this I came into the world, to testify to the truth." Whereupon Pilate asked his famous question, "What is truth?"

After the interrogation, Pilate, in his confrontations with the public, three times over (in John's narration) ascribes the title "King of the Jews" to Jesus; and when finally Pilate allows Jesus to be crucified, he has the inscription placed above his head, "Jesus of Nazareth, the King of the Jews." Matthew, Mark, and Luke tell of the taunting that this inscription evoked from hangers-on and passers-by: "He saved others; he cannot save himself. Let the Messiah, the King of Israel, come down from the cross now, so that we may see and believe" (Mark 15:31–32). John does not report the taunting but instead reports the chagrin of the chief priests. They had brought Jesus to Pilate on the charge that he was claiming to be king; they wanted Pilate to know that they themselves "had no king but the emperor." But now, rather than executing Jesus for the charge lodged against him, Pilate was apparently announcing that Jesus was in fact their king. So they asked Pilate to change the inscription from "King of the Jews" to "This man said, I am King of the Jews." Pilate would not budge. "What I have written, I have written," was his reply.[10]

What would a Jew of the day, informed by the prophetic literature of the Old Testament, have believed if he thought that Jesus was to be king in the imminent kingdom of God? He would of course have believed that the reign of all other kings was now threatened. But more generally, he would have believed that this king would usher in an era of justice and righteousness, *mishpat* and *tsedeqa*—an era in which justice would reign and everyone would do what is right. In short, identifying Jesus as king in the kingdom of God comes to the same as identifying Jesus as Messiah. For the Messiah was expected to be king; recall Mark's report of the shout of the taunters at the crucifixion, "Let the Messiah, the King of Israel, come down from the cross."

---

[10] The narrative as given above follows John 18:33 through 19:22.

In chapter 3 I quoted the classic description of the good king in Psalm 72. Let us have it before us again:

> Give the king your justice, O God,
>> and your righteousness to a king's son.
> May he judge your people with righteousness,
>> and your poor with justice.
> May the mountains yield prosperity for the people,
>> and the hills, in righteousness.
> May he defend the cause of the poor of the people,
>> give deliverance to the needy,
>> and crush the oppressor. . . .
> For he delivers the needy when they call,
>> the poor and those who have no helper.
> He has pity on the weak and the needy,
>> and saves the lives of the needy.
> From oppression and violence he redeems their life;
>> And precious is their blood in his sight.

Expanding the Scope of Justice

I have been arguing that justice is the inextricable context and content of the witness of the New Testament writers concerning Jesus and what God was doing in and by his life, death, and resurrection; and that Jesus, in their narrative, carries forward the prophetic sensibility to injustice—that is, the conviction that the fate of the vulnerable low ones is to be interpreted in terms of justice rather than charity and that their condition is to be given priority in the struggle against injustice. It would be a mistake, however, to locate what is new exclusively in the claim that in the coming of Jesus, the age of justice is inaugurated. What is also new is an expanded vision of the downtrodden.

One Sabbath day a leader of the Pharisees invited Jesus to join him and his friends for dinner (Luke 14:1ff.); the host must not have realized that he had invited an uncaged tiger into the house. The dinner was scarcely under way when Jesus noticed a man with dropsy (edema) standing in front of him—not a welcome visitor in the house of someone concerned to preserve ritual purity. Jesus asked the lawyers and Pharisees present whether it was permissible to heal someone on the Sabbath. Getting no response, he healed the man and sent him on his way.

A bit later it struck Jesus that some of the guests had seen to it that they were seated in "places of honor"—close to the host, no doubt. That led Jesus to remark that

> When you are invited by someone to a wedding banquet, do not sit down at the place of honor, in case someone more distinguished than you has been invited by your host; and the host who invited both of you may come and say to you, "Give this person your place," and then in disgrace you would start to take the lowest place. But when you are invited, go and sit down at the lowest place, so that when your host comes, he may say to you, "Friend, move up higher"; then you will be honored in the presence of all who sit at the table with you. For all who exalt themselves will be humbled, and those who humble themselves will be exalted.

Let me take a brief excursion to say something about this theme of social inversion that Jesus here introduces. Metaphors common in present-day discourse about society are those of *the margin* and *the outside*. We speak of people as outsiders and as living on the margins. The image in the background is that of a circle with center and circumference. Some people are at the center, some are on the circumference, some are outside.

I noted in our discussion of the Old Testament that its writers worked instead with the image of up and down: some are at the top of the social hierarchy, some are at the bottom. Those at the bottom are usually not there because it is their fault. They are there because they are downtrodden. Those at the top "trample the heads of the poor into the dust of the earth" (Amos 2:7).

When *center* and *circumference* are one's basic metaphors, the undoing of injustice will be described as *including* the outsiders. When *up* and *down* are one's basic metaphors, the undoing of injustice will be described as *lifting up* those at the bottom. The poor do not have to be included within the social order; they have always been there, usually indispensable to its functioning. They have to be lifted up. God

> raises the poor from the dust,
>> and lifts the needy from the ash heap
> to make them sit with princes. (Psalm 113:7)

All this is also true of the New Testament. But a striking feature of the New Testament writings, and of Jesus' preaching as they report it, is the frequency with which the up-and-down metaphor common in the writings of the Old Testament is employed to say something that the Old Testament writers at most hint at. The rectification of injustice requires not only *lifting up* the low ones but *casting down* the high ones. The coming of justice requires social inversion.

The theme was sounded already in Mary's Magnificat.

> My soul magnifies the Lord,
>> and my spirit rejoices in God my Savior,
>> for he has looked with favor on the lowliness of his servant. . . .

> He has brought down the powerful from their thrones,
>   and lifted up the lowly;
> he has filled the hungry with good things,
>   and sent the rich away empty. (Luke 1:46–53)

The theme was implicit in the fact it was to lowly shepherds that the elevated heavenly host delivered its "good news of great joy for all the people: to you is born this day in the city of David a Savior who is the Messiah, the Lord" (Luke 2:10–11). It was implicit in the fact that the shepherds found their Lord lying in a manger in a barn. And it was picked up in Luke's report of the Beatitudes. Jesus does not only say, "Blessed are you who are poor"; he adds, "Woe to you who are rich." And he does not only say, "Blessed are you who are hungry now." He adds, "Woe to you who are full now" (Luke 6: 20–25).

What is the import of this theme of social inversion? Part of its import is unmistakable. For the coming of justice it is not sufficient to raise up the ones at the bottom, leaving everything else the same. Something must also happen to those at the top; they must be cast down. Justice for the downtrodden requires casting down the ones who tread them down. The coming of justice can be a painful experience.

But what exactly does this lifting up and casting down come to? Was Jesus instructing his followers to invert social positions? That is to say, was he instructing them to push those at the top down to the bottom and lift those at the bottom up to the top, keeping everything else intact? We do not know with any certainty the social status of Jesus and his disciples. Jesus was a homeless itinerant rabbi who lived on alms; what status would such a person have had in his society? We do not know. But suppose that Jesus and his disciples were at the bottom of the social hierarchy. Was Nietzsche right to interpret this theme of social inversion as the expression of envy and resentment by those at the bottom against those at the top?

Jesus did not mean, literally, that justice requires that beggars become kings and kings become beggars. The beggars would soon start acting like kings. The clue to the meaning of the theme of social inversion lies in his sentence, "all who exalt themselves will be humbled and those who humble themselves will be exalted." The coming of justice requires the humbling of those who exalt themselves. The arrogant must be cured of their arrogance; the rich and powerful must be cured of their attachment to wealth and power. Only then is justice for all possible.

Over and over and in a variety of ways Jesus sounds the theme. One day he heard his disciples discussing who would be greatest in the kingdom of heaven. He called a child over, put the child among them, and said, "unless you change and become like children you will never enter the kingdom of heaven. Whoever becomes humble like this child is the greatest in the kingdom of heaven" (Matt. 18:1–4, 19:13–14; cf. Mark 9:33–37 and 10:13–16).

Back to the dinner party. Having declared that the hierarchical seating arrangements at the dinner were all wrong, Jesus turned to his host and said,

> When you give a luncheon or a dinner, do not invite your friends or your brothers or your relatives or rich neighbors, in case they may invite you in return, and you would be repaid. But when you give a banquet, invite the poor, the crippled, the lame, and the blind. And you will be blessed, because they cannot repay you, for you will be repaid at the resurrection of the just [*dikaios*].[11]

This barbed remark of Jesus to his host is usually interpreted as teaching that we are to practice a generosity that goes beyond all calculations of reciprocity. No doubt this was one of the points Jesus was making. But I think it likely that his host would have heard the main point as a different one. Inviting the poor, no problem—no problem in principle for a Pharisee, that is. Inviting the crippled, the lame, and the blind is a different matter.

The crippled, the lame, and the blind, along with those suffering from dropsy, are defective, malformed human beings. And in the legislation of Leviticus and Deuteronomy, anything malformed, be it human or animal, could not adequately mirror the holiness of God. The malformed were on that account to be excluded from the precincts of the temple and other holy places. It was apparently an important part of the piety of the Pharisees of Jesus' day to follow the regulations for the temple in their own private lives, especially in their homes. Their homes were to be little temples. Jesus' barbed remark to his host was a direct attack on this religious exclusivism.

The tension would have been thick enough to cut with a knife. So one of the guests tried to distract attention from what Jesus had said by propounding a platitude that all could agree on. Yes, we have our disagreements over who will be eating bread in the kingdom of heaven. But surely we can all agree that whoever does eat bread in the kingdom will be blessed: "Blessed is anyone who will eat bread in the kingdom of God."

Jesus is not to be distracted. He responds by telling the parable that has come to be known as the Parable of the Great Banquet:

> Someone gave a great dinner and invited many. At the time for the dinner he sent his slave to say to those who had been invited, "Come,

---

[11] The NRSV has "the righteous."

for everything is ready now." But they all alike began to make excuses. The first said to him, "I have bought a piece of land, and I must go out and see it; please accept my regrets." Another said, "I have bought five yoke of oxen, and I am going to try them out; please accept my regrets." Another said, "I have just been married and therefore I cannot come." So the slave returned and reported this to his master. Then the owner of the house became angry and said to his slave, "Go out at once into the streets and lanes of the town and bring in the poor, the crippled, the blind, and the lame." And the slave said, "Sir, what you ordered has been done, and there is still room." Then the master said to the slave, "Go out into the roads and lanes and compel people to come in, so that my house may be filled. For I tell you, none of those who were invited will taste my dinner.

You and I hear this as a morality tale about ingratitude. Once again, it is unlikely that those at the dinner party would have heard this as the main point.

For ancient Israel, the battlefield was second only to the temple as a place where God's holiness was to be reflected. Thus it was that the Deuteronomic legislation instructs the officer before a battle to address his troops as follows:

Has anyone built a new house but not dedicated it? He should go back to his house, or he might die in the battle and another dedicate it. Has anyone planted a vineyard but not yet enjoyed its fruit? He should go back to his house, or he might die in the battle and another be first to enjoy its fruit. Has anyone become engaged to a woman but not yet married her? He should go back to his house, or he might die in the battle and another marry her. (Deut. 20: 5–7)

Note that everything mentioned is incomplete in some significant way; the incomplete is like the malformed in not reflecting the holiness of God. And now notice that all those in Jesus' parable who plead that they cannot come to the banquet do so because they are in the middle of some incomplete project—exactly the sort of excuse that a pious Pharisee would find not ungrateful but obligatory. It is their exclusivist piety, not their ingratitude, that prevents them from accepting the invitation.

What are we to make of this? I think we have to conclude that Jesus' understanding of who are the downtrodden has been expanded well beyond the Old Testament understanding, to include not just the victims of social structures and practices—widows, orphans, aliens, the poor, the imprisoned—but also those excluded from full participation in society because they are defective, malformed, or seen as religiously inferior. The coming of God's just reign requires that these too be lifted up.

So prominent and pervasive in the gospels is Jesus' attack on exclusion of those regarded as religiously inferior that it seems almost pointless to cite examples. "Woe to you, scribes and Pharisees," he says, "for you lock people out of the kingdom of heaven [but] you do not go in yourselves, and when others are going in, you stop them" (Matt. 23:13–14). It was the point of the story about the pious arrogant Pharisee and the humble tax collector praying together in the temple: "I tell you," says Jesus, that this tax collector "went down to his home justified rather than the other; for all who exalt themselves will be humbled, but all who humble themselves will be exalted" (Luke 18:14). It has to be at least part of the point of Jesus' healings. Rather than avoiding the malformed as ritually unclean, Jesus touched them and healed them: the deaf, the dumb, the blind, the crippled, the paralytics, the possessed, those issuing bodily fluids—the whole lot.[12] And it lies behind Jesus' practice of eating with "sinners and tax collectors"—the sinners being prostitutes and other unsavory people who had run afoul of the moral law, the tax collectors being those Jews who had gone over to the other side and were now in the service of Rome. In Luke's telling of the story about a woman of the night who intrudes into a dinner that Jesus was having at the house of a Pharisee and anoints his feet with ointment, his host reproaches Jesus on the ground that if he were a prophet, "he would have known who and what kind of woman this is who is touching him—that she is a sinner" (Luke 7:39).

Indeed, so striking was Jesus' inclusion in his company of those perceived as religiously defective or inferior, and in his message of the coming of God's just reign, that it became part of his reputation.

As he sat at dinner in [Matthew the tax collector's] house, many tax collectors and sinners came and were sitting with him and his disciples. When the Pharisees saw this, they said to his disciples, "Why does your teacher eat with tax collectors and sinners?" But when he heard this, he said, "Those who are well have no need of a physician, but those who are sick. Go and learn what this means. 'I

---

[12] This is how N. T. Wright, among others, interprets the healings in his *Jesus and the Victory of God* (Minneapolis: Fortress Press, 1996). "For a first-century Jew, most if not all of the works of healing . . . could be seen as the restoration to membership in Israel of those who, through sickness or whatever, had been excluded as ritually unclean. The healings thus function in exact parallel with the welcome of sinners, and this, we may be quite sure, was what Jesus himself intended. . . . Jesus' healing miracles must be seen clearly as bestowing the gift of *shalom*, wholeness, on those who lacked it, bringing not only physical health but renewed membership in the people of YHWH" (191–92).

desire mercy, not sacrifice.' For I have come to call not the upright [*dikaioi*] but sinners." (Matt. 9:10–13; cf. Mark 2:15–17)[13]

Women were among those that Jesus ate with and included in his company and his message. Gentiles were included as well. He healed them, conversed with them, and included them too in his message. The well-known story in John 4 is about someone who is a member of both out-groups at once: a woman from Samaria.

Jesus and his disciples were on the way from Judah in the south to Galilee in the north. To get there, they had to travel through Samaria, an area populated with people whom the Jews, at least, regarded as ethnically distinct; John remarks pointedly (4:9) that "Jews do not share things in common with Samaritans." By noon the little band was tired and hungry. So the disciples went off to the neighboring village to buy some food while Jesus stayed behind and sat down at a well—by reputation, Jacob's well. A woman from the area, thus a Samaritan woman, came to draw water. Jesus asked her for a drink. That led to a deep religious conversation at the end of which Jesus identified himself to her as the Messiah. Now let me quote John's words: "Just then his disciples came. They were astonished that he was speaking with a woman, but no one said, 'What do you want?' or 'Why are you speaking with her?' "

In an episode reported in all three of the synoptic gospels, a term is used that captures the pattern of Jesus' engagement with those he came in contact with: he showed "no partiality." The episode is that in which some opponents of Jesus tried to trap him with the famous trick question about the morality of paying taxes to the Roman emperor. In all three narrations, the interrogator prefaces his question with a reference to Jesus' reputation. Let me quote Matthew's version: "Teacher, we know that you are sincere, and teach the way of God in accordance with truth, and show deference to no one; for you do not regard people with partiality" (Matt. 22:16).[14] The reference to Jesus' reputation for teaching the truth is flattery; the reference to his not showing deference to people and not regarding them with partiality is preparation for setting the trap. How far is he willing to go in showing deference to no one? Is he willing to go all the way to the emperor?

---

[13] Cf., among other such passages, Luke 15:1–2: "Now all the tax collectors and sinners were coming near to listen to him. And the Pharisees and the scribes were grumbling and saying, 'This fellow welcomes sinners and eats with them.' "

[14] Cf. Mark 12:14: "Teacher, we know that you are sincere, and show deference to no one; for you do not regard people with partiality, but teach the way of God in accordance with truth." And Luke 20:21: "Teacher, we know that you are right in what you say and teach, and you show deference to no one, but teach the way of God in accordance with truth."

Jesus was not at all impartial as between the humble and the arrogant; he favored the former and denounced the latter. But among the humble he played no favorites. The ritually unclean, the malformed, those engaged in illicit or unsavory occupations, the Jews who collected taxes for Rome, women, Gentiles, the wealthy, the poor—he freely conversed and ate with the whole lot of them. The coming of justice requires no deference to persons, no partiality.

The One Who Brings Justice Falls Victim

A description of the role of justice in the thought of the gospels would be seriously incomplete if we did not pick up a point made at the beginning of this chapter. That very same Jesus who is identified as the one sent by God to inaugurate the reign of justice himself became a victim of gross injustice. Though innocent of the charges lodged against him, he who came to lift up the downtrodden was himself handed over to be executed in the company of a pair of common criminals, thereby being consigned to the lowest rung of the downtrodden. Were it not for Jesus' resurrection, the entire story would have been profoundly ironic, with massive delusion at its core. As it is, Jesus' becoming the victim of injustice proved not the end of the story but a central episode in a larger story of victory rather than defeat for the cause of justice. For one who accepts Chalcedonian Christology, the victim was not only human but divine.

The Recognition of Rights in the New Testament

Our project in this chapter has been to show how two themes that we identified in the Old Testament are carried forward into the gospels: the theme of God's commitment to acting justly and to bringing about justice among human beings and the theme of God holding human beings accountable to himself for doing justice. The latter theme is part of the ever-present background in the gospels, the former is given a decisive new development. Jesus is the one chosen by God to inaugurate the reign of justice.

In concluding our discussion in chapter 3 of justice in the Old Testament, I argued that the Old Testament writers, in their development of the two themes mentioned, assumed that God has subjective rights— God can be wronged—and that those rights are not conferred but inherent, grounded in God's worth. I refrain from repeating those arguments here. The testimony of the entirety of Christian Scripture concerning God and justice assumes that God has inherent rights.

But what about human justice? Is there any indication that the gospel writers were assuming that human beings have inherent rights?

In the preceding chapter I argued that it is the attribution of forgiveness to God by the Old Testament writers that constitutes the most decisive indication of their assumption that God has subjective rights. One can forgive someone only if he has wronged one and only *for* the wrong he has done one. Forgiveness presupposes that one has been deprived of that to which one has a right. It presupposes the existence of subjective rights.

In his emphatic declaration that we are to forgive as God forgives, Jesus goes well beyond the Old Testament. Indeed, Jesus regards our willingness to forgive those who wrong us as a manifestation of the repentance that God requires for his forgiveness of those who wrong him. Luke reports Jesus as saying, "Forgive, and you will be forgiven" (6:37). Matthew reports him as making the connection even more explicit: "if you forgive others their trespasses, your heavenly Father will also forgive your trespasses" (6:14–15).

Peter was disturbed by the open-endedness of Jesus' injunction to forgive. So one day he posed to Jesus the *reductio ad absurdum* question, "Lord, if another member of the church sins against me,[15] how often should I forgive him? As many as seven times?" Jesus first gave a hyperbolic answer: not seven times but seventy-seven times. Then he told the parable about the king who, out of mercy, forgave the large debt owed him by one of his servants who, in turn, mercilessly refused to forgive the much smaller debt owed him by one of his fellow servants. The point of the story, in Jesus' words, is that you are to forgive your brother and sister out of mercy, from your heart, as often as proves necessary (Matt. 18:21–35).

Is there any indication of the gospel writers taking the next step, beyond the recognition of subjective rights that forgiveness presupposes, to the recognition of human beings as having worth and of that worth as grounding how they are to be treated? There is indeed. Luke and Matthew both report Jesus as encouraging his disciples on various occasions not to be anxious about their lives. "Consider the ravens," Luke reports him as saying; "they neither sow nor reap, they have neither storehouse nor barn and yet God feeds them. Of how much more value are you than the birds" (12:24)? Matthew's report is essentially the same: "Look at the birds of the air; they neither sow or reap nor gather into barns, and yet your heavenly Father feeds them. Are you not of more value than they" (6:26)? On another occasion Jesus says, "Do not be afraid; you are of more value than many sparrows" (Matt. 10:31). And

---

[15] Note the locution "sins against me." This is surely a synonym of "wrongs me."

Matthew (12:11–12) reports Jesus as justifying healing on the Sabbath with the words, "Suppose one of you has only one sheep and it falls into a pit on the Sabbath; will you not lay hold of it and lift it out? How much more valuable is a human being than a sheep?"

To be a human being is to have worth. Jesus does not indicate what that worth is, other than to say that it is much greater than the worth of birds and sheep and to suggest that it is a worth one has *qua* human being. Presumably, the worth he had in mind was that of bearing the image of God. What is to be noted, then, is that in these passages Jesus appeals to our worth as human beings to explain God's care for each and every one of us, and to the sick person's worth as a human being to explain why he himself heals on the Sabbath. Not only do we have an echo here of the Old Testament's celebration of the worth of human beings; we also have an echo of that passage from Genesis, quoted in chapter 3 in which one's right not to be murdered is grounded in one's worth. It seems safe to infer that it was these ideas that lay behind Jesus' practice of showing no partiality as between those who did and those who did not pass the Pharisees' test for being holy and ritually clean, as between those who had and those who lacked wealth and power, as between those who were and those who were not members of Israel, and so forth.

PART II

Fusion of Narrative with Theory:
The Goods to Which We Have Rights

Chapter Six

LOCATING THAT TO WHICH
WE HAVE RIGHTS

TRANSITION FROM NARRATIVE TO THEORY

We are ready to begin developing our theory of rights. A fundamental thesis of my discussion will be that that to which one has a right is always a good of some sort, with the exception of those cases of conferred rights in which the one who conferred the right mistakenly thought it was to a good, or correctly thought it was not to a good but conferred it in order to appease those who believed it was.[1] Not every good is of the right sort, however, for someone to have a right to it. So the first step in developing our theory of rights will be identifying the sort of goods to which one can have a right. We do that in this part of our discussion, part II. In Part III we give an account of what it is to have a right to a good of the sort we have identified.

We will not yet put narrative entirely behind us, however. The obvious question left hanging by our counter-narrative is whether the assumption and recognition of inherent rights can be traced back into pagan antiquity as well as into the biblical writings. The answer is that they can be—not at all surprising if one holds, as I do, that inherent rights belong to the furniture of the moral universe rather than being an idea devised by some overly imaginative theorists. We need look no further than to a passage from Aristotle's *Nicomachean Ethics*. In the course of his discussion of justice as equality, Aristotle said, "Awards should be according to merit; for all men agree that what is just in distribution must be according to merit in some sense, though they do not all specify the same sort of merit, but democrats identify it with the status of freeman, supporters of oligarchy with wealth (or with noble birth), and supporters of aristocracy with excellence" (*Nichomachean Ethics*, 1131a 23–28). Though Aristotle does not use the concept of rights here or elsewhere, there can be little doubt that he has his eye on the phenomenon of something

---

[1] Chris Eberle called my attention to the need for the latter of the two qualifications. His example was that of a legislative body that confers the right to polygamous marriages on the citizenry, even though it believes, correctly, that polygamous marriages are not a good thing. It does so in order to quiet the clamor.

being due a person on account of his worth; and that is exactly the phenomenon that we would conceptualize with the idea of inherent rights.

When introducing our discussion of justice in Scripture, I noted that in the biblical writings there is no theory of justice or of rights, nor indeed of anything else. There is a background framework of conviction providing some of the materials needed for a theory of justice as inherent rights; but no theory. The writings of pagan antiquity are unlike the biblical writings in that here there is theory in abundance, including ethical theory, Aristotle being a prime example. I would say, in fact, that ancient ethical theory was as profound and intellectually creative as ethical theory has ever been. Yet there is no theory of rights to be found in ancient ethical theory. That, in my judgment, was no accident. The ancients conducted all their ethical theorizing within the framework of eudaimonism. A theory of rights, so I contend, cannot be developed within that framework.

For this there are several reasons. Given the nature of the goods to which we have rights, a theory of rights requires, as we shall see shortly, a conception of the good life. Not all theorists conceive of the good life in the same way, however. That is to say: theorists do not merely espouse different views as to the content of the good life, while nonetheless conceiving of it in the same way; they conceive of it differently. The most important reason why a theory of rights cannot be developed within the framework of eudaimonism is that the conception of the good life with which eudaimonism works is not of the right sort to comprehend all the goods to which we have rights. An adequate theory of rights would not have been possible had the grip of eudaimonism on the intellectual imagination of the West not been broken. One can watch that grip being broken in Augustine's struggle against the Stoics.

These remarks bring into the light an assumption, not previously highlighted, underlying my argument in the preceding three chapters. In Scripture the good life was conceived in such a way as to make possible the recognition of rights in general and of inherent rights in particular. It was Augustine's reading of Scripture that forced him to break with eudaimonism in such a way as to make possible a theory of rights. The incursion of Scripture into the thought world of late antiquity made possible the rights culture that we are all familiar with.

The reader will now have anticipated why it is that, even though our counter-narrative is concluded and we are beginning theory, we will not yet leave narrative entirely behind us. We must see just why it is that the conception of the good life that eudaimonism works with cannot serve as the conception necessary for a theory of rights. So as not to beat up on a straw man, it will be important to have eudaimonism at its best before us; and never has eudaimonism been articulated as well as it was by the ancient theorists. It will then be instructive to see why and how Augustine, under the pressure of Scripture, found himself compelled to break with eudaimonism in such a way as to create space for a theory of rights.

Our systematic considerations in this part will proceed in three stages. In this chapter we determine the ontological category of those goods to which we have rights. Then for three chapters our goal is to pick out, from those entities that belong to that ontological category, the subset whose members are the goods of the relevant sort. Finally, in chapter 10 we consider attempts to give a general account or characterization of those goods.

The Ontology of That to Which We Have Rights

I have a right to receive a polite answer from the receptionist when I ask where I must go for my X ray, a right to not being hindered by thugs from strolling on the New Haven Green, a right to not being spied on out of prurient interests.

My receiving a polite answer to my question is an event, a happening, an occurrence. My not being hindered from strolling on the Green and my not being spied on are states, conditions. I suggest that everything to which one has a right is an event or a state, a happening or a condition. Let me follow the current philosophical practice and call both happenings and conditions *states of affairs*. Rights are to states of affairs. We customarily specify states of affairs by means of gerunds: my receiving a polite answer, my being free to walk on the Green, and so forth.[2]

We do, of course, speak of having a right to a dog; and a dog is not a state of affairs. But I take it that by "a right to a dog" one means a right to own a dog or to have a dog around. There are millions and millions of dogs in existence; that is not the problem. What is missing, when you are not enjoying your right to a dog, is some sort of relationship between yourself and some dog. What is missing is *your owning* a dog or *your having* a dog around. And those are states of affairs.

The events or states to which one has a right are always happenings *to* oneself or conditions *of* oneself; they are states of affairs of which one is,

---

[2] I assume that one can have a right to a state of affairs that does not presently exist, and hence that there are such states of affairs. Though this is highly controversial among metaphysicians, here is not the place to defend the assumption. Another way to go would be to conceive of states of affairs as entities that can either obtain or not obtain. On that conception, what I am assuming is not that one can have a right to a state of affairs that does not presently exist but to the obtaining of a state of affairs that exists but does not presently obtain.

in that way, a constituent. I do not have a right to the aurora borealis' *being in full glory tonight*. That is indeed a state of affairs; but it is not a state of affairs of the correct sort for me to have a right to it. I am not a constituent of it, let alone being a constituent in the right way. *My being free to view a display of the aurora borealis* is different in just this respect. It is of the correct ontological sort for me to have a right to it. If someone contends that I do not have a right to it, they cannot base their contention on the claim that it is ontologically impossible that I should have a right to it.

I said that the events to which a human being has a right are happenings *to* that person. An obvious question is whether some of them are not instead actions *of* that person, things the person does, happenings of which the person is agent rather than patient. Do I not have a right, for example, to walk on the New Haven Green?

I think not. Though I am *permitted* to walk on the Green, the claim-right I have—and all along it is claim-rights that we are talking about—is that of my not being hindered from walking on the Green. So too, by saying that you have a right to own a dog you might mean that you are permitted to do so, that you have a permission-right to own a dog. But if instead you mean to affirm a claim-right, that would be your right to being free to own a dog, to not being hindered from doing so.

And now a further large step: one's claim-rights are one's right to persons treating and refraining from treating one in certain ways. All my examples have been of this sort: my right to receiving a polite answer to my question, my right to being free to stroll on the New Haven Green, my right to not being spied on, my right to being free to view a display of the aurora borealis, your right to being free to own a dog. The argument for my contention that all rights are like this will have to come later, in our discussion in chapter 11.

The point made earlier, that the events or states to which a human being has a right are always happenings *to* that human being or conditions *of* him or her, must not be taken in an individualistic direction. On account of our solidarities with each other, by wronging one human being, one often wrongs others as well. By murdering one member of the family, one wrongs the other members. The point above remains intact, however. My wife's not being assaulted is not only a state in her life to which she has a right; it is also a state in *my* life to which *I* have a right. For she is *my* wife. By wronging her, you wrong me.

It will not always be evident from how we describe an event to which one has a right that it is an event in one's own life; on the surface, it will sometimes appear to be an event wholly in someone else's life. Suppose, for example, that you promised me that you would put out some corn for the wild turkey in the neighborhood while I was gone. I then have a right to your doing that—to your putting out some corn for the wild turkey. And that action on your part to which I have a right does not in any way involve me. Nothing in what I have to say subsequently requires that I treat as loose talk the statement that I have a right to your putting out corn for the turkey. What I do contend, however, is that this does not make fully explicit the structure of the situation. What I have a right to is *your keeping your promise to me* by putting out corn for the turkey. And that is an occurrence of which I am the recipient.

RIGHTS, LIVES, AND HISTORIES

Consider now the totality of those happenings of which I am the recipient and those conditions that I am in; and then pick out those to which I have a right. Do these all belong to my life? Are they all constituents of that rather long and complex entity that is my life?

First a cautionary word about the concept of life that I will be using. In the theory of material objects that he develops in his book *Material Beings*, Peter van Inwagen makes heavy use of the notion of a *life* under-stood as a biological event.[3] A life, as he understands it for the purpose of his theory, is "the events and processes that constitute an organism being alive" (87). He observes that it is the business of biologists to tell us what a life, thus understood, is.

The concept of a life that I be working with in my discussion is not the biologist's concept but the ordinary concept.[4] Anybody using the ordinary concept would regard my being treated impolitely by the receptionist as an episode in my life. But it is not an episode in my biological life; no biologist would take note of it in his theory. What the biologist calls a *life* is an abstraction from that vastly richer totality that is a life according to our ordinary concept. So too a *biographical* life, understood as what a biographer is interested in, is an abstraction from that richer totality. That richer totality is what we need for our purposes.

So once again our question: do the happenings and conditions to which I have a right all belong to my life? They do not. One can be wronged by things that happen to one after one's death, and by coming to be in certain conditions after one's death. One's reputation can be maliciously impugned, a promise made to one can be broken, a cause to which one devoted one's life can be ruined out of jealousy, one can be bad-mouthed at one's funeral, and so forth.

[3] Ithaca: Cornell University Press, 1990.
[4] In chapter 17 I make the ordinary concept more precise at a certain point.

Some philosophers disagree with my assumption that things can happen to a living organism after its death and that it can come to be in certain conditions that it was not in before. They would concede that we speak this way when speaking with the vulgar. We talk about paying tribute to those who have fallen in war, about showing disrespect for one's deceased predecessor, and the like. But they would insist that we should not understand what goes on in such cases as the dead human being undergoing something or coming to be in a state that he was not in before. For there is no such entity as a dead human being. No such entity appears in the inventory of the universe. There is no such entity to be referred to, no such entity to be talked about, no such entity to be treated with either respect or disrespect. Our doing what we call "honoring him" does not have, as its corollary, *his* being honored. To say that our ancestors "are no more" is not to refer to our ancestors and say about them that they are no more; it is to say that there is no such entity as a deceased ancestor of ours.

It would be a happy state of affairs if we could be noncommittal on these ontological issues. But we cannot. For as indicated, I hold that among the events and states to which one has a right are undergoings and conditions that occur after one's death. You wrong me if you fail to keep the promise you solemnly made to me when I was on my deathbed—which implies that I have a right against you to the event of your keeping your promise to me. Depending on what happens to a human being at death, it may be the case that I am not *hurt* or *harmed* by such actions on your part. But wronging is not to be equated with harming, with impairing a person's perceived well-being, as we shall see shortly in more detail and for less controversial cases.

Some will think rights-talk has gone completely berserk when it speaks of the rights of the dead—though it appears to me that some who think this have no problem with speaking about the rights of future generations. But rather than trying to argue them down—beyond continuing to give what seem to me compelling examples of such rights—let me observe that the view I am affirming here is a close relative of a view that goes back into antiquity. Aristotle did not talk about rights. But it was his view that one can be the patient of undergoings after one's death, and that those undergoings can be either goods or evils. "Both good and evil," he says, "are thought to exist for a dead man, as much as for one who is alive but not aware of them; e.g. honours and dishonours and the good or bad fortunes of children and in general of descendents" (*Nichomachean Ethics* I, 10; 1100 18–22).[5]

---

[5] I am using the translation in *The Complete Works of Aristotle: The Revised Oxford Translation*, ed. by Jonathan Barnes (Princeton: Princeton University Press, 1984).

So the events and states to which I have a right do not all belong to my life. My being maligned at my funeral is not an event in my life. My life is over. What is not over at my death is my *history*. Not only do we never leave history if we are ever in it; our individual histories continue to undergo alterations after our lives are over. Consider an analogue: decades after the Treaty of Versailles was signed, it became true that the Treaty had sowed the seeds of World War II. The historian who writes a history of the Treaty of Versailles does not end his narrative with the final signing. So too for us: our lives cease but our histories continue. Our histories include our lives but more besides, much more. The event that is one's life and the event that is one's history begin at the same point, namely, at the point at which the human being that one is comes into existence. The event that is one's life then ceases with one's death, whereas the event that is one's history continues as long as time continues. The events and states to which one has a right all belong to one's history; some, but only some, belong to one's life as well.

Some will question the claim I just made, that while one's history continues after one's life is over, they begin at the same time. Do not our histories precede the beginnings of our lives as well as succeed the endings; and can we not, on that account, be wronged before our lives begin as well as after they have ended? I think not. Before my life began I was not to be found in the inventory of the universe; so nothing could happen to me. There is an asymmetry in how we fit into time. But I acknowledge that there is no extant philosophical theory of time according to which persons whose lives are over are to be found in the inventory of the universe, while persons whose lives have not begun are not.[6] So I will let theory win out over intuition to the following extent: though my own examples of rights are all of rights of the living and of the dead, I do not at any point deny that there are entities not yet alive and that they have rights.

I shall speak of the events that involve me, as patient of some undergoing or possessor of some state, as *belonging to* and as *constituents of* my history or my life. What sort of relation is this? I suggest that the lives and the histories of human beings are events. They belong to the same ontological category as World War I; it too was an event. And just as that event that was World War I had many states of affairs as its constituents,

---

[6] A good introduction to the issues here is the chapter on "Presentism" in Trenton Merricks's *Truth and Ontology* (Oxford: Oxford University Press, 2007). Merricks would hold that a good deal of what I say about time in the section above is ontologically indefensible, because every extant theory of time entails the falsehood of at least some of those things. My response is that a condition of adequacy for a theory of time is that it not entail the falsehood of any of these things. My view is that there is not now and never has been an adequate theory of time.

so too those events that are the lives and histories of human beings have many states of affairs as their constituents. The relation between, on the one hand, the state of affairs of my receiving a polite answer to my question and, on the other hand, my life is that of a state of affairs being a constituent of an event. Of course, there is an important ontological difference between the sort of event that is a human life or a human history and the sort of event that World War I was. A human life or history is an event *of* an Aristotelian substance, namely, a certain human being; World War I was an event that was not *of* anything in that way.

The Worth of Lives and Histories Distinguished from the Worth of Human Beings and Persons

When I explain, in part III, what it is to have a right to something, I make much use of the fact that what makes for the excellence of a human being is not the same as what makes for the excellence of that human being's life or history. A particular human being might not be a particularly good specimen of The Human Being—physically clumsy, diabetic since childhood, prone to temper tantrums, and so forth—and yet have an excellent life. Conversely, he might be a superb specimen of The Human Being while yet having a very inferior life, whether because of his own doing or because of misfortune.

The fundamental reason these two modes of excellence must be distinguished is that neither the life nor the history of a human being is identical with the being whose life or history it is.[7] A human being is not an event but a substance—a *suppositum*, to use medieval Latin terminology. As such, a human being is not comprised of states of affairs but of blood, muscle, bones, and the like. I have a weight, and I can find out what that weight is by standing on a scale. My life and my history, by contrast, are weightless; they cannot be placed on a scale. They are, indeed, comprised of states of affairs that have *constituents* that can be placed on a scale. My life is comprised, among other things, of the state of affairs of my owning an automobile, this in turn having me as a constituent; and I and the automobile can be put on a scale. But *my owning an automobile* is not the sort of entity that can be placed on a scale.

Though a human being is ontologically distinct from his life and his history, there are, of course, close connections between the human

---

[7] Shelly Kagan, in an interesting article called to my attention by Kelly Sorenson, finds it important for an understanding of well-being to distinguish, as I do, between a person and the person's life. The use he makes of the distinction is quite different from mine, however. See "Me and My Life," *Proceedings of the Aristotelian Society* 94 (1994): 309–24.

being, on the one hand, and his life and history, on the other. Interesting things might turn up if we probed those connections. Some connections will come to light in later chapters. Here I note only that corresponding to the *state of affairs* in my life of my enjoying a conversation with friends is the *property* I have of enjoying a conversation with friends, corresponding to the *state of affairs* in my history of my being maligned at my funeral is the *property* I have of being maligned at my funeral—and in general, corresponding to the *state of affairs* in my life or history of my doing or being K is the *property* I possess of doing or being K.

The preceding point, about the lack of tight connection between the worth of a human being and the worth of his life or history, can now be put more precisely as follows. From the fact that the state of affairs of *my being K* is a good in my life, it does not follow that my having the property of *being K* makes a positive contribution to my worth as a human being. And conversely: from the fact that my having the property of *being K* makes a positive contribution to my worth as a human being, it does not follow that *my being K* makes a positive contribution to the worth of my life. This will all become clear in later chapters.

UNDERSTANDING THE GOOD

We have seen that the entities to which one has a right are always states of affairs—happenings or conditions—within one's life or history. And earlier I suggested that what one has a right to is always a good, with the qualifications mentioned. It follows, of course, that it is certain states of affairs within one's life and history that are the goods to which one has a right.

Let me be more precise about the connection here. Lives and histories are non-instrumentally excellent or disexcellent to varying degrees. "He had a good life," we sometimes say; on other occasions, "His life was miserable." The degree of non-instrumental excellence that a human being's life or history possesses is determined by the states of affairs that comprise that life or history. These happenings and conditions are what give his life or history the degree of non-instrumental excellence that it has. They are themselves, in that way, good or evil, to varying degrees. We can say that they are good or evil *for* the human being—meaning by the locutions "good for" and "evil for" that they contribute positively or negatively to the non-instrumental worth of the human being's life or history. (In the contemporary discussion, as we shortly see, the locution "good for" is also applied to *lives*, not just to the states of affairs that comprise lives; a life is spoken of as *good for* the person whose life it is. I refrain from speaking thus. I speak only of states of affairs within a human being's life as *good for* that human being.)

Before proceeding farther, let me make a few comments on how I understand the good. Good things, even things that excel in goodness, are all about us. There are excellent sunsets, excellent baseball games, excellent philosophy papers, excellent prayers, excellent meals, excellent automobiles, excellent musical works, excellent mutual investment funds, excellent specimens of the dachshund, excellent specimens of the white oak—and excellent human lives and histories.

I take the good to be that which is worthy of approbation, understanding approbation to be a general stance or attitude manifested in many different actions and attitudes: praise, worship, admiration, love, care, concern, and so forth. A thing may be worthy of one sort of approbation and not worthy of another. As we shall see in the next two chapters, the recognition of this last point is indispensable to understanding such thinkers as Augustine and the Stoics, to mention no others.

Augustine never hesitated to affirm that many "earthly" things are worthy of that mode of approbation that consists of enjoying them: the changing colors of the Mediterranean, conversation among friends, church music. But he denied that enjoyment of such "earthly" things is ever worthy of desire for its own sake, and ever worthy of the sort of pursuit that such desire often gives rise to. Only enjoyment of God is worthy of desire for its own sake. If enjoyment of some earthly thing comes your way, praise God for it; but do not desire it, do not seek it for its own sake. That way lies unhappiness.

A theory of the good would proceed from this identification of the good as that which is worthy of approbation to a general account of what it is about things that makes them approbation-worthy. I do not attempt to develop such an account. Doing so would overwhelm our project here of understanding the nature of justice.[8] And for our purposes, it is not necessary. The person who attempts to develop a theory of the good has to be able independently to identify examples of good and non-good things against which to test his theory for adequacy. We will do the same.

Three Distinct Conceptions of the Good Life

I said that the goods to which one has a right are all states of affairs within one's life or history that contribute positively to the worth of that life or

---

[8] The best theory of the good presently available, in my judgment, is that developed by Robert Adams in his *Finite and Infinite Goods: A Framework for Ethics* (Oxford: Oxford University Press, 1999).

history, making for its being as good a life or history as it is. Let us now set our histories off to the side for a moment and concentrate on lives. From philosophical literature of the past and the present one discovers that philosophers have conceived of a good life in different ways; they have different things in mind when speaking of a good life. Those who conceive of it in the same way also offer competing accounts of what it is that makes something a good life, as they conceive it; but a deeper divide than those disagreements is that among those who have different things in mind. The phrase "good life" is ambiguous.

The difference amounts to this: when thinking and speaking about a good life, philosophers have their eye on a certain *subset* of those states of affairs that comprise a human being's life or history; and they have not all had their eye on the same subset. What we have to do, then, is determine which of these subsets, if any, is suitable for our purposes here. If one or more is such that certain of the goods to which we have rights are not to be found within that subset, then that way of conceiving of a good life will not serve our purposes. It may be useful for discussing other topics in philosophy, but it will not be of use to us. We would find ourselves plunged into confusion if we did not clearly identify that subset and set it off to the side. Only after we have arrived at the appropriate way of conceiving of the good life can we ask the next question, whether it is possible to give a general account of what it is that makes a life, thus conceived, good.

In the philosophical literature of past and present one finds, so I suggest, three distinct ways of conceiving of the good life—never, to my knowledge, clearly and explicitly distinguished from each other. I call them the conception of the good life as the *experientially satisfying life*, the conception of the good life as the *happy* life, and the conception of the good life as the *flourishing* life. What I mean by "the experientially satisfying life" is clear enough from the phrase itself. By "the happy life" I mean the life that is lived well; by "the flourishing life" I mean the life that is both lived well and goes well.

The place to look to find out how contemporary philosophers conceive of a good life is to discussions of what they call "well-being," "welfare," or "utility." To the best of my knowledge, these discussions invariably proceed on the assumption that everybody has the same thing in mind by "welfare" or "well-being" and that the disagreements are disagreements over what it is, in general, that constitutes well-being.[9] James Griffin, in his book *Well-Being*, after rehearsing many of the perplexities

---

[9] This is true, for example, of the subtle, thorough, and up-to-date discussion of well-being in chapter 2 of Mark C. Murphy's *Natural Law and Practical Rationality* (Cambridge: Cambridge University Press, 2001).

and confusions in the literature, entertains the possibility that what accounts for some of these is that he and others are operating with different conceptions of well-being: "Perhaps we need two notions of life's going well, one with and one without the Experience Requirement."[10] But after briefly considering this possibility, Griffin rejects it. That rejection was a mistake, in my view. To understand what is going on in discussions of the good life, we do need two conceptions of a life's going well, one with and one without the "experience requirement." And we need a third conception as well, that of the life that is lived well. Unraveling and explaining these three conceptions, and determining which will serve our purpose of locating those life-goods and history-goods to which we have rights, will occupy us for the remainder of this chapter and the next several.

Let us begin with the easy case: the conception of the good life as the experientially satisfying life. The native home of this conception is the modern utilitarian tradition. It would be possible to develop a theory that resembles standard utilitarianism in certain respects—in its consequentialism, in its insistence that one's own well-being is not to be given priority, and so on—but does not conceive of well-being as the experientially satisfying life. Nonetheless, this is the understanding that those who identify themselves as utilitarians almost always work with. The question for us is whether a theory that does so understand well-being can serve as a framework for developing a theory of rights. My contention is that it cannot; the goods to which we have rights are not all to be found among the states of affairs that contribute to a life's being experientially satisfying.

Before pinpointing why that is, I should perhaps offer some evidence that this is indeed a prominent understanding of well-being. The official explanation of well-being that Griffin offers in the book I mentioned is that it consists of a life being "good for such-and-such a person" (37). It consists, he says, of "a life's being valuable . . . to the person who lives it" (21). This is also how Robert Adams, in *Finite and Infinite Goods*, thinks of well-being. In the third chapter of the book, a chapter that he titles "Well-Being and Excellence," Adams says, "Within the realm of what is good for its own sake, and not just instrumentally good, most contemporary ethical thought focuses mainly on well-being or welfare—that is, on the nature of human flourishing or what is good for a person" (83). A bit later he remarks, "It is one of the more difficult tasks of ethical theory to explain what human well-being consists in—what it is for something to be good for a person" (84). From these passages it is clear not only

[10] James Griffin, *Well-Being* (Oxford: Clarendon Press, 1986), pp. 317–18, n. 5.

that Adams himself understands well-being as consisting in a life being good *for* the person whose life it is but that this, in his judgment, is how "most contemporary ethical thought" understands it.

And how, in turn, are we to understand this idea of a life that is good *for* or good *to* the person whose life it is? Griffin never explicitly says. But it is clear what he has in mind. An occurrence or condition within a person's life contributes positively to that life's being good *for* the person whose life it is only if that occurrence or condition is something that the person experiences. Griffin speaks of the life that is good *for* the person whose life it is as satisfying what he calls "the experience requirement." Though Adams is no more explicit on the matter than Griffin, it is clear that this is also how he understands the idea of a life that is good *for* the person whose life it is. After disposing of the so-called informed desire account of welfare, Adams offers as his own account of welfare that a life is good *for* one insofar as one enjoys the excellent; and then he says that "enjoyment is internal to my life, and even to my consciousness, in a way that the satisfaction of my desires need not be. Even though *what* I enjoy is often external to myself, the enjoyment itself must be an event in my experience. . . . [T]he enjoyment criterion helps to assure that what we are assessing is *my* good rather than some other good that I care about" (100).

And now to pinpoint why this conception of the good life as the experientially satisfying life is not adequate for our purposes. The reason is simple: a great many of the goods to which we have rights are not to be found among the states of affairs within a person's life that contribute to its being an experientially satisfying life. Suppose, for example, that malicious rumor-mongers are ruining your reputation behind your back but that you never hear about this and it has no noticeable effect on how others treat you; neither the rumor-mongering nor its effects enters or alters your experience. You have been wronged, deprived of a good to which you have a right, but the deprivation of that good has no impact whatsoever on how experientially satisfying your life is. Or suppose that someone spies on you for prurient reasons but keeps what he learns entirely to himself. Then too you have been deprived of a good to which you have a right; yet the deprivation of that good has no impact on how experientially satisfying your life is. These are but two of many examples of the point: many of the life-goods to which one has a right make no contribution whatsoever to how experientially satisfying one's life is. They fall outside the net.

It goes without saying that the good life understood as the experientially satisfying life will not include those history-goods to which one has a right.

Our Project in the Next Chapter

Before the modern period, almost no one thought of the good life as the experientially satisfying life. Eudaimonism, the ethical framework favored by the ancients, conceived of the good life as the well-lived life, not as the experientially satisfying life. But conceiving of the good life as the well-lived life proves no more satisfactory for our purpose of developing a theory of rights than conceiving of it as the experientially satisfying life; there are goods to which one has a right that make no contribution whatsoever to how well one's life is lived.

To see why this is so will take considerably more work than it took to see why the conception favored by our modern-day utilitarians is not satisfactory for our purposes. Not only is eudaimonism far less familiar to most of us; the reasons for its inadequacy are more subtle. Furthermore, whereas the claim that utilitarianism cannot serve as framework for an account of rights is by no means uncommon, that claim has seldom if ever been made against eudaimonism. Many contemporary eudaimonists will strongly resist the claim. So the case has to be laid out in detail and with care.

Chapter Seven

WHY EUDAIMONISM CANNOT SERVE AS FRAMEWORK FOR A THEORY OF RIGHTS

THERE ARE IMPORTANT contemporary eudaimonists; Alasdair MacIntyre comes immediately to mind. But all contemporary eudaimonists, MacIntyre included, acknowledge the ancient eudaimonists as the source of their thought; all of them employ generous citations from the ancients. So I propose going to the source.

A word about terminology before we set out on our exploration of the employment by ancient eudaimonism of the conception of the good life as the life that is well lived. The ancient philosophers who wrote in Greek used the term "*eudaimonia*" for the well-lived life. The term is customarily translated in our texts as "happiness." Unfortunately, in present-day English "happiness" has a meaning different from what "*eudaimonia*" had for the ancients, and distinctly different connotations.[1] Whereas it was not linguistic nonsense for the Stoics to contend that the virtuous person would be *eudaimōn* on the torture rack,[2] it would be linguistic nonsense for someone speaking contemporary English to contend that a person— *any* person—could be happy there. Speakers of present-day English mean by a "happy" life pretty much what I have been calling an *experientially satisfying* life. Nonetheless, there is near-consensus among present-day commentators on the ancients that "happiness" is the best we can do in translating "*eudaimonia*."[3] So I will follow the crowd, speak of the well-lived life as the happy life, and do what I can to forestall misunderstanding by reminding the reader every now and then that it is the well-lived life that we are talking about.[4]

---

[1] See Martha Nussbaum, *The Fragility of Goodness* (Cambridge: Cambridge University Press, 1986), p. 6, n.

[2] Aristotle remarks that "those who say that the victim on the rack or the man who falls into great misfortunes is happy if he is good, are, whether they mean to or not, talking nonsense" (*Nichomachean Ethics*, VII.13; 1153b 19–21). From the context it is clear that what he has in mind is not that they are speaking linguistic nonsense and hence asserting no proposition, but that the proposition they are asserting is patently false.

[3] The only dissenter of whom I am aware is John M. Cooper, who proposes translating "*eudaimonia*" as "flourishing." See his *Reason and Human Good in Aristotle* (Indianapolis: Hackett, 1986).

[4] A masterful discussion of ancient eudaimonism, beginning with Aristotle, is Julia Annas's, *The Morality of Happiness* (Oxford: Oxford University Press, 1993). In her more recent

Most contemporary eudaimonists adhere to the Aristotelian or Peripatetic version of ancient eudaimonism; in fact, I know of no contemporary Stoic eudaimonist. What I need for my purposes, however, is an understanding of eudaimonism generally. Thus I will be offering a composite picture of the eudaimonism of the ancients. Since it is a composite, the picture will not capture the full texture of the thought of any particular figure. That is especially the case for the truly creative figures, Aristotle, for example.

I will be defending two theses concerning this composite picture: that eudaimonism, as I describe it, cannot serve as framework for a theory of rights, and that all the ethical thinkers of antiquity either fit my description of eudaimonism or, if some fit the description only when certain qualifications are added, those qualifications are not such that my main thesis does not hold for them. Given that my main goal in this book is to develop a systematic theory of rights, more is at stake for me in the systematic claim, that eudaimonism as I describe it cannot serve as framework for a theory of rights, than in the historical claims. Nonetheless, I arrive at the structure of thought that I take eudaimonism to be by looking closely at the thought of the ancients, under the tutelage of contemporary guides whose competence no one would question.

What Is Eudaimonism?

The eudaimonist holds that the ultimate and comprehensive goal of each of us is that we live our lives as well as possible, the well-lived life being, by definition, the happy life, the *eudaimōn* life. As Aristotle puts it, "It is thought to be a mark of a man of practical wisdom to be able to deliberate well about what is good and expedient for himself, not in some particular respect, e.g. about what sorts of thing conduce to health or to strength, but about what sorts of thing conduce to the good life in general" (*Nichomachean Ethics* VI, 5; 1140a 25–28). The disagreements we have about happiness—and they are many and deep—are disagreements over the content of the well-lived life, not over whether or not to aim at living one's life well.

---

book, *Platonic Ethics, Old and New* (Ithaca, N.Y.: Cornell University Press, 1999), Annas discusses the eudaimonism of Plato and the Platonic tradition. My understanding of eudaimonism in general, and of Stoic eudaimonism in particular, is heavily indebted to these two books. I have also very much benefited from two books by Martha Nussbaum: *The Therapy of Desire: Theory and Practice in Hellenistic Ethics* (Princeton: Princeton University Press, 1994); and her recent *Upheavals of Thought: The Intelligence of Emotions* (Cambridge: Cambridge University Press, 2001).

It is important to understand what sort of goal happiness is. "Happiness" is not the name of experiences of a certain sort. "Pleasure" names experiences of a certain sort; "happiness" does not. The eudaimonist is not saying that one's sole end in itself is or should be bringing about experiences of a certain sort, everything else being a means. Happiness does not belong to the content of the good life; it *characterizes* the content. The good life is constituted of activities; and what characterizes those activities is that together they make one's life a well-lived life.

Some of the activities that constitute a well-lived life will be, in the scheme of one's purposes, ends in themselves. Acquiring knowledge of certain sorts, maintaining friendship with various people—these activities are life-goods that are appropriately pursued as ends in themselves; their having that place in one's life contributes to making one's life as a whole well lived. From among all the good activities that *could* function as ends in themselves in the structure of one's intention and action, one makes a selection by using, as one's criterion, whether performing or aiming to perform those activities as ends in themselves will contribute to making one's life as a whole well lived. One does not make a selection by asking, say, which actions will produce the greatest desire-satisfaction of the greatest number.

Thus one's own happiness is one's ultimate goal in the sense, and only in the sense, that it is one's ultimate reason for selecting as one does from among all the good things one could do, whether as ends or as means. To aim at happiness is to aim at bringing it about that the entirety of one's activities possesses the character of being a well-lived life. Here is how Aristotle puts some of these points:

> Verbally there is very general agreement [on the highest of all goods achievable by action]; for both the general run of men and people of superior refinement say that it is happiness, and identify living well and faring well[5] with being happy; but with regard to what happiness is they differ, and the many do not give the same account as the wise. For the former think it is some plain and obvious thing, like pleasure, wealth, or honour; they differ, however, from one another—and often even the same man identifies it with different things, with health when he is ill, with wealth when he is poor; but, conscious of their ignorance, they admire those who proclaim some great thing that is above their comprehension. (*NE* I, 1; 1095a 17–26)

Two explanatory comments are in order. In the first place, the ancient eudaimonists focused not on individual actions but on lives, differing

---

[5] Annas translates this last phrase as "doing well"; that seems to me definitely the better translation. *Morality of Happiness*, p. 44.

sharply in that way from the bulk of present-day ethical theorists. Their fundamental question was not "What shall I do?" but "How shall I live?" And they did not regard the question "How shall I live?" as "in origin a philosopher's question; it is a question that an ordinary person will at some point put to herself. Many ordinary people may of course be too unreflective, or too satisfied with convention, or just too busy, to pose the question. But it is assumed that people of average intellect with a modicum of leisure will at some point reflect on their lives and ask whether they are as they should be, or whether they could be improved" (Annas, *Morality of Happiness*, 27).

Second, the ancient eudaimonists insisted that *eudaimonia* is activity. Happiness does not consist in what happens to one but in what one makes of what happens to one. Living well consists of acting well. The life-goods comprising a well-lived life are all actions on one's part, doings. In the words of Julia Annas, fine scholar of philosophical figures and movements in classical and late antiquity, "Happiness is . . . thought of as active rather than passive, and as something that involves the agent's activity, and thus as being, commonsensically, up to the agent. This kind of consideration would rule out wealth, for example, right away. Happiness cannot just be a thing, however good, that someone might present you with. At the very least it involves what you *do* with wealth, the kind of *use* you put it to" (*Morality of Happiness*, 45). She quotes Arius's rephrasing of Aristotle: "[Since the final good is not the fulfilment of bodily and external goods, but living according to virtue], therefore happiness is activity. . . . Happiness is life, and life is the fulfilment of action. No bodily or external good is in itself an action or in general an activity."[6]

Eudaimonism is commonly charged with being a form of egoism. The term "egoism" means so many different things that unless further explanation is forthcoming, the charge is void for vagueness. Those who make the charge seem usually to take an egoist to be a person who always asks, when considering some course of action, "What's in it for me?" that is,

---

[6] Cf. Annas, *Morality of Happiness*, p. 37: "My final good could not be a good thing, but neither could it just be a good state of affairs. These are ruled out right from the start by the fact that they have no essential connection to my activity; somebody else could get and present me with a good thing or state of affairs, but this would be irrelevant to my final good, which it must be up to me to get."

The passage from Aristotle that Arius was rephrasing is to be found in *Nichomachean Ethics* I, 7; 1098a 16–19: "Human good turns out to be activity of soul in conformity with excellence, and if there are more than one excellence, in conformity with the best and most complete. But we must add, 'in a complete life.' For one swallow does not make a summer, nor does one day; and so too one day, or a short time, does not make a man blessed and happy."

"What personally satisfying experiences for myself is this likely to bring about?" If that is how one understands egoism, then it is clear that eudaimonism is not, as such, a form of egoism. A particular eudaimonist might employ the framework in an egoistic way; but as such, eudaimonism is not egoism.

For example, most of the ancient writers held that a prominent place will be found in the life that is lived well for friendships; and it was certainly not their view that when presented with the possibility of establishing or nurturing a friendship, the question to ask is, "What's in it for me?" Most of them understood friendships as a natural good for human beings. And part of what goes into that complex activity that is friendship is seeking to promote natural goods of various sorts in the life of one's friend. So "What's in it for me?" is the wrong question. The right question to ask is, will maintaining this friendship contribute to making my life as well-lived as it would be if I did not maintain it? If I conclude that it will, then I go for it, even if I recognize that it might possibly require the sacrifice of my life; I go for that whole complex package that is friendship. It would be strange, indeed, if I did not anticipate getting some satisfaction out of this friendship. But there is more to friendship than self-satisfaction.

So eudaimonism is not egoism. Nonetheless, it is undeniably agent-oriented. I am confronted with a whole array of good actions as candidates for inclusion within my life, including such actions as *my* seeking to enhance *your* good. I must choose. Some actions that I choose will be chosen by me as ends in themselves. Others will be chosen by me as means to those I choose as ends in themselves. I choose among candidates on the basis of which, in my judgment, will contribute most to my living my life well. That is the test that every candidate for action on my part must pass. Not whether it contributes to *your* living *your* life well, but whether it contributes to *my* living *my* life well. And let it be said, once again, that "contributing to" must be understood as *being a constituent of.* Happiness is not some experiential state that we bring about causally. Happiness is the abstract feature that a life possesses of *being well-lived.*

In defense of the eudaimonists against the charge that they are egoists, Annas remarks that "the good of others ought to matter to me *because* it is the good of others, not because it is part of my own good." She adds that it is no part of the ancient theories that "its forming part of my good is the reason why I should care about the good of others" (*Morality of Happiness*, 224). This strikes me as obscuring the structure of eudaimonism that Annas herself lays out in rich detail. I can appraise some state of affairs in your life as being a natural good in your life—your being in good health, for example. But so far forth, that is purely descriptive; it does not imply anything as to the role of that recognition in my living of my life.

I can then take the next step of considering the action of *my seeking to bring about* that state of affairs in your life. I take it to be of the essence of eudaimonism to claim that my recognition that your being healthy would be a natural good in your life is not sufficient reason for me to seek to bring it about—not sufficient reason for me to incorporate into my life the good deed of *my seeking to bring about the natural good of health in your life.* The only consideration that is sufficient reason for me to incorporate that action into my life is my judgment that doing so would make for my life being as well lived as it would be otherwise. So it is true that *your health* does not somehow have to form part of my good for me to pursue it; I do not have to think, for example, that your health will cause my wealth. But *my pursuing your health* does have to form "part of my good." I include that action in my life if and only if I judge that it is a good action and that performing it will make *my* life as least as well lived as it would be otherwise.[7]

I take this to be what Aristotle is driving at in the following passage from *Nichomachean Ethics,* in which he is reflecting on whether the lover of virtue is a lover of self:

> Those who use the term [lover of self] as one of reproach ascribe self-love to people who assign to themselves the greater share of wealth, honours, and bodily pleasures. . . . [I]t is just . . . that men who are lovers of self in this way are reproached for being so. That it is those who give themselves the preference in regard to objects of this sort that most people usually call lovers of self is plain; for if a man were always anxious that he himself, above all things, should act justly, temperately, or in accordance with any other of the excellences, and in general were always to try to secure for himself the honourable course, no one will call such a man a lover of self or blame him. But such a man would seem more than the other a lover of self; at all events he assigns to himself the things that are noblest and best, and gratifies the most authoritative element in himself and in all things obeys this. (IX, 8; 1168b 13–31)

---

[7] Cf. the following passage from Alasdair MacIntyre, pre-eminent among our present eudaimonists: "What constitutes a good reason for my doing this rather than that, for my acting from this particular desire rather than that, is that my doing this rather than that serves my good, will contrribute to my flourishing *qua* human being." *Dependent Rational Animals* (Chicago and LaSalle: Open Court, 1999), p. 86. On page 159 of the same book, MacIntyre argues that once my virtue of generosity is in place, I will find in "gross and urgent need sufficient reason to act." But I will have cultivated the virtue for the above agent-centered reason.

Stoic Eudaimonism

"The framework for ancient ethics," says Annas, "is given by claims about the form my final end should take and the place in it that virtue should have, rather than by claims about actions that are required or permitted or about ways to bring about certain consequences" (*Morality of Happiness*, 136). More specifically, almost all the eudaimonist philosophers of antiquity agreed that acting virtuously is necessary and sufficient for living one's life well.[8] They also agreed that virtue, that is, *being* virtuous, is necessary for living one's life well. The big topic of debate was whether virtue—not virtuous activity but virtue itself—is sufficient as well as necessary for happiness, the Stoics saying that it is, the Peripatetics (Aristotelians), that it is not. Let us see why each party said what it did. That will take some time!

Ancient eudaimonism eventually settled down into the two major traditions just mentioned, the Stoic and the Peripatetic. Rather than give these two traditions equal time, I concentrate on the Stoics, partly to keep the discussion from getting out of bounds, partly because that is the version of eudaimonism Augustine struggled with, partly because the Stoics seem to me eventually to have given the sharpest formulation to most of the major issues, and partly because Aristotelian eudaimonism is so prominent on the contemporary scene that the more general contours of eudaimonism get lost from view. Given that the Stoic position is often initially counter-intuitive, I also judge it easier to expound the Stoics and point out where the Peripatetics differed than vice versa. Where the Peripatetics did differ on a major point relevant to my purposes, I will point that out. My contention is that eudaimonism in general cannot serve as framework for a theory of rights.

Several times in preceding chapters I have observed that being wronged occupies a distinct role in our emotional lives. The appropriate emotional response to being wronged is *anger.* "Appropriate" is too weak a word. One has a *right* to be angry with the wrongdoer on account of his wrongdoing; his wronging generated that right. Often there are emotions in addition to anger that are appropriate when one has been wronged—grief, for example. And we do not get angry only when we think we have been wronged. The thought of being wronged may not enter the head of the angry person. But between anger and the perception of being wronged there is a special connection. The anger of God over injustice is unmistakable in Israel's testimony. The writers assumed that God is wronged by injustice.

---

[8] According to Annas, the small group of Cyrenaics was the only exception.

The Stoics held that anger is never appropriate. More generally, it was their view that it is never appropriate to have negative emotions of any sort whatsoever, differing in this regard from the Peripatetics, who held that negative emotions must be kept in check rather than eliminated. I propose using what the Stoics said about emotional disturbance as the scarlet thread through the intricacies of their thought. There are other threads one could follow. But not only is this as good as any, it is better, I am inclined to think. The propriety and impropriety of emotional upset was at the heart of Augustine's polemic with the Stoics.

Seneca's classic essay *On Anger* (*de Ira*)[9] is cast in the form of a letter addressed by Seneca to his brother Novatus, who, in Martha Nussbaum's words, was "a non-philosophical public man who is depicted as having characteristic Roman concerns about military strength and success, about the safety and dignity of one's family and home, about strength and dignity and manliness and greatness of soul generally" (*Therapy*, 405). Seneca urges Novatus to eliminate anger from his life; and he suggests strategies for achieving that.

He leads off his argument by quoting the Peripatetic philosopher Theophrastus as saying, "A good man cannot help being angry at bad people" (I, 14; p. 31). Not at all, is Seneca's response. If that were so, "the better a man is, the more prone he will be to anger. Are you sure that he will not, on the contrary, be the calmer and free from affections, someone who hates no one?" (I, 14, pp. 31–32). "But against enemies," Novatus is represented as saying, "there is need for anger" (I, 11; p. 28).

"Nowhere less," Seneca replies. "The requirement there is not for impulses to be poured out, but to remain well tuned and responsive" (I, 11; p. 28). But "is the good man not angry if he sees his father slain and his mother ravished"? Novatus protests (I, 12; 30). No, says Seneca firmly, "he will not be angry. He will punish and protect. Why should not filial devotion, even without anger, be enough of a stimulus? . . . Anger for one's friends is the mark of a weak mind, not a devoted one. What is fine and honourable is to go forth in defence of parents, children, friends

---

[9] I quote from the edition and translation by John M. Cooper and J. F. Procopé, *Seneca: Moral and Political Essays* (Cambridge: Cambridge University Press, 1995). There is an analysis of *de Ira* in chapter 11 of Martha Nussbaum's, *The Therapy of Desire*. I have some general disagreements with Nussbaum's account of Stoicism. I think, for example, that the therapy the Stoics recommended was more directly a therapy of value judgments than a therapy of desires. Nonetheless, I have found Nussbaum's analysis of *de Ira* very helpful. I have also found very helpful Terence Irwin's essay, "Socratic Paradox and Stoic Theory," in *Companions to Ancient Thought*, vol. 4: *Ethics*, ed. Stephen Everson (Cambridge: Cambridge University Press, 1998), pp. 151–92. A useful survey of Stoic thought on action and the emotions is Brad Inwood's *Ethics and Human Action in Early Stoicism* (Oxford: Clarendon Press, 1985).

There is a very helpful collection of Stoic texts in *Hellenistic Philosophy*, 2nd ed., trans. Brad Inwood and L. P. Gerson (Indianapolis and Cambridge: Hackett, 1997).

and fellow-citizens, under the guidance of duty itself, in the exercise of will, judgment and foresight—and not through some raving impulse" (I, 12; p. 30).

Seneca regularly cites extreme manifestations of anger as if they were typical: the other emotions "have something quiet and placid in them, whereas anger is all excitement and impulse. Raving with a desire that is utterly inhuman for instruments of pain and reparations in blood, careless of itself so long as it harms the other, it rushes onto the very spearpoints, greedy for vengeance that draws down the avenger with it" (I, 1; p. 17). Some have described anger as "brief insanity." They are right, says Seneca; "it is just as uncontrolled."[10] We can recognize the correctness of Seneca's central point without being carried along by his hyperbole. Anger is an emotional disturbance. It need not be violent, it need not rage with an inhuman lust for blood and vengeance; but it is an emotional disturbance. No emotional disturbance, no anger.

Why must we try to eliminate anger from our lives? The answer the Stoics give to this question is the clue to vast stretches of their thought and an essential element of their polemic against the Peripatetics. "The better a man is, . . . the calmer and free from affections," said Seneca. The clue is there. Emotional disturbance is incompatible with happiness, incompatible with *eudaimonia*. Insofar as a person is worried, anxious, fearful, angry, or jealous, that person's life is not happy. Happiness requires peace of mind. The truly happy life is a life of *apātheia*, as the Stoics called it—a life free of passions, free of negative emotions. Freedom from emotional disturbance is not indeed sufficient for one's life to be well lived; one must be experiencing joy or satisfaction of a certain sort.[11] But

---

[10] The hyperbole continues: "The sure signs of raving madness are a bold and threatening look, a gloomy countenance, a grim visage, a rapid pace, restless hands, change of colour, heavy and frequent sighing. The marks of anger are the same: eyes ablaze and glittering, a deep flush over all the face as blood boils up from the vitals, quivering lips, teeth pressed together, bristling hair standing on end, breath drawn in and hissing, the crackle of writhing limbs, groans and bellowing, speech broken off with the words barely uttered, hands struck together too often, feet stamping the ground, the whole body in violent motion 'menacing mighty wrath in mien,' the hideous horrifying face of swollen self-degradation—you would hardly know whether to call the vice hateful or ugly" (I,1; pp. 17–18). In describing anger, Seneca appears to have had his eye on the person who has lost his temper!

[11] See Diogenes Laertius in Inwood and Gerson, *Hellenistic Philosophy*, pp. 198–99: "There are also three good states [of the soul], joy, caution, and wish. And joy is opposite to pleasure, being a reasonable elation; and caution to fear, being a reasonable avoidance. For the wise man will not be afraid in any way, but will be cautious. They say that wish is opposite to desire, being a reasonable striving. So just as there are certain passions which are forms of the primary ones, so too there are good states subordinate to the primary; forms of wish are good will, kindliness, acceptance, contentment; forms of caution are respect, sanctity; forms of joy are enjoyment, good spirits, tranquillity."

in their writings, the Stoics pay much more attention to the absence of disturbance than to the presence of joy.

To be happy, one must be at rest, at peace. One's life must be calm, serene, tranquil. These are the words the Stoics use, over and over.[12] "There is no surer proof of greatness," says Seneca, "than to be unprovoked by anything that can possibly happen. . . . [A] lofty mind [is] ever at rest in its calm anchorage, stifling anything which might induce anger" (III, 6; p. 82). Augustine agreed. At the end of the opening paragraph of his *Confessions*, he famously said, "Our souls are restless, Lord, until they find their rest in thee."

So instead of indulging anger, why not "gather your brief life together, calming it for yourself and for others?" Seneca asks his brother. The "end, and that right early, looms alike over victor and vanquished. In peace and quiet, rather, let us pass what is left of our lives" (III, 43; p. 115). "Summon up endurance, seeing what a prize awaits us—the unbroken calm of a happy mind. Think what it means to escape the greatest of evils, anger, . . . and the other affections that accompany it" (II, 12; p. 53).

How is the life of *apātheia* to be achieved? Recall the situation Seneca invited us to imagine: a son witnesses his father murdered and his mother raped. He is angry. The anger is an emotional disturbance. How can the son eliminate that disturbance—or rather, how can he forestall it? How can he get tranquility within his grasp?[13]

Many people today would say, "Get good locks on the doors, keep a gun handy, and sign up for martial arts exercises." That might help in some cases. But if the assailant is one's instructor in the martial arts course and he puts a gun to one's head before one has a chance to open the gun cabinet, it would be to no avail. The activist answer works only now and then.

If one has enough money available, one could achieve tranquility by keeping sufficient alcohol in one's bloodstream to maintain a state of semi-stupor. The Stoic strategy was as far from that as anything could be. Tranquility is not the only thing necessary for a happy life; the Stoics shared with all their fellow philosophers the conviction that acting virtu-

---

[12] Sextus Empiricus reports the Stoics Cleanthes and Chrysippus as saying that happiness is "a smooth flow of life." See text in Inwood and Gerson, *Hellenistic Philosophy*, p. 256. So also Diogenes Laertius: "the virtue of the happy man [is] a smooth flow of life." Text in ibid., p. 191.

[13] Cf. Seneca's *Letters to Lucilius*, 72, 4–5: "It is those who are still short of perfection whose happiness can be broken off; the joy of a wise man, on the other hand, is a woven fabric, rent by no chance happening and by no change of fortune; at all times and in all places he is at peace. For his joy depends on nothing external and looks for no boon from man or fortune. His happiness is something within himself; it would depart from his soul if it enter in from the outside; it is born there."

ously is also necessary. Happiness requires both virtue and tranquility. "Virtue alone is exalted and lofty. Nor is anything great which is not at the same time calm" (I, 21; p. 41). The drunk, need it be said, is not acting virtuously. His life is calm, perhaps; but his calm is not the calm of virtue.

To get virtuous tranquility within our grasp we must restructure our judgments about life-goods and life-evils, that is, our judgments about the things that enhance our happiness and those that diminish it. My anger over the murder of my father and the rape of my mother indicates that I judged that that murder and that rape diminished my happiness— my happiness, let us recall, being my ultimate comprehesive *telos*. I thought my happiness depended on my father not being murdered and my mother not being raped. I must rid myself of those value judgments. I must get myself to the point where I no longer regard that murder and that rape as evils in my life, events that diminish my happiness, impair how well I am living my life. I must get myself to the point where I regard them as *indifferent* to my happiness. If I judge that my father's murder and my mother's rape are life-evils, that they diminish my happiness, then of course I will desire that they not happen and will get emotionally upset if they do. Tranquility will go out the window. I must rid myself of those judgments. I must reshape my judgments of life-goods and life-evils, of things that enhance my happiness and of things that diminish my happiness, in accord with the overarching aim of getting tranquility within my grasp. For tranquility, to say it yet again, is necessary for happiness. The well-lived life is a tranquil life.

THE STOICS ON EMOTION

To grasp fully the import of this line of thought, we must take a glance at the Stoic theory of emotions and understanding of virtue. Let me take the topics in that order.

I will ignore the refinements of the Stoic theory of emotions, its sometimes obscure details, the variations from writer to writer, and confine myself to essentials.[14] The heart of the Stoic theory was that negative emotion occurs when one gets the impression (*species*) that some evil has befallen one or is about to do so or is threatening to do so, and when one judges that impression to be accurate.[15] What the Stoics uniformly

[14] The most thorough discussion of the Stoics on emotion is now Richard Sorabji, *Emotion and Peace of Mind: From Stoic Agitation to Christian Temptation* (Oxford: Oxford University Press, 2000).

[15] I will not enter the tangled question of what these "impressions" are. The Stoics uniformly regarded them as not the product of volition; the way they usually speak of them implies that they have propositional content.

meant by *an evil* is what for several paragraphs now I have been suggesting they meant: an evil is a state or event in one's life that diminishes one's happiness.[16] Some Stoics held that emotions are the *consequence* of the impressions and the judgments; others, such as Chrysippus and Seneca, *identified* them with the judgments. And some added that to be an emotion the judgment has to be "fresh."

The Stoics held that even in the absence of the concurring judgment, sometimes even in the face of a dissenting judgment, the impression of a life-evil befalling or threatening to befall one may all by itself induce a bodily reaction: pallor, trembling, flushing of the face, a cold feeling in the limbs, tingling in the spine, and the like. But such reactions are not yet emotions, they insisted.[17] Emotions presuppose judgments.

> Anger is undoubtedly set in motion by an impression received of wrongs (*injuriae*). But does it follow immediately on the impression itself and break out without any involvement of the mind? Or is some assent by the mind required for it to be set in motion? Our view is that it undertakes nothing on its own, but only with the mind's approval. To receive an impression of wrong (*injuria*) done to one, to lust for retribution, to put together the two propositions that the damage ought not to have been done and that punishment ought to be inflicted, is not the work of a mere involuntary impulse. That would be a simple process. What we have here is a complex with several constituents—realization, indignation, condemnation, retribution. These cannot occur without assent by the mind to whatever has struck it. (*de Ira* II, 1; pp. 42–43)[18]

Apart from the observed fact that one may be in grief, say, without having any particular "feelings" and that, conversely, one may have the "feelings" typical of grief without being in grief, the Stoics had a reason connected with their ethical position for insisting that bodily reactions to impressions are not yet emotions: one's value judgments, so they held,

[16] Cf. Irwin, "Socratic Paradox," p. 172: "The Stoics assume (with Aristotle) that every good must contribute to happiness, and hence that every good in itself must be a part of happiness."

[17] What exactly these immediate reactions, these pre-emotions (*propatheiai*), are remained obscure in the Stoics. I am persuaded by an article of Sarah C. Byers that Augustine, mainly in his sermons, advanced beyond the Stoics on this point. See "Augustine and the Cognitive Cause of Stoic 'Preliminary Passions' (*Propatheiai*)," *Journal of the History of Philosophy* 41, no. 4, (2003): 433–48. The article was brought to my attention by Eric Gregory.

[18] Cf. *de Ira* II, 3: "Thus it is that even the bravest man often turns pale as he puts on his armour, that the knees of even the fiercest soldier tremble a little as the signal is given for battle, that a great general's heart is in his mouth before the lines have charged against one another, that the most eloquent orator goes numb at the fingers as he prepares to speak" (p. 44).

can be brought under the control of the will, whereas by and large one's immediate bodily reactions cannot be.[19]

So here is a way to determine whether or not one is implicitly regarding something as a genuine life-good: would I be emotionally upset should that condition or happening not be present in my life or threaten not to be present? If so, then I judge it to be a good. Would I be emotionally upset were my son killed in an accident? If so, then I judge his continued life to be a good in my life, something that enhances my happiness. The issue is not whether I would feel a momentary shock running through my system on being told of his death. Most people would. The issue is whether I would experience an enduring emotional upset.

GOODS, PREFERABLES, AND VIRTUE

A page or two back I said that, on the Stoic view, if one is to get tranquility within one's grasp, one must so reform one's value judgments that one no longer views the murder of one's father and the rape of one's mother as life-evils but rather as simply *indifferent* to one's happiness. They cut no ice one way or the other. I was there using the word "indifferent" as the Stoics used it. "Things indifferent . . . do not contribute to happiness or unhappiness."[20] Living until full of years, enjoying warm family relationships, friendships, good health, satisfying work, music and books are all indifferents. To judge them as genuine life-goods, thereby to invest oneself in them emotionally, is to run the risk of emotional disturbance: quarrels erupt in families, friends become enemies, health deteriorates, jobs become redundant, eyesight deteriorates—the list goes on and on.

---

[19] Cf. *de Ira*, II, 2: Anger "will never, if it comes to birth against our will, yield to reason. Involuntary movements can be neither overcome nor avoided. Take the way that we shiver when cold water is sprinkled on us, or recoil at the touch of some things. Take the way that bad news makes our hair stand on end and indecent language brings on a blush. Take the vertigo that follows the sight of a precipice. None of these is in our power; no amount of reasoning can induce them not to happen. But anger *is* put to flight by precept. For it is a voluntary fault of the mind, and not one of those which occur through some quirk of the human condition and can therefore happen to the very wisest of men, even though they include that first mental jolt which affects us when we think ourselves wronged. . . . But these [sensations] are not cases of anger, any more than it is grief which makes us frown at the sight of a shipwreck on stage or fear that runs through the reader's mind as Hannibal blockades the walls after the battle of Cannae. No, all these are motions [*motus*] of minds with no positive wish to be in motion. They are not affections, but the preliminaries, the prelude to affections" (pp. 41–42).

[20] Diogenes Laertius, in Inwood and Gerson, *Hellenistic Philosophy*, p. 195.

But though all such things will be indifferents for us if we keep clearly in mind that happiness requires tranquility, some of these indifferents are nonetheless *preferable*. We prefer them.[21] From antiquity critics have charged that the Stoic distinction between goods and preferables is purely verbal. Cicero and Augustine were of this view. In *The City of God* Augustine remarks that "when [the Stoics] say that these things are not to be called goods but advantages [*commoda*], we are to regard this as a dispute over words, not as a genuine distinction between things. For what does it matter whether it is more appropriate to call them goods or advantages, when Stoic and Peripatetic alike tremble and grow pale with the fear of losing them? They do not call them by the same names, but they hold them in the same esteem."[22] My own assessment is that the Stoics said exactly what they should have said on this point and that their distinction between goods and preferables was substantive, not verbal. Whether they managed to live what they believed is another matter.

The Stoics thought of virtues on the model of skills (*technai*) of a certain sort: to become courageous is to acquire a certain sort of skill (more about this shortly). And those skills that are the virtues are ways of dealing with the indifferents of one's life. The indifferents are, as it were, the stuff or material that the virtues work on. They are the matter of the virtues. Annas makes the point frequently, quoting various Stoics. "The indifferents," she says, "conventional goods and evils—have value for happiness only in being the materials for and context within which the virtuous life is lived. On their own they neither add to the happiness of a life nor subtract from it" (*Platonic Ethics*, 43).

The Stoics unwaveringly insisted that the value of virtue is of a kind different from that of the preferables. Probably most of us share the intuition; how can courage be compared with good health, for example? Thinking of the virtues as working on the matter of the indifferents gives a rationale for the intuition. Virtue has to do with the kind of life that one makes out of the indifferents that come one's way.[23]

We have to step carefully here, however. In explicating Plato and the Stoics, Annas sometimes says that the indifferents have no value in them-

---

[21] Diogenes Laertius, in ibid., cites life, health, pleasure, beauty, strength, wealth, good reputation, and noble birth as examples of preferables, and death, disease, pain, ugliness, poverty, bad reputation, and low birth, as examples of non-preferables.

[22] I am using the translation by R. W. Dyson published by Cambridge University Press, 1998. Augustine is expressing his skepticism concerning the Stoic claim that the trembling and the pallor are not genuine emotions but only immediate bodily reactions. Cicero's views (along with Carneades's) are cited in Irwin, "Socratic Paradox," p. 153.

[23] Bowlin, in *Contingency and Fortune,* says throughout his book that whereas Aquinas worked with a "functional" view of the virtues, the Stoics did not. That seems to me mistaken. Bowlin's Stoics look more like modern Kantians than like ancient virtue theorists.

selves; such value as they have depends "on the use made of them by virtue or vice" (*Platonic Ethics*, 42). If to have value is to be a life-good, then, as we have just seen, this is true. But it is not true if we take "value" more generally.[24] Of course, one can consider *the worth to oneself* of some indifferent by noting its role in the living of one's life. But we cannot do without the additional idea of the indifferents having *intrinsic* degrees of worth. If the worth of friendship were entirely determined by whether or not it was taken up into a virtuous life or a vicious life, if friendship were not intrinsically preferable to social isolation, then there would be no reason to choose friendship over social isolation, and no reason to regard cultivating the former as a virtue. Annas says that the indifferents "motivate us to pursue and avoid them," adding that "this is natural, since we are following our human nature in doing this" (*Platonic Ethics*, 43). But if having friends is preferable for X because X lives a virtuous life among friends, if being socially isolated is preferable for Y because Y lives a virtuous life in social isolation, and if that is the end of the matter, then friendship and social isolation lose their motivational function. There will be no reason to aim at friendship and none to avoid isolation.

In short, certain of the indifferents must be *intrinsically* preferable to others if the over-arching aim of the virtues is to be what the Stoics say it is, namely, promoting the preferables in our lives and forestalling the non-preferables. Seneca makes the point clearly: "Indeed, which of our sages—I mean of our school, for whom the only good is virtue—will deny that these things we call indifferents also have some value in themselves [*aliquid in se pretii*] and that some are preferable to others?"[25] To this we can add the voice of John Stobaeus: "What is between virtue and vice is indifferent, but not [indifferent] with respect to selection and rejection; . . . some have selective value, and some have rejective disvalue, but make no contribution at all to the happy life."[26]

How do we determine which indifferents are preferable to which? I find the Stoics' answer to this question one of the weakest links in their chain of argument. What they do say on the matter goes as follows. By

---

[24] Admittedly, some Stoics did apparently take it as true. Consider, for example, Sextus Empiricus's way of speaking of the indifferents: "that which can be used well and badly would be indifferent. Virtue is always used well; vice is always used badly; but health and bodily things can be used sometimes well and sometimes badly, and that is why they would be indifferent." In Inwood and Gerson, *Hellenistic Philosophy*, p. 256; see also Diogenes Laertius on p. 195.

[25] From *de Brevitate Vitae* 22.4; quoted by Irwin, "Socratic Paradox," p. 176.

[26] In Inwood and Gerson, *Hellenistic Philosophy*, p. 213. Cf. Sextus Empiricus: "the preferred are those which have considerable value, the rejected are those which have considerable disvalue." In ibid., p. 256. The point is not that *all* preferables have intrinsic value; some have only instrumental value—but that *some* must have intrinsic value if the Stoic way of thinking of virtue is not to be fundamentally incoherent.

virtue of our human nature we are naturally inclined to seek certain things and to avoid others. What we must all do is take the things that we are naturally inclined to pursue and, by the use of reason, organize them into a coherent system of priorities. The place of a given item in that rational system of priorities will then constitute that item's intrinsic degree of preferability. What the Stoics called the *fitting, due, appropriate,* or *right* action in a given situation will be the action that seeks to promote the items that, in that situation, have as great a preferability as any. Here is how Diogenes Laertius put it:

> An appropriate [action], they say, is that which, when done, admits of a reasonable defence, such as what is consistent in life, and this extends also to plants and animals. For appropriate [actions] are observable in these too. . . . [An appropriate action] is an action congenial to arrangements which are according to nature. For of actions performed according to impulse . . . , some are appropriate and some inappropriate and some are neither appropriate nor inappropriate. Appropriate [actions], then, are those which reason constrains [us] to do, such as honouring our parents, brothers, fatherland, and spending time with friends. Inappropriate are those which reason constrains [us] not [to do], such as things like this: neglecting our parents, ignoring our brothers, being out of sympathy with our friends, overlooking [the interests of] our fatherland and such things. Neither appropriate nor inappropriate are those which reason neither constrains us to perform nor forbids, such as picking up a small stick, holding a writing instrument or scraper and things similar to these. (Inwood and Gerson, *Hellenistic Philosophy,* 196–97)

Not very impressive, one must admit, if one is looking not just for a *description* of how the Stoics used the concept of an appropriate (fitting, due, right) action but for an *explanation* of what the concept comes to. One looks for more; but nothing more is forthcoming.[27] One might forgive this lack were it not for the fact that the notion of the fitting action is at the basis of the entire system. To act virtuously, as we will see shortly, is to perform the fitting action in a certain way.

In contrasting ancient with modern ethics, Annas several times over makes the point that the ethical theories of the ancients were not hierarchically ordered; there is, she says, no particular priority among concepts and principles. But this cannot be entirely right. For virtue is at the heart of ancient ethical theory; and the concept of virtue presupposes the con-

---

[27] See the discussion in Irwin, "Socratic Paradox," pp. 160–64; and in Annas, *Morality of Happiness,* pp. 96–115.

cept of the action that is as fitting as any other in the situation. That much hierarchy is built into the very concept of virtue; the concept of the fitting action is conceptually prior to the concept of virtue. An account of virtue cannot get off the ground without appealing to the concept of a fitting action; and you and I cannot set about becoming virtuous if we do not know how to pick out actions that fit the situation. As Annas herself puts it,

> A virtue is a disposition to do the right thing, in various areas of life, and to have the right feelings and emotions about it. But how does the agent discern what is the right thing to do? Unless she is *correct* about what to do, she will not have a virtue. If she is wrong about what courage requires for example, then she will not be courageous, but merely foolhardy; she will do the wrong thing, and will have inappropriate feelings and emotions. So it is crucial to have an answer to the question: what here is the standard of rightness? What does the virtuous agent appeal to in working out what is the right thing to do? (*Morality*, 108–9)

The Stoics were not entirely silent on the topic of the right or fitting action, but what they had to say was, to repeat, not impressive.

Though living virtuously requires that one perform the action that fits the situation as well as any, the converse is not the case: performing fitting actions is not sufficient for living virtuously. One must perform the right actions out of a fully virtuous disposition.

What sort of disposition is that? Let me quote Annas: virtue "is a complex disposition to do the morally right thing for the right reason in a consistent and reliable way, in which one's emotions and feelings have so developed as to go along with one's decisions" (*Morality*, 441). Every phrase in that formulation could be unpacked; in Annas's discussion it comes as the summary of a long and rich discussion. I think it would distract from our purposes to do that unpacking. The formulation is sufficiently lucid as it stands for making the point that, given this understanding of virtue and the Stoic understanding of the right or fitting action, it would be irrational not to cultivate the life of virtue. Once one has ordered that to which one is naturally inclined into a rational system of priorities, what possible reason could there be for not taking the next step of cultivating those dispositions that are the virtues? The well-lived life will perforce be the virtuous life.[28]

---

[28] Cf. Diogenes Laertes: "happiness lies in virtue." Text in Inwood and Gerson, *Hellenistic Philosophy*, p. 192. And John Stobaeus: "They say that being happy is the goal for the sake of which everything is done and that it is itself done for the sake of nothing else, and this consists in living according to virtue." Text in ibid., p. 212.

THE STOIC UNDERSTANDING OF VIRTUOUS ACTION

To fully understand the Stoics, we must raise a question about the nature of virtuous action that Annas's formulation does not attempt to deal with. Has one in fact performed a virtuous act if one has not succeeded in doing what one tried to do? Is an act of courage to be chalked up to my credit if I do not succeed in stopping the assailant?

As mentioned earlier, the Stoics often used the model of a skill, a *technē*, for thinking about those dispositions that are the virtues. Among other points that they used the model to make, they argued that virtues should be understood as *stochastic* skills or practices, in distinction from non-stochastic skills.[29] What did they mean?

Well, certain skills are such that one can distinguish between two distinct things that one might aim at as one engages in them; call them the *objective* (*skopos*, target) of the skill and the *end* (*telos*) of the skill.[30] Given the competitive nature of games, the ancients did not like to think of virtues on analogy to games; nonetheless we can use a game such as basketball to illuminate their distinction.[31] The *objective* in playing basketball, the target, is to score more points than one's opponent. The *end* is to play well. Not only are these two aims conceptually distinct; the end of playing well can be achieved without achieving the objective of scoring more points than one's opponent, and vice versa. A team may play well and fail to score more points than its opponent; it may score more points than its opponent without playing well.

Other skills are such that either this distinction between end and objective cannot be made out or, if it can be made out, achieving the end ensures achieving the objective. Simple children's board games are examples of the first sort; they do not allow for playing the game well or poorly. The skill of performing arithmetical calculations is an example of the second sort. Though one can distinguish between the end and the objective, achieving the end ensures achieving the objective. If one fails to achieve the objective of getting the right answer, that is because one did not do a sufficiently good job of employing the skill.

The Stoics called those skills in which achieving the end does not ensure achieving the objective, "stochastic" (*stochastikē*, aiming). And virtues, they held, are stochastic skills. "A virtue is similar to a stochastic craft, in so far as it has an objective (achieving the natural advantages) and an end (doing all one can to achieve the natural advantages), and

---

[29] On this point I am following especially Irwin's discussion in "Socratic Paradox," pp. 164–68.

[30] I am using Irwin's translation of the Stoic terminology. See ibid., pp. 164ff.

[31] They themselves were fond of using archery as their example.

achieving the end is not sufficient for achieving the objective" (Irwin, "Socratic Paradox," 166). I might endeavor to act courageously as I struggle with the intruder and yet fail to achieve the objective, the target, of my action, namely, preventing him from achieving his dastardly purpose.

And now for the point of introducing this idea of the virtues as stochastic skills. Suppose that I endeavored to act courageously in attempting to stop the assailant. I will then have had a dual aim: I will have aimed at employing that skill that is the virtue of courage, and I will have aimed at stopping the assailant. How does living my life well relate to success in achieving that second aim? If I did in fact act courageously, then I will perforce have achieved my end; but must I also achieve my objective to act courageously? Can one act courageously and not achieve one's objective?

Working with roughly Kantian notions of intention, you and I might want to interrupt at this point with the observation that one could also fail to enact the intention to act courageously; one might be paralyzed by fear. The ancients would reject the idea; finding oneself paralyzed by fear is a sure sign that one has not yet fully acquired the virtue of courage; and if one does not have the virtue, one cannot act courageously. So once again: suppose that one achieves one's end (*telos*) of acting in the courageous manner but not one's objective (*skopos*) of saving one's parents. Has one performed an act of courage? Has one succeeded in performing an act of virtue? The Stoics emphatically said that one has succeeded; the Peripatetics, though in general less decisive on the matter than the Stoics, made the common sense response that in a way one has and in a way one has not.[32]

But once we have in hand the distinction between the *skopos* and the *telos* of an act of employing some virtue, is it not then a purely verbal matter whether we say that one has acted virtuously when one fails to achieve one's *skopos*? Use the words whichever way you want.

Strictly speaking, it is a verbal issue. But beneath the verbal issue is a substantive issue: does living one's life well depend on achieving the *skopos* of one's action or does it not? If I act in the courageous manner but fail to deter my assailant, have I lived my life well in this regard or have I not? Have I brought about a good in my life or have I not? None of the ancients would be willing to use the words "virtue" and "virtuous" in such a way as to make it true to say that though I did not act virtuously, I did nonetheless live my life well.

---

[32] Especially valuable is the detailed discussion by Annas of the dispute in *Morality of Happiness*, Part IV. The reason Bowlin, in *Contingency and Fortune*, thinks the Stoics did not have a functional view of the virtues is that he, in effect, interprets the Stoics as holding that virtuous action has an end but not an objective. As Bowlin argues, that is not a coher-

The Stoic case for holding that achieving the *skopos* of one's act is not necessary for living one's life well rested on their thesis that tranquility is a condition of happiness—a thesis not shared by the Peripatetics. Recall the Stoic analysis of the emotions. And now suppose that I regard success in achieving the objective of my action as a genuine good, that is, as contributing positively to my happiness. To evaluate something as a genuine good is to be emotionally disturbed should that good slip away or threaten to slip away. But all too often the objectives of our virtuously performed actions are not in fact achieved. So if tranquility is to be within our grasp, we must regard achieving those objectives as mere preferables, not genuine goods. Should my courageous endeavor fail in its objective of stopping the assailant, I would not be emotionally upset. It is indifferent to my happiness.[33] Achieving one's objective when acting in a virtuous manner will multiply the preferables in one's life; it will not enhance one's happiness. Likewise, failure to achieve one's objective will reduce the preferables but not diminish one's happiness. In Seneca's words, "The sage is self-sufficient, not in the sense that he wants [*vult*] to be without a friend, but in the sense that he can do without him. And when I say 'can,' I mean that he bears it with his mind undisturbed [*aequo animo*]."[34]

None of us is Master of the causal order of the universe; we are no more than cogs in the cosmic machine. By act of will we initiate some bodily motion; from there on we are at the mercy of external causality. And it is our experience that even our best-laid plans go awry. We do not know enough to be able to anticipate in any detail the effects of our actions—to which I would add, as the Stoics did not, that causality covers only some of what happens. In addition to causality there is both chance and free agency. Be that as it may, however, it is our common experience that we can seldom be entirely sure of the consequences of

---

ent view. But the Stoic view was not that view, but rather the view that success in achieving one's objective is not a condition of having acted virtuously.

[33] Cf. *de Ira* III, 34 (p. 109): "Believe me, they are trivial things which make us flare up in a far from trivial way, the sort of things which rouse children to quarrels and brawls. None of those things, which we handle with such ill humour, is serious or important. And there, I tell you, lies the start of your insane anger. You attach great value to little things. 'He wanted to take my inheritance.' 'He denounced me to the man whom I had long been courting for his last will and testament.' 'He fancied my mistress.' "

[34] Letters 9.5; quoted by Irwin, "Socratic Paradox," p. 184. Cf. Irwin, ibid., p. 175: "The relevant success is not success in reaching the preferred external results. . . . The virtuous person's doing the appropriate actions for the right reason, because of their appropriateness, constitutes the distinguishing feature of virtue, and therefore constitutes the success proper to successful action. Hence happiness and virtue are constituted by 'acting reasonably (*eulogistein*) in the selection of things according to nature' and by 'living completing (*epitelounta*) all the appropriate actions.' "

our enacted intentions. So do not invest yourself in those consequences, said the Stoics.[35]

THE DISPUTE BETWEEN THE STOICS AND THE PERIPATETICS

If one shares the conviction of Aristotle and most of the Peripatetics that full success in one's endeavor to act virtuously requires achieving both the objective and the end of one's action, then whether or not one is managing to live one's life well depends in part on external circumstances, not just on inward intentions. The Peripatetics were probably less impressed than the Stoics with the gap between end and objective. The virtues are skills for securing preferables and avoiding dispreferables; by and large they are successful in that. Indeed, if we regularly failed to achieve the objectives of our actions, developing skills for achieving our objectives would be out of the question. Nonetheless, nobody supposes that even the skilled person is always successful; skill reduces but does not eliminate the chance of failure. Thus for the Peripatetics, the well-lived life—happiness—is at the mercy of fortune in a way that it is not for the Stoics.

Virtuous activity, and thus happiness, was seen by the Peripatetics as vulnerable in another way as well. An issue that was much discussed was whether or not living in straitened circumstances necessarily impairs virtuous activity, thereby diminishing one's happiness. The issue was dramatically posed by the question, "Can one be happy on the torture rack?"

The Peripatetics in general, and Aristotle in particular, held that though the person living in straitened circumstances can act virtuously rather than viciously, nonetheless his virtuous activity is necessarily of a pinched and deficient sort. Here is how Aristotle makes the case:

> [happiness] needs the external goods . . . ; for it is impossible, or not easy, to do noble acts without the proper equipment. In many actions we use friends and riches and political power as instruments; and there are some things the lack of which takes the lustre from blessedness, as good birth, satisfactory children, beauty; for the man

---

[35] Kant thought of the moral life primarily in terms of obligation rather than virtue, and thus in terms of will rather than skill; but allowing for those differences, what he says in Section I of *Grounding for the Metaphysic of Morals* is pure Stoicism: "Even if, by some especially unfortunate fate or by the niggardly provision of stepmotherly nature, [the] will should be wholly lacking in the power to accomplished its purpose . . . yet would it, like a jewel, still shine by its own light as something which has its full value in itself. Its usefulness or fruitlessness can neither augment nor diminish this value." Trans. J. W. Ellington (Indianapolis: Hackett, 1981).

who is very ugly in appearance or ill-born or solitary and childless is hardly happy, and perhaps a man would be still less so if he had thoroughly bad children or friends or had lost good children or friends by death. (*NE* I, 8; 1099a 31–1099b 5)[36]

Aristotle's words suggest the following analogy for the dispute. Imagine a skilled woodworker who finds himself with nothing but defective wood available. The Stoic position is that as long as the woodworker has wood available, whatever its condition, he can practice his craft, and his labors will be far more admirable than those of the person who works on the same wood without the abilities of the skilled woodworker. Naturally, he would *prefer* better wood; but as long as he has some wood available, he can practice his craft and practice it well. The position of the Peripatetics was that though the skilled woodworker can indeed practice his craft on wood of poor quality, and do so in such a way that we admire his efforts, nonetheless his doing what he does is a very deficient display of skilled woodworking. He still possesses the skill, but very little of it can come through in this situation. It would be ridiculous to say that he can practice his skill equally well with bad wood as with fine.[37]

The case of the Stoics for their position on this point is the same as the case for their position on the preceding point. Tranquility is a condi-

---

[36] John M. Cooper fleshes our Aristotle's thought here as follows:

> Apparently the disfiguring of the virtuous man's happiness that the lack of [external] goods causes is traceable to some way in which his virtuous activities are impeded if he lives without them. How is this to be understood? Aristotle's thought, I believe, is this. Some external conditions (being good-looking, having good children, coming from a good family), while not used by the virtuous person as means to achieve his purposes (as, e.g., his money or personal influence might be) put him in the position where the options for action that are presented to him by his circumstances allow him to exercise his virtues fully and in ways that one might describe as normal for the virtues. Thus if one is physically quite unattractive . . . people will tend to avoid you, so that you will not be able to enter into the normally wide range of relationships that pose for the virtuous person the particular challenges that his virtue responds to with its correct assessments and right decisions. Such a person, let us assume, may in fact develop all the virtues in their fully perfected form and actually exercise them in ways that respond appropriately and correctly to his circumstances; but the circumstances themselves are restricted by his ugliness and the effects this has on others, so that his virtue is not called upon to regulate his responses and choices in all the sorts of circumstances that the more normally attractive person would face, and so its exercise is not as full and fine a thing as that more normally attractive person's would be.

John M. Cooper, "Aristotle on the Goods of Fortune," *The Philosophical Review* 94, no. 2 (April 1985): 182–83. The article is reprinted in Terence Irwin, ed., *Aristotle's Ethics* (New York and London: Garland, 1995).

[37] Cooper, in ibid., p. 181, offers the analogy of a skilled woodworker who lacks proper tools.

tion of happiness. It is agreed by all parties that one's life is lived well insofar as it is lived virtuously; the life-goods constitutive of one's happiness are composed entirely of virtuous actions on one's part. But to evaluate something as a genuine life-good, as opposed to a mere preferable, implies that if that which is the good should be endangered, one would be emotionally upset. So to regard virtuous action as contingent on fortune is perforce to allow the possibility of emotional disturbance in one's life. If virtuous action were dependent on fortune, then, should one find oneself in circumstances so straitened that it is impossible for one's virtue to flourish in virtuous action, one would be emotionally upset. But the well-lived life is free of emotional disturbance. So we must regard circumstances as irrelevant to virtuous action.

Speaking of the Stoics, Martha Nussbaum says that "if we imagine a wise person living in the worst possible natural circumstances, so long as she is good—and once good she cannot be corrupted—her *eudaimonia* will still be complete. She will be living as valuable and choice worthy and enviable a life as a human being could" (360). Yes and no. She will indeed be living her life as well as a life can be lived; it is as worthy as a human life could be. Her *eudaimonia* is complete. She is tranquil, not emotionally upset. But the Stoics would not say that she is living as choiceworthy a life as a human being could. Though she can live her life well, and thus be happy, on the torture rack, life on the torture rack is not to be preferred. The fully virtuous person, the sage, will not be upset should she find herself on the torture rack. But she will not prefer it; she will not choose it.

It will now be clear why the Stoics affirmed and the Peripatetics denied that virtue was sufficient for happiness. All agreed that *virtuous activity* is necessary and sufficient for the well-lived life, the happy life; they disagreed over whether *virtue* (*being virtuous*) is necessary and sufficient. The Stoics believed that circumstances could not prevent the virtuous person from acting virtuously; the Peripatetics believed they could. If the objective of my virtuous activity is not achieved, or if I am living in such straitened circumstances that the scope for virtuous activity on my part is narrow, then my virtuous activity is impaired, said the Peripatetics. I am not living my life as well as it could be lived. So whereas neither Stoics nor Peripatetics believed that one's *virtue* is hostage to fortune, the Peripatetics did believe that one's *virtuous activity* is hostage to fortune.[38] And because the happy life is the life of virtuous activity, happiness is hostage to fortune.

[38] Aristotle was of the view that *becoming virtuous* is also heavily dependant on fortune, especially the good fortune of living in a virtuous community; Aquinas followed him in this regard. See Bowlin, *Contingency and Fortune*, 168ff.

Is Tranquility Achievable?

Achieving tranquility was a two-part program for the Stoics: emotional detachment was one part, steadiness in virtue was the other. With respect to the indifferents, one aims at emotional detachment by getting to the point of no longer judging any of them to be genuine goods. With respect to virtue, one aims at becoming so skilled and habituated that one never deviates. "Let us give the mind that peace that we shall only give it by constantly practising wholesome precepts," says Seneca, "by good conduct, by concentrating our attention and desire on virtue alone. Let us meet the demands of conscience, and not toil for reputation. Let even ill-repute come after us, so long as we have deserved well" (III, 41; p. 114).

The Stoics did not conceal the fact that achieving emotional detachment and steadiness in virtue requires intense dedication to a long training program. Nobody becomes virtuous casually or overnight. Merely believing that virtue is necessary and sufficient for happiness and that virtuous activity is invulnerable to circumstances does not make one a sage. Nor does dedication to a training program make one a sage. One must actually achieve emotional detachment and steadiness in virtue. What the Stoics did not emphasize is something that is a clear implication of their view: until one actually achieves emotional detachment and steadiness in virtue, thus becoming a sage, one is upset over one's failure to do so; one's dedication to the supreme good of becoming virtuous and acting virtuously is frustrated. Where once one cried out against the fates, now one lacerates oneself.

Think of Augustine's narration of his anguished conversion, in chapter VIII of his *Confessions*; and of St. Paul's anguished description, in his letter to the church at Rome, of the person in moral bondage: the good that I would, that I do not, and the evil that I would not, that I do; O wretched man that I am (cf. Romans 7:14–25). The eyes of Paul and Augustine were on the unsettling fact that sometimes we find ourselves knowing what we ought to do and yet strangely and helplessly unable even to try to do it.

Augustine presses the point in his late writings that not only do we sometimes find ourselves in this predicament; here, in this life, nobody ever manages to act in a fully virtuous manner.[39] It became an important part of his polemic against the Stoics. Apparently, some of the pagans were of this view as well; there are no sages, it is only an ideal. If this is

---

[39] See especially *City of God*, XIX, 4. There is a superb analysis of Augustine's thought on this matter in chapters 2 to 4 of James Wetzel, *Augustine and the Limits of Virtue* (Cambridge: Cambridge University Press, 1992).

right, then to commit oneself to the Stoic program for achieving tranquility is to commit oneself to a program that yields not tranquility but its own peculiar kind of disturbance. Tranquility, where art thou?

THE STOIC "RESERVATION"

I have presented the Stoic way of thinking as compellingly as I could. Given the conviction that virtue is necessary and sufficient for happiness and the thesis that happiness requires peace of mind, everything follows. Nonetheless, when we look closely, do we not spy an incoherence? Virtuous activity has as its objective the promotion of those indifferents that are preferable and the avoidance of those that are non-preferable. It is true that the virtuous person knows how to live virtuously in poverty as well as in plenty. But that implies not that plenty is not to be preferred to poverty but that, in situations of poverty, there are still preferables. There could be no virtuous activities if none of the indifferents was intrinsically preferable. Virtue has to touch ground somewhere. It cannot float in the air.

But now look again at those virtuous activities. When I exercise my virtue of courage, I try to bring about something in the world, that being the objective, the target, the *skopos*, of my action. I may not be emotionally invested in my father and mother being saved from the assailant; should that objective of my action not come about, I might experience no emotional disturbance. Nonetheless, I try to bring it about. That is my objective. That is what I desire to happen. Now suppose that my desire is not satisfied. How could I not feel disappointment over my desire not being satisfied? Is not the disappointment of unsatisfied desire, unachieved endeavor, a kind of negativity incompatible with tranquility? In a fully tranquil life there would be no such experience. So though I may have reshaped my value judgments so that I am not upset over the murder of my father, I have not reshaped myself so as not to be upset over my failure to satisfy my *desire to bring about* his not being murdered.

The point is general. To engage in the practice of the virtues is perforce to have intentions of certain sorts. An intention is the intention to do something. Enacting the intention to do something presupposes the desire that it come about. Sometimes one may feel decidedly ambivalent about what one is trying to bring about, so that one feels relieved when one has tried and failed. But with that exception, one is disappointed over one's failure. Such disappointment is a species of disturbance. So the Stoic picture is incoherent.

The Stoic response is fascinating. We live in a universe governed by divine reason. To save ourselves from disappointment we must align our intentions with the divine plan.

> "To live according to virtue" is equivalent to living according to the experience of events which occur by nature, as Chrysippus says. . . . For our natures are parts of the nature of the universe. Therefore, the goal becomes "to live consistently with nature," i.e., according to one's own nature and that of the universe, doing nothing which is forbidden by the common law, which is right reason, penetrating all things, being the same as Zeus who is the leader of the administration of things. And this itself is the virtue of the happy man and a smooth flow of life, whenever all things are done according to the harmony of the daimon in each of us with the will of the administrator of the universe.[40]

What help is this? one asks. To eliminate from our lives the negative emotion of disappointment over frustrated desire we must align our intentions with the divine plan. But we do not know the divine plan—not in advance anyway, and not in detail. Afterward, yes. Should my intention to prevent my father's murder prove unsuccessful, that shows that my preventing his murder was not in the divine plan. But that is no help to me when I am forming and enacting my intentions.

The solution the Stoics proposed is that, except perhaps for those intentions so modest as to be assured of success in advance, we should always act with what they called "reservation." What they meant is that to all our enacted intentions we should attach the qualifier *deo volente*, God willing. With the reservation in mind, *God willing that I succeed*, I try to flick the dagger from the assailant's hand, thus to save my father's life. If I do not succeed in achieving that objective, that indicates that it was not part of the divine plan that I should flick the dagger from the assailant's hand.[41] So I feel no disappointment. If it had been my goal to flick the dagger from the assailant's hand, period, then I would feel disap-

---

[40] Diogenes Laertius in Inwood and Gerson, *Hellenistic Philisophy*, pp. 191–92. Cf. John Stobaeus in ibid., p. 212: Being happy "consists in living according to virtue, in living in agreement, and again (which is the same thing) in living according to nature. Zeno defined happiness in this manner: 'happiness is a smooth flow of life.' . . . So it is clear from this that [these expressions] are equivalent: 'living according to nature' and 'living honourably' and 'living well' and again 'the honourable and good' and 'virtue and what participates in virtue.' "

[41] Thus also the Stoic admiration for the icy coldness of the response to the news of the death of his son attributed to Anaxagoras by our sources: "I was already aware that I had begotten a mortal." For the sources, see Nussbaum, *Therapy of Desire*, p. 363, n. 19.

pointment over my failure. But my goal was not that; it was instead to flick the dagger from the assailant's hand *provided that doing so fits within the divine plan.* The desire presupposed by my enactment of my intention has not been frustrated; I remain undisturbed.[42]

We must endeavor to achieve only what we can be assured of achieving, always being ready to add the reservation *deo volente.* If "the mind [is to] have peace," says Seneca, it must not attempt such things "as are beyond its powers."

> Straightforward and manageable tasks follow your directions, unlike the huge tasks that are out of proportion to your capacity. The latter do not yield easily. If you take them on, they weigh you down; they distract you as you carry them out. Just when you think that you have them in your grasp, they fall and bring you down with them. That is why frustration is frequently the fate of one who, instead of undertaking what is easy, finds himself wishing that what he *has* undertaken were easier! Every time that you attempt something, you should make a reckoning of yourself, of what you are preparing to do and what has prepared you yourself to do it, since a change of heart at failure to get the job done will make your peevish. . . . So our actions should neither be petty [*parvus*] nor overconfident [*audax*] and unprincipled. Our hopes should not stray far. We should attempt nothing which leaves us, even at the moment of success, wondering how we did it. (*On Anger* III, 8; pp. 83–84)

---

[42] Seneca's standard formulation of the reservation in *de Ira* is "if nothing happens to prevent it." (In the selection from his *On Peace of Mind*, in Inwood and Gerson, *Hellenistic Philosophy*, p. 243, the reservation is translated as "unless something intervenes" and "unless something interferes.") But given the Stoic view of divine providence, this comes to the same as *deo volente.*

Inwood, *Ethics and Human Action*, pp. 119–20, gives a good formulation of the issue: It is a person's "duty to adapt himself to this cosmos, to want events to occur as they in fact will. Ideally a man should never be in the position of wanting something different from the actual course of events, since what happens in the world is the will of Zeus, is the best possible way for things to occur, and since man as a rational agent should assimilate his will to that of the supremely rational agent, who is Zeus. Moreover, if one does try to resist the will of Zeus, one will never succeed. . . . But the problem of man is that he is not prescient, he does not know for sure in every case what Zeus has in store for him. . . . The problem of the rational agent is to act in pursuit of one's reasonable goals in such a way that one does not commit oneself to anything which might be shown by events to be contrary to the plan of Zeus. . . . If one goes ahead in one's uncertainty about the future, acting in pursuit of one's own health, one may avoid conflict with the will of Zeus if one acts with a tacit reservation: if nothing comes along to interfere, i.e., if it is really fated to turn out so. . . . Acting with this reservation . . . brings it about that the agent is never frustrated, filled with regret, or required to change his mind."

The Inadequacy of Eudaimonism for a Theory of Rights

We are now in a position to see why eudaimonism cannot serve as framework for a theory of rights. Eudaimonism thinks of non-instrumental goods as consisting of life-goods, and it thinks of life-goods as activities; hence we get its understanding of well-being as the well-lived life. Its rule of application is that each of us is to aim at performing such activities as will make one's own life well lived. Eudaimonism is inadequate as a framework for a theory of rights both on account of its understanding of well-being and on account of its rule of application.

I have a right against others to the good of their treating me in certain ways—for example, a right against my university to the good of their paying me what they have contracted to pay me and a right against many others to the good of their not preventing me from strolling on the New Haven Green. These goods are life-goods of mine. But they are not activities on my part; they are "passivities." Hence they are not constitutive of my happiness, of how well my life is lived. So it is in general. Rights against others are rights to the good of being treated by them in certain ways. None of those goods is constitutive of one's happiness, for none of them is an activity on one's part.

May it be that though such goods are not *constitutive* of the well-lived life, they are nonetheless *conditions* thereof or *means* thereto and, hence, in the eudaimonist framework, instrumental goods? The only way this could be true on the Stoic view is that *becoming* virtuous requires being treated in certain ways by others; the person who is already virtuous is not susceptible to having his virtuous activity impaired by others.[43] The Peripatetics parted from the Stoics on this point. They held that virtuous activity by the virtuous person can also be impaired and impeded. Either way, might it be that those ways of being treated by others to which we have rights are all conditions or means of becoming virtuous or of acting virtuously? Are they all, in that way, instrumental to the well-lived life?

They are not. Our now-familiar examples can be trotted out once again. If your reputation is ruined behind your back but everybody continues to treat you as they always did, you have been deprived of a good

[43] There is a passage in Seneca's *de Ira* that says, in the Cooper and Procopé edition I have been using, that the sage can be wronged but that he takes no note of it: "A mighty mind with its true self-awareness will not avenge, since it has not noticed the wrong done to it. Weapons rebound from a hard surface; a blow to a solid object hurts only the man who delivers it. In the same way, no wrong done to a great mind will make itself felt, being weaker than its object. How much better it looks as though impervious to any weapon, to brush off wrongs and insults! Retribution is an admission of pain. A mind bowed by wrong done to it is not a great mind" (III, 5–6; 82). The term "wrong" occurs four times in this translation of the passage; in each case the Latin term is *injuria*. Therein, I suggest, lies the

to which you have a right even though your virtuous activity has in no way been impaired. Counter-examples go well beyond cases in which one does not know that one has been wronged, however. I have a right to a polite answer from the receptionist in the medical center; yet a grumpy answer will have no effect whatsoever on how well I live my life. Sometimes recognizing that one has been wronged even provokes one into living one's life better.

The conclusion is inescapable: the conception of well-being that the eudaimonist works with, well-being as living well, cannot serve as the conception of well-being for a theory of rights. None of those goods of being treated a certain way to which one has a right against others are *constitutive* of one's living well; and only some are *conditions* of one's living well.

When we look at eudaimonism from the side of its rule of application, a different deficiency comes to light. My living my life well may require that I seek to promote your happiness in some respect; it may even require that I do so for its own sake and not because I think it a means to my happiness. But always when the choice confronts me whether to perform a certain action or implement a certain plan of action, the question I ask is, what contribution will this make to my own life being well lived? This feature of the eudaimonist's way of thinking comes through lucidly in John Bowlin's description of the action of the Danes in World War II:

> When the truly courageous among Denmark's gentiles concluded that their Jewish neighbors deserved rescue despite the grave risks involved, they did not simply choose one course of action over another or express their preference for some ends and not others. . . .[T]he truly courageous Danes participated in the rescue precisely because they believed their chances of leading a noble and honorable life, one qualitatively better in kind than other possibilities, would be forever sacrificed by refusing to assist a group of fellow citizens in need. Refusal, they concluded, would transform them into the cowards they regarded with contempt, into the sort of people who have little chance of leading a praiseworthy and fulfilling human life.[44]

But suppose you have a right against me to the good of my treating you a certain way. Whether or not performing that action would make for greater happiness on my part is simply irrelevant to what I should do.

---

clue to interpreting the passage. The sage can be injured, harmed; but he cannot be wronged, that is, deprived of life-goods.

[44] Bowlin, *Contingency and Fortune,* p. 206.

I am to do what you have a right to my doing, period. Rights de-center
the agent. Instead of the agent's happiness determining his action, the
worth of the recipient and of those others who will be affected by the
action is to determine what the agent does.

It will be said that I am ignoring the fact that to treat you justly is to
act in accord with virtue, and so, to live my life well. Activity in accord
with virtue is constitutive of the well-lived life. So the eudaimonist's rule
of application does after all require that I treat you as you have a right
to my treating you. Treating you unjustly cannot be a way of living
my life better.

Not so. Recall Aristotle's celebration of the virtue of magnanimity. Suppose that justice toward one person conflicts with magnanimity toward
many, as it often does. What reason does the eudaimonist have for saying
that choosing justice over magnanimity always makes for the better-lived
life? And in general, what reason does the eudaimonist have for saying
that justice always takes precedence over the other virtues? What reason
does he have for assigning to the goods to which we have rights the
trumping role that such goods do in fact have?

None, so far as I can see. Recall that virtues, for the eudaimonist,
are habituated skills for rightly pursuing the rightly ordered natural
goods or preferables available to one. How are we to extract, from that
understanding of virtue, the trumping role of those goods to which we
have rights?

Your argument has to be mistaken, some will say. Aquinas was a eudaimonist, siding with the Peripatetics on most issues of dispute between
them and the Stoics.[45] And though rights-talk was certainly not big in
Aquinas, nonetheless the idea of rights was there. We quoted him in
chapter 1 as saying that justice is "rendering to each his right. . . . A man
is said to be just because he respects the rights [*ius*] of others" (*Summa
theologiae* II-II, 58, 1). Furthermore, in the course of arguing that respect
of persons is a sin, Aquinas remarks that "respect of persons is opposed
to distributive justice. For the equality of distributive justice consists in
allotting various things to various persons in proportion to their personal
dignity" (II-II, 63, 1). There, within the context of his eudaimonism,
Aquinas introduces and employs the idea of a person having a right to a
good on account of that good befitting the person's worth. That is the
idea of an inherent right.

So it cannot be true that eudaimonism cannot serve as framework for
a theory of rights. Grant that an adequate theory of rights requires the
idea of a person having a right to the good of being treated a certain way
on account of her worth. This idea received little or no recognition in

---

[45] This is the main argument of ibid.

classical eudaimonism; that has to be conceded. But Aquinas is testimony to the fact that nothing stands in the way of adding this idea.[46]

I reply that to add the idea is to give up eudaimonism. A theory of rights needs the idea of a person's worth requiring that she be treated in certain ways. The eudaimonist speaks only of the worth of life-goods and of conditions and means for those; the worth of persons and human beings has no place in his scheme. What he says about life-goods is that they are all activities and that each of us must choose among them with the goal in mind of enhancing one's own happiness. There is no room in this scheme for the worth of persons and human beings, and hence none for one's right against others to their treating one a certain way on account of one's worth.

---

[46] In chapter 1 I noted that though Aquinas thinks of justice as rendering to each what is due him or her, he nowhere gives an account of something's being due a person. (The same is true for MacIntyre's discussion in *Dependent Rational Animals*.) I think that this lacuna is not accidental.

Chapter Eight

AUGUSTINE'S BREAK WITH EUDAIMONISM

Only Love of the Immutable Can Yield Tranquility

Had the spell of ancient eudaimonism not been broken, an adequate theory of rights would have been impossible. We can witness in Augustine the struggle to break free of that spell. It was a struggle provoked by his reading of Christian Scripture; the incursion of Christianity into late antiquity created space for a theory of rights. I do not claim that Augustine was the only one in late antiquity to break with eudaimonism in such a way as to create that space. But it will be singularly instructive to see just how and why he made the break.

In A.D. 390, four years after his conversion and a year before his ordination as priest, Augustine wrote *Of True Religion*. Seven or so years later (397–98), very shortly after his appointment as bishop in 396, he wrote his *Confessions*. More or less simultaneously he wrote the first three books of *On Christian Doctrine*.

The dominant question guiding the discussion in all three books is how happiness is to be attained. There are differences among the three books in the terminology used to answer the question, and differences in emphasis, especially between the earlier *Of True Religion* and the somewhat later *Confessions* and *On Christian Doctrine*. But the structure of Augustine's answer remains the same.

Augustine shared with the Stoics the thesis that rest, tranquility, freedom from negative emotions, is necessary for happiness. Our goal, he says, is to "attain the things that make us happy and rest in them" (*On Christian Doctrine*, book I, chap. 3, sec. 3).[1] His view as to how tranquility is to be achieved was strikingly different from that of the Stoics, however, and closer to the views of the neo-Platonists.[2] Recall the Stoic analysis of

---

[1] I am using the translation by J. F. Shaw in *Nicene and Post-Nicene Fathers*, ed. Philip Schaff, vol. 2 (rpt., Grand Rapids, Mich.: Eerdmans, 1979).

[2] Whether Augustine's early thought is more Stoic or Platonist is a matter of much controversy; see James Wetzel, *Augustine and the Limits of Virtue*, for a very good discussion of the issue. I agree with Wetzel's judgment that, in his early career, "Augustine's sensibilities in ethics are fundamentally Stoic. He refuses to accept the intrusion of fortune into the idea of beatitude" (50). But I think that Augustine incorporated rather more Platonic and neo-Platonic themes into his Stoic outlook than Wetzel concedes or takes note of.

the root of our emotional disturbances: in judging things outside our control to be authentic goods, or conditions of or means to authentic goods, we make ourselves emotional hostages to those things. When they slip away or never happen, we get disturbed. The solution is to value as an authentic good only that which is within one's own control, namely, one's own virtue, and to understand virtue in such a way that virtue is sufficient for virtuous activity and virtuous activity is sufficient for happiness. Augustine insists that the way to achieve tranquility is instead never to put one's emotional life at the mercy of that which can fail one. And where the Stoics said that we put our emotional lives at the mercy of something when we judge it to be good, Augustine says that we do so when we love it. As we shall see, Augustine thought that one can judge something to be good without loving it. So if tranquility is what you want, love only that which cannot fail you—not that which lies entirely in your own hands, but that which cannot fail you.

And what, among all the things we can love, cannot fail us? God, and God alone. Recall again that famous sentence from the opening paragraph of the *Confessions*: "Our souls are restless, Lord, until they rest in thee." To love anything other than God is to court disturbance. Many are the passages in which Augustine makes the point. Here are just a couple. The soul that "clings to [mutable] things of beauty . . . only clings to sorrow." The love of such things "must not be like glue to bind [one's] soul to them. For they continue on the course that is set for them and leads to their end, and if the soul loves them and wishes to be with them and find its rest in them, it is torn by desires that can destroy it. In these things there is no place to rest, because they do not last" (IV, 10). One's virtue, too, must not be what one loves; for true virtue is impossible to achieve in this life. God alone "is the place of peace that cannot be disturbed; and he will not withhold himself from your love unless you withhold your love from him. . . . [So] stand with him and you shall not fall; rest in him and peace shall be yours" (*Confessions* IV, 11–12).[3]

The thought is perhaps most fully and lucidly stated in Augustine's answer to question 35 of the so-called *Eighty-three Different Questions*: "what else is it to live happily but to possess an eternal object through knowing it? For the eternal is that in which alone one can rightly place his confidence, it is that which cannot be taken away from the one who loves it, and it is that very thing which one possesses solely by knowing it. For of all things, the most excellent is what is eternal, and therefore we cannot possess it except by that part of ourselves in which lies our excellence, i.e., by our mind. But whatever is possessed by the mind is had by know-

---

[3] I am using the translation by R. S. Pine-Coffin in St. Augustine, *Confessions* (1961; rpt., London: Penguin Books, 1984).

ing, and no good is completely known which is not completely loved."[4]
To this we may add a sentence from *On Christian Doctrine*: "no one is so
egregiously silly as to ask, 'How do you know that a life of unchangeable
wisdom is preferable to one of change?' " (*On Christian Doctrine*, book I,
chap. 9, sec. 9).[5]

The influence of the Platonic tradition, with its central metaphor of
the ascent of the soul and its insistence that the soul's ascent requires
release from attachment to the earthly, is unmistakable in these writings
from the time of Augustine's ordination. The metaphor comes to the
surface most obviously and systematically in a passage in *Of True Religion*
(XXIX, sec. 52ff.) where Augustine describes "how far reason can advance from visible to invisible things in its ascent from temporal to eternal things."[6] It comes to the surface most movingly in the famous description in *Confessions* IX of the mystical vision that he and his mother shared
while looking out the window at the seaport in Ostia. The ascent metaphor had been prominent in some of Augustine's early writings, those
composed in 388 very shortly after his conversion.[7] In the writings we are
considering, it was still present but already losing its prominence. In the
City of God, written at the end of his career, it has all but disappeared.

ENJOYING WITHOUT LOVING

When Augustine is warning that love for anything mutable is always susceptible of disappointment, he can sound exceedingly astringent. That
astringency is considerably tempered by his insistence that it is possible
to enjoy things without loving them, and hence without the threat of

---

[4] *Eighty-three Different Questions*, trans. David L. Mosher (Washington, D.C.: Catholic University of America Press, 1977), p. 66.

[5] Cf. *De beata vita* 2.11. Question: "What must a person take to himself in order to be
blessed?" Answer: "It must be something ever enduring, that neither hangs on fortune, nor
is exposed to any mishaps."

[6] Translation of John H. S. Burleigh in *The Library of Christian Classics*, vol. 6: *Augustine's
Earlier Writings* (Philadelphia: Westminster Press, 1953), p. 251.

[7] Here is a passage from one of those earliest works, *de Quantitate Animae*. Augustine is
describing the seventh and final stage of the ascent of the soul: "We have now arrived at
the vision and contemplation of the truth, which is the seventh and final step. Nor is it a
step any longer, but a kind of stopping place to which these steps lead up. What its joys
are, what the full enjoyment of the highest and true good is like, what serenity and eternity
is in the air—how can I describe all this? It has been described by certain great and incomparable souls, insofar as they thought it ought to be described, souls whom we believe to
have seen these things, and to be seeing them still" (76). I am using Nussbaum's translation, *Upheavals of Thought*, p. 534.

emotional disturbance rearing its head.[8] The test of whether one is loving a thing or merely enjoying it is whether one would be emotionally upset should it die or change radically: "We have a thing without loving it when we can let it go without grieving."[9] We will seriously misunderstand Augustine's attitude toward the world if we neglect what he has to say about enjoyment and focus only on what he has to say about love.

When the thing enjoyed is itself excellent, enjoyment is appropriate, perhaps even called for. "If the things of this world delight you," says Augustine, "praise God for them" (*Confessions* IV, 12). Praise God for them because "these things of beauty would not exist at all unless they came from" God (ibid., IV, 10). The parallel with the Stoic distinction between two fundamentally different sorts of value is obvious: where the Stoics distinguished between the good and the preferable, Augustine distinguishes between the love-worthy and the enjoyment-worthy.

In the *Confessions* Augustine reports that he wept at the funeral of his seventeen-year-old son Adeodatus. He chastised himself for the tears he shed at his mother's funeral and for those he shed on the death of a boyhood friend; not so for those he shed at Adeodatus's funeral.

> The tears flowed from me when I heard your hymns and canticles, for the sweet singing of your Church moved me deeply. The music surged in my ears, truth seeped into my heart, and my feelings of devotion overflowed, so that the tears streamed down. But they were tears of gladness. (IX, 6)

The difference between these tears and the others is that those were tears of disappointed love, whereas these were tears of intense enjoyment of something worthy of enjoyment: the music of the church.

Augustine's clear distinction between love and enjoyment is what allows him to combine stern warnings against love of the mutable with lyrical celebrations of the beauty of those very same things. Consider, for example, this passage from *The City of God*:

> What discourse can adequately describe the beauty and utility of . . . creation, which the divine bounty has bestowed upon man to behold and consume. . . ? Consider the manifold and varied beauty of sky

---

[8] Throughout the subsequent discussion, I use "enjoy" to stand for an experience that is positively valorized (I explain this shortly), not as a synonym for the Latin "*fruere*" as that is used by Augustine in his famous formula "*uti, non frui*" (*On Christian Doctrine*, Book I). Augustine explains "*fruere*" as follows: "to enjoy a thing is to rest with satisfaction in it for its own sake" (*OCD* I, 4). Augustine consistently held the view that though other things may be enjoyed, in my sense of "enjoy," only God is to be the object of *fruere*. What confuses those of us who read Augustine in English is that a number of different words in Augustine's Latin are translated as "to enjoy," including, then, "*fruere*."

[9] *On True Religion*, xlvii, sec. 93.

and earth and sea; the plenteousness of light and its wondrous quality, in the sun, moon and stars and in the shadows of the forests; the colour and fragrance of flowers; the diversity and multitude of the birds with their wings and bright colours; the multiform species of living creatures of all kinds, even the smallest of which we behold with the greatest wonder—for we are more astonished at the feats of tiny ants and bees than we are at the immense bodies of the whales.

Consider also the grand spectacle of the sea, robing herself in different colours, like garments; sometimes green, and that in so many different shades; sometimes purple, sometimes blue. And what a delightful thing it is to behold the sea when stormy. . . . Who could give a complete account of all these things? (XXII, 24; pp. 1164–65)[10]

Enjoyment is not without its dangers, however. Though in the nature of the case enjoying without loving does not harbor the possibility of grief and disappointment, enjoyment tempts us to love the thing enjoyed. We must stand ever at guard against that temptation. Hence the wariness with which Augustine regards the pleasures of eating and drinking:

There is another evil which we meet with day by day. . . . For we repair the daily wastage of our bodies by eating and drinking, until the time comes when [God] will bring both food and our animal nature to an end. . . . But for the present I find pleasure in this need, though I fight against it, for fear of becoming its captive. . . . I look upon food as a medicine. But the snare of concupiscence awaits me in the very process of passing from the discomfort of hunger to the contentment which comes when it is satisfied. For the process itself is a pleasure and there is no other means of satisfying hunger except the one which we are obliged to take. And although the purpose of eating and drinking is to preserve health, in its train there follows an ominous kind of enjoyment, which often tries to outstrip it, so that it is really for the sake of pleasure that I do what I claim to do and mean to do for the sake of my health. . . . [U]nder the pretence of caring for health [my soul] may disguise the pursuit of pleasure. (*Confessions* X, 31)

Pleasure in eating is "an ominous kind of enjoyment"; it tempts us to eat for the love of the pleasure.

---

[10] One finds a similarly lyrical passage in another of Augustine's late writings, *de Trinitate* VIII, iii, 4–5. For a lyrical passage on the wonders of human creativity, see *City of God* XXII, 24.

UNDERSTANDING ENJOYMENT

Understanding the relation between enjoyment, on the one hand, and desire and its satisfaction, on the other, is crucial to understanding Augustine; so let me halt our exposition for a moment and engage in some systematic reflection on the topic. In speaking of enjoyment, we are touching on a dimension of our lives difficult to describe; the language available serves the purpose poorly. But let me do my best.

We do things and things are done to us. Some of what we do and undergo, we experience. And these experienced doings and undergoings are, as it were, valorized—the best word I can find. I mean that some of them we find enjoyable; we like them. Some we find not enjoyable; we do not like them. And some we find neither one nor the other; they are neutral, neither here nor there. Almost all of Brahms's chamber music I very much enjoy listening to, provided, of course, that it is well performed; to almost none of Wagner's music do I enjoy listening. I recognize certain excellences in some of it. But I do not like to listen to it; it makes me feel uneasy.

Among the things we like and dislike are feelings and sensations. But it would be a serious mistake to identify enjoyment with the having of pleasurable sensations and disliking with the having of painful sensations. For one thing, there are many more things we like and dislike, enjoy and disenjoy, than feelings and sensations. I enjoy working in the garden; but working in the garden is not a feeling or sensation, nor is woodworking, which I also enjoy. And though most of us dislike most pain, some people apparently like some pains. I do not mean that they are glad to be having the pain because they recognize that it cannot be separated from attaining something enjoyable. They find the pain itself an enjoyable experience. Or actually—generalizing from my own case— I would guess that this is true for most of us. When there is something mildly wrong with one of my fingers, I sometimes rather enjoy the slight pain that results from pressing on the sore spot; it is rather like enjoying now and then the taste of mildly bitter food—a salad of young dandelion greens, perhaps. I doubt that I am peculiar in this regard. And as to pleasurable feelings: the jaded sensualist finds himself no longer liking the pleasurable feelings and sensations he once so much relished.

These were comments on the nature of enjoyment. Let us move on to some reflections on the relation of enjoyment to the fulfillment of desire.

Enjoyment, I have said, consists in liking some experienced undertaking or undergoing. Desire is different. Desire is a mode of our investment in reality. More specifically, desire is a mode of our investment in the occurrence of some event or state of affairs, be it the continued occurrence of a presently occurring event or state of affairs or the occurrence of an event or state of affairs not now occurring. The object of one's desire is always that something happen. I desire that the semester be over, that clouds not obscure the predicted display of aurora borealis, that the Dutch win the World Cup, that the weather during our visit to Copenhagen be pleasant, and so forth.

Now for the relation between desire and enjoyment. Prominent among what we like and enjoy is the fulfilling of our desires. I do not mean that we like and enjoy the *occurrences* that we desire—the Dutch winning the World Cup, and so forth. We may also enjoy those. But I mean that we enjoy this other thing: the *fulfilling* of the *desire* for that occurrence. The Dutch winning the World Cup is one thing; the fulfilling of my desire that the Dutch win the World Cup is another thing. If what one desired was some experience of one's own, then both the desired experience and the experience of that desire being fulfilled are candidates for enjoyment. Were the conative, desiring, dimension of one's self somehow removed or were none of one's desires ever (so far as one knew) fulfilled, then one's enjoyment would be radically diminished in scope. Though it would not be eliminated, there would be much less of it.

We do not always enjoy a desire's being fulfilled. Sometimes the fulfilling proves bitter in the taste; the occurrence desired proves so repulsive—a "Dead Sea apple," as Sidgwick calls it, "mere dust and ashes in the eating"[11]—that we do not even enjoy the fulfilling of the desire for it. And sometimes the fulfilling of one's desire does not enter one's cognizance, either at the time or ever; one never learns that one's endeavor has succeeded. So of course its fulfillment brings no enjoyment.

We could drop our discussion concerning the relation between enjoyment and the fulfilling of desire at this point and conclude this interlude were it not for complications introduced by belief. Sometimes one believes that one's desire has been fulfilled when it has not been; perhaps some mix-up in the admissions office at Yale results in some high school senior in Wyoming believing that she has been admitted to Yale when she has not. The falsehood of her belief makes no difference to her enjoyment, so long as she remains in ignorance. Though her desire for admission has not been fulfilled, she believes it has, and that is enough to give her joy. Conversely, if she has been admitted but through some mix-up is led to believe that she has not, that is enough to make her sad.

Note that when the student is in Wyoming, experiencing her admission is not a possibility for her; nor, consequently, is experiencing the

<hr>

[11] Henry Sidgwick, *Methods of Ethics*, 6th ed. (London: Macmillan, 1901), p. 110.

fulfilling of her desire. That too does not prevent her joy. On the other hand, a person may experience the occurrence he desired, and hence experience the fulfilling of his desire, while nonetheless experiencing no joy—if he misinterprets his experience in such a way that he believes his desire has not been fulfilled.

In short, it appears to be both necessary and sufficient for the kind of enjoyment we are discussing to *believe* that one's desire has been fulfilled. If one does not believe that it has been fulfilled, then whether or not it has in fact been fulfilled, there is no joy—not even if one has experienced its fulfillment (failing to recognize it as such). And conversely, if one does believe it has been fulfilled, then one has joy whether or not it has actually been fulfilled and whether or not one has experienced its fulfillment.

So consider the case in which one believes that one's desire has been fulfilled when it has not been. What is it that one enjoys in such a case? The fulfillment of one's desire? There is no such fulfillment. The experience of the fulfillment of one's desire? There is no such experience. And consider the counterpart case in which one believes that one's desire has not been fulfilled when it has been. What is it that one dislikes in such a case? That one's desire has not been fulfilled? But it has been.

Recall the student who falsely believes she has been admitted to Yale; and now imagine that she learns the sad truth. How would she, in retrospect, describe her former state? She would say that what made her joyful was believing that she had been admitted. Or if she were speaking with a philosopher's precision, she would say that what made her joyful was believing that her *desire* to be admitted had been fulfilled; believing that one has been admitted to Yale is not, all by itself and as such, something that one either enjoys or disenjoys. What she had then, and now no longer has, was the joyful experience of believing that her desire for admission had been gratified. On account of how our believings are tied up with our desirings, among the things we dislike are certain believings and disbelievings.

I suggest that the core component of that particular kind of enjoyment that desire adds to our lives is the enjoyable experience of believing that one's desire is, was, or will be fulfilled. In some cases there will be another component of one's enjoyment, in addition to this core component; namely, the enjoyable experience of the desire being fulfilled.

In what follows I will not always highlight the rather complex structure of this analysis. When one's desire is fulfilled and one believes that it is, I shall speak with the vulgar and say that one is enjoying the fulfilling of one's desire (for those cases in which enjoyment is in fact the quality of one's experience).

A point made earlier in our discussion of Augustine, and which my analysis assumes, is worth stating in terms of this analysis: the enjoyable experience of the fulfilling of one's desire, and the enjoyable experience of believing that one's desire is, was, or will be fulfilled, are just two species of enjoyment among many. For one thing, one can enjoyably experience something for which one had no desire whatsoever: suddenly and unexpectedly the clouds part and I am gripped by the light of the sun on the trees with the dark sky behind. And second, when we experience joyfully a desire's being fulfilled, often we enjoy the occurrence that fulfills the desire, the occurrence that was the object of the desire. These latter two sorts of enjoyments are the pleasures that in his analysis of the aesthetic Kant calls "disinterested."

The distinction I have been emphasizing, between joyfully experiencing what one desired (if one did desire it) and joyfully experiencing the fulfilling of one's desire, enables us to understand some otherwise puzzling cases. Usually, people who voluntarily engage in athletics enjoy doing so. But certain extreme athletic performances—climbing Mouth Everest, swimming the English Channel, running the Boston Marathon in winning time, doing the mountain climbs in the Tour de France—give great satisfaction to the athlete even though he finds what he is doing extremely unpleasant, even painful. When I speak of the satisfaction the athlete feels, I do not have in mind his savoring of the accomplishment once it is over, though such savoring is indeed enjoyable. I have in mind the satisfaction he feels at the time. The climber finds climbing Mount Everest a deeply satisfying undertaking *while* he is doing it, even though the experience itself is excruciatingly painful.[12] The way to understand this, I suggest, is that even though the activities he is performing in fulfillment of his desire to get to the summit are not enjoyable, nonetheless he is getting great enjoyment from the fulfilling of his desire. All of us have been in similar situations without the extremity: feeling satisfaction in accomplishing something that was unpleasant. We enjoyed accomplishing the unenjoyable task.

What Is Love in Augustine?

We now go back to Augustine. Slide one's own virtue out of its place in the Stoic scheme, slide God into the vacated spot; think of everything that is of worth other than God as enjoyment-worthy rather than desire-

---

[12] In his discussion of such cases in *Finite and Infinite Goods*, Robert Adams appears to hold that it is only the subsequent savoring of such experiences that we find enjoyable. See p. 96.

worthy; and keep all the rest the same. This appears to be Augustine's alternative form of eudaimonism.

In fact it is not, as will be evident when we have all the evidence before us. What will emerge is that, rather than espousing an alternative version of eudaimonism, Augustine broke with eudaimonism. To get to the point of seeing how and why the break took place, I must say a word about the role of love in Augustine's thought and how he understood it. The topic could be, and has been, explored at length.[13] I shall say no more than is necessary for our purposes.

I know of no passage in Augustine in which he explains what he has in mind by love. But clearly the Platonic and neo-Platonic doctrine of love as *eros* is the essential context. *Eros* is attraction: being in the grip of something, being drawn to it, attracted to it: persons, animals and plants, landscapes, institutions and groups, projects, ideals, God, whatever. We love persons and things for something about them. Sometimes it is difficult, even impossible, to put into words what that is: an indescribable something draws one. But whether describable or not, it is for some features of mind, of character, of body, of commitment, of achievement, that we love the person. Something about her makes her love-worthy in one's eyes, something about the tree makes it love-worthy, something about the institution.[14]

I think there can be no doubt that Augustine also thinks of love in another way, however, never explicitly distinguished by him from love as attraction. Love can take the form of attachment. A bonding process has taken place and I now find myself attached to a child, a house, a cat, a photograph. If I can manage to view the situation objectively I might concede that were I just going for excellence, I would not fasten onto this child, this house, this cat, this photograph. But it was not the recognized excellence of the thing that caused my attachment. In one way or another I became bonded with it. I may recognize that your cat is better, *qua* cat, than mine. No matter; mine is the one I am attached to.

If the thing to which one is attached is susceptible to variations in well-being, love as attachment is invariably accompanied, so far as I can see, by love as benevolence. One seeks to preserve or enhance the well-being of the child, the cat, whatever. On the other hand, love as benevolence can occur in the absence of both the love of attachment and the love of

---

[13] See, especially, Hannah Arendt, *Love and Saint Augustine* (Chicago: University of Chicago Press, 1996); John Burnaby, *Amos Dei: A Study in the Religion of St. Augustine*, 3rd ed. (London, 1960); and Oliver O'Donovan, *The Problem of Self-Love in Augustine* (New Haven: Yale University Press, 1980).

[14] Nygren interprets Platonic *eros* as self-love. When expounding Nygren in chapter 4, I did not call attention to the fact that that interpretation, on my view, is a serious mistake. When I am gripped by some piece of music, it is the music that I love, not myself.

attraction. I may seek the well-being of someone to whom I am neither attached nor attracted. I may do so out of duty.

Love of all three sorts, attraction, attachment, and benevolence, is manifested in desires with respect to the thing loved. Love is not to be identified with desire, however, certainly not the love of attraction and attachment. For one thing, love is manifested not only in desires but in admiration, in praise, in reveling in the presence of the person or thing loved, and so forth. And second, love typically gives rise to desires that come and go while the love abides. The desires I now have with respect to my wife, on account of my love for her, are considerably different from those I had thirty years ago, and different when she is here at home than when she is gone.

Diminutions in the worth of something to which one is attached need not weaken one's attachment; they may, in fact, intensify it. Typically, they will cause grief, however, as will death or destruction of the thing loved. Love as attraction is different. If the qualities that drew one to the object disappear or are impaired and not replaced by other qualities that one finds equally attractive, one's attraction may weaken to the point of disappearing. The emotion one then feels is not so much grief as disappointment or regret; so too one feels disappointment when the object is destroyed or taken away.

Our loves of attraction and attachment account for some of our deepest joys and deepest sorrows. That feature of the person or thing that grounded one's attraction changes, so that one finds it no longer lovable: the beloved dog now limps, the beloved rose is blighted, the beloved person's wit has slowly changed to cruelty, the beloved friend has fallen ill and died. And even when the thing has not changed, remaining as lovable as ever, the desires that manifest one's attraction or attachment may be frustrated. Either way, love in this world of ours yields grief and disappointment. If we loved less or loved differently, we would be less upset, much less.

Depending on the passage, Augustine might have in mind any one of the three forms of love I have distinguished: love as attraction, love as attachment, love as benevolence. When he speaks of our love of God, it is principally love as attraction that he is thinking of, though love as attachment is by no means out of the picture. Love of God as benevolence is impossible on Augustine's view; God's well-being cannot be enhanced by us. God necessarily flourishes to the maximal degree. When Augustine speaks of his love for his boyhood friend, love as attachment is dominant, with benevolence as its accompaniment and attraction almost certainly in the picture.

Given this ambiguity, how shall we proceed? It would be boring and frustrating to try to determine, in each case, what precisely Augustine had in mind by love. And it would be pointless, because usually he would regard what he says as true for both attraction and attachment, and sometimes for benevolence as well.

To be human is to love, on Augustine's view. We are cast into love. We are born and destined to love. It is our nature to love. We can choose what to love; we cannot choose whether to love. It is an anthropology close to the Platonists and the neo-Platonists, very different from that of the Stoics. The emphasis of the Stoics was on the intellectual side of the self; Augustine's emphasis was on the affective side of the self.

This different anthropology is connected with a different theology. The Stoic god, cosmic Reason, was something to align oneself with; Augustine's God was someone to love. The different anthropology is also connected with a different analysis of our fundamental human ailment. What ails us, at bottom, is not false judgments of worth but misplaced loves. Our loves must be reoriented. If tranquility is what we are after, we must so love that our loves will not be disappointed.

The Stoic ideal was the sage. The Augustinian ideal was the lover of God. The sage finds joy in the success of his endeavor to become virtuous; the lover finds joy in the presence of that to which he is attracted or the well-being of that to which he is attached.[15]

But while the differences are real and large, we must not lose sight of the similarity. In both Augustine and the Stoics, tranquility is of looming importance. They offer different analyses of the roots of our restlessness. But they agree that happiness requires tranquility, equanimity, peace of mind, absence of negative emotions.[16]

IS LOVE OF THE IMMUTABLE NECESSARY AND SUFFICIENT FOR TRANQUILITY?

Augustine's claim that love of God and only love of God is disappointment-proof is dubious. Granted that if God is immutable, one's love for God will not be disappointed by changes in the object of one's love; nonetheless, the desires in which one's love gets expressed may certainly be frustrated. Augustine would respond that, in such a case, one's love and desires are malformed; one should not love God in that way. This is true. But the point is this: the fact that God is immutably perfect does not guarantee that one's love is perfect and immutable. It is a point Augustine himself began to emphasize. And not only may one's imper-

---

[15] *Confessions* X, 21–22.

[16] Cf. Wetzel, *Augustine and the Limits of Virtue*, p. 124: "the ideal of invulnerability in ethics remains the lodestone of Augustine's philosophical interests."

fect love of God give rise to malformed desires; the love itself may cool or become plagued by doubts, so that the joy once experienced in love of God is no longer there.

Not only is our love imperfect. In a passage quoted earlier, Augustine says that God alone "is the place of peace that cannot be disturbed; and he will not withhold himself from your love unless you withhold your love from him. . . . [So] stand with him and you shall not fall; rest in him and peace shall be yours" (*Confessions* IV, 11–12). It is the testimony of Israel's psalmist and of mystics through the ages that in the dark night of the soul, God does withhold himself. Of course, Augustine did not believe that God would *ultimately* withhold himself. But one's death may occur before the clouds part.

Objections arise from the opposite end as well. Yes, the sun and the mountains change; but they change so imperceptibly that those who worship them do not find their love disappointed on account of perceived changes in the thing worshipped. The issues relevant to our purposes lie elsewhere, however; so let me not press these considerations further.

MUTABLE HUMAN BEINGS ARE ALSO LOVE-WORTHY

I have reported Augustine's steady insistence that love of God and only love of God is grief-proof and disappointment-proof. I have not interpreted him as saying that God alone is love-worthy. Given his affirmation that happiness is what we all ultimately desire, and given his conviction that tranquility is a condition of happiness, one would expect him to say exactly that; probably most readers of my discussion up to this point have inferred that he did say that. And there are passages in which he does say that, or certainly appears to. This one, for example, part of which I quoted earlier: "If the things of this world delight you, praise God for them but turn your love away from them and give it to their Maker, so that in the things that please you, you may not displease him" (*Confessions* IV, 12). But when we put everything together, we have to conclude that that was not Augustine's view. What he says instead is that though "everyone wants to be happy," nonetheless "we must [not] arm ourselves against compassion. There are times when we must welcome sorrow on behalf of others" (*Confessions* III, 2).[17]

---

[17] "[A]lthough a man who is sorry for the sufferings of others deserves praise for his charity, nevertheless, if his pity is genuine, he would prefer that there should be no cause for his sorrow. . . . Sorrow may therefore be commendable but never desirable" (*Confessions* III, 2).

A remarkable statement—remarkable for us, that is. In the context of the philosophy of antiquity, it would have seemed not just remarkable but astonishing to the point of madness. Given that everybody's ultimate goal is his or her *eudaimonia*, what could possibly lead Augustine to say that there are times when we must welcome sorrow? We have heard him saying, in agreement with the eudaimonists, that happiness requires free-dom from such emotional disturbances as grief, fear, and worry. So what sense does it make for him to say that there are times when we must welcome sorrow?

That the sentence I quoted cannot be dismissed as a slip of the pen on Augustine's part is clear from the fact that the same thought is expressed rather more elaborately in Book X of the *Confessions*. Let me quote:

> Let all who are truly my brothers love in me what they know from your teaching to be worthy of their love, and let them sorrow to find in me what they know from your teaching to be occasion for re-morse. . . . [M]y true brothers are those who rejoice for me in their hearts when they find good in me and grieve for me when they find sin. They are my true brothers because whether they see good in me or evil, they love me still. To such as these I shall reveal what I am. Let them breathe a sigh of joy for what is good in me and a sigh of grief for what is bad. The good I do is done by you and by your grace: the evil is my fault; it is the punishment you send me. Let my brothers draw their breath in joy for the one and sigh with grief for the other. Let hymns of thanksgiving and cries of sorrow rise to-gether from their hearts. (*Confessions* X, 4)

Compassionate joy over the moral and religious excellence of one's fellow human beings and compassionate grief over their turpitude: that is what Augustine is urging. My true brothers (and sisters), he says, will love me even when they find something bad or evil in me and, given their love, are disturbed by that.

Clearly, Augustine means to praise such love, not just describe it. So there is something determining his judgments about the love-worthy other than just the thesis that the good that cannot disappoint us is love-worthy, some other consideration leading him to concede that something may be love-worthy even though our love for it yields grief. What might that other consideration be? What drove Augustine, in spite of his evident longing for tranquility, to speak up on behalf of emotional disturbance?

Probably, he was influenced by some passages from St. Paul, for exam-ple, Romans 12:15: "Rejoice with those who rejoice, and weep with those who weep." And I Corinthians 12:26: "If one member [of the church] suffers, all suffer together with it; if one member is honored, all rejoice together with it." But in Book I of *On Christian Doctrine*, it becomes clear that something deeper is going on than the influence of scattered biblical passages. Augustine found himself confronted with Christ's injunction "to love the Lord your God with all your heart and soul and mind and to love your neighbor as yourself" (*On Christian Doctrine* I, 26, sec. 27; quoting Matthew 22: 37–40). It was Christ's injunction to love not only God but one's neighbor as oneself that roiled the waters of Augustine's eudaimonism.

In the Stoic universe, the only thing worthy of one's love is oneself—or more precisely, one's own virtue. That is not how the Stoics stated their view; they did not think in terms of love. But armed with the Augustinian category of love, that is surely the right way to describe it.[18] From Christ, however, we have this astonishing teaching: as we love ourselves, so also we are to love our neighbors. Had Christ said only that each is to love himself, that already would have forced Augustine to hold that though the love of God alone is invulnerable to disappointment on account of change in the thing loved, nonetheless we are to love ourselves as well, thus becoming vulnerable. But Christ said this much more radical thing: love your neighbor along with loving yourself—love both. Loving oneself in the right way requires—so Augustine assumed—desiring one's moral and religious flourishing, the consequences of such desire being that one rejoices in success therein and grieves over failure therein. Augustine hears Christ saying that just as *my own* moral and religious condition is disturbance-worthy for me, so also *my neighbor's* moral and religious condition is to be disturbance-worthy for me.

Paul and Jesus are paradigms for us in emotional disturbance. The "citizens of the City of God" behold Paul

> rejoicing with those who rejoice and weeping with those who weep, troubled by fighting without and fears within, desiring to depart and be with Christ. They behold him longing to see the Romans. . . . They behold him jealous for the Corinthians. . . . They behold him suffering great heaviness and continual sorrow in his heart for the

---

[18] "At all events the mind must be withdrawn from all externals into itself. Let it trust in itself, rejoice in itself, esteem its own possessions, retreat as much as it can from things not its own, devote itself to itself, feel no damage." Seneca, *On Peace of Mind*, in Inwood and Gerson, *Hellenistic Philosophy*, p. 243. Cf. John M. Rist, "The Stoic Concept of Detachment," in John M. Rist, ed., *The Stoics* (Berkeley: University of California Press, 1978), pp. 264–65: "It is clearly incumbent on each man to be emotionally committed to one human being, or rather one human phenomenon alone, namely, one's own moral character and moral dignity. . . . Each man has one and only one object of value to be cherished, namely, his own higher self. . . . There is only one canon by which the wise man is able to judge his own behavior: Is it conducive to my own virtue, or does it risk compromising the moral self which it is my unique prerogative to preserve" (p. 265).

Israelites. . . . They behold him as he declares not only his pain, but also his mourning for certain persons who had sinned already, and not repented. (*City of God* XIV, 9; pp. 598–99)[19]

And they behold Jesus displaying

> emotions in circumstances where He judged that they ought to be displayed. For human emotion was not feigned in him. . . . He was grieved and angry at the Jews' hardness of heart. . . . He even wept when He was about to raise Lazarus. . . . [A]s his passion drew nigh, His soul was grieved. Truly, He accepted these emotions into His human mind for the sake of His own assured purpose, and when He so willed. (ibid., p. 599)

In short, "if *apatheia* is . . . defined as a condition such that the mind cannot be touched by any emotion whatsoever, who would not judge such insensitivity to be the worst of all vices?" If it is "a condition such that there is no fear to terrify and no pain to torment, then it is a condition to be avoided in this life if we wish to live rightly, that is, according to God" (ibid., p. 600). Christians, citizens of the Holy City of God, live "according to God during the pilgrimage of this present life. Such citizens feel fear and desire, pain and gladness, but in a manner consistent with the Holy Scriptures and wholesome doctrine, and because their love is righteous, all these emotions are righteous in them" (ibid., p. 597). A "righteous life will exhibit all these emotions righteously, whereas a perverse life exhibits them perversely" (ibid., p. 601).[20]

LOVE OF SELF AND NEIGHBOR EXPANDS BEYOND LOVE OF SOULS

It will not have missed the reader's notice that the neighbor-love Augustine urges in the passages quoted from the *Confessions*—and they are typical of his writing in the 390s—is of a decidedly pinched scope, as is the scope of the compassion that he urges. One's love for the neighbor is to take the form of desire and longing for the moral and religious excellence of his or her soul. In the passage quoted from Book X of the *Confessions*, the joy over himself that Augustine praises in his "true brothers" is joy over the good that he does, and the grief over himself that he praises in them is grief over the evil that he does. Let my true

---

[19] I am using the translation by R. W. Dyson in Augustine, *The City of God against the Pagans* (Cambridge: Cambridge University Press, 1998).

[20] Cf. Wetzel, *Augustine and the Limits of Virtue*, p. 104: "Augustine's sharpest break from the Stoic ideal of *apatheia* comes with his recognition that virtue and grief are compatible. Often, in fact, grief is the necessary and appropriate affective form of virtue."

brothers "grieve for me when they find sin" in me, he says, let them "sigh with grief" when they find evil.

Why does Augustine hold that love for the other should be confined to desires for the religious and moral flourishing of his or her soul? His answer is most vividly and provocatively expressed in the following passage from *Of True Religion*:

> Only he is overcome who has what he loves snatched from him by his adversary. He who loves only what cannot be snatched from him is indubitably unconquerable. . . . He cannot lose his neighbour whom he loves as himself, for he does not love even in himself the things that appear to the eyes or to any other bodily sense. So he has inward fellowship with him whom he loves as himself. . . .
>
> If a man were to love another not as himself but as a beast of burden, or as the baths, or as a gaudy or garrulous bird, that is for some temporal pleasure or advantage he hoped to derive, he must serve not a man but, what is much worse, a foul and detestable vice, in that he does not love the man as a man ought to be loved. . . .
>
> Man is not to be loved by man even as brothers after the flesh are loved, or sons, or wives, or kinsfolk, or relatives, or fellow citizens. For such love is temporal. We should have no such connections as are contingent upon birth and death, if our nature had remained in obedience to the commandments of God and in the likeness of his image. . . . Accordingly, the Truth himself calls us back to our original and perfect state, bids us resist carnal custom and teaches that no one is fit for the kingdom of God unless he hates these carnal relationships. Let no one think that is inhuman. It is more inhuman to love a man because he is your son and not because he is a man, that is, not to love that in him which belongs to God, but to love that which belongs to yourself. . . .
>
> If we are ablaze with love for eternity we shall hate temporal relationships. Let a man love his neighbour as himself. No one is his own father or son or kinsman or anything of the kind, but is simply a man. Whoever loves another as himself ought to love that in him which is his real self. Our real selves are not bodies. . . . Whoever, then, loves in his neighbour anything but his real self does not love him as himself. (XLVI, sec. 86–XLVII, sec. 90).[21]

It is a curious argument. We are to love the souls of our neighbors because their souls are what is eternal in them. Yet our love for their immor-

---

[21] In his *Retractions*, Augustine discusses this passage and says that he should not have said "hate temporal relationships." Had our forebears done this, we, their descendents, would never have been born and God's company of the elect would not have been filled up. I find it surprising that Augustine makes no corrections in the doctrine of love that he expounds in the passage.

tal souls is to take the form of investing ourselves in the highly mutable religious and moral condition of their souls.

Now leap to Augustine's last work, *City of God*. We do not "so much ask whether a pious soul is angry," Augustine now says,

> as why he is angry; not whether he is sad, but whence comes his sadness; not whether he is afraid, but what he fears. For I do not think that any right-minded person would condemn anger directed at a sinner in order to correct him; or sadness on behalf of one who is afflicted, in order to comfort him; or fear for one in peril, lest he perish. The Stoics, indeed, are wont to reproach even compassion. But . . . what is compassion but a kind of fellow feeling in our hearts for the misery of another which compels us to help him if we can? This impulse is the servant of right reason when compassion is displayed in such a way as to preserve righteousness, as when alms are distributed to the needy or forgiveness extended to the penitent. (IX, 5; p. 365)

Coming from reading *Of True Religion*, one is not surprised to find Augustine speaking well of anger "directed at a sinner"; one is surprised, however, to find him praising sadness "on behalf of one who is afflicted" and fear "for one in peril." So too, one is not surprised to find him saying in another place in *City of God* that those who love God will "feel pain for their [own] sins and gladness in their [own] good works" and will have the same feelings "on behalf of those whom they desire to see redeemed and fear to see perish" (*City of God* XIV, 9; pp. 597–98). Nor is one surprised to find him saying that a person "will take care to ensure that his neighbor also loves God" (*City of God* XIX, 14; p. 941). But one is surprised to find him saying, with no hint of disapproval, that we are "anxious lest [our friends] be afflicted by famine, war, pestilence, or captivity, fearing that in slavery they may suffer evils beyond what we can conceive" (*City of God* XIX, 8, p. 929).

Clearly, Augustine was no longer of the view that we are to love only the souls of our neighbors and be concerned only for the religious and moral well-being of their souls. That has to be the import of these passages. The point is made even more emphatically in the following passage:

> The more friends we have, and the more places we have them in, the further and more widely do we fear that some evil may befall them out of all the mass of the evils of this world. . . . And when such things do happen (and the more numerous our friends the more often they happen) and the fact is brought to our knowledge, who, save one who has experienced the same thing, can understand the burning sorrow which then afflicts our hearts? Indeed, we would rather hear that our friends were dead; although this also we could

not hear without pain: for if their life delighted us with the solace of friendship, how could it be that their death should not bring us grief? Anyone who forbids such grief must forbid, if he can, all friendly conversation: he must prohibit or extinguish affection; he must with ruthless disregard sever the ties of all human companionship, or else stipulate that such companionship must merely be made use of, without giving rise to any delight of soul. But if this can in no way be done, how can the death of one whose life has been sweet to us not bring us bitterness? For this is why the grief of a heart which is not inhuman is like a kind of wound or ulcer, healed by the application to it of our loving words of consolation. And though healing takes place all the more quickly and easily when the soul is well conditioned, we must not suppose that there is nothing at all to heal in such a case (*City of God* XIX, 8; pp. 929–30).

The rhetorical mode of the passage, for the most part, is purely descriptive: we do in fact love friends for their companionship, we do in fact care for their physical welfare, we do in fact suffer the grief that all too typically ensues upon such love and care. But what is striking to anyone who comes to this passage from reading *Of True Religion* is that Augustine expresses no disapproval of these facts.

There has been a sea-change in his thinking. The break with Platonism and Stoicism is now complete: virtue is not sufficient for happiness. That which is disturbance-worthy for me is not just the moral and religious condition of my own soul; neither is it the moral and religious condition of your soul along with mine and everybody's else as well. Famine, war, pestilence, captivity, the rupture of friendship—all these and more are worthy of getting upset over.[22]

Why? Why are we no longer enjoined to love our neighbor for her soul alone, and no longer enjoined to confine our desires to desires for the religious and moral well-being of her soul? And why, correspondingly, has the scope of laudable emotional disturbance been so drastically enlarged? To the best of my knowledge, Augustine never explicitly says. In the passage last quoted he drops a hint, however, as he does in other passages in *City of God*. In his early work, *Of True Religion*, he had rather defensively said, about his doctrine that we should love only the souls of our fellows, "Let no one think that is inhuman. It is more inhuman to love a man because he is your son." Now notice the phrase "a heart which is not inhuman" in the passage just quoted from *City of God*. And notice

---

[22] In my interpretation of Augustine on this point I am disagreeing with Wetzel, who interprets Augustine as saying, "When the Christian saint grieves, it is not for the loss of material well-being, but for personal failures of vision and love" (*Augustine and the Limits of Virtue*, p. 109).

the phrase "loss of their humanity" in the following passage from *City of God*: "Some of [the Stoics], with a vanity as monstrous as it is rare, are so entranced by their own self-restraint that they are not stirred or excited or swayed or influenced by any emotions at all. But these rather suffer an entire loss of their humanity than achieve a true tranquility. For a thing is not right merely because it is harsh, nor is stolidity the same thing as health" (*City of God* XIV, 9; p. 602).

I suggest that by the time he wrote *City of God*, Augustine had come to the view that the sort of love that he described as "not inhuman" in *Of True Religion* was in fact inhuman. That sounds pretty thin.[23] But maybe there is more here than meets the eye. After remarking, in another passage in *City of God*, that negative emotions belong to this life and not to the life to come, including those emotions that "are righteous and according to God," and after adding that because of our present "infirmity" we often find ourselves yielding to our emotions "even against our will" and breaking out into tears "when we do not wish to do so," Augustine goes on to say that, nonetheless, "if we felt no such emotions at all while subject to the infirmity of this life, we should then certainly not be living righteously. For the apostle condemned and denounced certain persons who, he said, were 'without natural affection.' The holy psalm also blames those of whom it says, 'I looked for some to take pity, but there was none.' Indeed, if, while in this place of misery, we were to be entirely free from pain, this, as one of this world's scholars [Cicero] has understood and said, 'would not be attained without a great price, savagery of mind, and stupor of body' " (*City of God* XIV, 9; pp. 599–600). "The grief of a heart which is not inhuman is like a kind of wound or ulcer, healed by the application to it of our loving words of consolation" (*City of God* XIX, 8; p. 930).

Augustine's ever deeper immersion in Scripture, from the time of his conversion onward, has brought him to the conclusion that our tendency to worry over the physical and mental well-being of family and friends, to weep at funerals for the loss of companionship, and the like is not to be ascribed to our fallenness but to our created human nature. God made us thus. To try to undo this dimension of ourselves is, "with ruthless disregard," to try to undo the work of the Creator.

---

[23] It sounds less thin when read in conjunction with the following story that Elie Wiesel told about himself, as reported by Martha Nussbaum in *The Therapy of Desire* (p. 403): "Wiesel was a child in one of the Nazi death camps. On the day the Allied forces arrived, the first member of the liberating army he saw was a very large black officer. Walking into the camp and seeing what was there to be seen, this man began to curse, shouting at the top of his voice. As the child Wiesel watched, he went on shouting and cursing for a very long time. And the child Wiesel thought, watching him, now humanity has come back. Now, with that anger, humanity has come back."

"[W]hose eloquence is sufficient, no matter how ready its flow, to depict all the miseries of this life?" asks Augustine. "Is there any pain, the contrary of pleasure, any disquiet, the contrary of rest, that cannot befall [even] a wise man's body? Certainly the amputation or decay of his limbs undermines a man's soundness; deformity ruins his beauty, sickness destroys his health, weakness his strength, lassitude his vigour, torpor or lethargy his activity." Similar things can be said about what befalls a person's mind. When we survey this destruction of body and mind, "when we contemplate or see people in this condition, and when we consider their plight fully, we can hardly refrain from weeping; perhaps we cannot do so at all" (*City of God* XIX, 4; pp. 919–20). And we should not try. We are so created as to grieve over human misery, over the misery of ourselves, our family, our friends, even over the misery of the "neighbor."

In the case that he makes for the propriety of emotional disturbance in life, Augustine nowhere (that I know of) offers the argument that we ought to imitate the passion of God in our own lives: if God is angry with the nations for the injustices they perpetrate, is it not right for us to be angry over those same injustices? If God listened to the cries of the enslaved Israelites, is it not right for us to listen to the cries of the enslaved and the abused? No doubt the reason Augustine did not offer this argument was that he did not believe there is disturbance in God's life. He knew that the biblical writers used the *language* of disturbance when speaking of God; but it was his view that with that language they were doing something other than ascribing negative affect to God.

Anticipation Replaces Ascent

I may have given the impression that Augustine discarded tranquility as a desideratum, that he began there but moved away. Not so; he never gave up his conviction that tranquility is a condition of happiness, nor his conviction that we all yearn for happiness. What happened, rather, is that over the course of his career his thought acquired an ever more prominent eschatological cast. The spatial metaphors change. Instead of looking up, we look ahead. Instead of ascending to the eternal, we journey to a new age. The eschatology was there at the beginning, but nowhere near as prominent as it became in *City of God*.

Our human existence comes in two stages: this present life and the life to come. In this present life, given all its miseries, we are not, in Stoic fashion, to seek tranquility but unflinchingly to acknowledge "the wretchedness of [our] condition" (*City of God* XIX, 6; p. 928), "the miserable condition of this life" (*City of God* XIX, 8; 929). We are to grieve and to bind ourselves together in a solidarity of grieving—and yes, of rejoicing and thanksgiving.[24] Even when it comes to vice we must acknowledge that, "no matter how much we may wish" to be free, "we cannot manage to achieve this in our present life" (*City of God* XIX, 4; p. 921). It was "stupid pride" of the Stoics to believe "that the Final Good is to be found in this life, and that they can achieve happiness by their own efforts" (*City of God* XIX, 4; p. 922).[25] In this present life, love trumps tranquility.

But this present life, with its "great mass of evils" (ibid., p. 930), is not the whole of our existence. There is also the life to come. For that life, God holds out the promise of joyful tranquility. The "emotions which we have, even when they are righteous and according to God, belong to this life, and not to the life to come for which we hope." (ibid., p. 599). "[W]hen there is no sin in man," then the condition of *apatheia* will "come to pass" (ibid.). For that day, we long. Peter Brown makes the point eloquently in his masterful biography of Augustine:

> Augustine is a man who has realized that he was doomed to remain incomplete in his present existence, that what he wishes for most ardently would never be more than a hope, postponed to a final resolution of all tensions, far beyond this life. Anyone who thought otherwise, he felt, was either morally obtuse or a doctrinaire. All a man could do was to "yearn" for the absent perfection, to feel its loss intensely, to pine for it. . . . This marks the end of a long-established ideal of perfection: Augustine would never achieve the concentrated tranquility of the supermen that still gaze out at us from some mosaics in Christian churches and from the statues of pagan sages.[26]

Our confident hope for life in the new age and for the happiness that we will there experience introduces a note of happiness into our life in this present age: we are "happy in the hope of the world to come, and in the hope of salvation"; in hope "we have been made happy." But it is no more than a *note* of happiness that hope brings into our present life. It remains true that "human life is compelled to be miserable by all the great evils of this world. . . . We are in the midst of evils, and we must

[24] Augustine's fullest treatment of "right feelings in the lives of righteous men" is in *City of God*, XIV, 9.

[25] Augustine continues in a bitingly caustic vein: "They believe that their wise man—that is, he whom, in their amazing vanity, they describe as such—even if he becomes blind, deaf and dumb; even if he falls victim to every other ill that can be described or imagined; even if he is compelled to put himself to death: that such a man would not shrink from calling such a life, beset with such ills, a happy one! O happy life, that seeks the aid of death to put an end to it!"

[26] Peter Brown, *Augustine of Hippo* (London: Faber & Faber, 1967), p. 156. The above is the theme of chapter 15 of Brown's biography.

endure them with patience until we come to those good things where everything will bestow ineffable delight upon us, and where there will no longer be anything which we must endure" (*City of God* XIX, 4).

Contra Nussbaum's Interpretation

I interpret Augustine's thought as a break with eudaimonism. In *Upheavals of Thought*, Martha Nussbaum interprets his thought instead as an important development within eudaimonism: "a major philosophical achievement and a decisive progress beyond the Platonic accounts; because it situates ascent within humanity and renounces the wish to depart from our human condition" (547). Let me explain where I think Nussbaum's account misinterprets the nature and motivation of the moves Augustine has made.

Nussbaum introduces her tracing of Augustine's thought with the remark, "In some manner Christian love has reopened the space within which fear, and anxiety, and grief, and intense delight, and even anger, all have their full force. And correct love promises no departure from these other emotions—if anything, it requires their intensification" (530). I very much agree. My disagreement is over how Augustine got to the point of saying these things.

Nussbaum interprets Augustine as coming to the view that the goal promised by the neo-Platonist ascent of the soul "is not attainable in this life" and that "it is not, in any case, a good or appropriate Christian aim" (535). The reason the goal is not attainable in this life is that a person "must depend for ascent not on her own self-control but on aspects of her personality that she neither governs nor fully understands. And these responsive elements in her personality depend, in turn, for their happy activation, on the mysterious ways of God's call. She cannot count on a stable perfection. Such progress as she does make is not made primarily through her own effort" (537).

The reason the Platonic goal of ascent is not appropriate in this life is that, rather than holding in memory one's prior self and confessing one's sins before God, the Platonist forgets his prior self and its misdeeds. And rather than living in humble dependence on God, the Platonist assumes that by his own efforts at self-control he can attain godlike invulnerability. The assumption is false; we are not in control of our moral and religious condition. A life so lived would be a life of pride. For "what is pride but an appetite for a perverse kind of elevation? ... [It] is a perverse kind of elevation indeed to forsake the foundation upon which the mind should rest, and to become and remain, as it were, one's own foundation" (*City of God* XIV, 13; p. 608).

There can be no doubt that Augustine, for the reasons Nussbaum cites, did regard Platonist ascent and Stoic invulnerability as impossible to achieve on one's own, and wrong for the Christian even to attempt. But notice, in the first place, that Nussbaum says nothing about the role of enjoyment in Augustine's thought. I have argued that one cannot understand Augustine's attitude toward the world if one focuses exclusively on what he says about love. More important, Nussbaum misses Augustine's affirmation of the goodness of what is natural to us. She says, "The deep need of all is for salvation, and appropriate emotions ultimately have that focus" (543). And she holds that "Augustine did not disagree with the Stoics that it is inappropriate to have emotions about earthly events and persons, seen as needed by the self. The other world is the object of . . . longing" (542). In the light of passages we have cited from *City of God*, this interpretation cannot be sustained. It is not only appropriate but morally required that we "have emotions about earthly events and persons."

Nussbaum does recognize that "Augustine's account restores compassion, along with other emotions, to a place of centrality in the earthly life" (551). But she sees Augustinian compassion as grounded in nothing more than awareness of human neediness and incompleteness: "Human beings are to relate to one another as needy and incomplete, and recognizing the need of another should give rise to Christian love" (551). Given her understanding of Augustine's attitude toward the world, she of course sees the neediness in question as entirely moral and spiritual. "Our sense of incompleteness is focused insistently on our sinfulness, and on our remoteness from God. What we see with compassion in our neighbors is this same sinfulness, this same need for God's grace. This means that Augustinian love is committed to denying the importance of the worldly losses and injustices to which my neighbor may attach importance, in order to assert the primacy of the need for God and the potential for grace" (552).

Not only is this a mistaken interpretation of the scope of compassion—admittedly accurate for the early *Of True Religion* but not for the late *City of God*—but it fails to explain why Augustine affirmed the worth of compassion. The ancient eudaimonists knew about human neediness and incompleteness. That did not shake them out of their eudaimonism. It did not lead them to affirm the worth of compassion. A eudaimonist contemporary of Augustine would have had no trouble understanding why, given Augustine's convictions about the impossibility of attaining self-sufficiency and the impropriety of even trying to do so, he would affirm the legitimacy of such emotions as fear, anxiety, regret, and anger; these all pertain to what happens to oneself. What he would not have understood is Augustine's affirmation of the worth of compassion. What could have led Augustine to say that "it is not only for their own sakes that the citizens of the City of God are moved by these feelings. They also feel them *on behalf of* others? (XIV, 9; p. 598; emphasis added). I see nothing in Augustine's thought that would explain his affirmation of compassion other than that he saw this as an implication of obedience to Christ's command to love one's neighbor as one loves oneself.

Nussbaum interprets Augustine as a chastened and humble eudaimonist. I think he has to be interpreted as parting ways with eudaimonism and entering territory untracked by the ancient philosophers. I have more to say about this in the next chapter.

Avoiding Inordinate Love

Augustine regularly calls attention to a certain way of loving one's neighbor that is to be avoided. Though he never settles on a preferred terminology for describing that way, the core idea is that we are to avoid loving our neighbor *inordinately*. One way he puts the point is that we are not to love our neighbor as though rest and happiness were to be found in such love.[27] In describing his inordinate love for his boyhood friend, he uses vivid similes to make the point: "I had loved him as though he would never die" (IV, 6). "I had poured out my soul upon him, like water upon sand, loving a man who was mortal as though he were never to die" (IV, 8).

Augustine's strategy for combatting inordinate love of neighbor was to insist that a person must turn "the whole current of his love both for himself and his neighbor into the channel of the love of God, which suffers no stream to be drawn off from itself by whose diversion its own volume would be diminished" (*On Christian Doctrine* I, 22, sec. 21). Christ teaches that we are to love God with our whole heart, soul, and mind. By that he "means that no part of our life is to be unoccupied, and to afford room, as it were, for the wish to enjoy [for its own sake] some other object, but that whatever else may suggest itself to us as an object worthy of love is to be borne into the same channel in which the whole current of our affections [for God] flows" (ibid.)

And how do we bring our love of neighbor into the channel of our love of God? One formula Augustine uses is that we are to love our neighbor *for the sake of* our love of God. Referring to Christ's command to love one's neighbor as oneself, Augustine asks whether this is an instrumental

---

[27] For example: "if the soul loves them and wishes to be with them and find its rest in them, it is torn by desires that can destroy it. In these things there is no place to rest" (*Confessions* IV, 10).

or a non-instrumental love—in his words, "whether man is to be loved by man for his own sake or for the sake of something else" (*CD* I, 22, sec. 20). His answer is that the neighbor "is to be loved for the sake of something else. For if a thing is to be loved for its own sake, then in the enjoyment of it consists a happy life, the hope of which at least, if not yet the reality, is our comfort in the present time. But a curse is pronounced on him who places his hope in man" (*CD* I, 22, secs. 20–21). It goes without saying that the love for the sake of which one is to love one's fellow human beings is one's love of God.

Augustine's employment of the language of utility here is offensive to us; we have ringing in our ears Kant's dictum about never treating a human being merely as a means. I infer from the following rather defensive remark that Augustine himself recognized that the language has an offensive ring to it: "if you ought not to love even yourself for your own sake, but for Him in whom your love finds its most worthy object, no other man has a right to be angry if you love him too for God's sake" (*CD* I, 22, sec. 21). Augustine sticks to his guns, however; one brings one's love of neighbor into the channel of one's love of God by loving the neighbor for the sake of one's love of God.

That is not the only way one does so. One also loves the neighbor *in* loving God; one's love of neighbor becomes a component within, a constituent of, one's love of God. And what is it to love one's neighbor *in* loving God? Augustine contents himself with giving an analogy: if you and I know next to nothing about each other except that we are both great admirers of some actor, then we love each other *in* loving the actor.

I will refrain from engaging critically the thought behind these vague and offensive locutions of loving the neighbor *in* and *for* one's love of God. Let me simply note that by Augustine's inclusion of love of self and love of neighbor within love of God, love of God proves to be a very different sort of thing from what we were led to think it was when we set out. The love of neighbor that is to be incorporated within our love of God is a love that not only rejoices in the neighbor's joy and virtue but grieves in the neighbor's sorrow and wrongdoing. Love of God in this present age thus incorporates emotional disturbance within itself. Love of God is vulnerable love.

One would have expected Augustine to employ an additional strategy for combatting inordinate love of what is other than God. An important component of the metaphysical and cosmological context of his thought was his conviction that there is in reality a continuum of excellence, with God, the supremely excellent, at the top, and everything else somewhere lower down on the continuum, its place determined by the degree to which it resembles God with respect to unity. Degree of unity determines degree of excellence. This picture is brought into the center of attention most elaborately and deliberately in *Of True Religion.*

Given this picture of reality, one would expect Augustine to combat inordinate love by introducing a doctrine of degrees of love, supplementing that with the doctrine that there can be fittingness and lack of fittingness between a degree of love for something and that thing's place on the continuum of excellence, and then arguing that one's degree of love for something should fit that thing's place on the continuum. There is one passage, in *On Christian Doctrine,* in which Augustine says exactly this. It is a passage that the fine Augustine scholar R. A. Markus puts at the center of his interpretation of Augustine on love.[28] Let me quote it in the translation Markus uses:

> [the righteous man is] the man who values things at their true worth; he has ordered love, which prevents him from loving what is not to be loved, or not loving what is to be loved, from preferring what ought to be loved less from loving equally what ought to be loved either less or more, or from loving either less or more what ought to be loved equally. (*On Christian Doctrine,* chap. 27, sec. 28)

A lucid statement of the view in question, so it would seem. But rather than developing the thought, Augustine immediately goes on to say that "every man is to be loved as a man for God's sake, but God is to be loved for His own sake." And that "all things are to be loved in reference to God." It is these ideas—the idea of loving someone for God's sake and of loving someone in reference to God, or as he usually puts it, loving someone "in God"—that preoccupy Augustine throughout the first chapter of *On Christian Doctrine.*

In short, counter to what you and I would have expected, Augustine scarcely ever appeals to the scale of being in combatting inordinate love. What he almost always appeals to is the doctrine that the non-human things of this world are to be enjoyed rather than loved and that our love of our fellow human beings is to be caught up into the stream of our love of God. These are the lines of interpretation that I have pursued in my interpretation of Augustine.

---

[28] In Markus's essay, "Marius Victorinus and Augustine," in *The Cambridge History of Later Greek and Early Medieval Philosophy* (Cambridge: Cambridge University Press, 1970).

THE INCURSION OF THE MORAL VISION
OF SCRIPTURE INTO LATE ANTIQUITY

SUMMARY OF THE ARGUMENT THUS FAR IN PART II

Let us take stock of where we are. Our project in this part of our discussion, part II, is to locate the goods to which we have rights. We concluded in chapter 6 that these are all goods in one's life or history, states or events that contribute to making one's life and history a *good* life and history. We then observed that in the philosophical literature there are different conceptions of the good life. That led us to ask which of these conceptions, if any, comprises all those goods to which we have rights.

We concluded rather quickly that the conception the modern utilitarian tradition works with, the conception of the good life as the experientially satisfying life, is not satisfactory for our purposes. We then set out to discern whether the conception of the good life as the well-lived life is satisfactory.

This conception of the good life is unfamiliar to most of us today, having been overwhelmed in the modern period by the conception of the good life as experientially satisfying. It was, however, the conception that the ethical theorists of antiquity, all of them eudaimonists, worked with. So we took time to get a grasp of eudaimonism in its most powerfully articulated versions, the Peripatetic and the Stoic versions of antiquity.

Our conclusion was that the conception of the good life as the well-lived life will also not serve our purposes; many of the goods to which we have rights are neither constituents nor conditions of the well-lived life. We noted, in addition, that the rule of application with which eudaimonism works will not allow for the recognition of inherent rights, the rule, namely, that says that each person's decisions on how to act are to be made by reference to whether or not the proposed action or pattern of action contributes to one's living one's own life as well as possible. To treat the other as one does because her worth requires it cannot be subsumed under treating her thus because so doing is required by living one's own life as well as possible. The recognition of rights in general, and of inherent rights in particular, would not have been possible had the agent-orientation of eudaimonism not lost its grip on the thought of the West.

The conclusion, that the grip of eudaimonism had to be broken for a theory of rights to become possible, invited the question, when and how was the grip broken? In the preceding chapter I argued that Augustine broke the grip (along perhaps with others) and that it was especially the influence of Scripture on Augustine that led to the break.

Not all readers will have found the argument as thus far developed, about Augustine's pivotal role in the history of rights, entirely compelling. So before we take the next step into theory, let us reflect a bit more on this episode in our intellectual history. Did it really have the import I have suggested it had? We start with Augustine's break with the eudaimonist's rule of application.

The Incompatibility of Christ's Command with the Agent-Orientation of Eudaimonism

Trained as was everybody in antiquity to think as a eudaimonist, Augustine was confronted after his conversion with the command of Christ to love one's neighbor as oneself. He might have interpreted Christ as informing us that there are significant satisfactions to be found in neighbor-love and that neighbor-love is thus to be included, along with friendship and family relations, among the natural goods or preferables. Alternatively, he might have interpreted Christ as informing us that loving one's neighbor is a virtue to be cultivated. Neighbor-love would then not belong to the "matter" that one tries to shape into a well-lived life for oneself but would be one of the skilled habits for shaping that "matter." A good many thinkers in the Christian tradition have adopted this latter interpretation—Aquinas, for example. Charity is added to the list of cardinal virtues that the pagans composed.[1] I think there can be little

---

[1] I am assuming, in this comment, that Aquinas was a eudaimonist. Those who do not find that obvious but want a defense of the claim should consult Scott MacDonald's essay, "Egoistic Rationalism: Aquinas' Basis for Christian Morality," in Michael D. Beaty, ed., *Christian Theism and the Problems of Philosophy* (Notre Dame: University of Notre Dame Press, 1990). MacDonald points out that Aquinas regarded concern for friends, family, countrymen, etc., as compatible with his eudaimonism; Aquinas's argument on this point is the same as that of the ancient eudaimonists. MacDonald concludes this part of his discussion by saying—speaking now in his own voice—that "there is no clear reason why an egoism of this sort cannot account for the apparent altruistic concerns of Christian morality. Aquinas' egoism is compatible, for instance, with the demand to love one's neighbor and to be concerned about his good" (340). What is striking about this comment is that MacDonald does not speak of the demand to love one's neighbor *as oneself*, but simply of the demand to love one's neighbor. I do not doubt that eudaimonism is compatible with the demand to love one's neighbor. My argument is that it is not compatible with the demand to love one's neighbor *as one loves oneself*.

doubt that Augustine found Christ's love command unsettling for his received way of thinking in a way that neither of these interpretations explains. Augustine interpreted Christ as saying that just as I am an object of my love, so also my neighbor is to be an object of my love.

Let me set Augustine's interpretation to the side for a moment and argue that this is the correct interpretation of Christ's love-command and that it is indeed incompatible with eudaimonism. The story of Christ issuing the command occurs in all three synoptic gospels in substantially the same form: Matthew 22:35ff., Mark 12:28ff., and Luke 10:25ff. A lawyer or scribe came up to Jesus one day and asked him which commandment in the Torah has priority—or as Luke has it, what one must do to inherit eternal life. Jesus' answer, as Mark reports it, is "The first is, 'Hear, O Israel: the Lord our God, the Lord is one; you shall love the Lord your God with all your heart, and with all your soul, and with all your mind, and with all your strength.' The second is, 'You shall love your neighbor as yourself.' There is no other commandment greater than these."

Jesus' reply blends together two passages from the Old Testament, one from Deuteronomy, "Hear, O Israel: The Lord is our God, the Lord alone. You shall love the Lord your God with all your heart, and with all your soul, and with all your might" (6:4–5), the other from Leviticus, "You shall not take vengeance or bear a grudge against any of your people, but you shall love your neighbor as yourself" (19:18). In Luke's narration, Jesus' answer is followed immediately by the lawyer asking, "And who is my neighbor?" to which Jesus responds with the parable of the Good Samaritan.

What is the force of the "as" in the command to love your neighbor as yourself? It can hardly mean love your neighbor *in the same way* that you love yourself. Love of different persons perforce takes different forms. I suggest that it has a double force. In the first place, the command is to be interpreted as an instance of the standard "just as . . . so also" rhetorical structure. You love yourself, right? Okay. Then love your neighbor as well. Just as you love yourself, so also love your neighbor. Add to the love of self, which you already have, your love of neighbor. But Jesus surely also means, place love of neighbor on a par with love of yourself. Weak neighbor-love combined with intense self-love would not qualify as satisfying the command.

In John 13:34 Jesus gives his disciples what he calls "a new commandment": "I give you a new commandment, that you love one another. Just as I have loved you, you also should love one another." Or as it reads in John 15:12, "This is my commandment, that you love one another as I have loved you." In the latter passage, the commandment is prefaced by a reference to Jesus' love of the Father: "As the Father has loved me, so

I have loved you; abide in my love. If you keep my commandments, you will abide in my love" (15:9–10).

The rhetorical structure of the new command is the same *just as . . . so also* structure as that of the former command. What is new is the content given to the structure. There the content was *your love of yourself . . . your love of your neighbor.* Here the content is (Jesus speaking to his twelve disciples), *my love of you . . . your love of each other.* A clear implication of the new command is that Jesus' love of his disciples is to serve as a paradigm for their love of each other. It would be most implausible to assume, in the case of the former commandment, that one's love of oneself is to serve as a paradigm for one's love of one's neighbor. Human self-love is much too defective to serve as paradigm.

The love command, thus understood, is incompatible with eudaimonism. Eudaimonism allows love of the other into one's life, but only if that love passes the test of contributing to one's own life being well-lived. As we have noted several times, that does not imply, and the eudaimonists did not take it as implying, that one is to love the other only if doing so serves as a *means* to the enhancement of one's own eudaimonia. To take it as implying that would be to misunderstand the nature of eudaimonia. Eudaimonia is not some state or condition that serves as one's sole end in itself. All sorts of things are candidates for serving as ends in themselves in one's life, including the well-being of friends and relatives. Eudaimonism is a principle for selecting, from among those things, the ones to adopt as one's ends in themselves. That principle of selection is to select something as an end in itself only if one believes that doing so will make for one's own life being lived well. Enhancement of how one's own life is lived is a condition on the acceptability of goals. Happiness is not an end in itself to be brought about by various means but a condition on the acceptability of candidates for actions on one's part that are ends in themselves.

Suppose Christ had said, "Love your neighbor as your friend," meaning love your neighbor along with your friends—the neighbor being understood as the person you just happen on, a mugged man lying half dead in a ditch, for example. That would not have been incompatible with eudaimonism, because eudaimonism had room for love of friends. The ancient eudaimonist would have found the injunction extremely puzzling. He understood how love of friends and relatives enhances happiness; how could one's happiness be enhanced by loving the person one just happens on? But he would not have found it incompatible with his eudaimonism.

But Christ did not say, "Love your neighbor along with your friends." He said, just as you love yourself, so also love your neighbor. Obeying this command requires rejecting the agent-orientation intrinsic to eudaimonism. Though eudaimonism is not egoism in the usual sense, none-theless intrinsic to it is a definite "me"-ism. The condition on my per-forming any action as an end-in-itself is that I judge that it will enhance *my* eudaimonia. As long as I continue to accept that condition on my choices, I am not loving my neighbor as I do myself. In my choices I am not giving enhancement of my neighbor's well-being the same status as enhancement of my own. Only when I give *your* well-being the same status in my selection of ends as *my* well-being will I be loving you as I do myself.

Let me add an additional consideration. Jesus makes clear in other passages that one's neighbor includes those who are one's enemies. As an application of the general commandment, he says, "love your enemies, do good to those who hate you" (Luke 6:27). Now we are unmistakably outside the pale of what any ancient eudaimonist did or could accept.

I can imagine an objection. Love of neighbor, contrary to what I have been assuming, does contribute to one's life being well-lived; even love of enemies contributes. There are goods in neighbor-love as well as in familial love that make one's life better lived, natural goods that make one's life richer, more satisfying. The ancient eudaimonist would find this suggestion implausible, and when he hears that the neighbor in-cludes one's enemy, would reject it out of hand. But that is because no-body in the ancient world had much acquaintance with true neighbor-love. Best to ask those who practice neighbor-love, the Mother Teresas of the world, whether they find that it enhances their lives. The ancient pagan world had no Mother Teresas to ask. We do.

The objection will not stand. For one thing, the objector has a far more sanguine view of neighbor-love than Jesus had. Jesus taught that obeying his commandment would be like carrying a cross on one's shoul-ders, perhaps even like being on a cross. Neighbor-love is very nearly the opposite of a "natural good." And second, the objector is still operating with the agent-oriented perspective, arguing that neighbor-love on my part enhances how *my* life is lived. But Christ says that as I love myself, so also I am to love my neighbor. I am not to raise the question of whether such love enhances my happiness; it may or it may not. As long as I continue to attach, as the condition of my accepting something as an end in itself, that it enhances how *my* life is lived, I am not treating love of the neighbor as I treat love of myself.

Give the objector one more chance. "Love your enemies," said Jesus, "do good, and lend, expecting nothing in return" (Luke 6:35). That sounds very anti-eudaimonist. But Jesus immediately goes on to say, "Your reward will be great, and you will be children of the Most High; for he is kind to the ungrateful and the wicked. Be merciful, just as your Father is merciful." What this suggests, to the person who wants both to be a

eudaimonist and to affirm Jesus' love command, is that one has to become an eschatological eudaimonist. If we consider only life in this
present age, then living one's life well often requires rejecting love of
neighbor; but God has so arranged human life and destiny that if we
consider human life in its totality, both in the age to come as well as in
this present age, then loving one's neighbor is indispensable to living
one's life well. For though neighbor-love may yield misery here in this
present age, God has so arranged things that in the age to come it will
be rewarded with abiding joy. Though neighbor-love may well turn out
to be neither a constituent nor a condition of the well-lived life in this
present age, its practice in this present life is a *means* to the well-lived life
in the age to come.

Can this be what Jesus meant, that neighbor-love, though it may not
enhance one's life here in this present age, is nonetheless to be practiced
because it is a means to abiding joy in the age to come? I find the suggestion implausible, even offensive. The love command is not prudential
advice on how to achieve future bliss; note that the "reward" Jesus promised was not some blissful experience but becoming like unto God in
loving one's enemies.

Does Eudaimonism Have Room for Compassion?

On my interpretation, one of the indications that Christ's injunction led
Augustine to break with eudaimonism, rather than try to incorporate
love of the other within eudaimonism, is the fact that Augustine's understanding of Christ's command led him to affirm the negative emotion of
compassion. In grief one sorrows over some misfortune that has befallen
oneself, that misfortune often being the misfortune of having one's
bonds of friendship and family destroyed. In compassion one sorrows
over the misfortune that has befallen the other, not over the fact that the
misfortune that befell the other is also a misfortune to oneself, because
it may not be. One sorrows *for* and *with* the other person. Augustine
shared with the Stoics the conviction that happiness requires tranquility.
Nonetheless, he understood Christ's command as requiring that we
allow the emotional disturbance of *compassion* into our lives—not just
grief but compassion. We are to be united in a solidarity of compassion
with family and friends and, beyond that, with whomever comes into our
lives—the "neighbor." Peripatetic eudaimonism had room for grief; it
was unlike Stoic eudaimonism in that regard. No version of eudaimonism has room for compassion.

The claim that eudaimonism has no room for compassion will not go uncontested. In her analysis of compassion in *Upheavals of Thought*,[2] Martha Nussbaum insists that it did have room. Let us consider her case.

Nussbaum opens her first chapter by declaring that emotions "involve judgments about important things, judgments in which, appraising an external object as salient for our own well-being, we acknowledge our own neediness and incompleteness before parts of the world that we do not fully control" (19). The theory of the emotions that Nussbaum alludes to here is that of the ancient eudaimonists, articulated most carefully by the Stoics and rehearsed in our chapter 7. Though from this opening sentence it is not clear whether she understands well-being as living well, her subsequent discussion leaves no doubt that she does.

> The value perceived in the object appears to be of a particular sort. It appears to make reference to the person's own flourishing. The object of the emotion is seen as *important for* some role it plays in the person's own life. I do not go about fearing any and every catastrophe anywhere in the world, nor (so it seems) do I fear any and every catastrophe that I know to be bad in important ways. What inspires fear is the thought of damages impending that cut to the heart of my own cherished relationships and projects. What inspires grief is the death of someone beloved, someone who has been an important part of one's own life. This does not mean that the emotions view these objects simply as tools or instruments of the agent's own satisfaction: they may be invested with intrinsic worth or value, as indeed my mother surely was. They may be loved for their own sake, and their good sought for its own sake. But what makes the emotion center around this particular mother, among all the many wonderful people and mothers in the world, is that she is *my* mother, a part of my life. (30–31)

Another way of putting the point she wants to make, says Nussbaum, "is that the emotions appear to be *eudaimonistic*, that is, concerned with the person's flourishing" (31). "Emotions [are] eudaimonistic evaluations" (300). She adds that "thinking . . . about ancient Greek eudaimonistic ethical theories will help us to start thinking about the geography of the emotional life. In a eudaimonistic ethical theory, the central question asked by a person is, 'How should a human being live?' The answer to that question is the person's conception of *eudaimonia*, or human flourishing, a complete human life" (31–32).

With this general account of emotion as background, Nussbaum uses Aristotle's definition and analysis of compassion as a template for her

[2] Cambridge: Cambridge University Press, 2001.

own discussion: compassion is "a painful emotion directed at another person's misfortune or suffering" (306).

What distinguishes compassion from pity, grief, fear, and the like, is its distinct cognitive components. One of those cognitive components is a belief or appraisal that the suffering of the other person is serious rather than trivial (306). "Compassion, like other major emotions, is concerned with value: it involves the recognition that the situation matters for the flourishing of the person in question" (307). If the suffering is too trivial to make any difference to the person's happiness, we do not feel compassion.

A second cognitive component is "the belief that the person does not deserve the suffering" (306). "Insofar as we believe that a person has come to grief through his or her own fault, we will blame and reproach, rather than having compassion. Insofar as we do feel compassion, it is either because we believe the person to be without blame for her plight or because, though there is an element of fault, we believe that her suffering is out of proportion to the fault" (311).

Aristotle held that there is a third cognitive component of compassion: "the belief that the possibilities of the person who experiences the emotion are similar to those of the sufferer" (306). Nussbaum regards this as not quite right. It is not that "compassion requires acknowledgment that one has possibilities and vulnerabilities similar to those of the sufferer" (316). What is at issue, rather, is "the eudaimonistic character of the emotions" (318).

For grief to be present, the dead person must be seen, and valued, as an important part of the mourner's own life, her scheme of goals and projects. Similarly, for compassion to be present, the person must consider the suffering of another as a significant part of his or her own scheme of goals and ends. She must take the person's ill as affecting her own flourishing. In effect, she must make herself vulnerable in the person of another. It is that *eudaimonistic judgment*, not the judgment of similar possibilities, that seems to be a necessary constituent of compassion (318–19).

In summary, the cognitive components of compassion are these three: "the judgment of *size* (a serious bad event has befallen someone); the judgment of *nondesert* (this person did not bring this suffering on himself or herself); and the *eudaimonistic judgment* (this person, or creature, is a significant element in my scheme of goals and projects, an end whose good is to be promoted)" (321).

The Stoics were enemies of compassion. Nussbaum states their case crisply and precisely: "the only way to be damaged by life with respect to one's flourishing is to make bad choices or become unjust; the appropriate response to such deliberate badness is blame, not compassion"

(357). Nussbaum notes that Epictetus "urges a tough, mocking attitude. One should try to get the sufferer not to moan about fortune in this undignified way, but to take charge of herself and her life. 'Wipe your own nose,' Epictetus tells the passive pupil. Marcus Aurelius, gentler, urges a lofty parental attitude: think of the person who is moaning about fortune as like a child who has lost a toy" (364).[3]

The eudaimonist need not be a Stoic, however; she can be a Peripatetic. And on the view of the Peripatetics, the "failure of external support can affect a person's capacity for virtue and choice itself" (372). "The Stoic would like to believe that no experience of worldly helplessness can touch us, that we are never victims" (372). What he overlooks is the extent "to which people who are malnourished, or ill, or treated with contempt by their society have a harder time developing their capacities for learning and choice" (ibid.)[4]

This, stripped of all its rich details, is Nussbaum's case for the compassionate eudaimonist. Her claim is not only that the eudaimonist can be compassionate but that compassion, along with the other emotions, can be understood only within a eudaimonistic framework. I hold, to the contrary, that affirmation of compassion requires rejection of eudaimonism.

Begin with Nussbaum's insistence that, as a eudaimonist, she can acknowledge that her mother has "intrinsic worth." A persistent theme in Nussbaum's exposition of Stoicism in *Upheavals of Thought* is that the "faculty of moral choice is the possession of all humans" and "vastly superior in dignity and worth to any other good thing" (357). It constitutes "the dignity of humanity in each person" (366)—a dignity that is "indestructible" (370) and "infinite" (359).

---

[3] Kant was expressing a very precise understanding of the Stoic position when he remarked, "It was a sublime way of representing the wise man, as the Stoic conceived him, when he let the wise one say: I wish I had a friend, not that he might give me help in poverty, sickness, captivity, and so on, but in order that I might stand by him and save a human being. But for all that, the very same wise man, when his friend is not to be saved, says to himself: What's it to me? i.e., he rejected commiseration." *Doctrine of Virtue* 34, trans. J. W. Ellington, in Immanuel Kant, *Ethical Philosophy* (Indianapolis: Hackett, 1983).

[4] The clarity with which the Aristotelian (Peripatetic) view concerning the worth of the natural preferables comes through in these passages of Nussbaum is striking. Serious shortfall in the natural preferables available to one diminishes one's "capacity for virtue and choice." This is also the conceptuality that underlies Nussbaum's presentation of "the capabilities approach" in her book *Women and Human Development* (Cambridge: Cambridge University Press, 2000). On p. 5 she says that "the best approach to [the] idea of a basic social minimum is provided by an approach that focuses on *human capabilities*, that is, what people are actually able to do and to be—in a way informed by an intuitive idea of a life that is worth of the dignity of the human being." The basic social minimum does not have worth in its own right; its worth is that it makes possible a life that is worthily lived.

I do not find the Stoics, or any other of the ancient eudaimonists, attributing any such dignity to the mere capacity of moral choice. The quasi-Stoic Immanuel Kant certainly did; but not the ancient eudaimonists. It is not hard to see why they did not. The eudaimonist focuses relentlessly on the question that, as he sees it, all of us ask implicitly if not explicitly: how shall I live my life? His way of understanding that question presupposes that lives have intrinsic worth; their worth is not purely instrumental to something else of worth. This intrinsic worth comes in varying degrees, the degree of a life's worth being determined by how well that life is lived. Now it is true, of course, that there could not be lives, in the sense that is relevant here, without the person whose life it is having the *capacity* for exercising moral choice. But the worth of lives is determined not by the agent's *capacity* for moral choice but by what he *actually does* with that capacity, along with all his other capacities. The eudaimonist admires the sage. He does not admire the *capacity* of certain beings for becoming sages, nor does he admire the *beings* who possess that capacity. He admires the person who actually is a sage. Or to speak more strictly, he admires the *life* of the person who actually is a sage.[5] In short, what the eudaimonist asserts is not that one's *mother* has intrinsic worth but that her *life* has an intrinsic worth of a certain degree, that degree determined by how well her life has been lived.

Suppose then that I am a eudaimonist. What do I do with the conviction that lives comes in varying degrees of intrinsic worth, the degree of worth determined by how well the life is lived? I aim at living my own life as well as possible. If on reflection I conclude that having a good relationship with my mother will enhance my own happiness, I will seek such a relationship. And no doubt that will include acts on my part of promoting goods in my mother's life. Promoting her happiness is an activity that contributes to my own life being well lived; that is why I include it within my goals and projects—though usually I will not have this reason in the forefront of my mind. Nussbaum speaks of "the eudaimonistic judgment that others . . . are an important part of one's own scheme of goals and projects, important as each in their own right" (32).

---

[5] In the following passage one sees Nussbaum moving back and forth between the worth of persons and the worth of the lives of persons: "To the pro-compassion tradition, differences in class and rank create differences in the worth or success of *lives*. To grant this much, the anti-compassion position holds, is to grant that the world and its morally irrelevant happenings can in effect forge different ranks and conditions of *humanity*. The believer in equal *human* worth should not acknowledge this: she should take her bearings from that basic human endowment that is not unequally distributed and she should honor that equal basic endowment by treating that, and that only, as the measure of a *life*" (359; emphasis added).

The two components that Nussbaum alludes to here must be held together in the precise conformation that she specifies. One treats others as important "each in their own right," on the condition that doing so is "an important part of one's own scheme of goals and projects" (32).

So suppose that promoting the well-being of one's mother is an important component in one's own scheme of goals and projects. And now suppose that some misfortune befalls her. If one is an Aristotelian eudaimonist, as Nussbaum is, how will one react? What will be the nature of one's emotional response?

The object of one's emotion, says Nussbaum, will be the evil that has befallen oneself, the damage that has occurred to one's own eudaimonia. Not the evil that has befallen one's mother but the evil that has befallen oneself. And what is the evil that has befallen oneself? The rupture of one's relationship with one's mother, this relationship including one's goal of enhancing the well-being of one's mother. Emotions, says Nussbaum in a passage quoted earlier, "make reference to the person's own flourishing. The object of the emotion is seen as *important for* some role it plays in the person's own life." Emotions are "concerned with the person's flourishing." And about compassion, specifically, she says that the person feeling the emotion must take the other "person's ill as affecting her own flourishing. In effect, she must make herself vulnerable in the person of another."

I submit that what Nussbaum has described here is not compassion but a species of grief. If the object of my negative emotion is the misfortune that has befallen me, then, even though the misfortune befalling me involves a misfortune befalling you, what I feel is grief. Compassion occurs when the object of my sorrow is not what has befallen me but what has befallen *the other.* Compassion is sorrow *for* and *with* the other, or as Augustine put it in one place, "on behalf of" the other (*City of God* XIV, 9; p. 598). Compassion is an alienation of the self from the self, a forgetfulness of self and an emotional identification with the other. An identification of this sort often happens in our engagement with fiction: we identify with one of the characters, feeling joy over the fortunes that come his way and sorrow over the misfortunes. We have entered into the life of the character. Joy and sorrow over what the fate of the character means for one's own life are not in view. Compassion is *kenotic*, to use a term common in contemporary theology; compassion is self-emptying.

In the story Jesus told to explain who is one's neighbor, the Samaritan, on seeing the mugged man in the ditch, was "moved with pity." I judge that "pity" is not the best translation, given its connotation in present-day English of condescension. The Samaritan was moved with sympathy, compassion. Yet the man had played no role whatsoever in the life of the

Samaritan; the Samaritan just happened on him. The eudaimonist theory of the emotions, accurately explained and defended by Nussbaum,
cannot account for this emotion of compassion. Unlike such emotions
as fear and grief, it does not have a eudaimonistic basis. Because it does
not presuppose any investment in the well-being of the other, it cannot
have as its basis the perceived or threatened impairment of one's investment. On being moved to compassion, the Samaritan proceeded to care
for the man in the ditch; he invested himself in his recovery. The compassion evoked the care, the investment, not the other way round.

To explain compassion, the eighteenth-century Scots moral theorists
postulated an innate "sentiment." Assume that they were right about
that.[6] Then no doubt at least some eudaimonists will feel compassion.
My claim is not that eudaimonists do not feel compassion but that *eudaimonism as a system of thought* has no place for compassion. And if the Scots
were right about that, then Jesus and the New Testament writers must be
interpreted as saying that we are not to stifle but to cultivate our in-
created "sentiment" of sympathy, compassion.

I imagine a response: why cannot a eudaimonist concede that not all
emotions have a eudaimonistic basis? Most do, but compassion does not.
And why can he not then embrace a Scots-type theory of compassion?
After all, when I specified what I regarded as definitive of eudaimonism,
I said nothing at all about a theory of emotions.

Well, yes; a eudaimonist could do that. But when I said that eudaimonism has no place for compassion, I did not mean that eudaimonism cannot incorporate an account of compassion; I meant that there is nothing
in the system that enables it to *affirm* compassion. It can affirm that species of grief on which Nussbaum has her eye; it lacks the resources for
affirming the sympathy of the Good Samaritan. Had Augustine remained
a eudaimonist, he could not have urged that we join together in a solidarity of compassion. The neighbor-love that Jesus enjoins consists of putting oneself in the place of the other; compassion is the emotional component of such love.

---

[6] In my judgment, the best analysis of the emotions currently available is that by
Robert C. Roberts in his *Emotions: An Essay in Aid of Moral Psychology* (Cambridge: Cambridge
University Press, 2003). Roberts's general analysis of emotions is a near cousin of the Stoic
analysis: emotions are "concern-based construals." Roberts devotes only one paragraph to
an analysis of compassion, saying, "Being based on a concern for the sufferer's well-being,
the construal is distressful to the subject and begets a consequent concern to alleviate the
suffering or make up the deficiency, or at least to see it alleviated or made up" (295). I
doubt that compassion is based on a concern; I think the Scots moral theorists were right
in appealing instead to a "sentiment" to explain it. But be that as it may, the concern to
which Roberts appeals in explaining the emotion is not one of Nussbaum's eudaimonistic
concerns; it has nothing to do with the well-being of the agent. Hence the argument I

Augustine's Break with the
Eudaimonist Conception of Well-being

Augustine's embrace of the moral vision of Scripture led him to break not only with the agent-orientation of eudaimonism but also with its conception of the good life as the well-lived life. The significance Augustine assigned to the natural preferables constitutes his break on this point. Let us begin by briefly recalling the views current in his day.

The Stoics held that the natural preferables are indifferent with respect to the well-lived life; hence they are not genuine life-goods. Many of them are not activities and are perforce not to be found among the activities that are the non-instrumental goods constituting a well-lived life. But all of them are such that their absence from one's life is no impediment to one's performing the activities of living well. Their absence is nothing to get upset over.

The Peripatetics disagreed. Though virtue is indeed the sole determinant of whether one's life is lived well, the virtues depend for their full exercise and flowering on external circumstances. External circumstances of various sorts are thus genuine goods, albeit instrumental goods. All eudaimonists agreed that actions of living well are the only non-instrumental goods. "According to Aristotle's account, [external goods] are needed as antecedently existing conditions that make possible the full exercise of the happy man's virtuous qualities of mind and character. In each case the value to the happy man consists in what the external goods make it possible for him, as a result of having them, to do. Any value goods other than virtuous action itself might have just for their own sakes is denied, or at least left out of account, on this theory."[7]

Late in his career Augustine rejected the attitude of the eudaimonists toward the natural preferables on the ground that that attitude is contrary to nature. He did not flesh out how he was thinking—not in any passage I know of. But in the preceding chapter I offered what seemed to me a reliable inference from some clues that he scattered about. Though the Stoics were the explicit target of his objection, his critique applies to the Peripatetics as well.

Recall the eudaimonist's thesis that it belongs to our nature as human beings to find certain things preferable and certain other things dis-preferable; among the things we find preferable are participation in families

---

offer above, about the inability of eudaimonism to affirm compassion, would have to be reformulated if Roberts is right on this matter, but it would not be essentially different.

[7] John M. Cooper, "Aristotle on the Goods of Fortune," in *Aristotle's Ethics*, ed. Terence Irwin (New York and London: Garland, 1995), p. 189. The article is reprinted from *The Philosophical Review* 94, no. 2 (April 1985).

and in friendships. No doubt what they were pointing to, at least in part, was the fact about ourselves that I noted in the previous chapter: our experiences are valorized, negatively, positively, and neutrally. The view of the eudaimonists was that some of this belongs to our nature; we have an in-built valorization structure. And when given a choice, we prefer (other things being equal) the positively valorized experience over the neutrally and negatively valorized experience.

Augustine's reaction to this picture was to affirm it but insist that it does not go far enough: not only does it belong to our nature as human beings to have preferences; it also belongs to our nature to be emotionally disturbed over the serious deprivation of preferables in ourselves and others. It is natural to cry at the death of one's child. Augustine saw the training in philosophy offered by the Stoics as aimed at altering the self in such a way that one's natural impulses toward emotional disturbance over deprivation of preferables were no longer operative. The person who is a successful product of the Stoic training program and remains dry-eyed on the death of his child is acting contrary to human nature.

As his career went along, Augustine became increasingly dubious about the claims made for the Stoic training programs. By the time he wrote *City of God* he insisted that the Stoic programs of emotion therapy were doomed to failure; success was impossible. More important, Augustine saw these programs as trying to undo how we were created by God. Admittedly, some of the things that are now natural to us are the consequence of our fallen condition; but Augustine saw no reason to think that our natural impulse to grieve over the death of family and friends and our natural impulse to feel compassion for those in misery are among those. These belong to our God-created nature. The Stoic program of self-reformation thus amounts to a radical critique of God's creation. God pronounced his creation good. We must do so as well. It is good to grieve over the death and misery of family and friends, good to feel compassion over the misery of the neighbor. One's life is more worthy if it contains such grief than if it does not. But if it is good to grieve over the significant deprivation of the natural preferables in our own lives and those of others, those preferables must themselves be genuine life-goods.

For this line of thought to apply to the Peripatetics, a point must be added about the character of the grief that is natural and good for us to feel over the misfortunes that befall ourselves and our family and friends, and about the character of the compassion that is natural and good to feel over the misfortunes that befall the mere neighbor. The Peripatetic, unlike the Stoic, grieves over the significant deprivation of natural preferables in his own life and in the lives of those to whom he is attached.

He does so, however, only because that deprivation makes it impossible for virtuous action to be fully achieved and to flower in his own life. What he is grieving over is the blow to his own virtuous action that such deprivations represent.

Augustine came to the conviction that it is not only natural for us to grieve over deprivations of natural goods in our own lives and those of others because we judge such deprivations to impair the flowering of virtue in our own lives, and because any blow to one's own virtue is grief-worthy. It is natural for us to grieve over the absence of those natural preferables for its own sake. It is natural to us to judge their intrinsic worth such that their absence is worth getting upset over. We are created thus. They are genuine life-goods independent of whatever positive role they may play in how one lives one's life. Their worth is not exhausted by the fact that the life of virtue cannot fully flower in straitened circumstances.

There is no place in eudaimonism for the biblical figure of Job. Job was the righteous lamenter. His friends suggested that his appearance of rectitude must be deceptive. Job would have none of it. He was upright. To use the language of eudaimonism, he was virtuous. Nonetheless, he lamented—lamented not that he could not *live* his life well but lamented all the ways in which his life was not *going well.* For the eudaimonist, Job was a cry-baby. Obviously, he was that for the Stoic; initially one thinks that the Peripatetic would have been more understanding. But not so. The Peripatetic would have understood Job had he lamented the impairment of his virtue by his straitened circumstances. But that was not Job's lament. Job lamented the fact that, though upright, he was suffering.

The early death of a beloved child may or may not impair the virtue of the parent. That has nothing to do with the parent's natural impulse to grieve. The parent is grieving over the fact that his or her life, in this crucial respect, is not *going well.* Whether or not it is lived well, it is not going well. The understanding of well-being presupposed by the moral vision of Scripture is that of well-being as the life that goes well—and beyond that, of the history that goes well. Call it the *flourishing* life and the *flourishing* history. To go well, one's life must be lived well; but it may be lived well without going well. The moral vision of Scripture speaks a good deal about living one's life well in whatever one's circumstances, straitened or ample. But it also speaks of what it is for one's life to go well and not to go well. Part of what it says is that the person who lives his life well when his life is not going well will not stifle the cry that this is not how life was meant to be.

Back in chapter 6 I observed that there are three distinct conceptions of well-being (the good life) to be discerned in the philosophical literature, adding that much of the confusion and futility in contemporary discussions of well-being are to be traced to the failure to distinguish these conceptions. The conception of the good life implicit in Augustine's late thought was that of the good life as the life that goes well— what I shall call the *flourishing* life.[8] It is this conception of the good life that we need for a theory of rights.

RIGHTS AND THE STRUCTURE OF THE GOOD LIFE

So as to get a deeper understanding of why neither the conception of the good life as the happy life nor the conception of the good life as the experientially satisfying life can serve for a theory of rights, why instead we need the conception of the good life as the flourishing life, let me now draw out some of the implications of the existence of rights for the structure of the good life.

The eudaimonists uniformly held that the well-lived life has two levels, a lower level consisting of the natural preferables and an upper level consisting of the virtues, the connection between the two levels being that the virtues are skills for dealing with the natural preferables and dis-preferables once those have been rationally ordered. Whether or not one's life is well lived depends entirely on the degree to which those skills are present and exercised.

An implication of the existence of rights for the structure of the good life is that the good life must be seen as having a tri-level, rather than a bi-level, structure. Its tri-level structure is a consequence of the relation of rights to life- and history-goods—a relation fundamentally different from that of virtues to life-goods.

Rights are not skills for dealing with preferables and dis-preferables in such a way as to produce a well-lived life. Rights are *normative relationships* that *incorporate* life-goods. Recall the points made in chapter 6 about the structure of rights. (The defense of the claim that this is their structure is still to come, in chapter 11.) The fundamental structure of a (claim) right is always that *X has a right against Y to Y's doing (or refraining from doing) Z.* For example, Paul has a right against Peter to Peter's making food available to him.

Should Paul actually enjoy this right, we can then distinguish the following:

---

[8] I mentioned, in chapter 6, that in his book *Well-Being* James Griffin entertains the suggestion that the problems and perplexities that he is confronting in his analysis are due to the fact that he and others are tacitly working with two distinct understandings of well-being. One of those is clearly that of the life that is good *for* the person whose life it is— the satisfying life, as I have called it. Apparently, the other is that of the life that goes well. On p. 7 Griffin himself speaks of well-being as "what it is for a single life to go well."

(i)   Paul's enjoying his right against Peter to his having food made available to him by Peter.

(ii) Paul's having food made available to him by Peter.

(iii) Paul's having food available to him.

Each of these is a state or condition in Paul's life. And each is distinct from the other two; the third could occur without the second occurring, and both the third and the second could occur without the first occurring. The second specifies the action on Peter's part that, according to the first, Paul is enjoying the right to, namely, Peter's making food available to Paul. And the third specifies what, according to the second, is the result of Peter's action, namely, Paul's having food available to him. It is possible for Paul to have food available to him without Peter's making it available; it is possible for Peter to make it available without Paul's having a right against him to his making it available.

Now recall the thesis to which I have often appealed, that what one has a right to is a life- or history-good of oneself—with the exceptions mentioned at the beginning of chapter 6. (I will save print by often speaking only of life-goods, though I mean what I say to apply to history-goods as well.) In subsequent chapters it will become clear why there is this connection between rights and life-goods. For the time being, let me just say that to deprive a person of that to which he has a right is to treat him with under-respect; and only if that of which one deprived him was a life-good would one be treating him with under-respect. One would not be treating him with under-respect if one deprived him of a life-evil—or of a life-neutral.

Given this thesis, that what one has a right to is always a life-good of oneself, the state of Paul's life specified by (ii) above is a good in Paul's life, namely, having food made available to him by Peter, or to put it in the active voice, Peter's making food available to him. And the fact that that is a life-good in turn implies, I take it, that the state specified by (iii), Paul's having food available to him, is also a life-good of his. But the state that (i) specifies, namely, Paul's enjoying the right, is likewise a good in Paul's life. It is, of course, a state of an ontological sort very different from the other two states. It is a *normative* social relationship, whereas the second is a non-normative social relationship, and the third, though a relationship, is not a social relationship but a relationship between Paul and some food. Nonetheless, it is surely a good in one's life that one enjoys that to which one has a right, just as it is an evil in one's life that one does not enjoy that to which one has a right, that one is wronged. So too, it is a good in one's life that one honors the rights of others and an evil in one's life that one does not honor them. The conclusion follows: an implication of the existence of rights is that the good life has a tri-level structure of goods.

The right that I have been using as an example, Paul's right against Peter to Peter's making food available to him, is a right that would traditionally be classified as a benefit right. Many so-called freedom rights have the same internal structure. Consider, for example, Paul's right against Peter to Peter's refraining from interfering with Paul's walking on the New Haven Green. The following three states that are goods in Paul's life can be distinguished in this case:

  (i) Paul's enjoying his right against Peter to his walking on the New Haven Green without Peter's interfering with him.
 (ii) Paul's walking on the New Haven Green without Peter's interfering with him.
(iii) Paul's walking on the New Haven Green.

Each of these states or events is distinct from the other two. And all three are goods in Paul's life.

Earlier, I argued that Augustine's conviction that God is the creator of our natural impulse to grieve over the serious deprivation of natural preferables in our lives and those of others carried the implication that the natural preferables are intrinsic life-goods—not merely intrinsically preferable, but intrinsically good, in the sense that their presence in one's life all by itself makes one's life better. It can now be seen that the fact that the natural advantages have this worth, of being intrinsic life-goods and not just intrinsic preferables, is also an implication of the recognition of rights.

The fact that Paul's having adequate food available is a good in his life is not the consequence of his having (or enjoying) the right against Peter to Peter's making adequate food available to him. It is the other way around: having a right to that action on Peter's part presupposes that it is a life-good in Paul's life. On the Peripatetic view, the natural advantages are goods in one's life *because* they make virtuous activity possible; they are instrumental to the non-instrumental good of virtuous activity. By contrast, the goods that rights incorporate, whether at level (ii) or level (iii), are goods in their own right; their incorporation within rights does not make them that. If they were not already that, I could not treat you with under-respect by depriving you of one or more of them. It follows that making space for the recognition of rights requires discarding the eudaimonist's understanding of well-being as living well.

Another argument for the same conclusion goes as follows. We noted just above that enjoying one's right to some action or restraint from action on the part of someone else is itself an important good in one's life or history, distinct from the life-good that is that action or restraint. But if one is thinking of well-being in terms of well-living, one has no way of acknowledging this state as a life-good. Enjoying one's right is not an aspect of how one's life is lived; it is of the wrong ontological sort to be that. Recall that "enjoying one's right" just means that one's right is honored, not violated. Enjoying one's right against X to A is a normative social relationship; and normative social relationships are ontologically distinct from those activities constitutive of how well a person's life is lived. Happiness, said Aristotle, consists in activity. The normative social relationship of enjoying one's right against X to A is not an activity on one's part.

But could the person working with the concept of well-being as happiness perhaps treat the enjoyment of rights as belonging among the natural preferables—a very strange natural preferable, but so be it? Could he place one's enjoyment of one's rights along with having adequate food available, having adequate shelter, and so forth, as among the preferables to be put into a rational order, and then to be treated as the matter that one takes into account as one exercises those life-skills that are the virtues?

Well, to treat them thus would perforce be to declare that one's enjoyment of a right is not in itself a good in one's life, only a preferable, when surely it is a good. But apart from that, while it might be possible to think of one's enjoyment of socially conferred rights this way, it makes no sense to think of one's enjoyment of natural rights this way. For recall the point, that if one thinks exclusively in terms of how one lives one's life, then what determines the worth of one's life is entirely what one does with the natural preferables and dis-preferables that come one's way. The worth of one's life is entirely determined by one's doings, one's actions. But if Paul has a right against Peter to Peter's making food available to him, then Peter's making food available to him is a good in Paul's life; and it has that status independent of whatever Paul may do with that state in living his life, whether he makes use of it virtuously or viciously. Suppose he makes use of it viciously. Then, if we concede that it does make a positive contribution to the worth of his life, we have to conclude that its positive contribution is toward how his life goes, not toward how his life is lived.

If one thinks of well-being in terms of the well-going life, one has no difficulty in recognizing virtues along with rights in one's moral framework. If one thinks of well-being in terms of the well-lived life, one cannot acknowledge the existence of rights.

THE MORAL VISION OF SCRIPTURE: EIRENÉISM

The moral vision of Scripture, by virtue of its recognition of rights in general and of natural and inherent rights in particular, presupposes the understanding of well-being as the well-going life, the flourishing life; and as we saw a bit earlier, the existence of rights implies that the flourishing life has the tri-level structure to which I called attention. The ultimate maxim of action in the moral vision of Scripture is, of course, the love command.

The philosophical tradition has no name for this particular moral vision. I have highlighed its differences from eudaimonism. But obviously, it is also not deontologism, nor is it consequentialism. If we want to name it, we need a new name. The flourishing life, thus understood, was called *shalom* by the Hebrew writers of the Old Testament, "*shalom*" being translated with the Greek "*eirenē*" in the Septuagint; the New Testament writers followed in the steps of the Septuagint translators. So if we need a name for this moral vision—this conception of the good life coupled with this maxim of action—best to call it *eirenéism.*

Vulnerability is intrinsic to eirenéism. My flourishing is not and cannot be in my own hands. The Peripatetics rejected Stoic self-sufficiency; only in certain conditions can one become virtuous to a significant degree, and thus happy. Stoics and Peripatetics agreed, however, that only one's own virtue is *constitutive* of one's happiness. The eirenéist holds that having adequate food available and decent shelter are constitutive of one's flourishing, not just instrumental to it; the natural preferables are constitutive of flourishing. And he holds that having one's rights honored is likewise constitutive of one's flourishing. Whether my flourishing is diminished by my being guilty of violating the rights of others is in my hands; whether my flourishing is diminished by my being wronged is not in my hands. My well-being is constituted in good measure by the actions and restraints from action of others. It is in their hands. Well-being is intrinsically social in a way that it is not for the eudaimonist.

Chapter Ten

CHARACTERIZING LIFE- AND
HISTORY-GOODS

MY ARGUMENT IN THIS PART has gone as follows. First, I argued that that to which one has a right is a good, specifically, a good in one's life or history—some state or event that contributes positively to one's life or history having the worth it does have. I then argued that there are life- and history-goods that are not included among the goods constitutive of the *experientially satisfying* life and that some of these are goods to which we have rights. I went on to argue that there are also life- and history-goods that are not included among the goods constitutive of the *well-lived* (happy) life and that some of these are goods to which we have rights. I completed this line of thought by arguing that all the life- and history-goods to which we have rights are to be found among those goods constitutive of the *well-going* (flourishing) life and history. I did not argue that all life- and history-goods are included among those constitutive of the well-going life, though I do in fact believe this to be the case; I argued only that all those goods to which we have rights are included among those constitutive of the well-going life, as are those goods that consist of enjoying one's rights. If we understand *well-being* in such a way that the degree of a person's well-being is identical with the worth of his life and history, then the argument as a whole can be formulated in terms of well-being and the adequacy or inadequacy of various understandings or conceptions thereof.

To conclude this part of our discussion, I want now to consider whether it is possible to give a general characterization of life- and history-goods. Up to this point I have simply declared or assumed that such-and-such was in fact a life- or history-good, and trusted that the reader would agree with my judgment. One could take this procedure to the next level by composing a representative list of such goods and then trying to compose a typology; recent discussions of so-called basic goods by Finnis, Nussbaum, and others are examples of this procedure. My question is whether it is possible to go beyond this and find some character that all these states and events share, a character such that their having that character is not analytically implied by their all being life- and history-goods, nor by their all being goods constitutive of the well-going life.

Let me approach the suggestion I wish to make by considering the strategies for arriving at such a general characterization that presently dominate the philosophical scene. There are two of them, one characteristic of the utilitarian tradition, one of the natural law tradition. The strategy characteristic of the utilitarian tradition gives pride of place to the notion of desire-satisfaction; the strategy characteristic of the natural law tradition gives pride of place to the notion of proper functioning.

The Failure of the Desire-Satisfaction Strategy to Yield a General Characterization of Life- and History-Goods

The desire-satisfaction strategy begins with the simple idea that a person enjoys well-being insofar as his or her desires are satisfied, and then proceeds by adding qualifications.[1] (Seldom if ever do those who follow this strategy acknowledge that there are history-goods that are not life-goods.)

The simple idea without qualification was considered and rejected more than a century ago by Henry Sidgwick in his well-known *Methods of Ethics*.[2] Sidgwick quotes the stark unqualified formulation offered by Hobbes: "whatsoever is the object of any man's Desire, that it is which he for his part calleth Good, and the object of his aversion, Evil."[3] And then Sidgwick offers what he calls "the obvious objection": "a man often desires what he knows is on the whole bad for him: the pleasure of drinking champagne which is sure to disagree with him, the gratification of revenge when he knows that his true interest lies in reconciliation" (110).

The reference to what the person himself knows, though relevant to combatting Hobbes's claim, is not essential. We all recognize, no doubt more in others than in ourselves, that the occurrence of something that satisfies a person's desire may diminish rather than enhance his or her well-being. The simple form of the desire-satisfaction account will not work. We "mistake our own interests. It is depressingly common that when even some of our strongest and most central desires are fulfilled, we are not better, even worse, off. Since the notion we are after is the ordinary notion of 'well-being,' what must matter for utility will have to

---

[1] Some theorists speak instead of preferences; others speak of interests. Desires, preferences, and interests seem to me distinct states of the self. Nonetheless, the criticisms I lodge against the desire-satisfaction theory have obvious analogues for preference-satisfaction and interest-satisfaction theories.

[2] 6th ed.; London: Macmillan, 1901.

[3] Quoted by Sidgwick, ibid., p. 109.

be, not persons' actual desires, but their desires in some way improved. The objection to the actual-desire account is overwhelming."[4]

A strategy one might explore for coping with the problem would be to take a person's actual desires and try to find some non-question-begging way of removing the unsatisfactory ones. I know of no writer who has in fact employed this strategy, in part, no doubt, because if desire-satisfaction is to be used to characterize well-being, we have not only to discard from consideration some of the things we do desire but to add desires for some of the things we do not desire. Sidgwick, more than a century ago, introduced what is now the standard strategy: one moves from speaking of a person's *actual* desires to speaking of the desires that he *would* have in his present situation if he no longer suffered from the defects that cause him to have desires for things whose satisfaction would not be a good in his life. One moves from description to philosophical fiction.

What are those defects? On this matter, too, Sidgwick's view has become standard for those working with the desire-satisfaction strategy. There is just one defect: lack of knowledge, broadly understood. I did not anticipate that champagne would cause this unpleasant reaction—or I did but failed to imagine the experience at all vividly. So in determining whether some state or event in a person's life contributes positively toward his well-being, we must ask whether it is something that he would desire in his present situation "if all the consequences of all the different lines of conduct open to him were accurately foreseen and adequately realised in imagination at the present point of time" (Sidgwick, *Methods*, 111f.). Well-being, to use Griffin's formulation, consists in "the fulfilment of desires that persons would have if they appreciated the true nature of their objects."[5]

In his book *Natural Law and Practical Rationality*,[6] Mark C. Murphy argues that the move by desire-satisfaction theorists from actual desires to desires that are "in some way improved"—those that an agent would have

---

[4] James Griffin, *Well-Being* (Oxford: Clarendon Press, 1986), p. 10.

[5] Ibid., p. 11. There is an ambiguity in this formulation. Does Griffin mean that we are to consider all the entities that are potential objects of desire on my part, that next we are to suppose that I am fully informed about all of those, and that, finally, we are to determine which of these I would desire in that situation? Or, rather than starting our thought experiment with all potential objects of desire on my part, does he mean that we are to start with the objects of my actual desires, that we are next to suppose that I am fully informed about all of these, and that, finally, we are to determine which of these I would desire in that situation? The latter determination, staggering though it is, is considerably less staggering than the former. Yet I think the evidence overall is that the former thought experiment is what Griffin has in mind. He says, for example, that "if I fully appreciated the nature of all possible objects of desire, I should change much of what I wanted" (11).

[6] Cambridge: Cambridge University Press, 2001.

in "a setting optimal for desiring" (51)—is confused. Murphy's argument is that the desire I have when I lack some information is, as such, no different from the desire I have when I possess that information, and conversely. The *object* of my desire is different; but not the desire itself.

I find Murphy's argument compelling. And there can be no doubt that it is on target. Witness Griffin's formulation above; he spoke of desires "that persons would have." Nonetheless, Murphy's argument does not score a lethal hit on the desire-satisfaction strategy as such. Rather than speaking of the desires that people *would have* in their present circumstances if they knew all the relevant things, the desire-satisfaction theorist can speak of *what it is* that people would desire if they knew the relevant things—what the *object* of their desire would be in that circumstance. This, in a somewhat roundabout way, is what Peter Railton has proposed. We should consider an agent's good to be, says Railton, "what he would want himself to want . . . were he to contemplate his present situation from a standpoint fully and vividly informed about himself and his circumstances, and entirely free of cognitive error or lapses of instrumental rationality."[7]

So by the term "informed desire," let me henceforth mean not what is usually meant in the literature on well-being, namely, a desire that one would have in one's present situation if one were appropriately informed, but rather, what one would desire in one's present situation if one were appropriately informed. The English word "desire" is ambiguous on this point. It may refer either to that state of the self that is a desire, or to the thing desired.

Now, the issue is this. Do the states and events of one's life and history that contribute positively to its worth all have the following character: they are what one *does* desire in case one possesses all the relevant information or what one *would* desire in one's present situation *if* one possessed all the relevant information? I have not considered what is to be understood by "relevant information." But presumably, it would have to come to something like what Griffin suggests: full information about all genuine candidates for objects of desire on my part in my situation.

One point to raise about this proposal is whether there is a truth of the matter as to what one would desire in one's present situation if one were fully cognizant of all relevant information—and if there is a truth of the matter, whether any of us is in a position to know what that truth is. I think the right answer to both questions is probably no. If so, there is no point in proceeding farther.

---

[7] "Facts and Values," in *Philosophical Topics* 14, p. 16. Quoted in Murphy, *Natural Law*, p. 51.

Suppose, though, that the right answer to both questions is yes. Then the main point to be made about the informed-desire account is that many of our desirings are themselves malformed. Robert Adams makes the point well in his discussion of well-being in *Finite and Infinite Goods*. It is not uncommon for human beings to have desirings that reflect ill-will toward themselves. "I may want things that are bad for me *because* they are bad for me, or because they are painful, if I hate myself or despise myself or am angry at myself, or if I feel guilty and want to punish myself" (89). Likewise, it is not uncommon for human beings to prefer what is low and base, morally or otherwise. "I may prefer money to friendship, idleness to creativity, casual commercial sex to love" (89). Our human condition is not that our desirings are all well formed but not all informed; our desirings are themselves malformed, deformed, fallen. We need reformation, not just information.[8] The informed-desire account, by virtue of its assumption that ignorance alone accounts for our desire of things that are not goods and for our failure to desire things that are goods, is inherently incapable of taking account of such desires

Adams imagines someone replying by insisting "that one who prefers money to friendship does not appreciate friendship as he should, and that this is a failure of imagination." His response is that there is indeed "a failure of appreciation here, in that such a person does not value friendship as highly as he should. But that is not a failure of imagination in the relevant sense; it is rather that which is supposed to be explained by a failure of imagination. And other explanations are possible. Sadly it sometimes happens that one who has tasted friendship comes to prefer money or some other form of power. Must he have forgotten what friendship is like, or can he just have come to like the power more than it deserves?" (91).

The myopic focus of the utilitarian tradition on lack of knowledge is motivated by the wish to have a morally neutral and non-paternalistic way of determining a person's well-being—the assumption being that we can make morally neutral determinations of whether or not a person's desires are informed and satisfied. Griffin is a good example of the point. What about irrational desires, he asks, compulsive hand-washing, for example? Should they not be excluded? No. "Since irrational desires cannot be excluded wholesale, why not let them in?" What about irrational desires that affect others and not just oneself, misogyny, for example? Should they not be excluded? Well, if some male is "upset or distressed" by "a woman's sitting next to him in the Senior Common Room," then

---

[8] There is an excellent discussion of deformed desires and the insuperable difficulty these pose for the informed-desire account of well-being in chapter 2 of Martha Nussbaum's *Women and Human Development* (Cambridge: Cambridge University Press, 2000).

"there is a utilitarian value at stake" (25). So such desires should also be allowed. What then about desires that are downright immoral? Sadistic desires, for example? Griffin first observes that sadistic desires tend to diminish a person's well-being. But then he says that "it would be a mistake simply to rule out sadistic desires. Not everyone is fairly normal. Perhaps there is someone for whom sadistic kicks are all he has" (26).

This is theory gone berserk. From the beginning Griffin has affirmed that the gratification of some desires proves not to be a good. The assumption that seems to be coming to the surface in these examples is that no matter what the desire, if the agent finds the gratification satisfying, then it is a good in the person's life. Some sadists have no other "kicks," he says. It is only when the agent does not find the gratification satisfying that the gratification of the desire is not a good. But this is to adopt the stance of the amoralist in judging the worth of person's lives. Surely the sadist's "kicks" do not enhance the worth of his life; they make his life less admirable, less estimable. Some desires, to say it again, are malformed desires. And note that those afflicted with irrational, addictive, and imnmoral desires often have strong higher level desires to be rid of those desires.

The Inability of the Proper-Function Strategy to Yield a General Characterization of Life- and History-Goods

The most sophisticated recent employment of the proper-function strategy for characterizing the human good is that by Mark Murphy in the book mentioned above, *Natural Law and Practical Rationality.* Murphy's discussion clearly assumes that well-being is identical with happiness—the well-lived life. Whether Murphy succeeds in characterizing the well-lived life in terms of proper functioning is an issue worth considering. I think we can see in advance, however, that life- and history-goods more generally cannot be thus characterized.

Aristotle's discussion of the proper function of the human being was set within the context of his eudaimonism. That was no accident. A proper function account of the human good fits well with the conception of well-being as the well-lived life; it fits not at all with the conception of well-being as the well-going life. The reason is straightforward. The functioning of an entity pertains to what it does. But many of the goods constitutive of how one's life is going do not consist of activities on one's part—not to mention those constitutive of how one's history is going. Some consist of things done to one—Paul's having food made available to him by Peter, for example. And some consist simply of being in a certain situation—Paul's having food available to him, for example, or Paul's not being prevented by Peter from walking on the New Haven Green.

The defender of the proper-functioning account will presumably reply that though things done to one are indeed not manifestations of one's functioning, they affect one's functioning and are in that way instrumental goods or evils. My response is that many do not affect one's functioning. Recall our now-familiar examples of being pruriently spied on or maligned when that has no impact on how one is treated nor does one ever find out about it. And once again, let us not forget the goods of which one is deprived after one's death.

I suppose someone might reply that though the presence of these evils in one's life does indeed not indicate malfunctioning on one's part, they are a manifestation of malfunctioning on the part of the person who brings about such evils in one's life. All evils in one's life are the manifestation either of one's own malfunctioning or of someone else's.

I think this reply rests on a serious mistake. Suppose I come across someone who is incapable of entering into friendships. And suppose I somehow discover that this abnormality in behavior is due to an abnormality of the person's brain. I would say what Murphy says when discussing this sort of case, namely, that this brain abnormality was not just an abnormality but a malfunction, and that as a consequence the person malfunctions. Or suppose that someone is forced to undergo a conditioning program whose outcome is that he is now unable to enter into friendships. I would say that in this case too there is something wrong with him, he is malfunctioning—though given the current state of science, I would not be able to pinpoint the malfunctioning part that accounts for *his* malfunctioning.

But now suppose I come across someone who has proved fully capable of entering into friendships, but has decided to forgo them. Perhaps he has dedicated himself to becoming a hermit on Mount Athos. I would not regard him as malfunctioning, and consequently would have no inclination whatsoever to look for an abnormality in some part of him that accounts for his unusual behavior. But if there is no abnormality in this respect in some part of him, then there is no *malfunction* in some part of him.

Deciding not to establish friendships when one is capable of friendship is not a malfunction, any more than not running when one is capable of running is a malfunction. But then, by the same token, deciding to establish friendships is not a case of proper functioning. Of course, one would not form friendships if one suffered from the malfunction of being incapable of forming friendships. But actually establishing friendships is not a case of proper functioning. It is, however, a life-good. The *capacity* for establishing friendships is a manifestation of proper functioning; actually establishing friendships is not. (I am assuming throughout that we should not think of the decision to forgo friendships on the model of a disease. The decision is neither a disease nor the symptom of a disease.)

What accounts for these paradoxes, if that is what they are, is the fact that human beings are capable of making free decisions. Neither the person who decides to enter into friendships nor the person who decides not to do so because he has chosen to be a hermit is malfunctioning. The difference between them is to be tracked not to some malfunction in the latter person but, in both cases, to the person's decision. Yet the person who forgoes friendships is forgoing a significant aspect of well-being.

Proper functioning radically under-determines well-being. One cannot read the contents of well-being off our proper functioning.

A REALISTIC FANTASY

An electric hand saw is a small machine designed to be used as a tool to saw wood and other materials. It can be used for other purposes; but that is what it is designed for. When working as designed to work, it is functioning properly; when not, it is malfunctioning. When it malfunctions, that is because some part is malfunctioning. Working as it was designed to work leaves wide scope for how it is used, even when used for the purposes for which it was designed. In that respect, it is like most tools. One can saw many different boards with a properly functioning electric hand saw; one can pound many different nails with a properly functioning hammer.

Let us now engage in some fantasy. Suppose that God brought into existence a creature of the following sort. The creature has an embedded design plan, so that when working in certain ways it is functioning properly and when not working in those ways, it is malfunctioning. Part of its design is a valorization structure: it finds some experiences enjoyable, some dis-enjoyable, some neutral. This valorization structure is in part innate and in part acquired. While some of the acquired valorization structure may be the consequence of malfunctioning, most of it will have come about in accord with a design plan for such acquisition. And the creature has desires, these desires likewise being in part innate and in part acquired.

The creature is like tools in general in that its proper functioning is compatible with its being used in a variety of different ways. But rather than leaving it to some other creature to decide how to use this one, God settled on the novel experiment of making this creature in such a way that it can itself decide how it will be used. Indeed, it must decide; proper functioning falls far short of being sufficiently determinative for action. Most of the time, possibly all of the time, the creature's making a decision consists of settling on something that it regards as a good outcome of its action and acting so as to bring that about.

Let us further imagine that God has desires with regard to this creature, preferences. For one thing, God desires that certain things happen to this creature and that other things not happen. But God also desires that this creature desire certain sorts of things and not desire others. And God desires that this creature will decide to use itself in certain ways and not decide to use itself in other ways. God had these various desires for his creature in mind when he created the creature; they are not an afterthought.

God admires this creature. And not only admires it but loves it, God's detailed desires with regard to this creature being an expression of God's love for it. What does love come to in this case? Well, love has the usual component of attachment; God is attached to this creature. But beyond that, God's overarching desire is that this creature not be treated by other members of its species as if it had less worth than it does have, and that this creature find those components of its life that fall within its cognizance to be satisfying, enjoyable, gratifying.

When God stands back to survey the states and events that comprise the life and history of this creature, which of those would God regard as good? Which would God regard as contributing positively to the overall worth of this creature's life?

Well, God will no doubt regard any malfunction of this creature as not a good in its life. Blindness, deafness, paralysis, these and many more of the same sort are contrary to the creature's embedded design plan and would be seen by God as evils. But beyond that, God regards as a good in this creature's life whatever transpires in accord with God's desire for how that creature's life should go.

Our fantasy is an example of fantasy realism. The creature is a human being.

THE HUMAN GOOD CHARACTERIZED IN TERMS OF DIVINE DESIRE

Our question in this chapter is whether it is possible to give a general characterization of those states and events that are goods in a human being's life and/or history. With the above fantasy in mind, consider the following passage from Robert Adams's discussion of well-being and excellence. Adams has in mind what I have called the *experientially satisfying* life. But if we generalize just a bit, what he says can also be applied to well-being in general.

The question, what would be best *for* a given person, is less characteristic of that person's own point of view (the point of view defined
by the whole system of his aims) than of the point of view of someone
who loves him. . . . The question "What would be best *for* him?" is
particularly apt to arise (perhaps indeed most apt to arise) in situations in which some measure of paternalism is inevitable, in which
we have to decide on behalf of a child or some other person whose
system of preferences is undeveloped or immature, or whose capacities for choice are in some way impaired. . . . In thinking about what
would be good for a child for whose education we are responsible,
. . . we must think about what interests and habits of choice to encourage and foster in her, and cannot presuppose a system of preferences and volitional tendencies already in her as defining the good
that we intend for her.[9]

I have argued that attempts to characterize the human good in terms
of proper functioning are bound to fail. And I have joined others in
arguing that attempts to characterize the human good in terms of desire-
satisfaction likewise show no promise. The suggestion Adams makes in
this passage, while still appealing to human desires, is a distinct improve-
ment over the standard desire-satisfaction accounts. Rather than looking
to the desires of the person whose well-being we are considering, we look
to the desires *for* that person of someone else who loves that person.

Yet this suggestion will also not work as a general account (Adams does
not present it as such). What a loving parent or teacher desires for the
child may prove, when the desire is satisfied, not to be a good in the life
of the child. What we need is someone who not only loves the child
but whose desires are not defective. I propose that we extrapolate from
Adams's suggestion to a *divine-desire* characterization: the goods constitutive of a person's well-being are what God desires for that person's life
and history.

Most of us most of the time, when considering whether something
constitutes a good in a person's life or history, do not explicitly appeal
to what God desires; perhaps most of us do not do so even implicitly.
Many would resist ever making such an appeal: they do not believe that
God exists, or they believe that God exists but do not believe that God
has desires, or they believe that God has desires but do not believe
that those desires are expressive of God's love for us, or they believe that
all talk about God's desires is vain because we have no way of knowing
what they are.

---

[9] *Finite and Infinite Goods*, p. 93.

Each of these types of skepticism would be important to address if I were to go beyond merely suggesting the divine-desire characterization of life- and history-goods to developing the suggestion into a full-blown theory. I will not do that. My goal in this book is to develop an account of justice and to say about the good only what is necessary for that purpose.

It is important, though, to take note of some of the things that a divine-desire account does not imply. It does not imply that when one is considering whether so-and-so is a good in the life of a certain person, one is tacitly asking whether God desires it. Nor does it imply that one should be asking that. Analogues will be helpful. Informed-desire accounts do not imply that when considering whether something is a life-good, one is tacitly thinking in terms of the complicated hypothetical situations that theorists have devised. Nor do they imply that that is how one should be thinking. Similarly, the divine-command theory of moral obligation does not imply that when considering what one is obligated to do, one is implicitly if not explicitly asking what God has commanded; neither does it imply that one should be doing that. It may be clear that something is a good in the life of someone even though the question of what characterizes all such goods has never crossed one's mind. It may be clear even if one happens to have considered the correct characterization and rejected it. A characterization of the human good implies next to nothing about an epistemology of our awareness of the human good.

PART III

Theory: Having a Right to a Good

Chapter Eleven

ACCOUNTING FOR RIGHTS

Preliminary Comments

We now leave narrative behind and attend exclusively to theory. The question before us is how to understand rights, specifically, *claim*-rights. What is it to have a right to something? What differentiates those actual and potential life-goods to which one has a right from those to which one does not? And not only differentiates: what *accounts for* the fact that one has a right to these life-goods and not to those? (From now on I will regularly use "life-goods" as short for "life- and history-goods.")

My aim is to give an account of those rights that make up *primary* justice. Every now and then in the course of our discussion I have alluded to the fact that, in my judgment, retributive rights are a blend of permission-rights and claim-rights. The person who has been wronged has the permission-right to be angry with the wrongdoer and to see to it that appropriately hard treatment is imposed on him, and the claim-right to be free to do so; but the fact that forgiveness is often appropriate, and sometimes even obligatory, implies that often no claim-rights are violated if one forgoes claiming one's retributive rights and forgives the wrongdoer. What I have to say about claim-rights in general will illuminate those intertwined with permission-rights to constitute retributive rights. But I will not be able to discuss that intertwinement.

Often human rights loom so large in discussions of rights that other rights are either obscured from view or understood on the model of human rights. The result is a very distorted picture of rights. Rights pervade the fine texture of our everyday existence. We need first an understanding of that fine texture. When we get to those very special rights that are human rights, we can then see how they fit within that texture, rather than that texture being obscured from us or distorted by our preoccupation with human rights. My aim is to develop an account of rights in general—an account that holds for human rights as well as rights we have on account of being particular sorts of human beings, rights that are socially generated as well as natural rights, inherent rights as well as conferred rights.

My focus, as I mentioned, will be on moral rights. Rights of other sorts—legal rights, for example—are of course deeply intertwined with moral rights. When deliberating whether to confer some legal right on citizens, the legislature must consider whether doing so is required by moral rights, and if not required, whether the proposed legislation is compatible with moral rights. And when legal rights have been justly conferred, then the state and its citizens have a moral right (other things being equal) to those legal rights being honored.

Not only are moral and legal rights intertwined. Amidst their differences are deep structural similarities; and it has been my experience that discussions of legal rights by legal philosophers often illuminate moral rights. In particular, I have found this to be the case for one of the classics in twentieth-century legal philosophy, W. H. Hohfeld's essay, *Fundamental Legal Conceptions as Applied in Judicial Reasoning.*[1]

The deepest divide among theories of legal rights is that between so-called *will* or *choice* theories and so-called *interest* or *benefit* theories. To over-simplify: those who favor will theories think of the conferral of legal rights as aimed at protecting or securing a certain zone of autonomy on the part of the right-holder; those who favor interest theories think of the conferral of legal rights as aimed at protecting or securing a certain range of interests or benefits on the part of the right-holder. I think that those of us interested in moral rights can learn a good deal from this debate among legal philosophers. Nonetheless, actually to enter the debate would require engaging a number of issues that, so I judge, would distract us from our purposes. Let me just say that the affinities of my theory are with interest theories of legal rights rather than with will theories.[2]

On the contemporary scene there are two principal ways of attempting to account for moral rights: one way tries to show that rights are grounded in duties, the other tries to show that rights are grounded in respect for persons.[3] I will develop and defend a version of the latter. But the claim that rights are grounded in duties is accepted in so many quarters, often without question, that I propose taking the time to explore in some detail why they are not. I should repeat a comment made earlier, that whereas in the idiolect of some legal and political philosophers, *obligations* are normative constraints socially generated, *duties* are "natural" normative constraints, I will be employing ordinary English and using "duty" and "obligation" as synonyms.

The suggestion that moral rights are grounded in duties comes in two main forms. One is common especially in theological writings, and holds that the goods to which one has claim-rights are those one must enjoy in order to fulfill one's duties. The other is common especially in philo-

---

[1] New Haven: Yale University Press, 1920.

[2] An excellent discussion of the two theories is to be found in the three essays in Matthew H. Kramer, N. E. Simmonds, and Hillel Steiner, *A Debate over Rights: Philosophical Enquiries* (Oxford: Clarendon Press, 1998).

[3] Though these are the principal ways, they are not, as we will see in chapter 14, the only ways.

sophical discussions about rights, and consists of three theses: (i) a good to which one has a claim-right is always the good of some agent or agents doing or refraining from doing something; (ii) if X has a claim-right against Y to Y's doing or refraining from doing A, then Y has a duty toward X to do or refrain from doing A; and (iii) that claim-right of X against Y is grounded in that duty of Y toward X.

W. N. Hohfeld's defense of the second thesis of the latter suggestion has acquired canonical status in the contemporary philosophical literature on rights. Let me accordingly call it the *Hohfeld thesis* or, rather, the *weak* Hohfeld thesis. (Why I call it "weak" will become clear later in this chapter.) As to the first suggestion, I know of no one who has articulated it better than the theologian Paul Ramsey. So let me call it the *Ramsey thesis.*

Whether Hohfeld also held the third thesis of the latter suggestion, the thesis that says that Y's duty toward X *accounts for* X's right against Y, is not clear; he is not explicit on the matter. And as to the first thesis of the latter suggestion, Hohfeld takes for granted without argument that what one has a right to is always an action or restraint from action on the part of some person, some group of persons, or some social entity. Hohfeld devotes no explicit attention to the relation between rights and the good.

In the Introduction, I made the point that a proposition of the form *X has a right against Y to Y's doing A* is not the simple analytic converse of the corresponding proposition of the form *Y has a duty toward X to do A.* Rights-talk and duties-talk are not just two different ways of saying the same thing; we need both if we are to bring to speech the two distinct dimensions of the moral order, the agent-dimension and the patient-dimension.[4] Our question now is whether these two dimensions are related in such a way that rights, which belong to the patient-dimension, are grounded in the duties of the agent-dimension.

Claims that one thing accounts for another can be notoriously difficult to assess. What we will see is that rights and duties are not related as they

---

[4] Matthew H. Kramer, in "Rights without Trimmings" (in Kramer et al., *A Debate over Rights*), insists that Hohfeld simply stipulated that, from among the various things called "rights," he would call "claim-rights" those that have duties as their correlatives. Thus for Hohfeld it is true by definition of "claim-rights" that these rights have duties as their correlatives. Though I do not find Hohfeld entirely clear on the matter, I doubt that this is how he should be interpreted. On Kramer's interpretation, the word "claim" does no work; Hohfeld might as well have stipulated that he would call those rights that have duties as their correlatives "D-rights"—"D" for duty. I think that, on the contrary, Hohfeld assumed that, in addition to our having the various concepts of what we ambiguously call "rights," we have the concept of *duty* and the concept of a *legitimate claim*; and he then affirmed, as a thesis, that duties and legitimate claims are related as correlatives. If that thesis about correlatives is not only true but necessarily true, then it is a synthetic necessary truth.

would have to be if duties were to account for rights—conversely, if rights were to be grounded in duties. The accounting question is cut off at the pass.

RAMSEY'S STATEMENT OF HIS THESIS

The Ramsey thesis holds that the goods to which one has a right are those one must enjoy in order to fulfill one's duties. Here is how Ramsey states the thesis in one place in his provocative essay, "The Created Destination of Property Right":[5]

> If human rights are the rights of fellow humanity, "inalienably" connected with this human nature in us and with our life with fellow man and with our duties to other men, then rights must be whatever it is necessary for me to have in order to be with and for fellow man. If I have an inalienable natural right to life simply by my being a man, this is because life is the single most basic precondition to human existence in covenant. (37)

It is of natural human rights that Ramsey is explicitly speaking in this passage. But that he means his thesis concerning the connection between rights and duties to be understood more generally is clear from an earlier passage:

> The state and its law as an ordinance of creation, natural justice, human and legal rights and social institutions generally, so far as these have a positive purpose under the creative, governing, and preserving purposes of God—all are the external basis making possible the actualization of the promise of covenant; while covenant or fellow humanity is the internal basis and meaning of every right, true justice, or law. (25–26)

Ramsey's employment in this passage of the distinction between "external basis" and "internal basis" is an allusion to Karl Barth's apothegm, that covenant is the internal basis of creation and creation the external basis of covenant. God's covenant dealings with humankind is the purpose and significance of creation; God's creation of humankind makes those covenant dealings possible.

God's covenant dealings with humankind have the overarching character, says Ramsey, of God's being *for* humankind; and as a component

---

[5] The essay is the first chapter in Ramsey's little book, *Christian Ethics and the Sit-In* (New York: Association Press, 1961).

of God's being *for* humankind, God asks of us that we be *for* our fellow human beings. God's being for us is God's mercy, God's charity, God's "steadfast covenant-love"; and our being for each other is correspondingly our mercy, our charity, our neighbor-love (26). It follows that "the requirements of charity, or of steadfast covenant-love, and the requirements of justice, or of natural right, are ultimately inseverable" (26).

> [I]n being *for* fellow man is revealed the internal basis of any sort of justice, or the meaning and intentionality there were present all along in that life of man *with* man which God directs in creating, preserving, and governing the world by means of the social order. His rights are a man's capability to covenant. (30)

Ramsey observes that if one looks at love through the lens of justice rather than looking at justice through the lens of love, then one has to acknowledge that "justice bears only the external marks of man's destiny for steadfast covenant-love. It provides only the external possibility of covenant, or a minimum sign and promise of this." Accordingly, "the fellow humanity of man that shows forth in the order of justice" can perhaps best be described "as the life of man *with* fellow man (not *for* him)" (26). Nonetheless,

> to be *for* fellow man (charity) and to be *with* fellow man (justice) indicates the permeability of justice to charity. Charity (*for* fellow man) is the internal basis and meaning of natural justice (*with* fellow man), as justice in turn is the promise and possibility of close meeting and steadfast covenant. This has to be said of every human right. . . . Human rights all bear the marks of the primal justice of man's creation for fellow humanity. (26–27)[6]

---

[6] I mentioned that the view being expressed by Ramsey is found rather frequently among theologians. One also finds it now and then in official ecclesiastical documents. Consider, for example, this passage from "The United Church Pronouncement on Human Rights" (text to be found in Appendix IV, p. 296, of Max L. Stackhouse, *Creeds, Society, and Human Rights* (Grand Rapids, Mich.: Eerdmans, 1984): "Because of God's claim upon all God's creatures human rights have to do with the basic answerability or responsibility of being a human creature. To be created in the image of God means . . . to be called to care for God's whole creation according to God's intention. Therefore the fundamental human right which gives the human being his or her dignity is also an obligation to serve and to help in the creation of the conditions for life in the whole creation. The fundamental human right is the right to be responsible to God. Human rights and human duties are two sides of the same coin. 'My rights' is an abstraction and in reality nothing without the 'rights of my neighbors,' which constitute my duty. In view of God's claim upon God's human creatures, rights are given by God as the means for all human beings to fulfill their duties before God's righteousness. Thus human rights are what people need in order to fulfill their fundamental task of becoming a human person, that is, fulfilling their calling as the image of God."

Why the Ramsey Thesis Is Untenable

The fundamental impulse that leads Ramsey to affirm his thesis seems to me profoundly correct. Ramsey is opposed to the idea that a person "has his humanity, his natural and human rights and justice due him, radically without his fellow man, half without him, and on some other basis than a man's own true manhood *with* other men" (31). "A man is never without his fellow man. ... [B]ecause his creatureliness is from the beginning in the form of fellow humanity and because . . . he has real being only by being *with* and *for* fellow man, we have to reckon with this in everything that is said about justice and about the rights of man" (31).

Already in the Introduction I made clear that I hold, in agreement with Ramsey, that rights are inherently social. In reflecting on Ramsey's thesis, the question to be considered, then, is not whether or not rights have to do with how we are and ought to be related to each other, but whether Ramsey and his fellow theologians have correctly located the way in which rights involve our sociality. To this question, the answer seems to me to be that they have not. Ramsey's thesis is that I have a claim-right to the enjoyment of certain goods just in case enjoying those goods is necessary for fulfilling my obligations. The thesis is untenable for at least four reasons.

In the first place, the totality of one's duties is too narrow, too pinched, too constricted, to account in this way for all of one's rights. It is indeed true, as Ramsey observes, that if one is to fulfill any of one's duties whatsoever, one must have adequate food and water, shelter from the elements, relatively clean air to breathe, and so forth. But not all the life-goods to which one has a right are ones that one must enjoy if one is to fulfill one's obligations.

Privacy rights are an example. We each have a right to not having our privacy invaded for prurient reasons. But if nothing whatsoever is done by the voyeur with the information garnered, then his invasion of one's privacy has no impact whatsoever on one's carrying out of one's obligations. Yet even in such cases, one has a right to not having one's privacy invaded.

Likewise, certain rights to respect are not accounted for by the Ramsey thesis. I have a right to a polite answer when I arrive at the clinic and ask where the internal medicine department is located. A gruff, impolite, disrespectful answer will in no way interfere with my fulfilling my obligations. An *incorrect* answer might interfere; but a gruff answer will not. A gruff answer might shatter the fragile egos of some persons and thus interfere with their carrying out their obligations. But it will not do that to me; I will be angry for a while and then get on with things. Nonetheless, I have a right to a polite answer.

And some of our rights are connected with what we take delight in; Ramsey's picture of human beings, in the essay under consideration, is altogether too stern. Here is an example of the point. Suppose I go off on a fishing trip with my buddies. I am just coming off a fine vacation with my family. None of the tensions that often erupt on family vacations has surfaced. The weather was fine. Everybody enjoyed everybody and everything. So I cannot plead that I need this fishing excursion; if I said to my wife that I needed it, she and I would both know that I was speaking ironically. I just expect to have fun fishing and talking philosophy and theology with my buddies for a few days. So off we go to one of those quiet wooded lakes in northern Minnesota. Then, a few hours after we have pitched our tent, a bunch of rugged outdoor types who have nothing but scorn for city slickers like us camp next door and play their rock-and-roll so loudly and spiel off their raunchy jokes so raucously that our attempt at philosophico-theological discourse is completely frustrated. I would say that we are deprived of our right to enjoy ourselves in our own way. But it can scarcely be argued that we are being prevented from carrying out our obligations. Life is not all duty.

Probably the best way for the defender of the Ramsey thesis to deal with such counter-examples is to move away from a claim about individual acts to a claim about practices and types of actions. In order that people in general may fulfill their obligations in general, it is important that there be the *practice* of not invading people's privacy, the *practice* of treating clients politely, the *practice* of not disrupting innocent enjoyments. But I myself have no idea how to articulate this rough idea so that it is both plausible and relatively precise. So let me move on to a second difficulty with the Ramsey thesis that seems to me at least as serious, if not more so, than the first.

The Ramsey thesis pictures our obligations as given, fixed; it then tells us how to determine our rights, given those obligations. Given my obligations, I ask which life-goods I must enjoy if I am to carry out those obligations; those are then the life-goods to which I have a right.

I submit that this is a very inaccurate picture of the relation between one's rights and one's duties. If I am deprived of some life-good through no fault of my own, whether by nature or humankind, with the consequence that I am not able to do what otherwise I would be obligated to do, then I am not obligated to do that. Suppose, for example, that it is indispensable to my fulfilling my obligations that I get to my office; then, by the Ramsey thesis, I have the right to be at liberty to get to my office. And suppose that this is correct; I do in fact have that right. But now suppose that a terrorist attack makes it impossible for me to get my office;

then I no longer have those obligations that I cannot fulfill without getting to my office. Nonetheless, I still have the right to get to my office;
I am wronged in being prevented from getting there. In short, which
obligations we have is determined to a considerable extent by whether or
not we are enjoying the life-goods to which we have a right—just the
opposite connection of rights to duties propounded by the Ramsey thesis.

A related point is the following. To a considerable extent we choose
our obligations; and often, when we do, we have the right to do so. But
it is implausible to suppose that in every such case, our right to the good
of choosing our obligations is indispensable to our carrying out some
other obligation that we did not choose. What I have in mind is that
every social role carries with it as an essential constituent, a certain complex of rights and duties: for example, the social role of a physician carries with it certain rights and duties, as does the social role of a university
professor. In our society we have the right, to a considerable extent, to
choose among such social roles, and thereby to choose the duties that
come along with them; and rather often it is the case that consulting
one's obligations does not settle one's choice, one way or another,
among available roles.

The point then is this: the path between rights and duties goes
both ways; it is not a one-way street. Some of the life-goods to which one
has a right are ones that one must enjoy if one is to carry out one's
obligations. But it is also the case that whether or not one is enjoying
the goods to which one has a right contributes to determining one's
obligations. It is true that I can only fulfill my obligations to my family if
I have adequate food; but if adequate food is unavailable through no
fault of mine, then I do not have those obligations. Nonetheless, I may
still have a right to the food.

The two final points can be made briefly. Some human beings, at certain times in their lives, have no duties because they are not then capable
of forming intentions; infants and persons in a coma are examples. Yet
such human beings have rights; they can be wronged. Ramsey might
propose dealing with the case of infants and certain of the people in
comas by adding to his thesis the sub-thesis that a human being has a
right to those goods that are necessary to his or her *coming to have* duties.
But that does not deal with human beings in a terminal coma. Yet such
human beings can also be wronged, as can those who are dead; one can
be wronged by being maligned at one's funeral.

Last, a comprehensive theory of rights will have to account for God's
rights as well as ours. But it is hard indeed to see any plausibility in the
Ramsey thesis when applied to God. God has a right to be worshipped.
Which obligation on God's part is such that God cannot carry it out
unless God is worshipped?

Hohfeld's Presentation of His Thesis

Let us turn now to the weak Hohfeld thesis, that if X has a claim-right against Y to Y's doing or refraining from doing action A, then Y has a duty toward X to do or refrain from doing A. Or to put the thesis less precisely but more epigrammatically: to every claim-right there is a correlative duty. If the weak Hohfeld thesis should prove untenable on account of our discovering some claim-rights to which there are no correlative duties, then of course the second way of trying to ground rights in duties will have failed. But I will be arguing that, when certain ambiguities are removed, the weak Hohfeld thesis is correct.

From our first chapter onward we have had to address certain aspects of the relation between claim-rights and duties. Up to this point we have probed no deeper into those relations than was necessary for the immediate task at hand. Now our address to the topic will be more comprehensive and systematic.

Hohfeld was exclusively concerned with the use of the term "a right" in law and legal theory; what he says is easily adapted to our purposes, however. The term "a right," he says, "tends to be used indiscriminately to cover what in a given case may be a privilege, a power, or an immunity, rather than a right in the strictest sense" (36). While thus recognizing that speaking of privileges, powers, and immunities as rights is common usage, Hohfeld nevertheless presses on to ask, "what clue do we find, in ordinary legal discourse, toward limiting the word in question to a definite and appropriate meaning?" (38). His answer is that the "clue lies in the correlative 'duty,' for it is certain that even those who use the word and the conception 'right' in the broadest possible way are accustomed to thinking of 'duty' as the invariable correlative" (ibid.). He goes on to say that "if, as seems desirable, we should seek a synonym for the term 'right' in this limited and proper meaning, perhaps the word 'claim' would prove the best" (ibid.).

I shall not affirm Hohfeld's insistence that to use the term "rights" for privileges, powers, and immunities is to use it loosely, improperly, or inappropriately; it is enough for my purposes that we distinguish its use for claims from those other uses, whether or not those other uses are strict and proper or loose and improper. My concern here is exclusively with what Hohfeld calls "claims," not with privileges, powers, and immunities And rather than following Hohfeld in taking the existence of correlative duties as the "clue" that the term is being used to pick out claims, let me construe Hohfeld as propounding the *thesis* that to every claim-right there is a correlative duty.

Hohfeld sets forth his thesis by offering an example that he intends the reader to generalize: "if X has a right against Y that he shall stay off the former's land, the correlative (and equivalent) is that Y is under a duty toward X to stay off the place" (38). The generalization is this:

> (1) X has a claim-right against Y that Y shall do or refrain from doing A if and only if Y has the duty toward X to do or refrain from doing A.

"A duty," says Hohfeld, "is the invariable correlative of that legal relation which is most properly called a right or claim" (39).

A significant question of interpretation is whether Hohfeld did mean to affirm this "if and only if" thesis, or whether his language was misleading in this passage and he meant to affirm no more than "only if." Did he mean to say that to every claim-right there is a correlative duty *and vice versa*, or merely that to every claim-right there is a correlative duty? Call these the *weak Hohfeld thesis* and the *strong Hohfeld thesis*, respectively. Many present-day writers would be willing to affirm only the weak Hohfeld thesis; it is often held, for example, that duties of charity have no corresponding rights. What about Hohfeld himself?

Incidentally, it should be noted that the strong Hohfeld thesis is close to, but not quite identical with, the principle that I introduced in the Introduction as *the principle of correlatives*: if Y belongs to the sort of entity that can have rights, then X has a right against Y to Y's doing A if and only if Y has an obligation toward X to do A. It is in that initial qualification, "if Y belongs to the sort of entity that can have rights," that my principle of correlatives differs from the strong Hohfeld thesis. The need for the qualification will become clear in chapter 17.

I judge that Hohfeld meant to affirm what I have called the *strong Hohfeld thesis*, though I concede the evidence to be less than decisive. Hohfeld's main concern, when discussing claim-rights, is to argue that to every such right there is a correlative duty. But the phrase "and equivalent" in the passage just quoted suggests that he has something more in mind. And as his discussion proceeds, one gets the clear impression that he sees himself as exploring the *inter*-relationships of rights and duties. Further, he cites no example of a duty one person has toward another for which there is not a correlative right of the second person against the first.

HOHFELD ON CLAIM-RIGHTS, PERMISSION-RIGHTS, AND DUTIES

Hohfeld apparently regards the strong Hohfeld thesis as self-evident, because rather than saying anything at all by way of defense, he moves on immediately to distinguish rights as claims from what he thinks they are all too easily confused with, namely, rights as privileges. A privilege, he says, "is the opposite of a duty, and the correlative of a 'no-right.' In the example last put, whereas X has a *right* or *claim* that Y, the other man, should stay off the land, he himself has the *privilege* of entering on the land; or, in equivalent words, X does not have a duty to stay off" (38–39).

Whatever be the situation in law, in ordinary usage I think what Hohfeld has his eye on here are better called *permissions* than privileges. When considering rights as claims, we were thinking of cases in which X has a right against Y that Y shall do or refrain from doing something; now our focus is on those cases in which X has the right *himself* to do or refrain from doing something. These are cases in which X is *permitted* to do or refrain from doing something.[7]

As suggested in the passage last quoted, Hohfeld's thesis concerning the relation of permission-rights to duties is this:

(2) X has the permission-right to do or refrain from doing A if and only if X does not have the duty to not do or refrain from doing A.[8]

To be permitted to do something is not to be obligated to not do it.

And what, if anything, is the relation between permissions and claims? Here is what Hohfeld says:

Passing now to the question of "correlatives," it will be remembered . . . that a duty is the invariable correlative of that legal relation which is most properly called a right or claim. That being so, if further evidence be needed as to the fundamental and important difference between a right (or claim) and a privilege, surely it is found in the fact that the correlative of the latter relation is a "no-right," there being no single term available to express the latter conception. Thus, the correlative of X's right that Y shall not enter on the land is Y's duty not to enter; but the correlative of X's privilege of entering himself is manifestly Y's "no-right" that X shall not enter. (39)

Generalizing from Hohfeld's example, the thesis he has in mind is this:

---

[7] Kramer et al., in *A Debate over Rights*, prefer to call Hohfeld's privileges *liberties*. But as will shortly become clear, what we would normally cite as an example of a liberty to which one has a right is a combination of a permission-right and a claim-right. My right to the liberty of walking on the New Haven Green is a combination of my permission-right to walk there and my claim-right to being free from interference in walking there.

[8] To the best of my knowledge, every present-day writer would affirm this thesis.

(3) X has the permission-right to do or refrain from doing A
if and only if neither Y nor anyone else has the claim-right to
X's not doing or refraining from doing A.

And so we get Hohfeld's summary formula: whereas to every claim-right
there is a correlative duty, to every permission-right there is a correlative
"no-right" (i.e., a correlative no-claim-right). It is especially this difference that shows "the importance of keeping the conception of a right
(or claim) and the conception of a privilege quite distinct from each
other"(39).

If X is permitted to do A, does X then also have the claim-right against
Y and everybody else to their *allowing* him to do A— that is, the claim-
right against Y and everybody else to their not trying to prevent him from
doing A? Hohfeld's answer is no. X's having that permission-right does
not imply that X has that claim-right. It may be that you are permitted
to do A—you violate no obligation in doing A and wrong no one—while
nonetheless it is also the case that you are not wronged should I try to
prevent you from doing A. Hohfeld offers an interesting example to illustrate the point. To some readers the example has seemed baffling; to
me, it seems extraordinarily acute. Imagine a situation in which a person
wants to eat a shrimp salad. We must distinguish, says Hohfeld,

> two classes of relations: *first*, the party's respective privileges, as
> against A, B, C, D and others in relation to eating the salad, or,
> correlatively, the respective "no-rights" of A, B, C, D and others that
> the party should not eat the salad; *second*, the party's respective rights
> (or claims) as against A, B, C, D and others that they should not
> interfere with the physical act of eating the salad, or, correlatively,
> the respective duties of A, B, C, D and others that they should
> not interfere.
>
> These two groups of relations seem perfectly distinct; and the priv-
> ileges could, in a given case, exist even though the rights mentioned
> did not. A, B, C and D, being the owners of the salad, might say to
> X: "Eat the salad, if you can; you have our license to do so, but we
> don't agree not to interfere with you." In such a case the privileges
> exist, so that if X succeeds in eating the salad, he has violated no
> rights of any of the parties. But it is equally clear that if A had suc-
> ceeded in holding so fast to the dish that X couldn't eat the con-
> tents, no right of X would have been violated. (41)

Hohfeld adds that "A 'liberty' considered as a legal relation (or 'right'
in the loose and generic sense of that term) must mean, if it have any
definite content at all, precisely the same thing as *privilege*." (42–43).
Given the distinction just made, between being permitted to do some-

thing and having the claim-right to be free to do it, it seems to me exceedingly unwise to use the word "liberty" as a synonym of "privilege" understood as *permission*.

The point made by Hohfeld with the example of the salad is that being permitted to do something does not imply the claim-right to be free to do it. If the first party eats the salad, the others are not wronged; if the others manage to stop him from eating the salad, he is not wronged. As in any fair contest, neither party is wronged by either outcome. Perhaps the law provides us with no examples of the converse: having the right to be free to do something that the law does not permit. But morality provides us with abundant examples of having the right to be free to do something which morally is not permitted—that is, examples of cases in which one would be wronged should someone prevent one from doing what is morally wrong to do. In our lives as members of families, in our lives as citizens, and in our relation to God, often we have the right to be free to make moral mistakes.

What remains is to say a word about Hohfeld's powers and immunities. Hohfeld's example of a power is the power of a judge to pronounce sentence on someone convicted of a crime. His emphasis, in his discussion of powers, falls on the fact that a power is the capacity to bring about an alteration in someone's claim-rights or permission-rights, either an alteration in one's own rights or in those of another. The judge has the capacity to alter the rights of the person standing before him.[9] Hohfeld understands immunities, then, as immunities to such alteration. Immunities are limitations on the scope of powers. A military commander has the power, the *potestas*, to generate obligations in his troops by issuing commands of certain sorts to them; because I am not in the military, he does not have the power to generate obligations in me in that way. I am immune to his doing so. In the law, freedom claim-rights and immunities both offer protections of a certain sort. Nonetheless, Hohfeld was right to distinguish them. It is not that I have a claim-right against the military commander to his generating obligations in me by issuing commands. I am *immune* to his doing so; he lacks the *power* to do so.

I think Hohfeld was correct in distinguishing powers from both claims and permissions. Claim-rights and permission-rights are closely related

---

[9] If it was Hohfeld's intent to *define* a "power" as the capacity to bring about an alteration in someone's claim-rights or permission-rights, rather than, assuming that we know what a power is, to observe that that capacity for alteration is characteristic of powers, then Hohfeldian powers are a very untidy class. Many Hohfeldian powers will be what the medieval Latins called a *potestas*. But we also alter people's claim-rights and permission-rights by giving them gifts and by wronging them. I think it likely that Hohfeld was thinking of a power as a *potestas*; and that, in spite of the fact that I can alter someone's normative status by giving them gifts or wronging them, he would not call such actions "powers."

to powers; but powers themselves are neither of those. The power the judge has to pronounce sentence is a capacity that comes with his status of judge; it is an essential component of that status. I, not having the status of judge, do not have that capacity. Given his power, his capacity, to pronounce sentence, the judge is now permitted to exercise that power in certain ways, and has the claim-right to be free to do so. But the capacity to do something is not to be identified with the permission or the freedom to exercise that capacity in certain ways.

An Objection from Feinberg to the Strong Hohfeld Thesis

Our topic in the remainder of this chapter is whether the weak Hohfeld thesis is correct. Is it true that to every claim-right there is a correlative duty? Before I set out on that exploration, however, let me briefly consider an objection to the converse thesis. The overall lie of the land will become more clear.

The objection I have in mind goes as follows. Hohfeld speaks of the relation between rights against persons or social entities, on the one hand, and obligations toward persons or social entities, on the other hand. But not only do we have obligations toward persons or social entities to perform such-and-such actions; we also have obligations to obey laws. And in at least some such cases so says the objector, the idea of somebody or something having a right against us is just inapplicable. Joel Feinberg puts the point this way:

> When a traffic signal directs me to stop, it is difficult to find an assignable person who can plausibly claim my stopping as his own due. The original legislators may be long dead, and if vision is clear and no other motorists are in sight, there is no other person to whose right of way I owe respect. In short, I have a legal duty of obedience that is correlated with no other person's rights against me.[10]

I am not convinced. It is true that one does not violate anyone's right of way if one proceeds cautiously through a red traffic signal at 3 o'clock in the morning when "vision is clear and no other motorists are in sight." It is also true that one does not violate any legislator's right to obedience by such action. But traffic laws are not commands issued by private persons; they are legislation issued by the state. It is true that the state issues legislation *by way of* persons doing one thing and another; nonetheless, the issuance of traffic laws is a matter of state action. Accordingly, it is

[10] Feinberg, *Social Philosophy*, p. 63.

the state to whom one owes obedience. Should one fail to render the state obedience, it is the state that one wrongs. The structure is exactly similar to my disobeying a valid command issued to me by an individual person. Yes, I disobey the command. But *in* disobeying the command, I disobey the person who issued the command, thereby wronging him.

INITIAL DEFENSE OF THE WEAK HOHFELD THESIS

Consider some rights that appear to lack correlative duties. Suppose X has the right to drive either way on Main Street. Is there a duty correlative to this right? It is not obvious on the face of it that there is.

But Hohfeld's discussion alerts us to the fact that the term "right" in the sentence "X has the right to drive either way on Main Street" might well be ambiguous as between a permission-right and a claim-right. What might be meant is simply that X is *permitted* to drive both ways on Main Street; there is nothing in law or morality forbidding X from doing so, nothing that makes it his duty not to do so. If that is what is meant, then neither the strong nor the weak Hohfeld thesis applies. These theses are theses concerning *claim-rights*, not concerning permission-rights. Hohfeld's claim concerning permission-rights, as it applies to the case at hand, is that X is permitted to drive either way on Main Street if and only if X does not have a duty not to drive one of the two ways.

But if the sentence "X has the right to drive either way on Main Street" is understood as referring to a claim-right rather than a permission-right, what might that claim-right be? And does it have a correlative duty?

One of the points that emerged in discussing Hohfeld is that the sentence might be used to say that X has a claim-right to *being free* to drive either way on Main Street. It might be used to affirm the existence of a *freedom-right*. Though Hohfeld acknowledges the existence of freedom rights in his example of the salad, in his theory he gives such rights no special attention; he regards them as special cases of claim-rights, which of course they are, and lets it go at that. Further, the freedom-right to which Hohfeld refers in his example is a *specific* freedom right: the right of someone to be free from interference by A, B, C, and D in eating the salad. The rights that are customarily cited as examples of freedom-rights are *generalized* rights; they are not rights to be free from interference by some specific person or persons. When I say that X has the right to be free to drive either way on Main Street, I do not mention anybody from whose interference X has the right to be free.

So suppose X has the claim-right to being free to drive either way on Main Street. Is there a duty correlative to this right? I would say there is. If X has the claim-right to being free to drive either way on Main Street, then *everybody* has the duty to refrain from trying to stop him from doing so. So too, I am not only permitted to walk the streets of Manhattan; I have the claim-right to *being free* to do so. And to that claim-right there corresponds the duty of everyone to refrain from trying to stop me from doing so; nobody has the permission-right to interfere with my walking. In short, generalized freedom-rights prove, on scrutiny, to fit the weak Hohfeld thesis.

ADDITIONAL DEFENSE OF THE WEAK HOHFELD THESIS

Consider cases of quite a different sort. Suppose that the person in prison is innocent; justice has miscarried. Suppose also that nobody in the criminal justice system has acted culpably in his case. All the evidence publicly available at the time pointed to his guilt; his innocence is not established, let us say, until ten years later by a DNA test not available at the time.

Persons not guilty of a crime have a claim-right to freedom of movement. Yet it is not the case that those who imprisoned this person are culpable. Quite to the contrary; they have done what they ought to have done. So this is a case in which a person has a claim-right to the life-good of moving about freely, while his jailers, by keeping him imprisoned, are not only not violating their obligations but fulfilling them. Had they *not* imprisoned him, they would have been culpable. A claim-right without a corresponding duty—so it would seem.[11]

Here is another example of the point, a bit more elaborate. The city statutes state unambiguously that for the months of May through September, the city park is to be open until 10 P.M. to anybody who is neither creating nor threatening to create a nuisance. Just as the hour strikes 8 o'clock one July evening, my family and I arrive to walk in the park and feed the ducks. But the gatekeeper peremptorily orders us to leave, demands that everybody already in the park get out, and once they are all out, locks up. We have been deprived of our right—of our statutory right, and thereby of our moral right. We have been wronged. But is the gatekeeper guilty of having violated his obligations?

That depends on his reason for locking up at 8 o'clock. If his reason was that he did not want to wait until 10 o'clock to have beer with his buddies, then he would have violated his obligations. But suppose his reason was instead the following. It was late on a hot and difficult day when the city superintendent of parks instructed his newly hired gatekeeper on his duties; in his weariness he quite excusably fell into absentmindedness while talking, forgot that the regulations had recently

---

[11] The example was offered to me by Robert Adams.

been changed by the city commission, and said that the park was to be locked up at 8 o'clock when what he should have said was that it was to be locked up at 10 o'clock. That is why the keeper locked the gate in our faces when I and my family arrived at 8 to stroll about and feed the ducks. The keeper has done his duty under difficult circumstances; he is not culpable for his ignorance of the statute. Yet we have been deprived of our rights.

I suggest that a deeper analysis of these examples, and others like them, points up an ambiguity in the weak Hohfeld thesis rather than showing that the thesis must be rejected. A distinction that is common in the literature of philosophical ethics is that between so-called *subjective* and so-called *objective* duty. Because these terms were already used in chapter 1 for other purposes, I suggested earlier that we call them, respectively, full-cognition obligation and culpability obligation. Here is an example. Thirty or so years ago the accepted treatment for a person who survived a heart attack was bed rest for some six or eight weeks. We now know that this is very bad treatment; better to begin moderate exercise almost immediately. So imagine a cardiologist thirty years ago who prescribed two months of bed rest to his patient, and then ask this question: did he prescribe the treatment that he ought to have prescribed? I think we are all inclined to say that in one sense he did and in another, he did not.

In one sense of "ought" he did exactly what a cardiologist in his situation ought to have done. He followed his best lights; he would have been culpable had he not done so. But in another sense of "ought," that is not how he ought to have treated his patient. The treatment he described was in fact a very bad treatment; it would have been much better had he prescribed a regimen of moderate exercise. That is how cardiologists ought to treat their patients. But he did not know that and could not have known that. So he was not culpable, not blameworthy.

Duty (obligation) as understood in the former response is culpability obligation, usually called subjective obligation: a person has the culpability obligation to do A when, should he fail to do A, he would on that account be culpable, blameworthy. Duty as understood in the latter response is full-cognition obligation, or as it is usually called, objective obligation.

To avoid counter-examples of the sort I mentioned above, "duty" in the weak Hohfeld thesis must be understood as full-cognition duty. The gatekeeper violated his full-cognition duty, not his culpability duty; so too, those whose activities conspired to put the innocent person in jail violated their full-cognition duty, not their culpability duty. If duties are indeed the correlatives of rights (and rights of duties), then it is full-cognition duties that are the correlatives, not culpability duties.

FURTHER DEFENSE OF THE WEAK HOHFELD THESIS

Thus far we have turned up no exceptions to the weak Hohfeld thesis, that to every claim-right there is a corresponding duty—provided one understands "duty" as full-cognition duty rather than culpability duty. So let us move on to cases of yet a different sort.

Suppose you are a lifeguard at the beach on a windy day and you see two people, at some distance from each other but equidistant from you, struggling for their lives in the surf. It is obvious to you that you cannot save both. But there appears to be a chance that you can save one if you plunge in immediately and head for one of them. Neither of these two swimmers, call them Rick and Rich, has a right to your trying to save him. If you try to save Rick but not Rich, it cannot be claimed that you have violated Rich's right to your trying to save him; and vice versa. Yet if you do nothing, you are guilty—guilty of not having carried out your obligation to try to save one or the other. You are guilty but nobody is wronged. A duty without a right—so it appears.

There are examples of a similar structure in which it appears that there is a right without a duty. Suppose you are the swimmer struggling in the surf and Mike and Matt are the lifeguards on duty, equally competent, and sitting together, equidistant from you. Suppose further that neither is the subordinate of the other and that they realize that if they both try to save you, they are likely to get in each other's way and make it less likely that you will be rescued. You appear to have a right to an attempt at rescue; if neither Mike nor Matt tries to save you, you have been wronged. Yet it appears that neither is such that if *he* fails to try to save you, then *he* has failed in *his* duty. If Mike refrains from trying to save you because Matt was just a second faster in his response, he is not guilty of failing in his duty to try to save you, and vice versa. You are wronged if neither tries to save you, but neither is guilty of failing in his duty to you if *he* does not try to save you. A right without a duty—so it appears.

The pair of examples strikes at not just the weak but the strong Hohfeld thesis. One response worth considering is that, rather than giving up on the strong Hohfeld thesis, we acknowledge the existence of types of rights and duties more complex than we have hitherto taken note of. If you are guilty for not having tried to save either Rick or Rich, that must be because you had an obligation to try to save either Rick or Rich—not an obligation to try to save Rick or an obligation to try to save Rich, but an obligation to try to save either Rick or Rich—that is, an obligation to try to save Rich if you do not try to save Rick and to try to save Rick if you do not try to save Rich. You had a conditional obligation to both Rick and Rich. But then, by the same token, Rick and Rich each has a conditional right to your trying to save him, that is, the right to your trying to save him if you do not try to save the other. If you make no attempt to save either, then each is deprived of that conditional right; each is wronged. If you try to save one, then neither has been deprived of that conditional right; neither has been wronged.

But now consider a variant on the first example. Suppose, again, that you are the lifeguard; and imagine this time that there is one swimmer off to your right struggling for his life in the surf and five off to your left who are struggling. And suppose it seems likely to you that if you plunge in immediately and head for the five, you can save at least two, though not all five, whereas if you head for the one, you will be able to save him but him alone. It seems obvious that your duty is to try to save as many as possible, and thus to head for the five. But of what right is this now the correlative duty? You are guilty if you do nothing; but who is wronged and of what right have they been deprived? Another example of a duty without a right—so it appears.[12]

Perhaps we could come up with rights of a sufficiently complex type to handle cases of this sort as well. But I think there is a better way to go. In this third case, as in the first, there is no one such that you have the duty *toward him* to try to save him; and in the second case, there is no one such that you have the right *against him* to his trying to save you. The Hohfeld theses should be interpreted as meant only for those cases in which there is a person or there are persons such that the right is a right against *that person* or against *those persons* and there is a duty toward *that person* or *those persons*.[13]

REFORMULATING THE HOHFELD THESES TO ACCOMMODATE THIRD-PARTY COMMANDS AND PROMISES

Valid third-party commands and promises bring to light a structural feature of rights and duties that is concealed by the examples I have thus far been working with. In a valid third-party command, X commands Y that Y do or refrain from doing A to Z, with the consequence that X then has a right against Y to Y's doing or refraining from doing A to Z, and Y has an obligation toward X to do or refrain from doing A to Z. In such a case, let us say that Z is the *beneficiary* of the action that Y is obligated to perform out of obedience to the command and to whose performance X has a right. Similarly, in a valid third-party promise, X promises Y that he will

---

[12] The example was offered to me by Geoffrey Cupit.

[13] It must be kept in mind that in such contexts, "person" is to be understood as short for "person or social entity."

do or refrain from doing A to Z, with the consequence that X has an obligation toward Y to do or refrain from doing A to Z, and Y has a right against X to X's doing or refraining from doing A to Z. Z is the *beneficiary* of the action to whose performance X has a duty and Y has a right. The structural feature of rights and duties that is ordinarily concealed from view but revealed by third-party commands and promises is the distinction between the holders of rights and the objects of duties, on the one hand, and the beneficiaries of obligatory/rightful actions, on the other.

So as to bring this structural feature to light, we can reformulate the strong Hohfeld thesis as follows:

> If X holds a right against Y to Y's performing or refraining from performing A, whether or not X be the beneficiary of the performance or restraint, then Y has the duty toward X to perform A; and if Y has a duty toward X to perform or refrain from performing A, whether or not X be the beneficiary of the action, then X has a right against Y to Y's performing or refraining from performing A.

THE WEAK HOHFELD THESIS IN THE CLEAR

The weak Hohfeld thesis is in the clear. I know of no reason for rejecting it that we have not already considered and disposed of. To every claim-right there is a correlative duty. I should add that sometimes it seems clear that a person has a right to some good without its being clear against whom he has that right—without its being clear who has which duties.[14]

Its converse is another matter. As I mentioned earlier, it is often claimed that there are duties of charity, the concept of a duty of charity being the concept of a duty to treat someone beneficently when that person does not have a right against one to such treatment. The duty to forgive, assuming there is such a duty, would be a prime example. In chapter 17, after I have completed my account of rights, I will argue that there is a plausible understanding of duties of charity such that they are not exceptions to the strong Hohfeld thesis.

The other matter to consider, in assessing the converse of the weak Hohfeld thesis, is whether we have duties toward entities other than persons and human beings for which there are no correlative rights on the part of those entities. Suppose it is true, as I have tacitly been assuming

---

[14] Kramer, in "Rights without Trimmings," considers, and effectively answers, other objections to the weak Hohfeld thesis. I have concentrated on those that are especially important for our discussion in subsequent chapters.

since chapter 6, that entities that do not have lives do not have rights; and suppose that we nonetheless have duties toward some such entities—works of art, perhaps, or wetlands—not third-party duties but two-party. Then the converse of the weak Hohfeld thesis would be false; we would have duties toward some things that do not have correlative rights against us. In chapter 17 I argue that this is in fact the case. Thus whereas the weak Hohfeld thesis is in the clear, the strong thesis will have to be rejected.

FURTHER OBSERVATIONS ON THE STRUCTURE OF RIGHTS

We are now in position to give greater specificity to a thesis that has governed our discussion from the very beginning, namely, that that to which one has a right is always a good of some sort. In chapter 6 I developed the thesis that the goods to which someone or something has a right are always states or events in that entity's life or history;[15] in chapters 7 to 10 I argued that only within the flourishing life and history are all those states and events to be found, not within the experientially satisfying life nor within the happy life. The point to be made now, discussed in anticipatory fashion in chapter 9, is that the states and events to which one has a right all consist of or are components of human actions or restraints from action toward oneself. Rights are normative social relationships of a certain sort, as, of course, are obligations.

A person's possession of a right always has the structure of X has a right against Y to Y's doing or refraining from doing A. Suppose that the right in question is a two-party right. Then, if X enjoys his right against Y by virtue of Y fulfilling his duty toward X of doing or refraining from doing A, *Y's doing or refraining from doing A* is a good in X's life or history—as is that distinct state of X *enjoying his right* to Y's doing or refraining from doing A. And in many cases, the thing done, namely, A, will also be some good in X's life or history. Recall our example from chapter 9 of Paul's enjoying his right against Peter to Peter's making means of sustenance available to him. The following life-states of Paul are all goods in his life:

(1) Paul's enjoying his right against Peter to having means of sustenance made available to him by Peter.
(2) Paul's having means of sustenance made available to him by Peter.
(3) Paul's having means of sustenance available to him.

And as for Peter, his honoring of Paul's right against him, that is,

---

[15] In chapter 17 I argue that the thesis holds good for social entities as well as persons and human beings.

(i) Peter's doing his duty toward Paul of making means of
sustenance available to Paul

is a good in Peter's life, because doing one's duty is always a good in
one's life. On the other hand, the activity that it is his duty to do, namely,

(ii) Peter's making means of sustenance available to Paul

may or may not be a good in Peter's life. Performing that action may be
such a heavy burden for Peter that it diminishes his flourishing. In general, doing that which one has a duty to do may diminish one's flourishing even though the whole thing—doing one's duty by doing that
thing—is a good in one's life.

Third-party rights are a variation on this basic structure. Suppose that
Paul issues a valid command to Peter to do A with respect to Polly, so
that Peter is now under obligation toward Paul to do what Paul requested
and Paul now has a right against Peter to Peter's doing that. Suppose
further that Paul enjoys the good to which he has a right; that is to say,
suppose that Peter obeys Paul's command. Then the following are all
goods in Paul's life:

(4) Paul's enjoying his right against Peter to Peter's obeying him
    by doing A with respect to Polly.
(5) Peter's obeying Paul by doing A with respect to Polly.

But that which Peter does in obedience to Paul, namely, A with respect
to Polly, is not a good in Paul's life, because it is not a state or event in
his life. It is an event in Peter's life and an event in Polly's life, but not
in Paul's.

As for Peter, his honoring of Paul's right against him to obeying Paul
by doing A, that is,

(iii) Peter's doing his duty toward Paul of obeying him by
doing A with respect to Polly

is a good in Peter's life. Doing one's duty, to say it again, is always a good
in one's life. But

(iv) Peter's obeying Paul by doing A with respect to Polly

may or may not be a good in Peter's life. Peter may find that obeying
Paul by doing A with respect to Polly imposes considerable harm on
himself; it may significantly diminish his flourishing. That will usually be
because

(v) Peter's doing A with respect to Polly

diminishes Peter's flourishing.

Last, what about Polly's having A done to her by Peter? Is that a good in *her* life? It might not be. If what Paul commands Peter to do is deliver to Polly the very sad news that she has not received tenure, then what Peter does with respect to Polly is not a good in Polly's life. It is an event in her life that diminishes rather than enhances her flourishing.

Amidst all these variations and subtleties, what remains true is that rights are claims to the good of being treated in certain ways. Rights are normative social relationships.

Chapter Twelve

RIGHTS NOT GROUNDED IN DUTIES

THE ISSUE NOW BEFORE US: ARE RIGHTS GROUNDED IN DUTIES?

We are trying to understand rights. What is it about certain of one's life- and history-goods that accounts for the fact that one has a right to those goods, whereas to others, one does not? In the preceding chapter we considered two suggestions to the effect that we have the rights we have on account of our having the duties we have.

One of these suggestions, the *Ramsey thesis*, as I called it, holds that the life-goods to which one has a right are those one must enjoy in order to fulfill one's duties. (The Ramsey thesis ignores those history-goods that are not life-goods.) We uncovered a number of reasons for rejecting the Ramsey thesis.

The other suggestion consisted of three theses: (i) the good to which one has a right always has the basic structure of being the good of some agent doing or refraining from doing something with respect to one; (ii) if X has a right against Y to Y's doing or refraining from doing A, then Y has a duty toward X to do or refrain from doing A; and (iii) that right of X against Y is grounded in that duty of Y toward X. Our discussion led us to affirm theses (i) and (ii). Along the way we also considered the strengthened version of (ii), which says that duties have correlative rights as well as rights having correlative duties. Our reason for suspending final judgment on that stronger thesis was twofold. It remains to be considered whether there are entities of certain sorts toward which we have duties without their having correlative rights against us. And it remains to be considered whether the widely held view is correct, that duties of charity lack correlative rights.

The fact that we found no rights without correlative duties means that we are now confronted with the third thesis, that what accounts for a right is the duty correlative to that right. If there are duties to which there are no correlative rights, then we can properly demand of any fully developed attempt to ground rights in duties that it explain why that is. If other duties have correlative rights that they ground, why not these? But because that issue becomes relevant only if the thesis can be sustained that claim-rights are grounded in their correlative duties, let us set it off to the side for the time being.

Suppose that X tortures Y solely for the pleasure X finds in doing so—the delicious sense of power it gives him to have Y totally at his mercy, to be able to extract screams whenever he pleases. In thus torturing Y, X has flagrantly wronged Y—deprived him of what he has a right to. What accounts for this wronging? X can do all sorts of things to Y that would not amount to wronging Y. What accounts for the fact that in this case, Y is wronged?

What accounts for it, so the thesis under consideration says, is that in torturing Y as he did, X did to Y what he ought not to have done to Y. Y is wronged by X because X violated his obligations toward Y. It was X's duty not to torture Y.

And what accounts, in turn, for the fact that in torturing Y as he did, X violated his duty? The success of the attempt to ground rights in duties depends on whether it is possible to offer a general account of subjective obligations that does not presuppose the existence of subjective rights but instead shows how and why subjective obligations are more basic than subjective rights and how the latter are grounded in the former.

My argument in this chapter will be that this cannot be done; no general account of obligation can achieve what is required. Or to speak more precisely and more modestly: none of the standard accounts of obligation satisfies the requirement. Who knows what new ones might come down the pike? Thus we finally get the systematic defense of the claim made in chapter 1, that the conception of justice as right order is untenable. Or to speak once again more precisely and more modestly: what I will show is that if the norm for right order is thought of as a matrix specifying in a general way the obligations of members of the social order, then the right order conception of justice is untenable. This is how all our present-day proponents of the right order conception do think of the norm. Because I hold that the conception of justice as inherent rights can be developed into a fully adequate account of justice, I do not propose hiring myself out to the right order theorist to try imagining alternative ways of thinking of the norm for right order that do not fall prey to fatal objections.

Our Focus Will Be on the Divine Command Theory

The requirement that the account show how and why obligations are more basic than rights and how the latter are grounded in the former removes certain accounts of obligation from consideration at once—the divine fiat account, for example. On the divine fiat account, God brings about obligations by simple fiat. God declares, "Let it be the case that so-and-so is obligatory," whereupon it is. The content of the fiats might be specific: "Let it be the case that John is obligated to respect his parents now." Or it might be general: "Let it be the case that children are obligated to respect their parents."

The account fails because it does not satisfy the requirement that it show how and why obligations are more basic than rights in the order of grounding. By virtue of the principle of correlatives, if Y belongs to the sort of entity that can have rights, then X has a right against Y to Y's doing A if and only if Y has an obligation toward X to do A. On the divine fiat theory of obligation, what would account for the grounding relation in each pair going from duties to rights rather than from rights to duties? What is it about the idea of God's bringing about normative facts by fiat that establishes this order of grounding? Why not think of God as bringing about rights by fiat, with duties then grounded in rights? Why not go for a divine fiat account of rights? Or better yet, if one favors a divine fiat account, why not be impartial and advertise it as a divine fiat account of rights and obligations?

The contemporary scene offers two views concerning the source of moral obligations that appear to hold more promise, for showing that rights are grounded in duties, than the divine fiat account. Both see subjective obligations as grounded in principles of obligation; to be guilty is to violate some prior principle of obligation. The *social contract* line of thought sees objective principles of obligation as the product of our agreeing (promising, undertaking) to act in accord with those principles. The *moral authority* line of thought sees those principles as the deliverances of some moral authority. The deliverances are commonly held to take the form of commands, requests, or legislation.

Let us begin with the latter line of thought. Rather than attempting a survey of moral authority views in general, I propose focusing on a particular species of such views, namely, that which holds that God is the relevant authority. This seems to me the only species with any plausibility. All candidates other than God that have been proposed for the relevant moral authority have patent deficiencies that undercut their candidacy. Durkheim argued that for each of us it is our society that is our moral authority. Given the flawed character of every society, I find it hard to view this proposal as anything other than an act of theoretical desperation.

One more preliminary matter is important. I have just now been speaking of views concerning *the source* of moral obligations; where do moral obligations come from? A full account of moral obligation will contain more than a thesis concerning the source of moral obligations; it will also contain a thesis concerning *the nature* of moral obligation. What *is it* to be morally obligated to do something? And at the center of any account of the nature of moral obligation has to be an account of the *requiredness* that is an ingredient of obligation. An act that I am obligated to perform is not merely an act that would be good for me to perform;

it is one that I am *required* to perform. Though the social contract theory of obligation purports to tell us the source of moral obligations, it makes no pretense of offering an account of the requiredness that is ingredient within obligation. So too, the divine command theory purports to tell us where obligations come from but does not purport to give us an explanation of the requiredness ingredient within obligation.

It is not the project of this chapter to develop an account of the nature of obligation; the project is the more limited one of determining whether rights are grounded in duties. Nonetheless, several of my arguments presuppose the falsehood of a certain account of the nature of obligation, namely, the so-called *social requirement* account. I judge that this is not the understanding of the nature of obligation that most of us tacitly operate with; I surmise that most readers will find the arguments I offer to the point, if not always compelling. However, those who hold some version of the social requirement account will not find all of them to the point; they will find an understanding of the nature of obligation being presupposed that they disagree with.

I think it best to delay presenting my own account of the nature of obligation—the *respect* account, I will call it—until chapter 17. After presenting my account, I will show why I think it is to be preferred to all social requirement accounts. What this means, for those readers who favor some social requirement account, is that, for them, the argument of this chapter will not be fully complete until chapter 17.

It seems intuitively plausible that if one can show that the divine command theory works as a general account of the source of moral obligations, then, given the principle of correlatives, one will have shown that rights are grounded in duties. For though it is true that by issuing a valid command one generates not only in one's addressee the obligation to obey by doing what one commanded but in oneself the right to his doing that, it seems intuitively correct to hold that one has the right because he has the obligation. Whether that initial intuition has a solid basis is something we would have to consider if the divine command account proved satisfactory in all other respects. I will argue that it does not.

I will pass over all the in's and out's of the divine command theory so as to concentrate on what is directly relevant to our purposes here.[1]

How Commands Generate Obligations

The divine command account of principles of moral obligation gets its initial plausibility from two facts. First, the Hebrew, Christian, and Muslim

---

[1] In chapter 6 of my *Divine Discourse* I discuss different aspects of the theory from those that I discuss here.

Scriptures pervasively present God as issuing commands to human beings. And second, by the issuing of commands, we human beings often generate in our fellow human beings obligations to do certain things that previously they were not obligated to do. By commanding his troops to start the bombardment, the officer places them under obligation to do so. Before he issued the command, they were not obligated to do that; the obligation was generated by the command. It is these two facts that the divine command theory of moral obligation takes and runs with. Let it be added that the issuing of commands and requests is not the only way in which we generate obligations in others. To cite just one other example: acts of charity typically generate duties of gratitude in the recipients.[2]

Evident as it is that obligations are generated by the issuing of commands, it is equally evident that some commandings do not generate obligations (and that some locutionary acts whose sentences have the grammatical form of a command do not count as illocutionary acts of commanding). An imposter commander does not generate in a body of troops the obligation to perform some military maneuver by commanding them to perform it, nor do I generate in you the moral obligation to surrender the desirable seat you found on the train by commanding you to surrender it.

What accounts for the difference? Well, an act of commanding can be defective in one way or another—malformed, not properly formed. Worse yet, the conditions for the performance of any act of commanding whatsoever, even of a malformed act, can be absent, so that, though imperative language was uttered, no act of commanding occurred. A condition of some illocutionary act's being a well-formed act of commanding is that it generate a (prima facie) obligation in the addressee to do what is commanded.

The imposter officer did not, by what he said, perform a well-formed act of commanding, a decisive sign thereof being that he did not generate in the troops the obligation to perform the military maneuvers that he commanded. Why not? What was lacking on his part, making his act of commanding—assuming that he did in fact succeed in commanding—malformed?

---

[2] This fact has led to the quixotic claim by Derrida and other participants in the recent flurry of discussions about "the gift" that one can never give a true gift, because always some return is required, if of nothing else, then at least of gratitude. See Jacques Derrida, *The Gift of Death*, trans. David Wills (Chicago: University of Chicago Press, 1995). My own view is that, rather than treating this argument as revealing the surprising truth, hitherto unnoticed, that there can be no true gift, one should instead treat it as a *reductio ad absurdum* argument against the assumption that something is not a true gift if gratitude is (morally) required.

Well, the imposter officer lacked the *power,* the *potestas,* to issue military commands to this body of persons; he lacked the *capacity* to do so. Hence he also lacked the *authority* to do so, that is, the permission-right to do so and the claim-right to be free to do so. That is why the command he issued was malformed in such a way that he did not generate in them an obligation to do what he commanded. To have the permission-right to issue a command to someone on some matter is perforce to have the permission-right to generate in them the obligation to do that. The legitimate officer possesses the capacity and the authority to generate obligations in his troops on military matters by commanding; the imposter does not.

If the legitimate officer has the *potestas* and the authority to generate obligations on military matters in his troops by issuing commands to them, then obviously the troops have the obligation to obey such commands of that sort as he may issue to them, by doing what he commands. And the corollary of that obligation on the part of the troops is the right, on the part of the officer, to his troops' obeying him by doing what he commands them to do—when he commands what he is authorized to command, when his command is a well-formed command.

Let me call the permission-right and freedom claim-right of the legitimate officer to issue commands to his troops on military matters *standing* rights on the part of the officer; let me likewise call the implied obligation of the troops to obey such well-formed commands as the offier may issue a *standing* obligation on their part, and the implied right of the officer to his troops obeying such well-formed commands as he may issue a *standing* right on his part. This standing obligation of the troops and these standing rights of the officer are not generated by the officer's commands; they were already there. It is because they were already there that the officer, by commanding his troops to do A, can now generate in them the obligation to do A, assuming that A is an example of the type of action that he has the authority to command. This standing obligation and these standing rights are the presupposed normative context for the officer's ability to generate in his troops specific obligations to do certain things by issuing commands to them. It is because the imposter officer lacks not only the authority but even the *potestas* to issue commands on military matters to these troops, with the consequence that the troops lack the standing obligation to do what he commands and he lacks the standing right to their obedience to his commands, that he cannot generate in them the obligation to perform some military maneuver by commanding them to perform it.

The fact that the legitimate officer has the *potestas* and the standing authority is of course not a coincidence; having that *potestas* and the standing authority is an intrinsic component of his office, his position, as officer of these troops. It comes along with the office.

The phenomenon of an *office* or *position* with powers intrinsic to it and with the authority to exercise those powers in certain ways is an important element of human affairs in general.[3] For example, there is the office of umpire in professional baseball, the office of judge in a court system, and the office of president of a university.

Having a certain office normally gives one the authority to do certain things that one could do even if one did not have that office. For example, having the office of President of the United States gives one the authority to move into the White House; but even if one did not have that authority, one could move into the White House if one had sufficient clout at one's disposal. On the other hand, having a certain office normally also enables one to do certain things that otherwise one simply could not do, no matter how much power, *potentia*, was at one's disposal. And along with that *potestas* comes the authority to exercise it in certain ways—that is, the permission-right to exercise it in those ways and the claim-right to be free to do so. Not only the authority but the power (*potestas*) itself comes as a component of the office.

In professional baseball, only someone who has the office of umpire is able to call a player out. Spectators in the stands can shout "out"; often they do. But only the umpire can *call* a player out; only the umpire has the power to *declare* him out. And not even someone whose profession is that of umpire has the power to declare a player out when off-duty and himself a spectator in the stands; he can do so only when acting in the office, the position, of umpire.

Furthermore, a person has the office of umpire with respect to certain players and not with respect to others; offices are typically *with respect to* specific groups of people. Only a person who has the office of judge has the power and authority to declare a person legally guilty. He has that power and authority only when functioning in his office as judge; and he has that power, and the authority to exercise it in certain ways, only with respect to certain people.

To have the authority to do certain things, so I have been suggesting, is to have the permission-right to do certain things and the claim-right to be free to do those things. Intrinsic to most offices, perhaps indeed to all, is such authority. What we have seen is that among the rights intrin-

---

[3] What I am here calling an *office*, I called, in chapter 5 of my *Divine Discourse* (Cambridge: Cambridge University Press, 1995) a *standing*. I have changed terminology so that here I could highlight the distinction between an office, on the one hand, and its attendant powers, obligations, and rights, on the other, and have the word "standing" available for the latter.

sic to an office will often be the authority to issue commands of a certain sort to a certain group of people.

The power and authority of a person to issue commands of a certain sort to a certain group of people is so familiar that we overlook how extraordinary it is. Given the connection noted between commands, on the one hand, and obligations and rights, on the other, the power and authority to issue commands implies the power and authority to generate in certain people the obligation to obey one by performing actions of a certain sort, the corollary of which is the claim-right on one's own part to their obeying one by doing that. Such power and authority, to generate obligations in others and rights in oneself by performing a speech act of a certain sort, is extraordinary!

It will be crucial for our subsequent discussion to keep in mind the distinction I have introduced and employed, between the *standing* obligations and rights that make it possible to generate obligations in others and rights in oneself by issuing commands, and the *new* obligations and rights thus *generated.* The issuing of commands does indeed generate in people obligations to do specific things that previously they were not obligated to do—or generate additional grounds for their being obligated to do things they were already obligated to do. But commands do not generate these obligations *ex nihilo.* For the generation to occur, the one who commands must already have the *potestas* and standing authority to place these people under obligation to do a thing of this sort by issuing to them a command to do a thing of this sort, and they must already have the standing obligation to obey him by doing such things as he validly commands them to do. The issuing of commands is not the sort of thing that can generate obligations outside the context of obligations and rights already there.

History is full of examples of illegitimate regimes issuing commands, and doing what looks like issuing commands, to the people they have subjected; the subjects are often well advised to submit. But given the fact that the regime does not occupy the "office" of legitimate government of these people, it does not generate in them the obligation to do something by commanding them to do that. So too, *mutatis mutandis,* is the case for legitimate regimes that issue commands outside the scope of their authority.

An Initial Objection to the Divine Command Theory

Let us now use what we have learned about the nature and import of human commanding to reflect on the divine command account of principles of moral obligation. The Hebrew, Christian, and Muslim Scrip-

tures present God as issuing commands to certain human beings to do
certain things; thereby God generates in them the obligation to obey
God by doing those things. The divine command theory extrapolates
from this biblical and koranic presentation to claim that all moral obligations are generated in this fashion. Every moral obligation, so the theory
claims, is the content of a command of God; every moral obligation is
what obedience to some command of God requires. It should be clear
from our discussion of the Old Testament in chapter 3 that this extrapolation goes well beyond what Scripture itself says. Of course that is not
to show that the extrapolation is false.

When we approach the theory with the previous discussion in mind,
two substantial objections come to the fore. The first is the following.
The theory proposes to illuminate how God generates moral obligations
by pointing to an analogous phenomenon in human affairs: we generate
obligations in each other by, among other things, issuing commands.
However, some of the obligations that we generate in each other by issuing commands are *moral* obligations. Hence it is not the case that all
moral obligations are generated by God's commands; some are generated by *human* commands. So the theory is not the general account of
obligation that it purports to be; it leaves unexplained the obligations
that we human beings generate. The very phenomenon in human affairs
that the theory uses to *illuminate* God's generation of moral obligation
is *incompatible* with the theory itself.

How might the divine command theorist respond to this objection?
One response would be to claim that the obligations we generate by
the issuing of commands are never *moral* obligations; they are military
obligations, legal obligations, game obligations, etiquette obligations, or
whatever, but not moral obligations.

This response to the objection strikes me as having no plausibility. Up
to this point in my discussion I have deliberately refrained from saying
anything at all about the sort of obligations generated by our well-formed
commands; in particular, I have not said that they are moral obligations.
But surely many of them are, maybe most of them. When a parent commands (requests, asks) his child to clean up his room, he generates in
the child the obligation to *obey* him by cleaning up his room—and hence
the obligation, if it was not already obligatory, to clean up his room.
Surely, at least the first of these, the obligation to obey, is a moral obligation, though perhaps only a prima facie one.

Another response to this initial objection to the divine command theory that the divine command theorist might consider is first to concede
that, by commanding someone to do so-and-so, we sometimes generate
in him the prima facie *moral* obligation to obey the command by doing
that, but then to go on to claim that the reason you and I are sometimes

morally obligated to obey the commands of our fellow human beings is that God has commanded us to obey those commands, thereby generating in us the moral obligation to obey God by obeying our fellow human beings. Absent that divine command and the moral obligation generated thereby, we would never be morally obligated to do what our fellow human beings command us to do. So yes, it is true that a human being, by commanding X that X do A, can generate in X the moral obligation to obey him by doing A; but such obligation-generation by a human being is entirely parasitic on, and derivative from, God's having generated in us the moral obligation to obey God by obeying our fellows.

On this view, the concept of a well-formed command does not include the property of generating an obligation in the person to whom it is addressed; it is not a conceptual truth that such speech acts generate obligations. That view seems to me clearly mistaken. But let me forgo pressing the point. The more important point to make is that, on this analysis of the situation, our human generation of obligations by the issuing of commands can no longer be used to illuminate *God's* generation of moral obligations by the issuing of commands. Given this analysis of our human situation, reasoning to God by analogy would suggest that we are morally obligated to obey God's commands because there is someone other than God commanding us to do what God commands; and so on, *ad infinitum.*

A Second Objection to the Divine Command Theory

A second objection to the divine command theory that comes to the fore, when we approach it with the preceding discussion of human commanding in mind, is more important for my purposes here. The theory holds that all moral obligations are generated by God's commands. It holds, thus, that God generates moral obligations where there were no such obligations before, none at all. By commanding, God generates moral obligations *ex nihilo.* Our previous discussion casts doubt on that claim. The essence of the objection to the divine command theory that I will now develop was already lodged by Samuel Clarke against Hobbes's account of obligation; so we can call it, if we want, the *Clarke objection.*[4]

---

[4] It was Terence Cuneo who called to my attention, quite some time after I had developed my objection to the divine command theory, that the core of the objection goes back at least to Samuel Clarke. Here is what Clarke says about Hobbes's attempt to derive obligations from the social contract: "To make these 'compacts' obligatory [Hobbes] is forced . . . to recur to an antecedent 'law of nature'; and this destroys all that he had before said. For the same law of nature which obliges man to 'fidelity,' 'after' having made a compact, will unavoidably, upon all the same accounts, be found to oblige them, 'before'

Suppose that God has commanded me to do A and that I now ask, what makes it morally obligatory for me to do what God commanded— not just prudent but obligatory? After all, it is by no means the case that everything everybody commands me to do is something that I am on that account morally obligated to do, even prima facie. So why in this case? What is it about God's having commanded me to do something that makes it morally obligatory for me to do it?

So far as I can see, the only answer is that, by virtue of God's "office" or "position" with respect to us, God has the power (*potestas*) and author- ity to place me and my fellow human beings under moral obligation to do something by commanding us to do it; as the consequence of that power, we have the standing moral obligation to obey God by doing such things as God may command, and God has the standing moral right to our obeying him by doing what he commands. But obviously, we cannot now say that that standing obligation of ours was in turn generated by some command of God—specifically, by God's command to obey God's commands. That would set us off on an infinite regress. God's generation of moral obligations on our part, by issuing commands to us, *presupposes* the existence of a standing moral obligation on our part *not thus gener- ated*—and a corresponding moral right on God's part.

How might the divine command theorist respond to this point? One response he might consider is to deny that there is that standing obliga- tion. There is no general obligation on our part to obey God by per- forming such actions as God may command, nor any general right on God's part to our obeying God by doing what God commands. There are only the specific obligations generated in us by God's actual com- mands, along with the specific rights thereby generated in God to our obeying him.

How shall we reply, in turn, to this response to our second objection? Well, notice that it leaves the divine command theorist without anything to point to that would account for why it is that God generates specific moral obligations in us by issuing commands to us. On this view, if God commands me to do A, then it is just a brute fact that thereby God has generated in me the moral obligation to obey God by doing A; if God commands me to do B, then it is just a brute fact that thereby God has generated in me the moral obligation to obey God by doing B; and in

all compacts, to 'contentment' and mutual 'benevolence.'" In "A Discourse concerning the Unchangeable Obligations of Natural Religion," in D. D. Raphael, *British Moralists 1650–1800*, vol. I (Indianapolis: Hackett, 1991), p. 219.

One of my readers for Princeton University Press has called my attention to the close similarity between my argument and H.L.A. Hart's argument, against the legal positivism of John Austin, that ordinary legal rights *presuppose* a legal right to rule or legislate. The basic text is Hart's *The Concept of Law* (Oxford: Oxford University Press, 1961).

general, for any act that God commands me to perform, it is a brute fact that I am morally obligated to obey God by performing that act. Nothing explains this. That is just how it is.

Instead of regarding this appeal to brute fact as a deficiency of his view, the person considering this line of response might go on the attack and insist that the absence of any suggested explanation is a virtue of his view; all attempts to offer an account here are misguided. Human beings can issue commands that do not generate obligations; accordingly, when a human being does generate an obligation in someone by commanding that so-and-so be done, there will always be something that accounts for that. Let it be conceded that what accounts for it is the speaker's power and authority to issue such a command to this person, along with the standing obligation and the standing right that that authority implies. But God could not possibly issue commands that do not impose obligations, because God could not possibly issue anything other than well-formed commands; so there is nothing to account for.

Two replies to this initial response to our second objection to the divine command theory are in order. If one is willing to rest with brute fact at this point, why not take the next step of simply eliminating reference to divine commands and holding the position mentioned earlier, that God creates moral obligations by fiat? Why not be a divine fiat theorist rather than a divine command theorist?[5] Why not hold that God's bringing about of moral obligations is a basic act on God's part? God does not *generate* my moral obligation to do A by performing some other action, namely, *commanding* me to do A, thereby generating my obligation to obey him by doing A, and thus my obligation to do A; God brings about my obligation to do A simply by deciding to bring it about. God says, *Let N.W. be morally obligated to do A*, whereupon N.W. is so obligated. Reference to the act of commanding is beside the point; commanding has nothing to do with it.

In short, the initial response to our second objection, the response that says that there simply is no standing obligation on our part to obey such commands as God may issue, effectively undercuts the divine command theory rather than supporting it, doing so in such a way as to pay a price that the divine command theorist wished not to pay. The divine command theorist assumed that, by pointing to the nature and effects of human commands, he could *illuminate* the source of moral obligation. Just as we human beings generate obligations by commanding, so too

---

[5] Philip Quinn has discussed the divine-fiat view in some of his essays. For references, and for critique, see Mark C. Murphy, "Theological Voluntarism," in *The Stanford Encyclopedia of Philosophy* (Fall 2002 edition), ed. Edward N. Zalta, http://plato.stanford.edu/archives/fall2002entries/voluntarism-theoological.

God generates obligations. But in human affairs there is nothing even remotely similar to the generation of moral obligations by fiat.[6] And as I observed earlier, if God can generate obligations by fiat, presumably God can also generate rights by fiat. So what basis remains for holding that rights are grounded in duties?

Furthermore, the argument that there is nothing to account for here, because God could not issue malformed commands, is not sound. Let it be agreed that God's office or position with respect to us, combined with God's nature, do imply that it is impossible for God to issue malformed commands to us; nonetheless, the fact that, by virtue of God's position or office, God has the power and authority to issue commands to us of a certain sort explains how it is that, by actually issuing a command to us to do so-and-so, God generates in us the new obligation to obey God by doing that.

Be all that as it may, however, the initial response to our second objection—the response that declares that there is no standing obligation on our part to obey God by doing such things as God may command and no counterpart standing right on God's part—is untenable for any theist of an Abrahamic sort. Intrinsic to such theism is the claim or assumption that we human beings *do* have that general obligation and that God does have the corresponding general right. Some of our obligations are obligations to do specific things: to help *this* blind person across *this* street at *this* time, to tell the truth to *this* person at *this* time, and so on. But other obligations of ours are obligations to perform actions of a certain type when an instance of the type becomes possible or relevant: to be of aid to blind people, to tell the truth, not to covet. The Ten Commandments are all of this latter sort. The obligation in question here is also of this sort; we have the general obligation to obey God by doing such things as God may command.

ANOTHER RESPONSE TO THE SECOND OBJECTION

We have been considering a response to our second objection to the divine command theory, the objection that, though well-formed commands do indeed generate obligations, commands are not the sort of thing that can generate obligations *ex nihilo*; they presuppose a normative

---

[6] The person who holds that God generates obligations in human beings by sheer fiat would presumably not want to say that this is true for all obligations; God does generate some obligations by the issuing of explicit commands. So one way of fitting things together would be to say that God generates by sheer fiat our standing obligation to obey such commands as God may issue, and generates all other obligations by the issuing of commands.

context of prior obligations and rights. The only other response by the divine command theorist to this second objection that I can think of is to concede that there is indeed the standing obligation on our part to obey God by performing such actions as God may command, but to insist that this is not a *moral* obligation. Though the obligations *generated* by God's actual commands are moral, the standing obligation is not a moral obligation. This, if I interpret him correctly, is the solution Robert Adams is proposing in the following paragraph from his discussion of the divine command theory in his book *Finite and Infinite Goods*:

> One central feature of the human practice of commanding is that persons to whom commands are issued have some obligation to obey them. If their relationships to the commander are not such as to sustain obligations, the command is not valid; perhaps it is not "really" a command. This feature of the practice is surely part of what is taken into the content of God's intentions in commanding. That might be thought to create a problem of circularity for the theory that the nature of obligation is to be understood in terms of divine commands. The solution to this problem is that the kind of obligation whose nature is to be understood in terms of divine commands is fully valid moral (and religious) obligations, whereas the obligation that is presupposed as involved in the practice of commanding is a premoral social or institutional obligation that may or may not have full moral validity. (266–67)

Let me expand a bit on what I take Adams's thought here to be. The root notion of obligation is *requirement*. Requirements come from many sources: from the laws of the land in which one lives, from the rules of the game one is playing, from the rules of politeness in one's society, from the rules of etiquette for a person of one's status, from one or another social role that one fills, and as we have seen, from some command issued to one. One of the tasks of the moral theorist is to determine where, in this panoply of requirements, *moral* requirements are to be found.

We can state in declarative sentences what is required of a person by one or another of these sources of requirement: "The rules of etiquette require that you place the fork to the left of the plate"—alternatively, "According to the rules of etiquette, the fork is to be placed to the left of the plate." But we can also express such requirements in imperative sentences using the language of "should," "ought," and "must": "You should (ought to, must) place the fork to the left of the plate."

Unlike the declarative sentences, such imperative sentences, all by themselves, leave obscure the source of the requirement expressed; sometimes the context makes that source clear, sometimes not.

Adams's suggestion is that there is another source of requirement, distinct from any of those I have just now mentioned, namely, the social-linguistic practice of giving and receiving commands. One of the rules governing that practice is that the addressee of a well-formed command is to obey that command by doing what is commanded. If you and I are now engaged in the social-linguistic practice of giving and receiving commands, you as the one issuing a command and I as the addressee thereof, then I am required by the rules of the practice to obey you by doing what you commanded, assuming the command you issued is well formed. I ought to do it, I should do it, I must do it, by virtue of the rules of the social-linguistic practice. I would be violating the rules of the practice if I did not obey you.

In the course of my discussion I have said, several times over and in several different ways, that it belongs to the *concept* of a well-formed command that it is a speech act that places its addressee under (prima facie) obligation to obey by doing what is commanded, To say that it is a rule of the social-linguistic practice of giving and receiving commands, that one is to obey such well-formed commands as are issued to one by doing what is commanded, is to get at the same point from a different angle, with this addition: to make the point in the second way is to specify the source of the requirement, to make it in the first way is to leave the source unspecified. Here is an analogy: one can say that the queen in chess is that piece that moves in such-and-such a way, or one can say that the rules for the movement of the queen in chess are such-and-such. The point is the same.

The application of the general point goes like this: there is indeed the standing obligation on our part to obey God by performing such actions as God may command—given that God is a loving God. But that is not a moral obligation; it is, instead, a requirement of that social-linguistic practice of giving and receiving commands in which God participates along with us. Moral obligations, by contrast, are what obedience to God's actual commands requires of us. The requirements of the social-linguistic practice of giving and receiving commands are contrasted with the requirements of God's commands. So it is true that God's commands do not generate moral obligations *ex nihilo*, that is, in the absence of any prior obligations whatsoever; they are, however, generated in the absence of all prior *moral* obligations.

How shall we appraise this second response to my second objection to the divine command theory? Well, let us suppose that God has commanded me to perform action A. Then I have the following obligations:

(2) the standing general obligation to obey God by performing such actions as God may command me to perform, and

(3) the generated specific obligation to obey God by performing the action A that God commanded me to perform.

The first of these is an obligation to perform actions of a certain type; the second is an obligation to perform an action of that type. So if I violate (2), then perforce I also violate (1); conversely, there is no other way to violate (1) than by violating either (2) or some other specific obligation that is like (2) in being an example of the type specified in (1). Now, on the analysis under consideration, the violation of (2) is a violation of a moral obligation, thus an act of moral wrongdoing; and so too for all generated obligations like (2). Hence all violations of (1) are perforce acts of moral wrongdoing. Yet (1) is said to be not a moral obligation.

I do not understand how this can be. Let it be conceded that (1) is a requirement of the social-linguistic practice of giving and receiving commands. That does not prevent its *also* being a moral obligation. (Cf. the final words in the passage from Adams: "a premoral social or institutional obligation that may or may not have full moral validity.") What else is needed to make it a moral obligation? If the fact that all examples of the type are moral obligations is not sufficient, and if it is not sufficient that there could not possibly be a violation of (1) that is not a case of moral wrongdoing, then what would be sufficient to make (1) a moral obligation? What is lacking?

Suppose that something I am legally required to do I am also morally required to do—whether or not I am morally required to do it apart from its being legally required of me. Then every violation of the legal requirement is also perforce a case of moral wrongdoing; it is both at once. There is nothing mysterious in that. One and the same act is a violation of two distinct sets of standing requirements, moral and legal.

The relation between (1) and (2) is different. Here there is only one standing requirement, namely, (1). It is the obligation to perform actions of a certain type whenever that becomes a live possibility. The type is: obedience to a command of God issued to us. We are obligated to bring about an instance of that type whenever there is open to us the possibility of doing so; and there is that possibility whenever God issues a command to us—and only when God does so. So suppose that God issues to me the command to do A. Then there is open to me the possibility of performing an instance of the type, specifically, this instance: obedience to *this* command of God to me that I do A. So given that I have the standing obligation to perform any instance of the type when the live possibility of so doing is opened up to me, I am obligated to perform *this* instance of the type.

I do not see how my obligation to perform this instance of the type can be a *moral* obligation when my obligation to perform *any* instance of the type that becomes possible for me is *not* a moral obligation.

My own view concerning the general relation between, on the one hand, the requirements of the social-linguistic practice of giving and receiving commands and, on the other hand, our moral obligations, runs along the following lines.[7] Certain things are required of us by the social roles we play, others by the rules governing the practices we employ. None of these is, as such, a moral requirement.

Well-formed commands are like such roles and rules in that, just as certain things are required of us by roles and rules, so also certain things are required of us by commands. But commands are unlike roles and rules in a fundamental way. Commands directly introduce *persons* into the situation; for every command issued to me, there is a person issuing the command. More specifically, commands introduce the possibility of *obedience or disobedience to a person* into the situation. What is enjoined on me by a command may be something that I was already required to do by role or rule; alternatively, it may not have been required of me by anything at all. Either way, the command, if well formed, introduces this new factor: if I fail to do what I am enjoined to do by this command, be that independently required of me or not, I perforce treat the person issuing the command in a certain way; I disobey her. That way of treating a person is always, prima facie, a case of moral wrongdoing—trivial moral wrongdoing in some cases, but moral wrongdoing nonetheless. It is a prima facie case of morally wronging a person. To disobey a valid command is prima facie to show a certain degree of disrespect for the person issuing the command.

So I agree that it is a rule of the social-linguistic practice of giving and receiving commands that one is to obey such well-formed commands as are addressed to one; the rule simply unfolds the nature, the essence, of a command. But I hold that obedience to well-formed commands is not only required by the rules of our social-linguistic practice; it is required by morality as well. When I depart from polite practice and put the fork to the right of the plate, no one is wronged. But when someone issues to me a valid request to place the fork to the left of the plate and I, for no good reason, refuse to do so, then that person has been morally wronged and I, who have done it, am on that account morally guilty. Perhaps not seriously guilty; but guilt does not have to be serious to be guilt.

My view, in short, is that not only is that standing obligation to obey God by performing such acts as he may command a *moral* obligation; the

---

[7] I elaborate this view much more fully in chapter 4 of my *Divine Discourse*.

much more general obligation, to obey persons in general by performing such acts as they may enjoin on us with well-formed commands, is also a moral obligation.

Generalizing to All Authority Accounts of Moral Obligation

The conclusion of our argument thus far is this. The person who holds that rights are grounded ultimately in duties owes us an account of moral obligation in which it is clear that rights are dependant on duties. The divine command theory of moral obligation does not fill the bill. It proves not to be a satisfactory general account of obligation because, though God's commands do indeed place us under obligation, their doing so presupposes the normative context of a standing obligation on our part to obey such commands as God may issue to us. It also proves not to be satisfactory for the purposes at hand, because a corollary of that standing obligation on our part is the standing right on God's part to our obedience to such commands as God may issue. There is no reason to suppose that either the standing right or the standing obligation is prior to the other.

We can safely generalize: every moral authority account of the principles of moral obligation will fall prey to the same objection . Commands, requests, and the like generate obligations only in the context of obligations and rights not generated by commands or requests.

Standing Rights, Standing Obligations, and Promises

Our consideration of social agreement accounts of the principles of moral obligation can be more brief. On such accounts, the principles of moral obligation are rules that we have agreed, promised, or in some other way undertaken to live by. They are imposed on us not by some moral authority but by ourselves.

In promising you to do something, I generate an obligation in myself to do that and a right of you to my doing it. Furthermore, it seems correct to say that you have the right to my doing that *because* I have taken on myself the obligation to do it; certainly it seems odd to say the opposite, that I now have the obligation because you have the right. So if the social agreement account works as a general theory of obligation, and if to every right there is a correlative duty, then we are well on the way to showing that rights are grounded in duties.

The truth of the matter, however, is that whatever the other objections to social agreement accounts—and they are legion—such accounts all fall prey to an objection wholly parallel to the main objection I lodged against the divine command theory. Let me take a somewhat circuitous path to this conclusion; what we learn on the way will prove of use in later chapters.

God is presented in the Hebrew, Christian, and Muslim Scriptures not only as issuing commands to us but as making promises to us and covenants with us. Promises and covenants work in the opposite way from commands. Whereas the one who issues a well-formed command generates in the addressee an obligation to obey by doing the thing commanded, and generates in himself the right to the addressee's doing that, the one who makes a well-formed promise generates in himself the obligation to keep his promise by doing the thing promised and generates in the addressee the right to his doing that.

In my discussion of commands I observed that commands sometimes generate in their addressees the obligation to obey and sometimes do not. I asked what accounts for the difference. A command that does not generate in its addressee the (prima facie) obligation to obey the command is defective in some way. The defect I pointed to was that the one issuing the command lacked the *power* (*potestas*) and/or *authority* to issue a command of that sort to these people—that is, he lacked the power and/or authority to generate in them the obligation to do a thing of that sort by commanding it. And I observed that a consequence of someone having the authority to command something of a certain person is that the addressee has the standing obligation to obey such well-formed commands as the speaker may issue to him—the corollary of this in turn being that the speaker has the standing right to that obedience.

The same things are to be said, *mutatis mutandis*, concerning promises and covenants. It is typically the case that there are things that the head of an organization, functioning in her capacity as head, can obligate herself or the organization to do, by promising or contracting to do them, that other members of the organization cannot thus obligate themselves or the organization to do; they lack the authority, and perhaps even the power, to do that. Likewise, there are certain actions that the officer of a body of troops can obligate himself to perform, by promising his troops to perform them, that an imposter officer cannot thus obligate himself to perform. Of course, the head of the organization has that power and authority only when actually functioning in her capacity as head; and the officer of the troops has that power and authority only when actually functioning in his capacity as officer.

I further observed that usually it is not coincidental that only the person in a certain office or position has the power and authority to issue commands of such-and-such a sort to such-and-such persons. Such power and authority are typically intrinsic components of the office or position that the speaker occupies: the power and authority come along with the office. The same thing holds, *mutatis mutandis*, for promises and covenants. The power and authority to make certain sorts of contracts come along with the position of head of the company; the power and authority to make certain sorts of promises come along with the position of officer of these troops.

It would be tedious to elaborate these points of similarity in more detail; let us move on to the application. An implication of the biblical and koranic presentation of God as making promises to us and covenants with us is that God has the power and authority to generate in himself the obligation to perform some action by promising or covenanting with us to perform that action. And a presupposition or implication of God's having that power and authority is that God has the standing general obligation to keep such promises and covenants as God may make, by doing what God promises or covenants, and that we have the standing general right to God's keeping such promises as God may make.

That standing obligation on God's part is a moral obligation, as is that standing right on our part. The obligation, let it be said, is also a requirement of the social-linguistic practice of offering and receiving promises and covenants. But promises and covenants are engagements between or among persons; when, for no good reason, I break a promise, I wrong *a person*, show him or her disrespect. The obligation to keep one's promises is both a requirement of the social-linguistic practice of making and receiving promises and a prima facie moral requirement.

To summarize: presupposed by the biblical presentation of God as *issuing commands* to us, thereby generating in us the moral obligation to obey by doing the thing commanded, is the standing general moral obligation on our part to obey such commands as God may issue by doing the thing commanded, and the standing general moral right on God's part to our obeying such commands as God may issue. And presupposed by the biblical presentation of God as *making promises* to us, thereby generating in himself the moral obligation to keep God's promise by doing the thing promised, is the standing general moral obligation on God's part to keep such promises as God may make by doing the thing promised, and the standing general moral right on our part to God's keeping such promises as God may make. Just as we have moral obligations toward God and God has moral rights against us prior to God's issuing of commands, so too God has moral obligations to us and we have moral rights against God prior to God's making promises to us and covenants with us.

I am well aware that many members of the Christian tradition, past and present, will find the latter suggestion abhorrent. Quite a few would be willing to concede that we have standing moral obligations toward God and that God, correlatively, has standing moral rights against us; but many would resist the view that God has standing moral obligations toward us and that we have standing moral rights against God. Some would deny that God has any moral obligations at all toward us; most of the others would hold that such moral obligations as God has toward us have been freely assumed by God by way of promising and covenanting. But if one reflects on the necessary conditions of promising and covenanting, one sees that that cannot be. If God has no standing obligations toward us and we have no standing rights against God, then the biblical and koranic presentation of God as making promises to us and covenants with us cannot be true—that is, not literally true. It must be, at most, a picture. Many in the tradition have been willing to "bite the bullet" and say exactly this.

Why have so many members of the Christian tradition found it abhorrent to think of God as having standing moral obligations toward us and of us as having standing moral rights against God? Assuming that this is indeed an implication of God's promising, why would they prefer to say that then God does not really promise? My guess is that it is because of the tendency, lodged deep in the tradition, to think of morality as consisting ultimately of principles of obligation to which moral agents are then subject. How could God be "subject" to such principles? The suggestion that I develop in the next two chapters is that it is a mistake to think of morality this way.

The application of the points made above to social agreement accounts of the principles of moral obligation will now be obvious. We do indeed generate obligations in ourselves, and thereby rights in those to whom we obligate ourselves, by making promises, agreements, and the like. But such generation cannot occur in a normative void. What accounts for the fact that, by making an agreement with each other, you and I generate in ourselves the obligation to do what we agreed and in the other the right to our doing that, is that there is a standing obligation for us to keep such agreements as we may make with each other. Absent that standing obligation and its correlative standing right, we might generate expectations in each other by striking an agreement, but we would not generate obligations. This is the Clarke objection.

Chapter Thirteen

RIGHTS GROUNDED IN RESPECT FOR WORTH

Recall one of the conclusions reached in chapter 11: the fundamental structure of claim-rights is that the life- or history-goods to which one has a right are actions or restraints from action on the part of persons or social entities.

We do not always have the fundamental structure in mind when we speak of rights. Some of the examples I gave along the way, of life- or history-goods to which one has a right, were not actions or restraints from action on the part of others; many of the examples given by other writers are also not of this sort. I have a right to walk on the New Haven Green. But walking on the Green is neither an action nor restraint from action on the part of others, nor an action such that I would wrong myself should I fail to accord myself the good of performing it. It is a permission-right. The claim-right in question is my right *to be free* to walk on the New Haven Green; and that consists of my right to others' refraining from interfering with my walking on the New Haven Green. The fundamental structure of the good to which I have a claim-right is thus not that of walking on the New Haven Green but that of others' refraining from interfering with my walking on the New Haven Green. This is the pattern for freedom rights in general. And as to benefit rights, though we speak of one's right to (the good of) a monthly Social Security check, the fundamental structure of the right is that it is a right to (the good of) of being sent a Social Security check monthly by the U.S. government. This is the pattern for benefit-rights in general.

It would be tedious always to express the fundamental structure of rights; not even philosophy could bear the burden. Nonetheless, to understand the nature of rights it is important to keep in mind their fundamental structure. Doing so makes clear, for example, that the mere fact that some event has resulted in the absence from one's life of some life-good is by no means sufficient to establish a violation of rights. When someone deliberately hits me over the head with a 2 x 4 while I am strolling on the New Haven Green, thereby causing brain damage, I am wronged; but when a tornado sends a 2 x 4 flying through the air that hits me on the head and causes the same brain damage, I am not

wronged. When Union Carbide's plant in Bhopal, India, emitted noxious fumes into the air, thereby depriving thousands of the inhabitants
in the valley of their lives, they were wronged; but when a volcano erupts
and spreads noxious fumes down a valley, they are not wronged. Injustice
is far from the only cause of human suffering. Clawing animals, biting
insects, floods, droughts, tornadoes, and poisonous plants all deprive us
of life-goods without wronging us thereby.

Justice and injustice are inherently social. Enjoying what one has a
right to, and being deprived of what one has a right to, are social engagements. Only if some person or social entity is accountable for one's lack
of some life- or history-good does that lack represent being wronged.
Among the goods in some people's lives are feats of great athletic skill;
if one were composing a eulogy of Bob Gibson's life, one would mention
his feats as a pitcher for the St. Louis Cardinals. There are no such goods
in my life; I lack athletic talent. I rather think my life would have been
more excellent had it contained a few such feats; but the lack of such
goods in my life is no indication that I have been wronged. I did not
have and do not have a right to such goods. On the other hand, there
are probably some people lacking such feats in their lives for whom that
lack is an indication of having been wronged. Imagine, for example,
someone whose great athletic talent has been maliciously impaired by
some jealous competitor, so that great athletic feats prove never again
within her reach. The reason the lack of such goods in my life does not
represent a violation of my rights is that, in my case, the lack cannot be
traced to the agency of someone who deliberately impaired me. In the
case of the natively talented person whose ability was maliciously impaired, the lack can be so traced.

So once again, the fundamental structure of a right is that it is a right
to the life- or history-good of some action or restraint from action on
the part of some person or social entity. Conversely, always, when one is
wronged, one is wronged by some action or restraint from action on the
part of some person or social entity—that is, by some action or restraint
from action that can be *laid to the account* of some person or social entity.
If I am hurled out the window in a train wreck and fall on you in such a
way that your spleen is ruptured, I do not thereby wrong you, because I
was not accountable for damaging your spleen; my agency was not involved in the right way for me to be accountable. "I didn't do it," we say.
It is important to add that "accountable" must be understood in such a
way that it does not imply blameworthiness or praiseworthiness. My
agency may account for your being deprived of some good to which you
have a right, so that I have wronged you; but if I acted out of non-culpable
ignorance, I am not blameworthy. Rights, let us recall, are the correlatives
of full-cognition obligations, not of culpability obligations.

Now for the converse: though a right is a right to be treated a certain way by persons and social entities, there are many ways of being treated by persons and social entities to which one does not have a right, not even when those ways of being treated would enhance one's flourishing. The greatest challenge facing any theory of rights is to explain the difference: why is it that we have a right to certain actions and restraints from action on the part of persons and social entities, whereas to other actions and restraints we do not have a right—even when those others would be life-goods for us enhancing our flourishing? Why do I have a right to a polite answer from the receptionist in the clinic when I ask where I must go for my flu shot, but not a right to her giving me that fine etching hanging on her wall, even though, over the long run, being given the etching would enhance my flourishing much more than a gruff answer to my question diminishes it?

THE SORT OF ACCOUNT WE ARE LOOKING FOR

The account of rights that we are looking for is an account of moral rights. Within the terrain of moral rights, we are looking for an account of primary rights, not of rectifying or retributive rights—though it would be surprising if an account of the former did not cast considerable light on the latter. And within the terrain of primary rights, we are looking for an account that will explain and illuminate both freedom rights and benefit rights, both natural rights and socially conferred and linguistically generated rights, both inherent rights and conferred rights. In addition, we are looking for an account that will explain and illuminate why we do respond, and why it is appropriate for us to respond, with such emotions as anger and indignation to the perception that one has been deprived of that to which one has a right. And we are looking for an account that will take due recognition of the situated character of rights.

What I mean by this last is that the right one has against one person to his doing A will usually be such that there are other persons against whom one does not have that right, at that time in that situation. And the right one has in certain situations against someone for doing A will often be such that, at other times and in other situations, one does not have that right against that person; one may not have it against anyone. The rights of the poor to which John Chrysostom pointed (recall chapter 2) provide an example of this last point. In most situations, people have a right to fair access to adequate means of sustenance; they have this right, so Chrysostom argued, just by virtue of being human. But when extreme widespread drought occurs and no food is available, nobody any longer has that right against anyone.

In chapter 6 I distinguished between the relative worth or excellence of a human being and the relative worth or excellence of a human being's life and history. A human being's life and history are made up of states and events; the worth or excellence of the life or history as a whole is determined by the worth or excellence of the states and events that make up that life or history. A human being, by contrast, is not a state or event, nor is he or she "made up" of states and events. A human being is an Aristotelian substance. And entities that have worth are by no means confined to the ontological category of states and events. Substances such as human beings have worth, worth in various respects. Some human beings are better than others with respect to their ability as swimmers, some with respect to their talent for mathematics, some with respect to virtue, and so forth. What we will now be seeing is that rights emerge from a certain interweaving of life- and history-goods and evils, on the one hand, and the worth of human beings, on the other. This is the delayed payoff of the distinction made in chapter 6.[1]

An Opening Example

Let us set out on our journey with an example of a socially conferred right, that is, a right conferred by the legislation of some organization or the rules of some social practice.[2] Imagine a piano competition in which the rule is that the person who performs best in the final stage of the competition is to be declared winner of the competition and given a prize of $100,000; no other considerations are to be used in determining who shall be declared winner and given the prize than just the quality of the final performance. Let us suppose that Frank constitutes the one-man jury in this competition, and that the finals have just been concluded. There were two finalists, call them No. 1 and No. 2. Finalist No. 1 is elderly; after a long and distinguished career as a performer, this may well be his last public appearance. He is famous, wealthy, and arrogant, brimming over with self-esteem. Finalist No. 2 is young and at the very beginning of his career; though of exceptional talent, he is not yet widely known. Frank has learned that he is destitute and of fragile self-esteem; he regularly falls into depression when people judge his performances inferior.

---

[1] For the sake of economy of words, I continue to speak of "life-goods," when what I have in mind is "life- or history-goods."

[2] The example was presented to me by Chris Eberle as a counter-example to an earlier attempt of mine to articulate an account of rights.

Frank judges that No. 1 gave the better performance overall. No. 2's performance showed enormous promise; there were passages of sheer brilliance that transcended anything in the performance of his competitor. But No. 1's performance was steady and overall superior. To Frank's surprise, as he is about to follow the rules of the competition and declare No. 1 the winner, he finds balance-of-good considerations welling up within him. He realizes that it is a good thing in the life of any pianist to have the honor of being declared the winner of a prestigious competition, and a good thing to receive $100,000 even if one is wealthy. He also recognizes that everybody is trusting him to go by the rules, and that it is a bad thing in the lives of people to have their trust betrayed. But on the other hand, there are all those good things that would ensue if No. 2 received the prize. Young talent would be encouraged, No. 2's fragile self-esteem would be bolstered, he would be liberated from having to wait on tables to make ends meet, and so forth. Frank is not required to give reasons for his decision. But he reflects that should he give the prize to No. 2 and later be asked why he made the decision he did, he could offer plausible-sounding reasons for the judgment that No. 2 had turned in the better performance. Hence there is no danger that the standard practice of piano competition will be undermined should Frank declare in favor of No. 2. Frank would in fact be vigorously opposed to doing anything that would undermine the practice; he regards it as a fine thing.

After a few minutes of such balance-of-good reflections, Frank makes his decision. He declares No. 2 the winner, his unstated reason being that the sum of life-goods and evils that will ensue from this declaration clearly outweighs in worth that of the life-goods and evils that would ensue from declaring No. 1 the winner.

I hold that even if Frank was correct in his judgment that greater good would be achieved by declaring No. 2 the winner, he should not have done what he did. That is to say, *morally* he should not have done what he did.

Why not? Is it because the *virtuous* person does not do that sort of thing—does not, for example, betray trust in the way Frank did? Well, just as the concept of a right, on my analysis, is conceptually posterior to the concept of the good, so also the concept of a moral virtue is conceptually posterior to the concept of a morally admirable act. A moral virtue is the habit of performing morally excellent acts of a certain sort in a certain way: courage is the habit of performing courageous acts in a certain way, in distinction from cowardly acts, on the one hand, and foolhardy acts, on the other. So before we can tell whether Frank did or did not act virtuously, we must make a judgment about the moral worth of what he did. And that is exactly what is in question.

Suppose we think of the moral virtues as those habits of action necessary for achieving the goods constitutive of a properly formed and properly functioning society. We can agree that trustworthiness is such a virtue. And Frank did not act as the person for whom the virtue of
trustworthiness is all-determinative would have acted. He proved himself
not to be trustworthy, or more precisely, not to be *unfailingly* trustworthy.
Is that why he should not have done what he did?

That is not at all clear. We live in a world in which we are often confronted with conflicts among good things to do and bad things to avoid;
the virtuous person is in the habit of doing the better thing in such
situations. Betraying trust is a bad thing to do—less bad, perhaps, if nobody other than oneself has any reason to suspect that one is betraying
trust; but, nonetheless, a bad thing to do. On the other hand, encouraging the cultural endeavors of the upcoming generation is a good thing
to do, as is giving arrogance its come-uppance. One can dispute whether
Frank made the correct judgment as to the overall balance of life-goods
and evils. But if he did, and if the only relevant consideration is such life-
goods and evils as he considered, then I see no reason to infer that he
did not act virtuously. What he did is what the virtuous person who thinks
in terms of life-goods and evils might well do in such a case.

I submit that the only way to bring to light just how Frank did what
morally he should not have done is to bring something other than life-
goods and life-evils into the picture. Frank violated the *rights* of No. 1;
No. 1 had *a right* to be declared winner. That is the new and decisive
consideration. In addition to weighing up life-goods and evils, Frank
should have taken note of a moral consideration of a different order; he
should have asked himself whether, in declaring No. 2 the winner, he
would be depriving No. 1 of what he had a *moral right* to. Given the correlatives thesis, in declaring No. 2 the winner Frank also did what he *ought
not* to have done; he violated his *moral obligations*. So in addition to
weighing up life-goods and life-evils, Frank might have asked himself
whether, in declaring No. 2 the winner, he would be violating his moral
obligations. It would not have mattered whether he picked up the stick
on the rights end or the obligations end; the decision would have
been the same.

We should take a minute here to consider the force of the word
"should" in the claim that Frank should not have done what he did. The
"should" here is the deliberative should, not to be identified with the
should of moral obligation. The question "What should I do?" is not the
same as the question "What is my obligation (duty) to do?" When thinking exclusively in terms of life-goods and evils, giving no thought whatsoever to obligations, Frank can nonetheless ask what he should do. And
if and when he does bring obligations into the picture, he can still ask

whether he should do what he is morally obligated to do. It may be necessarily true that he should do what he is morally obligated to do; but it is not analytically true, that is, not true by virtue of the meaning of the terms "should" and "morally obligated." It is not like asking whether he should do what he should do, or whether he is obligated to do what he is obligated to do.

Our example of Frank and the piano competition is useful for correcting an impression given by many discussions on rights. Many such discussions give the impression that rights are violated for ignoble reasons, such as greed, spite, jealousy, pride, rage, or lust for power or status. But Frank's reasons were noble reasons; he wanted to encourage young talent, give a come-uppance to arrogance, and the like. I think the structure of rights is probably better illuminated by analyzing examples of noble than of ignoble violations.

Rights, and Goods That Trump

What is it that Frank does when he violates the rights of No. 1? What are rights? Begin with the apothegm that rights are trumps.[3] I take this to mean that if I have a right against you to the good of some action on your part, then your performing that action is to take precedence for you over whatever balance of life-goods and evils might ensue from not performing that action, provided no one has a right to any of those life-goods. You are not to consider whether not performing the action might make a greater contribution to my flourishing, to your flourishing, or to the flourishing of others. Such considerations are off the table. If your doing what I have a (prima facie) right to your doing violates no rights of others and conflicts with none of yours or mine, then you should do what I have a right to your doing, *period.* Rights are peremptory.

How does it happen that the good of certain actions and restraints from action acquires this trumping import, this peremptory significance? It is important to recall, as we attempt to answer this question, that we are beginning our analysis of what it is to have a right with socially conferred rights; the answer to the question will be somewhat different when we are speaking of natural and inherent rights.

Take an example of a socially conferred right different from the one I have been using, a real-life example that I have cited previously in my

---

[3] To the best of my knowledge, it was Ronald Dworkin who first used the metaphor of rights as trumps. See his article, "Rights as Trumps," in Jeremy Waldron, ed., *Theories of Rights* (Oxford: Oxford University Press, 1984). An older way of making the same point is to say that rights are *peremptory.*

discussion. I have a right to the good of a monthly Social Security payment from the U.S. government. My having a right to that good implies
that the government, in the person of its officials, is not to go through
eudaimonistic or utilitarian calculations when deciding whether to send
me the payments; they are to put all such calculations out of mind and
do what I have a right to their doing, namely, send me the payment.

Why do I have this right, when most other human beings do not have
it? I have it because I have the status of being a U.S. citizen who is age
sixty-five or older (plus a few other conditions that for our purposes we
can afford to ignore). The right comes along with the status; anyone who
has that status has that right.

How did that right get attached to that status? It got attached to it by
the Social Security legislation of the United States. The legislation may
not have used the *language* of rights or entitlement. It may simply have
said that the government *shall* send a payment of a certain size each
month to those of its citizens who are at least age sixty-five (and satisfy a
few other conditions). But everyone understands those words as meaning that the government shall send this payment to such persons, *period.
No questions asked.* It is not to send the payment to such persons when the
government believes, in the person of its Social Security administrators,
that it would serve the greater good to do so or the good of the recipients.
It is to send the payment, *period.* With respect to all those who have the
status of being U.S. citizens age sixty-five or older, the legislation gives
trumping import to the good of their receiving a monthly payment.

The same sort of thing holds for the piano competition. Here the
relevant status is the competitive ranking of having turned in the best
performance in the judgment of the jury. The rules of the competition
attach, to the person who acquires this status, the right to being declared
winner and receiving the designated prize. The relevant rule, perhaps
explicitly formulated somewhere, is that the person who, in the judgment of the jury, has turned in the best performance in the final stage
of the competition *shall be* declared winner and receive the prize, no
further questions asked.

RIGHTS, GOODS THAT TRUMP, AND WRONGING

Though this is the beginning of the explanation of what constitutes a
right, it is by no means the end. Frank knew very well that it was a rule
of the practice that whoever in the eyes of the jury acquired the competitive status of having turned in the best performance in the finals was to be
declared the winner of the competition and given the prize, no further
questions asked. He knew that the goods of being declared winner and

receiving the prize had this trumping import for whoever had acquired the requisite status. He knew about this intra-practice trumping import. But in his calculation of goods and evils, what he did is to put the good of following the rule of the practice on this occasion in the balance with all the other life-goods and evils that would ensue from his declaration. Knowing full well that the rules of the practice gave trumping import to being declared winner and receiving the prize for whoever acquired the status of turning in the best final performance in the judgment of the jury, he put the practice itself in the balance on this occasion.

The trumping import of a good to which one has a moral right is not a purely intra-practice or intra-legislation phenomenon. It is possible that some justice-as-right-order theorists think of socially conferred rights as nothing more than intra-practice or intra-legislation trumps. But if that was all they were, we would have no explanation of why Frank morally should not have done what he did. If the rules of a certain practice or the laws of a certain organization, in combination with my having a certain status, give me a moral right against you to some life-good, then among the considerations that are off the table for you is whether, in this case, following or violating the rule or law would yield the greater overall positive balance of life-goods and evils. The trumping force of goods to which we have moral rights is *supra*-practice and *supra*-legislation.

How do we explain this transcending dimension of the trumping force of those goods to which we have rights? Only by bringing into the picture a factor distinct from any of those I have thus far represented Frank as taking into consideration. In doing what he did, Frank *wronged* No. 1. That is to say, he wronged that *person* who was No. 1. He altered the moral condition of that person in that way. If you have a moral right against me to my doing A with respect to you and I do not do A, then not only do I fail to render you some life-good to which the rules of some practice or some piece of legislation gives trumping import for persons of your status; I have *wronged you*. To our failure to render people certain life-goods comes attached the all-important significance of thereby *wronging* them; to other examples of such failure, that significance does not come attached. That significance, *wronging*, is the source of rights. We begin to see why, from the very beginning of our discussion, I have given prominence in our reflections on justice to the phenomenon of *being wronged*.

But how does *wronging human beings* get into the picture? I argued, first, that what accounts for one's having a socially conferred moral right to some life-good is that a law of some organization or a rule of some social practice gives trumping import to that life-good for all who have a certain status, and that one has that status. I then observed, however, that the trumping import of a good to which one has a moral right transcends those laws and those rules that confer the right on those of a certain status. And I went on to suggest that what accounts for this is that, when someone has a right against me to my performing A and I do not perform A, then I have morally wronged that person; I have altered his moral condition in that regard. But how does that phenomenon of wronging a human being get into the picture? Why isn't the fact that a law or rule has been violated the end of the matter?

The U.S. Social Security legislation says that all U.S. citizens of age sixty-five or over *shall* receive a monthly Social Security payment. Should some bureaucrat, whether out of noble utilitarian considerations concerning the greater good or because he wishes to practice a bit of embezzling, decide not to send me a payment for a couple of months, he would be violating the legislation. By saying that all who have the status of being U.S. citizens age sixty-five or older *shall* receive a monthly payment, the law declares that even considerations of greater good are off the table for those responsible for sending out the payments; the good of my receiving the monthly payment is to trump all those considerations. But nothing is said or suggested in the law about *wronging me*. How does that get into the picture? How does violating the legislation acquire this extra significance?

In the example of the piano competition, the rules of the social practice say that the jury *shall* declare the person who turns in the best final performance in the judgment of the jury to be winner of the competition and *shall* offer him the prize, no further questions asked. That good, for the person who has that status, is to trump all others. Nothing is said in the rules about the fact that if the rules are violated, the person who has performed best has been *wronged*. How does wronging a human being get into the picture?

In short, what is the connection between the trumping import of goods to which we have rights, brought about in the case of socially conferred rights by the laws of some organization or the rules of some social practice, and the fact that, by violating the rules, some *human being* is *wronged*?

I suggest that at least one of the connections in such cases is trust and betrayal of trust. Everybody involved in the piano competition, competitors and audience alike, trusted that the jury would make its declaration of winner in accord with the rules of the competition. Frank not only violated the rules; by violating the rules he did this other thing: he betrayed trust. So too, the bureaucrat who acts in violation of the legislation does not only violate the rules; thereby he betrays trust, and thereby the government also betrays trust.

To betray a person's trust is to wrong the person—at least prima facie. The betrayer of trust does something quite different from miscalculating the relative worth of life-goods and evils; likewise he does something else than act out of accord with some legislation or social practice. He *wrongs a human being*. It makes no difference whether anyone discovers the betrayal.

I assume that I do not have to defend the claim that to betray someone's trust is to wrong that person. The fact that we all feel angry when we discover that our trust has been betrayed indicates our conviction that betrayal of trust wrongs us.

I suggest that what we have just concluded about the two cases considered is true in general for rights conferred by legislation or social practice. If on account of some social practice or legislation someone has a right against me to my treating them a certain way and I do not treat them that way, then in acting out of accord with the practice I do this other thing as well: I betray their trust, and thereby I wrong them. If this is correct, then underlying every socially conferred right is a natural right; for our right not to have our trust betrayed is a natural right, not a right we have on account of the action of human beings. Or if some strange piece of legislation does confer the right on some people, they would have had the right even if it had not been conferred.

Wronging and Respect

And what is it to wrong someone? Obviously it cannot simply be doing to the person what one should not do, where the "should" is the purely deliberative should, or we will not have advanced a single step. Let me take my clue from the chapter by the late Jean Hampton, "Forgiveness, Resentment, and Hatred," in the book she wrote with Jeffrie G. Murphy, *Forgiveness and Mercy*.[4] Hampton asks, "What is it that really bothers us about being wronged?" Her answer:

> It is not simply that wrongdoings threaten or produce physical or psychological damage, or damage to our careers, interests or families. However much we may sorrow over bad fortune, when the same damage is threatened or produced by natural forces or by accidents, we do not experience that special anger that comes from having been *insulted*. When someone wrongs another, she does not regard her victim as the sort of person who is valuable enough to require better treatment. Whereas nature cannot treat us in accord with our moral value, we believe other human beings are able and required to do so. Hence when they do not, we are insulted in the

[4] Cambridge University Press, 1988.

sense that we believe they have ignored the high standing that value gives us. (43–44)[5]

What follows this passage is an extraordinarily insightful discussion of demeaning, degrading, and the difference between them (degrading consists of reducing the value of the other). Hampton concludes by remarking, "*A person wrongs another if and only if (while acting as a responsible agent) she treats him in a way that is objectively . . . demeaning, that is, disrespectful of [that person's] worth*" (52).

This seems to me correct: to wrong a human being is to treat her in a way that is disrespectful of her worth. But what is it to treat someone in a way that is disrespectful of her worth?

Three ideas are at work when we judge that someone has been treated disrespectfully, or as I shall often call it, treated with *under-respect*. First, we assume that human beings have non-instrumental worth; if that were not the case, there could be no such thing as treating *them* with disrespect. To deny that human beings have non-instrumental worth is to deny by implication that they have moral rights; conversely, to deny that human beings have moral rights is to deny by implication that they have non-instrumental worth. Second, we assume that certain of our actions with respect to our fellow human beings have what may be called *respect-disrespect import*; that is to say, they are cases of treating someone as being of a certain worth. And third, we assume that the respect-disrespect import of one's action may or may not fit the actual worth of the human being who is the object of the action. Let me say something about each of these assumptions, beginning with the second.

THE RESPECT-DISRESPECT IMPORT OF ACTIONS

Treating a human being in a way that is disrespectful of her worth— alternatively expressed, in a way that shows disrespect for her worth—is not to be identified with *not* treating her in a way that shows respect for her worth. Most human beings are not treated by me in any way whatsoever. They fall completely outside my ken; in no way whatsoever do I

---

[5] Hampton goes on to quote a passage to the same effect from the chapter by Jeffrie G. Murphy that preceded hers in the book: "One reason we so deeply resent moral injuries done to us is not simply that they hurt us in some tangible or sensible way; it is because such injuries are also *messages*—symbolic communications. They are ways a wrongdoer has of saying to us, "I count but you do not," "I can use you for my purposes," or "I am here up high and you are there down below." Intentional wrongdoing *insults* us and attempts (sometimes successfully) to degrade us—and thus it involves a kind of injury that is not merely tangible and sensible. It is moral injury, and we care about such injuries."

treat them or engage them. So perforce I do not treat them in a way that shows respect for their worth. But that is not to wrong them.

Disrespect is active. Mere absence of showing respect is not, as such, showing disrespect—though in certain situations, not to do what we call "pay respect" is to treat with disrespect, as when, for example, one says nothing in a situation where words of praise or approbation are expected. Disrespect comes in the form of demeaning or insulting remarks, belittling or dismissive comments, physical or emotional abuse, silence when words are expected, acting as if the other person were not present. Treating a human being with disrespect is treating her in a way that is incompatible with acknowledgment of her true worth.

Treating someone with disrespect, as I shall understand it, does not require *feeling* disrespect. We speak of *showing* someone respect and of *showing* someone disrespect. It is natural to think of these along expressivist lines: I have a feeling (attitude) of respect or disrespect for you, and I now *show* that feeling by my comportment and actions—I express it, I manifest it, I reveal it. This is indeed one meaning of the phrases "showing X respect" and "showing X disrespect": by one's comportment and actions, one expresses one's feeling (attitude) of respect or disrespect for the other. But that is not the concept relevant to our purposes here.

When I speak of showing someone respect or disrespect, I just mean *treating* her with respect or disrespect. One can treat someone with respect or disrespect without having *feelings* of respect or disrespect for her, and so without showing or manifesting such feelings. By the expressions "treating a person with disrespect" and "showing a person disrespect," I shall mean acting in a disrespectful manner toward the person, treating her disrespectfully, whatever one's feelings and attitudes. The point is that one's actions may be respectful even when one feels no respect, when one feels disrespect; one may be dissembling. And one's actions may be disrespectful even when one feels respect. We say sometimes, "I didn't mean to be disrespectful" or "I didn't mean to show disrespect," when we realize that, though we have nothing but feelings of respect for the person, we nonetheless treated her disrespectfully.

An equally important point is that treating with respect or disrespect is not to be identified with *acting out of* respect or disrespect. To act out of respect or disrespect is to be motivated in what one is doing by one's respect or disrespect for him or her. One may have treated someone with disrespect or under-respect without having acted out of disrespect—one may even have acted out of respect. This last would be the case if one had so low an opinion of his or her worth that one's acting out of respect for this human being nonetheless resulted in treating him or her as would only befit someone of less worth. The phenomenon of treating someone with respect or disrespect has no direct connections with motivation, hence none with acting out of respect or disrespect. Most actions are performed neither out of respect nor out of disrespect; treating with respect or disrespect is not confined to that small range of actions that are so motivated.[6]

Somewhat similar points have to be made about the connection between treating someone with disrespect, on the one hand, and the recipient or agent *believing* that that is what is happening, on the other. A person's own estimate of her worth may be out of accord with what is in fact her worth; so too, a person's negative interpretation of how she has been treated may be an incorrect interpretation. Thus a person may believe that she is being treated with disrespect when she is not; she incorrectly believes that her worth has been slighted. And conversely, she may be treated with disrespect without believing that she is, even believing that she is not. Thomas E. Hill Jr., in his article "Servility and Self-Respect," offers a vivid example of this last point.[7] Hill is imagining a servile black man whom he calls "Uncle Tom":

> He always steps aside for white men; he does not complain when less qualified whites take over his job; he gratefully accepts whatever benefits his all-white government and employers allot him, and he would not think of protesting its insufficiency. He displays the symbols of deference to whites, and of contempt toward blacks: he faces the former with bowed stance and a ready "Sir" and "Ma'am"; he reserves his strongest obscenities for the latter. Imagine, too, that he is not playing a game. He is not the shrewdly prudent calculator, who knows how to make the best of a bad lot and mocks his masters behind their backs. He accepts without question the idea that, as a black, he is owed less than whites. He may believe that blacks are mentally inferior and of less social utility, but that is not the crucial point. The attitude which he displays is that what he values, aspires for, and can demand is of less importance than what whites value, aspire for, and can demand. He is far from the picture book's carefree, happy servant, but he does not feel that he has a right to expect anything better.

Just as the recipient of an action may have a mistaken view as to her worth, so too the *agent* may have a mistaken view as to the worth of the recipient, or a mistaken view as to whether his way of treating the recipi-

---

[6] The locution "respecting a person" seems to me ambiguous as between *treating with respect* and *acting out of respect.*

[7] Reprinted in David Lyons, ed., *Rights* (Belmont, Calif.: Wadsworth, 1979), p. 112.

ent is disrespectful of the recipient's worth. The agent may have treated the recipient with disrespect when he does not believe he did, and may not have treated her with disrespect when he fears he has.

Disrespect, and thereby also wronging, is determined, on the one hand, by the *actual* worth of the recipient, not by what agent or recipient happens to *believe* to be that worth; and on the other hand, by whether or not the respect-disrespect import of the action is such as to befit a person of this worth, not by whether the agent or recipient believes it does, or by whether the agent's actions express his feelings of disrespect. By contrast, whether or not a recipient *feels* angry over her treatment is determined not by whether she was in fact treated with disrespect but by whether she believes she was.

Sometimes the disrespectful action is performed by the performance of another action, typically in itself innocuous, that *counts as* the disrespectful action. For example, by virtue of convention a variety of typically innocuous actions have come to *count as* "paying respect" to the person: tipping the hat, bowing, curtsying, kneeling, rising when the person enters the room, opening doors for the person, inviting the person to go through a door first, addressing the person as "Sir" or "Madam." In each of these cases, the action cited counts as (generates) the illocutionary action of "paying respect." And "paying respect" is, of course, one way among others of showing respect; it is that inherently, intrinsically. Further, in many situations, failure to perform some conventional action of "paying respect" to a person counts as performing the illocutionary action of "paying disrespect"; and that in turn may constitute treating him with disrespect, or under-respect. Of course, our ways of "paying disrespect" to people are by no means confined to *refraining* from performing some action that, by convention, counts as "paying respect." "Scum," the one person calls the other, thereby performing the illocutionary act of insulting him, and hence paying him disrespect.

In defense of my claim that Frank should not have declared No. 2 the winner of the piano competition, I said that Frank wronged all who participated in the competition, whether as contestants or audience, by betraying their trust. But he also wronged No. 1 in particular, assuming that he was correct in his judgment that No. 1 performed best. In the situation as I described it, declaring someone the winner of the competition *counts as* asserting that he turned in the best performance. And Frank's asserting that No. 2 turned in the best performance when in fact No. 1 did, is a way of showing No. 1 disrespect. What No. 1 deserved is that Frank would declare that he had performed best.

In many cases of treating someone with disrespect, no illocutionary act is involved—no phenomenon of one act counting as another by virtue of some convention, the latter act being a case of showing disrespect. One just does something to the person without doing anything that counts as doing that thing: tortures him, kills him, invades his privacy, mutilates her, rapes her. And the thing done is a case of treating the person with disrespect; acting thus toward the person is incompatible with acknowledging her true worth.

Determining whether or not one person has treated another with disrespect (under-respect) usually requires taking a number of factors into consideration. A passage in Allen Wood's discussion of Kant's ethics makes the point well.[8] "Proper expression of respect," he says, "is a contextual matter; it is not evident that it could be reduced to any set of rules or generalizations that could serve as premises in a deductive argument. It might instead be something that has to be apprehended in each set of particular circumstances, perhaps by a sort of educated moral perception. Allan Gibbard is doubtless correct that it is impossible to codify 'respect for persons' into any determinate set of unexceptionable rules" (150–51). Interpreting the import of "actions regarding their respect or disrespect of the dignity of rational nature" is a hermeneutical enterprise. And "there can be no neat algorithms or decision procedures for the interpretation of human actions" (154–55).

The thing done that shows disrespect for a human being will always be a case of imposing on that human being some life-evil or depriving her of some life-good. Rape is that, betraying trust is that, performing the illocutionary action of "paying" the person disrespect (insulting her) is that. Of course, the mere inaction of not bowing before the king is harmless—no skin off the king's nose. It is what that inaction counts as, namely, the illocutionary action of "paying disrespect," that is the deprivation of a life-good.

A final point worth making about showing under-respect or disrespect is that one's showing of disrespect will be focused on some good-making feature of the person. One treats him or her with disrespect *as such-and-such*, though it will not always be immediately clear just what that aspect is. The disrespect I show the king, when I refuse to pay him respect by kneeling before him, is focused on his social rank; I belittle him *as king*. The disrespect shown Lance Armstrong, by those who cast aspersions on his record of winning the Tour de France seven times in a row by suggesting that he must have been taking performance-enhancing drugs, is focused on his achievement as a cyclist; they belittle him *as a competitive cyclist*. The rapist demeans his victim *as a Bosnian*, say, or *as a woman*— and in any case, *as a human being*.

[8] Allen W. Wood, *Kant's Ethical Thought* (Cambridge: Cambridge University Press, 1999).

Human Worth

From these reflections on what it is to show disrespect for the worth of a human being, let me move on to some brief comments on human worth itself. As with any other entity that falls within the Aristotelian category of substance, the worth of a human being is determined by various features of that human being—accomplishments, native endowments, and the like. And as Hampton observes in the chapter mentioned, which features count in giving worth to a human being, and how much they count for, are notoriously controversial matters. Does a person's membership in the aristocracy give him worth? Is he, so far forth, a more admirable human being on that account? Does a person's standing in the guild of philosophers give him, so far forth, a certain worth?

Accounts of human worth also differ in their overall structure, not just in what they regard as imparting worth. Hampton quotes Hobbes as saying that any worth human beings have is purely instrumental: "The value, or worth, of a man is, as of all other things, his price; that is to say, so much as would be given for the use of his power."[9] Hampton represents Kant as holding, by contrast, that our worth is entirely non-instrumental, and both objective and equal; our worth is determined solely by our capacity for rational agency.

One might disagree with Kant on equality while agreeing with him on non-instrumentality and objectivity, holding, for example, that men are objectively and non-instrumentally worth more than women, or kings more than subjects, or Caucasians more than Africans, or Americans more than members of the Taliban, or Israelis more than Palestinians, or adults more than children, or the upright more than the felon. Alternatively, one might agree with Kant on non-instrumentality while disagreeing on objectivity, denying that there is anything about human beings that is of intrinsic value; appraisals of human worth reflect nothing more than value schemes expressive of power relationships.

If one disagrees with Kant that the only thing that gives any of us worth is our capacity for rational agency and holds instead, as I do, that many things about us give us worth—this person here is admirable for his intelligence, that person there for her courage, and so forth—then the idea looms before us of determining "our overall value as persons," to quote Hampton (48).

I dare say that most of us are reluctant to make such overall evaluations, and even more reluctant to rank human beings with respect to

---

[9] From Thomas Hobbes, *Leviathan*, ed. C. B. Macpherson (Harmondsworth: Penguin, 1965), chap. 10, para. 16.

their overall worth. When it comes to ranking, we prefer to rank the excellence of human beings with respect to their intelligence, with respect to their musical abilities, with respect to their athletic abilities, with respect to their virtue, and so on, and let it go at that. Fortunately, employing the conceptuality of rights does not require making overall evaluations of the worth of human beings. If we concede that Lance Armstrong's athletic feats contribute to his worth, then if someone belittles or bad-mouths those feats, that person has treated Armstrong as having less worth than he does have *as an athlete,* and has thereby wronged him. No need to determine what Armstrong's overall worth is, and certainly no need to determine how he ranks among human beings generally in overall worth.

FITTINGNESS BETWEEN THE RESPECT-DISRESPECT IMPORT OF ACTIONS AND THE WORTH OF HUMAN BEINGS

The third assumption underlying the conviction that human beings can be, and often are, treated with under-respect is that there can be a fit or lack of fit between, on the one hand, the respect-disrespect import of our actions, and, on the other hand, the worth of human beings. One treats a human being with under-respect when the respect-disrespect import of one's action would only fit someone of lesser worth in regard to the focus of one's disrespectful action.

Our disagreements over whether someone has been treated with disrespect, and hence whether she has been wronged, have their source either in different estimations of the import of our actions or in different estimations of the worth of the person, or both. The rapist who thinks what he did is okay may either think that rape is "not so bad" or that, while it shows disrespect for the worth of some women, it does not show disrespect for the worth of this woman. One guesses that most of the Serbian soldiers who raped Bosnian women in the conflict of the 1990s regarded rape as incompatible with the worth of Serbian women. But Bosnian women were different; they were scum. Raping them was not treating them with disrespect, though killing them might be. And probably those members of the American military who were guilty of torturing and sexually humiliating Iraqi prisoners in the Abu Ghraib prison complex near Baghdad would have thought it wrong to treat an upstanding American this way. The Iraqi prisoners were a lower grade of human beings. In treating them thus, one was not treating them with disrespect for their worth. They did not have much worth to show disrespect for. And most if not all of the whites in the U.S. South who thought it okay to enslave blacks were not of the view that slavery is really "not so bad"; they were opposed to enslaving whites. It was their view that blacks were not of much worth.

The lower in worth I regard the human being before me, the fewer will be the ways of treating her that I regard as showing her under-respect, and thereby the more will be the ways of treating her that I regard as subject to nothing but greater good considerations. If I regard the worth of the human being before me as so low that torturing her does not amount to treating her with under-respect, then I will make the decision of whether to torture her purely on considerations of the greater good.

An important point to be made here is that often it will be the case that one cannot simply take a person in one hand, a certain way of treating her in the other, and determine whether the respect-disrespect import of that treatment fits or does not fit her worth. The determination requires making comparisons among persons with regard to their relative worth, or comparisons among actions with regard to their relative respect-disrespect import, or both. Suppose, for example, that I am invited to nominate a student for a philosophy prize and that I have responsibly arrived at the judgment that, while three are worthy of nomination, X is superior as a philosopher to Y and Y is superior to Z. Then I do not treat either Y or Z with under-respect if I nominate neither of them for the prize. However, if X is for some reason removed from the picture, then I do treat Y with under-respect if I do not nominate him.[10]

Obvious as is the principle of relativity when applied to such cases as the one just offered, it also produces some of the deepest quandaries for those who think in terms of rights. Suppose that I find myself in the tragic situation of having to choose between being accountable for either the torture of A or the torture of B and C; and let us suppose that the three are of equal worth. Then the worth of B and C together is presumably a good deal more than the worth of A alone. So it appears that in choosing to be responsible for torturing A, thus avoiding being responsible for torturing both B and C, I do not treat A as of less worth than he is.

The Interaction between the Worth of Life-Goods and the Worth of Human Beings

Let us stand back a bit so as to get a somewhat broader perspective on the conclusions at which we have arrived. All about us are things of excellence, among them human beings, and human lives and histories. Human lives and histories vary in excellence; some are more flourishing

---

[10] The examples I gave in chapter 11, about life guards and drowning swimmers, are also apropos here.

than others. Likewise, human beings vary in excellence. Some excel in a particular respect; some excel overall. A principle underlying our discussion in this chapter is that one is never to treat a human being as of less worth than she is in the relevant respect. But the same is true for the states and events that comprise a human being's life and history; one is also not to treat those as of less worth than they are. And these are just two specifications of a fundamental, all-embracing principle for human action: one is never to treat anything as of less worth than it is. We also sometimes go astray by treating something as befits a thing of greater worth; the recognition of lack of fit of this sort pervades Augustine's thought. Our focus on rights has led us to concentrate on under-respect and to ignore over-respect.

The principle that we are never to treat any entity as befits an entity of lesser worth presupposes that our actions have respect/disrespect import not only with regard to the worth of human beings but with regard to the worth of other entities as well. Choosing one course of action over another has such an import: it is to treat the former course of action as of more worth than the latter. Praising one thing more highly than another has such an import: it is to treat the former thing as of more worth than the latter. And so forth.[11] Rights are introduced into our practical reasoning when we go beyond taking the relative worth of life-states and life-events into account and bring the worth of human beings and social entities into consideration—and perhaps that of some other sorts of entities as well.

---

[11] A close relative of what I call the "respect/disrespect import" of an action is what Allen W. Wood calls the "expressive meaning" of an action in his discussion of Kant's ethics (*Kant's Ethical Thought* [Cambridge: Cambridge University Press, 1999]). Though Wood employs this terminology mainly when discussing the expressive meaning of actions with regard to the worth of human beings, he recognizes that the idea applies generally: "every action that is done for a reason (as distinct from being merely a response to an impulse) is based on regarding something as objectively *valuable*. When it is done for that kind of reason, the performance of the action is most fundamentally an expression of esteem for that value, and this expressive reason for performing the action is therefore the ground of any other reason we may have for performing it. . . . From the standpoint of reasons for action, even our furtherance of an end to be effected is fundamentally a piece of expressive behavior" (142).

The difference between Wood's concept of the expressive meaning of an action and mine of the respect/disrespect import of an action is that the expressive meaning of an action is the evaluative judgment that the action expresses. It is an expression of the agent's "esteem for [the] value" of the entity concerned. By contrast, the respect/disrespect import of an action is not decisively determined by the agent's evaluations or intentions; it may not "express" his evaluations and intentions. He may treat an entity with under-respect even though he does not under-esteem it.

It appears to me that the idea needed for an exposition of Kant's thought is actually mine of respect/disrespect import, rather than Wood's of expressive meaning.

Of course, the only way to treat a human being with due respect, under-respect, or over-respect is to bring about states and events in her life or history; and each of those will contribute to determining the degree of that human being's flourishing, some contributing more, some less. But the point is that some of those very same states and events that determine the degree of a human being's flourishing perforce have another significance as well: they fit or do not fit that human being's worth.

In short, each of those states and events that we bring about in a human being's life, whereby we treat her in a way that fits or does not fit her worth, participates in two orders of significance. It contributes to determining the degree to which the life of that human being is a flourishing life; and it exhibits due respect or lack of due respect for the human being herself.[12] Rights exist at the intersection of two systems of evaluation and treatment: the life-goods system and the human-being system. Most of the obstacles to understanding how they work have that duality as their source. (I remind the reader that, in my discussion, "lives" is usually short for "lives and histories" and that entities other than human beings have rights.)

A fundamental feature of how the human-being system interacts with the life-goods system is that the former always trumps the latter. No matter how great the balance of life-goods over life-evils that Frank would bring about if he declared No. 2 the winner of the competition, doing so would wrong No. 1, and hence Frank is not to do it. Once he recognizes that it would wrong No. 1, there is no point in his thinking further about the balance of life-goods. He may as well put it out of mind.

THE TRUMPING PRINCIPLE VERSUS THE BOOSTING PRINCIPLE

But is there not something deeply paradoxical about allowing the human-being system to intrude into the life-goods system? Does it not produce profound distortion in the latter? If Frank decides to declare No. 1 the winner on the ground that No. 1 has a right to this declaration, is he not then treating all those life-goods that would come about if he declared No. 2 the winner as of less worth than they are? He is acting exactly like the person who has weighed up the two sets of life-goods,

---

[12] Allen Wood, in *Kant's Ethical Thought*, says that "as [Christine] Korsgaard has emphasized, Kantian ethics breaks with the utilitarian tradition most fundamentally by denying that the most basic objects of value are states of affairs, and [by denying] that 'the business of morality is to *bring something about*" (141). I agree with what Wood is getting at here; but this is not the right way to put it. It is the business of morality to bring something about, because there is no other way to acknowledge the worth of entities than by bringing something about.

mistakenly decided that the balance tilts in favor of those that come along with declaring No. 1 the winner, and resolved on that ground to declare him winner.

If there were nothing at stake other than external behavior, Frank would indeed be acting like such a person. But external behavior is not the full story. When a person trumps in and takes the hand in a game of cards, he has not totaled up the face value of the cards and made an error in doing so. The face value of the cards makes no difference.

But why is it that the goods to which we have rights have trumping force over all other goods? Well, what would be the alternative to the trumping principle? It would presumably be the *boosting* principle. Having a right to some life-good *boosts* the value of that life-good, gives it added value. Rights do not remove considerations of greater good from the table; always one is to seek the greater good. But in weighing up life-goods and evils, one must take into account the fact that some life-goods have enhanced value on account of someone having a right to them, and that some life-evils likewise have enhanced disvalue.

On this view, what would it be to have a right to some good? Presumably, someone would have a right against another to their treating one a certain way just in case their failure to treat one that way, *considered all by itself* apart from accompaniments and consequences, would constitute treating one with under-respect. The fact that the *act as such* has that significance boosts the value of that way of being treated.

I hold that the boosting principle proves untenable on close inspection; it makes an assumption that cannot be justified. My defense of the trumping principle is that its alternative is untenable. Here is my case.

I suggested that, at bottom, the reason Frank would wrong No. 1 should he not declare him the winner is that he would be violating his trust and that of the other participants in the event, and that to violate someone's trust is to treat him or her with under-respect. Now the idea behind the boosting principle cannot be that should Frank break trust with No. 1 he would be treating him with under-respect, but that that is okay, provided a great many life-goods result therefrom. It is never acceptable to treat anything at all with under-respect, be it a person, an animal, a life-good, or whatever. The idea has to be that breaking trust with No. 1, when there are all those goods to be achieved by doing so, would not be a case of treating him with under-respect. Breaking trust with someone *considered all by itself* would be a case of treating him with under-respect; that is how breaking trust, which is already a life-evil, receives a boost in disvalue. But whether, in a given case, breaking someone's trust constitutes treating him with under-respect has to be determined by considering the action itself, with its boosted disvalue, along with all its accompaniments and consequences in life-goods and life-evils.

It is that entire package that has an actual respect-disrespect import; the action considered all by itself is a mere abstraction.

So does contestant No. 1 have a right against Frank to Frank's keeping trust with him? The initial idea of the person inclined to affirm the boosting principle is that No. 1 does indeed have that right, but that it can be over-ridden. But that, as we now see, is not the correct way to put it. If Frank can bring about a great many life-goods by breaking trust with No. 1, then in that situation No. 1 does not have a right against Frank to his not breaking trust; and he does not have that right in that situation because Frank's breaking trust in that situation would not constitute treating No. 1 with under-respect. It is not that he has the right but that the right is over-ridden; he does not have the right in this situation. The boosting principle affirms the inviolability of rights just as much as does the trumping principle.

But now consider the thesis that it is the entire package, consisting of the act and its accompaniments and consequences, that has actual respect-disrespect import. The act of breaking trust with someone, considered all by itself, would constitute treating that person with under-respect; hence, if it ever occurred all by itself, the person would have a right to not being treated that way. But actions never occur all by themselves. They come dragging along accompaniments and consequences.

Now for the crucial question: why does bringing all those life-good accompaniments and consequences into the picture change anything? Remember, nobody has a right to those consequences; the situation in which one is dealing with conflicting or apparently conflicting rights is a totally different matter. But if none of those life-good accompaniments and consequences has anything to do with due respect—they are just nice to have—how can it possibly be that the package consisting of those plus an act of betraying trust is not a case of wronging, not a case of treating with under-respect? How can *the package* have that respect-disrespect import if everything in the package, other than betraying trust, has no such import? How can adding zero to one not yield one? It is because I cannot see any plausible answer to this question that I regard the boosting principle as untenable.

We could drop the discussion at this point. But I think we gain some important additional insight into the issues at stake if we reflect a bit further on the implications of the boosting principle. An advocate of the principle could hold that there are some ways of treating human beings that, considered in abstraction from accompaniments and consequences, amount to treating them with such severe under-respect that the disvalue thereby imparted to those actions cannot be outweighed by any amount of accompanying and resultant life-goods. For such actions, if there are any, there is no point in even considering the accompanying and resultant life-goods—which is exactly the situation for all rights as the advocate of the trumping principle sees the matter. A pure version of the boosting principle would deny that this can be. No matter how much disvalue an action may carry considered all by itself, on account of someone having a right to it considered all by itself, it is always possible for that action to occur in a situation where it can be justified by accompanying and resultant life-goods.

Now if the pure version of the booster principle were true, then the following would also be true: the worth of every human being would be such that, for every way of treating that human being, it is always possible that the life-goods and evils accompanying and resulting from that treatment be such that treating that human being that way does not constitute treating him as if he had less worth than he does. There is always a tipping point at which, for example, the action of breaking trust with someone is no longer treating him as if he had less worth than he does. Nobody has a worth such that due respect for that worth requires keeping trust with him at all cost of life-goods and evils. Nobody is worth that much. Every human being has a price, a price in terms of life-goods and life-evils. Once you know how much disvalue breaking trust with someone possesses on account of that person having a right, considered in abstraction, to not being treated thus, and once you know how many life-goods you have to put on the other side of the scale in order to outweigh the disvalue of breaking trust, then you know the price that human being has in terms of life-goods and life-evils.

By contrast, the trumping principle affirms that if someone has a right to their trust not being broken, then no matter how many life-goods can be achieved and life-evils avoided by violating his trust, one would treat him as if he had less worth than he does if one violated his trust. No human being has a price. Each is priceless.

The proponent of the boosting principle could hold that some human beings have less worth than others—those not of one's kind less worth than those who are of one's kind, for example. Then, though it might still be seen as wrong wantonly to betray the trust of those not of one's kind, the resultant life-goods necessary to make it acceptable would be fewer. Alternatively, one might hold that the trumping principle holds for some beings and the boosting principle for the others. One might hold, for example, that the trumping principle holds for God, whereas the boosting principle holds for human beings. Or that the trumping principle holds for those beings who are persons, whereas the boosting principle holds for those entities that are not persons—social entities, animals, those human beings who are not capable of functioning as persons, and so forth. In short, all sorts of combinations are possible.

But all of this is hypothetical. The boosting principle is untenable, for the reasons given. If one allows the worth of persons to enter into one's deliberations on how to act, there is no alternative to allowing the life-goods to which one has rights to trump those to which one does not. That is how it has to be. And one does have to allow the worth of persons to enter into one's deliberations. For if one does not, one will all too often treat them with under-respect. And we are not to treat anything with under-respect.

KANT'S FORMULA

"So act," said Kant, "that you use humanity, whether in your own person or that of another, always at the same time as an end, never merely as a means." Though the rhetorical power of the apothegm is undeniable, its meaning is dark. We customarily think of an end as some event that one aims to bring about.[13] So what can Kant mean when he says that *humanity in a person* should be our end? Humanity in a person is not an event, and it already exists in all the persons that there are.

Allen Wood explains Kant's point as follows:

Consequentialist theories represent the fulfillment of our duties as bringing about desirable *states of affairs*. Deontological theories . . . represent them as obedience to an obligatory *rule* or *commandment*. [Kant's principle of respect for humanity], however, bases duties instead on the *absolute worth* of rational nature as an end in itself. Though [the principle] takes the form of a rule or commandment,

[13] The background to Kant's terminology is his distinction between an *existent*, or *self-sufficient*, end and an end *to be effected*. Allen Wood, in *Kant's Ethical Thought*, puts the distinction this way: an existent end is "something that already exists and whose 'existence is in itself an end,' having worth as something to be esteemed, preserved, and furthered. Kant opposed this sort of end to an *end to be effected*, . . . that is, some things or state of affairs that does not yet exist but is to be brought about through an agent's causality"(115). On pp. 362–63, n. 4, Wood cites a number of philosophers who charge that Kant is misusing the word "end" here; an end is always something that one seeks to bring about. Wood responds by insisting that Kant's use of the word is not a misuse. My own response to the charge would be different. I would concede to the critics that Kant's usage is, if not quite a misuse, at least only marginally correct; but that this does not make any difference. One can see what he was getting at. Philosophy would be impossible if philosophers were required to stick to "standard English" or "standard German."

That Kant means what Wood says he means is unambiguously clear, I would say, in the following passage from his *Groundwork of the Metaphysic of Morals* (Academy 428): "Suppose, however, there were something *whose existence* has *in itself* an absolute value, something which as *an end in itself* could be a ground of determinate laws." (H. J. Paton translation [New York: Harper Torchbooks, 1956], p. 95).

> what it basically asserts is the existence of a *substantive value* to be respected. This value does not take the form of a desired object to be brought about, but rather the value of something existing, which is to be respected, esteemed, or honored in our actions. (141)

In short, to treat a person as an end, or more precisely, to treat humanity in a person as an end, is to treat it with the respect, esteem, and honor appropriate to something of non-instrumental worth.

And what is the contrast? What is it to treat a person, or humanity in a person, as a means? This too becomes clear in the course of Wood's discussion (though not in the passage quoted). To treat a human being as a means is to treat her in some way other than what respect for her non-instrumental worth requires. One would so treat her if one treated her as a means to, or a constituent of, one's respect for the non-instrumental worth of something else. That "something else" will often be life-goods, be it goods in one's own life, goods in the life of the human being concerned, or goods in everybody's life. If one's treatment of a human being is determined solely by reference to life-goods, one is treating that human being as a means.

So what the principle says is that one is always to act in accord with what respect for the non-instrumental worth of the human being requires, or what respect for humanity in the human being requires. One may *also* introduce balance of life-good considerations into how one treats human beings. But one is never to treat a human being with under-respect. In short, Kant's famous principle—act always in such a way as to treat human beings as ends and never merely as means—comes to the same as the principle I have been defending: always act in such a way as to allow respect for the worth of human beings to trump balance of life-good considerations.

Chapter Fourteen

THE NATURE AND GROUNDING OF NATURAL HUMAN RIGHTS

MY DISCUSSION TO THIS POINT has been of rights in general. As context for an analysis of rights of special sorts, I have tried to give a general account of rights. Now I turn to that species of rights that has attracted most attention on the contemporary scene, natural human rights. In this chapter I explain what I take natural human rights be and what we are trying to do when we try to discover how they are grounded. In the following two chapters I critique various grounding proposals and offer my own.

THE VIOLATION AND RECOGNITION OF HUMAN RIGHTS IN THE TWENTIETH CENTURY

The twentieth century was a horror. "In total, during the first eighty-eight years of the century, almost 170 million men, women, and children were shot, beaten, tortured, knifed, burned, starved, frozen, crushed, or worked to death; buried alive, drowned, hanged, bombed, or killed in any other of the myriad other ways governments have inflicted deaths on unarmed helpless citizens and foreigners. Depending on whether one used high or more conservative estimates, the dead could conceivably be more than 360 million people. It is as though our species has been devastated by a modern Black Plague."[1]

The horror was intensive as well as extensive. Ahmad Qabazard was a nineteen-year-old Kuwaiti held by the Iraqis during their invasion of Kuwait. An Iraqi officer told his parents he was about to be released. "They were overjoyed, cooked wonderful things, and when they heard cars approaching went to the door. When Ahmad was taken out of the car, they saw that his ears, his nose, and his genitalia had been cut off. He was coming out of the car with his eyes in his hands. Then the Iraqis shot him, once in the stomach and once in the head, and told his mother to be sure not to move the body for three days."[2]

---

[1] Israel W. Charney, ed., *Encyclopedia of Genocide* (1999), p. 28. Quoted in Michael Perry, *Toward a Theory of Human Rights* (Cambridge: Cambridge University Press, 2007), chapter 1.

[2] Report by Julie Flint, *Observer* (March 3, 1991). Quoted by Jonathan Glover, *Humanity: A Moral History of the Twentieth Century* (New Haven: Yale University Press, 2000), p. 32.

The moral history of the twentieth century would be incomplete, however, if in addition to reciting the horrors, we did not take note of the emergence of a powerful human rights culture whose great documentary achievements are the UN Universal Declaration of Human Rights (1948), the UN International Covenant on Civil and Political Rights (1966), and the UN International Covenant on Economic, Social and Cultural Rights (1966).

The story of how the first of these came into being has recently been wonderfully told by Mary Ann Glendon in *A World Made New: Eleanor Roosevelt and the Universal Declaration of Human Rights*.[3] Glendon concludes her narrative with a brief statement of the significance of the declaration. "The Universal Declaration charted a bold new course for human rights by presenting a vision of freedom as linked to social security, balanced by responsibilities, grounded in respect for equal human dignity, and guarded by the rule of law. That vision was meant to protect liberty from degenerating into license and to repel the excesses of individualism and collectivism alike. By affirming that all its rights belong to everyone, everywhere, it aimed to put an end to the idea that a nation's treatment of its own citizens or subjects was immune from outside scrutiny" (235). The declaration's statement of human rights comprises twenty-nine articles. That there could be agreement on such an extensive list of the rights that "belong to everyone, everywhere" is amazing.

The declaration has often been charged with being a manifestation and instrument of Western imperialism, more often, it appears to me, by those enjoying the rights cited than by those who are not. Glendon discusses this charge in some detail in her chapter 12, "Universality under Siege." The story of how the document came into existence belies the charge. Participants in the formation and ratification of the declaration were not all from the West and its colonies. What the participants discovered is that, while their diverse religious and philosophical perspectives yielded quite different accounts of human rights, a remarkable consensus emerged when they set those disagreements aside and just said what they thought all human beings had a right to.[4]

The documents go a bit beyond merely listing human rights. They are all what Glendon calls "dignity-based rights instruments." They declare human rights to be grounded in "the inherent dignity" of "all members of the human family." No account is given of what constitutes this inherent dignity; any such account would have proved controversial. But there

---

[3] New York: Random House, 2001.

[4] This aspect of the story was told by Jacques Maritain, who was a participant in the discussions at a certain stage. See his *Man and the State* (Chicago: University of Chicago Press, 1951), chapter 4.

was consensus on the claim that all members of the human family have inherent dignity and that human rights are grounded in that dignity.

I should speak a bit more precisely here. Though the declaration strongly suggests that human rights are grounded in inherent dignity, it does not actually say this; it simply conjoins a reference to dignity with a reference to rights. The preamble opens with the declaration that "recognition of the inherent dignity and of the equal and inalienable rights of all members of the human family is the foundation of freedom, justice and peace in the world." And Article 1 announces, "All human beings are born free and equal in dignity and rights." The later covenants make explicit the grounding connection that was implicit in the declaration. Both open by repeating the first clause of the preamble of the declaration, quoted above, and then go on to speak of "recognizing that these rights derive from the inherent dignity of the human person."[5]

What Is a Human Right?

What are we talking about when we talk about human rights? A human right, so I suggest, is a right attached to the status of being a human being, a member of the species *Homo sapiens*. It makes no difference how or why the right is attached to the status. Being a human being gives one the right.

It is important to repeat a point made in an earlier chapter. Alasdair MacIntyre understands the idea of a human right as "a conception of individuals both stripped of all social status and yet bearers of rights"; and then argues that there could not be such individuals.[6] MacIntyre is right in claiming that there could not be a human being who has no social status. But when we speak of human rights, we are not imagining individuals stripped of all social status and then asking what rights these naked individuals have. We take human beings as they come, in all their social embeddedness. We notice that each of them has many different statuses to which rights are attached. It occurs to us to wonder whether the status that all these beings necessarily share, namely, that of being human beings, also has rights attached to it. That is the question we ask. We do no stripping.

---

[5] Article 1 of the Declaration reads in its totality as follows: "All human beings are born free and equal in dignity and rights. They are endowed with reason and conscience and should act towards one another in a spirit of brotherhood." The ideas of equality, of being endowed with reason and conscience, and of acting toward one another in a spirit of brotherhood are not picked up in either of the two Covenants.

[6] Alasdair MacIntyre, "Are There Any Natural Rights?: The Charles F. Adams Lecture of February 28, 1983," published by Bowdoin College, Bowdoin, Maine.

It appears to me that there are relatively few positive rights that are truly human rights. Recall the distinction. A positive or benefit right is a right against others to their treating one a certain way; a negative or freedom right is a right against others to their refraining from treating one a certain way. Now consider the right cited in Article 26 of the declaration: "Everyone has a right to education." This is a positive right. And from what the article goes on to say, it appears that what the drafters had in mind was the right to the benefit of a *formal* education.[7] But surely it is not true that the only status required for having a right to a formal education is that of being a human being. One has to be a human being of a certain sort, namely, one who is *capable of being formally educated*. Not all human beings are of that sort; if they are not, they are not wronged if they do not receive a formal education, even though a system of formal education is in place in their society. So the right to a formal education is not a truly human right. Or consider a right cited in Article 24: everyone "has the right to . . . periodic holidays with pay." The concept of a holiday with pay does not apply to the self-employed of the world, because they are not on salary—as of course it does not apply to children, to Alzheimer patients, and so forth. Hence the right to periodic holidays with pay is also not a truly human right; it is not attached to the status of being a human being but, at most, to the status of being a human being who works for a salary.

The same is true for most benefit rights, because for most benefits, some human beings are incapable of receiving or utilizing the benefit. Even the benefit right of fair access to adequate means of sustenance is not, strictly speaking, a human right, because not every case of turning off the life-support system of a terminally ill patient constitutes wronging him or her. Prominent among those benefit rights that are truly human rights are rights to the benefit of protection against bodily assault; every human being is capable of utilizing such a benefit.

Those of a philosophical bent of mind will raise the following question. Consider the right of being formally educated if capable of being so educated. Not the right of being formally educated, period, but the right of *being formally educated if capable of being so educated*. That is a truly human right, is it not?

My reply is twofold. If there really were this conditional human right, then presumably we could generalize to the conclusion that to every non-

---

[7] Here is the article's full statement of the right to education: "Everyone has the right to education. Education shall be free, at least in the elementary and fundamental stages. Elementary education shall be compulsory. Technical and professional education shall be made generally available and higher education shall be equally accessible to all on the basis of merit." The article then goes on to make some comments about the goals of education.

human right there is a corresponding human right. One simply tucks the status into a conditional clause within the right. Human rights would be everywhere. Corresponding to the right to receive a monthly Social Security check from the U.S. government, this being a right attached to the status of being a U.S. citizen age sixty-five or older, there is the right to receive a monthly Social Security check from the U.S. government if one is a U.S. citizen age sixty-five or older. This now is a right attached to the status of being a human being; it is a human right.

But these are fake rights, pseudo rights. Consider the purported human right to the good of being formally educated if capable of being so educated. Now consider a human being who is in fact not so capable. What is the difference between this human being enjoying this life-good to which he supposedly has a right, and not enjoying it? What is the difference between my wronging him by depriving him of this life-good to which he supposedly has a human right, and my respecting his purported right by bestowing on him this life-good? There is no difference.

The question of whether a certain right is a human right is not to be confused with the question of whether it is a universal right—that is, whether every human being always has that right against somebody or other.[8] I speak of a right as "attached" to a certain status if, when one has the right, one has it on account of having that status. But one may have the status and yet, in a given situation, not have the right; having the status is not sufficient for having the right that is attached to the status. The main reason for this is that it is true of rights in general that one does not have a right against someone to the good of some action or restraint from action on their part if they are incapable of bestowing that good on one—or capable only at the cost of violating rights.

For example, consider once again the right to a formal education, attached, as we saw, to the status of being a human being capable of being formally educated. If one has that right in a given situation, it is on account of having that status; the only status one has to present to establish that one has the right, when one does have it, is the status of being a human being capable of being formally educated. But now suppose that one lives in a society that has no system of formal education; most societies have been of that sort. Then even though one is a human being capable of being formally educated, one does not have a right to the life-good of receiving a formal education. Because no one is capable of bestowing that good on one, there is no one against whom one has that right. In that situation, one is not wronged by not receiving such

---

[8] This is the best way to think of what it is for a benefit right to be universal. As for negative or freedom rights, the best way to think of what it is for them to be universal is that everybody always has the right against everybody.

an education. In short, not only are the two ideas, human rights and universal rights, distinct ideas; there can be human rights that are not universal rights.

It is easier to find examples of negative rights that are truly human rights than of benefit rights that are. The right not to be tortured for the pleasure of the torturer is one. This is a right against others that they refrain from this action; hence it is a negative right. It comes attached to the status of being a human being; hence it is a human right. One does not have to be some particular sort of human being to have the right. And it is a universal right. Every human being always has it against somebody or other; in fact, every human being always has it against everybody.

It may be that the right not to be tortured for any reason whatsoever is not universal; the matter is controversial. Some writers hold that if a person possesses information that I and others can use to save the lives of many persons, if there is no other way to acquire the information than to get it out of this person, and if there is no other way to get it out of this person than by torturing him, then torturing him is morally permissible—which is to say, that he does not have a right against us to our refraining from torturing him. If this is correct, then the negative right not to be tortured for any reason whatsoever, though it is a human right, is not a universal right.

Let us be clear about the situation, however. The fact that some great good can be achieved by torture does not make it permissible. What makes torture sometimes permissible, if it is, is only that, if one did not torture, one would be committing a serious violation of rights. One would be treating with under-respect all those whose lives one could save; one would be acting as if the worth of all those people together was less than the worth of this single person. The reason that he would not have a right against me or anyone else not to be tortured is that, in this situation, we would not be treating him with under-respect.

NATURAL RIGHTS AND HUMAN RIGHTS

In chapter 1 I explained what I meant by "natural" rights. Some of our rights are possessed by us on account of human action of some sort; they have been conferred on us (generated within us) by human legislation or practice, by human speech acts, by human acts of generosity, and so forth. Call such rights *socially conferred* rights. Natural rights are rights that are not socially conferred, plus those that are socially conferred but that we would have even if they had not been socially conferred.

This way of characterizing natural rights follows standard usage. But as I observed in chapter 1, when we bring God into the picture, it is obvious that additional distinctions are in order. Some of our natural rights have been conferred on us by some action on God's part independent of God's action of creating us, by some divine speech act. These are *divinely conferred* rights.

And then there are those rights of God and human beings that in chapter 12 I called *standing rights*. These too are natural rights, obviously. They are what I called, in chapter 1, *inherent* natural rights. The argument of chapter 12 establishes that they are not divinely conferred rights. An implication of my argument in the next two chapters is that they are also not "conferred" on God and us by some matrix of principles of obligation. They "inhere" in God and in us, on account of the worth that God has by virtue of some status that God has, and in us by virtue of some status that we have. Rather than something or other *conferring* the right on entities that have this status, the worth of the status grounds the right.

Though my way of characterizing natural rights follows standard usage, it is my impression that most of those theologians who profess to be hostile to natural rights are in fact not hostile to natural rights as such; they are not hostile to *divinely conferred* natural rights. It is *inherent* natural rights that they do not like.

It is one thing for a right to be inherently attached to a certain status, or as I have also put it, a bit misleadingly, for a right to be inherently attached to someone on account of their having that status; it is quite another thing for that status to belong to human nature and thus for human beings to have it essentially. Inherent rights and human rights are not the same. The rights of parents, as traditionally conceived, offer an example. The rights of a parent with respect to his or her child are thought to be inherent to the status of parent. They may in fact have been conferred on the parent by both human and divine legislation; but they would be attached to that status even if there had not been that legislation. Yet the status of being a parent does not belong to human nature; obviously one can be human without being a parent.

A good deal of confusion in talk about natural rights has been caused by failure to note the distinction just made, between a right being inherent to a certain status and that status being intrinsic or essential to the human being who has that status. The idea of *nature* enters the discussion at two distinct points. Sometimes the issue under discussion is whether it is by "nature" or by conferral that this right is attached to this status; sometimes the issue is whether there is such a thing as human nature and, if so, whether this status belongs to that nature.

Not only is the idea of a natural right distinct from the idea of a human right; natural rights and human rights do not necessarily coincide. It may be that, as a matter of fact, there are no human rights that are not natural rights. But one can easily imagine some international treaty conferring on all human beings a right that was not a natural right of theirs. The status to which the right was attached would then be that of being a human being. But the right would be attached to that status by the treaty; it would not be a natural right.

The converse, that there are natural rights that are not human rights, is among the most common convictions of human beings. Belief in the natural right of kings comes at once to mind, and in the natural right of parents. Other examples are nowadays more important.

Some of the Southern slave owners of the nineteenth century appear to have believed that their slaves had few if any rights; it was quite okay to deal with them entirely in terms of expediency. Many of the Nazis thought of the Jews the same way. Stalin seems to have thought of most Russians this way. And probably some Serbs regarded Bosnian Muslims this way. A mere smattering of knowledge of human history provides many other examples of the same point.

In his analysis of cases such as these, Richard Rorty suggests that the oppressors do not regard their victims as human. "The moral to be drawn," he says, from stories about cruelties perpetrated in the '90s by Serbs on Bosnian Muslims,

> is that Serbian murderers and rapists do not think of themselves as violating human rights. For they are not doing these things to fellow human beings, but to *Muslims*. They are not being inhuman, but rather are discriminating between the true humans and the pseudohumans. They are making the same sort of distinction as the Crusaders made between humans and infidel dogs, and the Black Muslims make between humans and blue-eyed devils. . . . They think the line between humans and animals is not simply the line between featherless bipeds and all others. They think the line divides some featherless bipeds from others: There are animals walking about in humanoid form.[9]

The word "human" has a number of meanings; and it may be true that the oppressors Rorty cites spoke as he says they did: these beings are "not human" or "not really human." But what I mean by "a human being" is a member of the species *Homo sapiens*. And I would be surprised indeed if any of the oppressors Rorty cites thought that their victims were not members of the species *Homo sapiens*. Rather, they regarded that as irrelevant to how these beings should be treated.

---

[9] Richard Rorty, "Human Rights, Rationality, and Sentimentality," in Stephen Shute and Susan Hurley, eds., *On Human Rights: The Oxford Amnesty Lectures 1993* (New York: Basic Books, 1993), pp. 112–13.

Now for the point. Deep in humanity is the impulse to regard those human beings who are members of one's in-group as having a right to be treated in certain ways that those human beings who are members of some or all out-groups lack. The rights of members of the in-group are seen as natural rights; they would have those rights even if there had been no human legislation that conferred those rights on them. There is something about Greeks, something about Athenians, something about white people, something about Aryans, something about Serbs, that sets them apart and gives them an inherent dignity that the others lack. That dignity grounds the rights of members of the in-group. Such purported rights are seen, then, as natural rights that are not human rights. The recognition of natural *human* rights was an achievement wrought against impulses deeply ingrained in human beings.

THE PROJECT OF SHOWING HOW HUMAN RIGHTS ARE GROUNDED

What is one trying to do when one tries to show that human rights are grounded in human dignity? To show how a right is grounded is to account for it, to explain why those who have it do have it. What status gives them that right? What accounts for that right being attached to that status?[10] For example, what status of mine gives me the right to a monthly Social Security check? And what accounts for that right being attached to that status?

In the preceding chapter we saw that a person's rights consist of what is required of others, by way of action and restraint from action, if that person is not to be treated as of less worth than she is. But worth or excellence or dignity is not something that just settles down here and there willy-nilly. An entity has worth on account of some property it has, some capacity it possesses, some activity it has performed or is performing, some relationship in which it stands. Its worth supervenes on its having certain properties (capacities, activities, etc.) or standing in

[10] What are we to make of the opening of the second paragraph of the U.S. Declaration of Independence (1776), which famously says, "we hold these truths to be self-evident, that all men are created equal; that they are endowed by their Creator with certain unalienable rights; that among these are life, liberty, and the pursuit of happiness"? I take it as a piece of epistemological bluster that, if it were true, would render my questions irrelevant. It is an aberration, albeit an important aberration, in the tradition of human rights thought. MacIntyre, in his skeptical discussion of natural human rights, takes it to be a canonical episode in the history of natural human rights thought, introduced because people like Jefferson and Robespierre could no longer accept any sort of theological account. But why regard Jefferson and Robespierre as representative, on this score, of eighteenth-century political thought? They were the odd men out. See p. 18 of MacIntyre's "Are There Any Natural Rights?"

certain relationships. The attempt to show that human rights are grounded in human dignity is thus the attempt to pinpoint some property or relationship whose possession by all human beings gives them all a certain worth—some property or relationship on which worth supervenes. If one succeeds in pinpointing one or more of such properties or relationships, then natural human rights are what is required by way of action and restraint from action in order that due respect be shown for the worth of all entities that possess those properties or stand in those relationships—namely, all human beings. Should the schedule of natural human rights that one arrives at in this way diverge markedly from standard lists of human rights, one would have reason to wonder whether one's endeavor was seriously flawed in some way. On the other hand, it would be surprising if those lists did not here and there require deletion, addition, revision, qualification, and so forth.

Richard Rorty, in "Human Rights, Rationality, and Sentimentality," insists that the enterprise in which I will be engaged in the next couple of chapters, namely, determining whether human rights can be grounded in human dignity—*rights foundationalism* he calls it—is "outmoded." He affirms the judgment of the Argentinian jurist and philosopher Eduardo Rabossi that a "new, welcome fact of the post-Holocaust world" is that a human rights culture is now firmly in place. Given this development, philosophers should "stop trying to get behind or beneath this fact, stop trying to detect and defend its so-called 'philosophical presuppositions.' " The world has changed; "the human rights phenomenon renders human rights foundationalism outmoded and irrelevant" (115–16).

Though the social practice of treating each and every human being as having certain rights on account of being human is now rather well entrenched and widespread, it is not yet universally employed. Not all human beings participate in the practice. So the need of the day, says Rorty, is to expand the scope of the practice, get more people to participate in it, get more people to embrace human rights culture. He holds that for that purpose, the philosophical project of trying to ground human rights is useless. Far more effective is telling "sad and sentimental stories" so as to evoke sympathy for the feelings of other people. (More about this in the Epilogue.)

The reason philosophical attempts to ground our human rights culture in human nature are outmoded and irrelevant is not just that such attempts are useless for spreading that culture—this being the need of the day. More fundamentally, what makes them outmoded and irrelevant is the decline of the belief that human beings have a nature.

We are much less inclined than our ancestors were to take "theories of human nature" seriously, much less inclined to take ontology or history as a guide to life. We have come to see that the only lesson of either history or anthropology is our extraordinary malleability. We are coming to think of ourselves as the flexible, protean, self-shaping animal rather than as the rational animal or the cruel animal. (115)[11]

There is no human nature for human rights to be grounded in. It is only the *social practice* of according certain rights to each and every human being that attaches rights to the status of being human. Human rights, as Rorty sees the matter, are all socially conferred. None of them is natural.

What we have here is exactly the confusion to which I pointed above, namely, confusion over the point at which the concept *natural* is employed. One does not have to believe in human nature to believe in natural human rights. Suppose human beings have no nature, no essence—whatever we take that to mean. It remains the case that they are human beings; they have that status. And even the person who does not believe in human nature can hold that the properties and relations composing that status just naturally have a worth that grounds human rights. Of course, if one's view is that the only thing that makes something a human being is, say, a certain "look," then presumably one will hold that there are no natural human rights; the human "look," after all, does not have much worth.

THE SORT OF PROPERTY WE ARE LOOKING FOR

A few things should be said about the sort of property (or relation) we are looking for. It will be a property that all human beings have, though not necessarily by virtue of their nature. It will be a property that no non-human animal has—more generally, that no non-human earthling has. It may or may not be a relational property, that is, a property that, as Aristotle put it, is a property *with respect to* (*pros ti*) something. It will be a property that gives human beings non-instrumental worth, that worth being of a degree sufficient to account for the standard schedule of human rights, or something very much like it. The non-instrumental worth it gives human beings will be greater than that which any animal has. No matter how far in the scale of excellence a human being may drop, she is still of greater excellence than any animal. It need not be the only property that gives a particular human being worth. And it

---

[11] There is of course an irony in claiming that we are "the flexible, protean, self-shaping animal" in the course of arguing that we have no nature.

may be a degreed property of such a sort that, the higher the degree, the greater the contribution that possession of that property makes to the human being's excellence. Of course, if there are other properties that contribute to a person's excellence, then one person may have a higher degree of this property than another while still being of less excellence overall.

If the property is a non-degreed property, then the worth conferred on human beings by their possession of this property will be equal, and so also the respect to which they are entitled on account of possessing the property will be equal. There will be a straightforward link between human rights, human equality, and equality of due respect. On the other hand, if the property proves to be a degreed property, the situation with respect to equality will be more complex. Call that which comes in degrees D. Human beings will be equal in that they all have the property of having some degree or other of D. That property will give them equal worth in that regard; and the respect to which they are entitled on account of having that worth will also be equal. But as to all the properties of the form *having degree x of D*, the worth human beings have on account of having one of those properties will not be equal, and the respect to which they are entitled on account of having one of them will likewise not be equal. The link between human rights and human equality will be complex, not to say, problematic.

Chapter Fifteen

IS A SECULAR GROUNDING

OF HUMAN RIGHTS POSSIBLE?

JONATHAN GLOVER opens his "moral history of the twentieth century" with a presentation of what he calls "Nietzsche's Challenge." The challenge occurs often in Nietzsche's writings. Glover quotes a passage from *The Genealogy of Morals* in which Nietzsche is reflecting on what we must expect when humankind no longer believes in God: "As the will to truth thus gains self-consciousness—there can be no doubt of that—morality will gradually *perish* now: this is the great spectacle in a hundred acts reserved for the next two centuries in Europe—the most terrible, most questionable, and perhaps also the most hopeful of all spectacles." Glover then remarks, "A century later, many people share Nietzsche's scepticism about a religious basis for morality" (12).

Glover is one of those who share that skepticism. He is skeptical not just about a religious basis for morality but about any objective basis. "The prospects of reviving belief in a moral law are dim," he says. In this situation, morality can either "be abandoned, or it can be re-created." He proposes that it be re-created and that the result be *seen* as a creation. Morality "may survive in a more defensible form when seen to be a human creation. We can shape it consciously to serve people's needs and interests, and to reflect the things we most care about" (41).

There are billions of people living today who have not lost faith in a moral law. One assumes Glover knows this. Perhaps he regards all such people as relics of an outmoded mentality: not yet come of age, not fully modern, not up to speed. In any case, Glover's eye is on a certain subset of secular Western intellectuals, that subset including himself. He thinks that the prospect of reviving belief in a moral law among these intellectuals is dim. It is these people who either have to abandon morality or set about creating a morality that, while more gentle and tolerant than the "hard" morality Nietzsche proposed, is yet seen for what it is, namely, a human creation.[1]

---

[1] Here is Nietzsche urging his hard morality, in vague but menacing language: "And if your hardness will not flash and cut and cut to pieces: how can you one day create with me? For creators are hard. And it must seem bliss to you to press your hand upon millennia as upon wax, bliss to write upon the will of millennia as upon metal—harder than metal,

It is obvious from Glover's own narration of the horrors of the twentieth century that the murderers of the twentieth century would have had
no interest whatsoever in the morality Glover creates. If morality is to be
created, they will create their own; and it will be more like Nietzsche's
than like Glover's. They did in fact create their own; it was more like
Nietzsche's.

Glover is by no means idiosyncratic in setting his discussion within the
context of Nietzsche's challenge. Present-day discussions by philosophers about morality in general, and human rights in particular, are
haunted by Nietzsche's challenge. Is it possible, without reference to
God, to identify something about each and every human being that gives
him or her a dignity adequate for grounding human rights? If not, then
what? Some think the challenge can be met. Many think it cannot.
Among the latter is the Australian philosopher Raimond Gaita, himself
a secularist. He thinks we are "whistling in the dark" if we suppose
Nietzsche's challenge can be met.[2]

> Only someone who is religious can speak seriously of the sacred, but
> such talk informs the thoughts of most of us whether or not we are
> religious, for it shapes our thoughts about the way in which human
> beings limit our will as does nothing else in nature. If we are not
> religious, we will often search for one of the inadequate expressions
> which are available to us to say what we hope will be a secular equiva-
> lent of it. We may say that all human beings are inestimably precious,
> that they are ends in themselves, that they are owed unconditional
> respect, that they possess inalienable rights, and, of course, that they
> possess inalienable dignity. In my judgment these are ways of trying
> to say what we feel a need to say when we are estranged from the
> conceptual resources we need to say it. Be that as it may: each of
> them is problematic and contentious. Not one of them has the sim-
> ple power of the religious ways of speaking.
>
> Where does that power come from. Not, I am quite sure, from
> esoteric theological or philosophical elaborations of what it means

---

nobler than metal. Only the noblest is perfectly hard. This new law-table do I put over you,
O my brothers: *Become hard!*" *Thus Spake Zarathustra*, Part Three, "Of Old and New Law-
Tables." Quoted in Glover, *Humanity*, p. 16.

[2] The "whistling in the dark" phrase occurs in the following passage: "The secular philosophical tradition speaks of inalienable rights, inalienable dignity and of persons as ends
in themselves. These are, I believe, ways of whistling in the dark, ways of trying to make
secure to reason what reason cannot finally underwrite. Religious traditions speak of the
sacredness of each human being, but I doubt that sanctity is a concept that has a secure
home outside those traditions." Raimond Gaita, *Thinking about Love and Truth and Justice*
(2000), p. 5. The passage is quoted in chapter 1 of Michael Perry's *Toward a Theory of
Human Rights*.

for something to be sacred. It derives from the unashamedly anthro-
pomorphic character of the claim that we are sacred because God
loves us, his children. (23–24)

I think Gaita is right about this. It is impossible to develop a secular
account of human dignity adequate for grounding human rights. Or
to speak more cautiously: given that, after many attempts, no one has
succeeded in developing such an account, it seems unlikely that it can
be done. But rather than simply offering this as a dictum and moving on
at once to an overtly theistic account, I propose looking at the most
important of secular attempts to ground human rights so as to see where
and why they fail.[3]

KANT'S GROUNDING PROPOSAL

Most, but not all, attempts at grounding human rights attempt to ground
them in human dignity; most of such attempts, in turn, adopt what may
be called the *capacities approach*.[4] The property proposed, as that on which
the relevant sort of dignity supervenes, is some capacity of human beings.
Kant remains the paradigmatic representative of this approach; we cannot do better than look at what he had to say.

I will use Allen Wood's *Kant's Ethical Thought* as my guide through this
part of the Kantian thickets.[5] Wood gives priority in his interpretation to
Kant's 1785 *Groundwork of the Metaphysic of Morals*. A somewhat different
picture of Kant's thought would emerge if one gave priority to his publication of three years later, *Critique of Practical Reason*. My reason for following Wood is that it was in the *Groundwork* that Kant gave what became
the classic formulation of the capacities approach.

Kant ascribes to human beings three fundamental capacities: animality, humanity, and personality. For our purposes here we can set animality
off to the side. "The predisposition to personality is the rational capacity
to respect the moral law and to act having duty or the moral law as the
sole sufficient motive of the will" (Wood, 118). "The predisposition to
humanity lies in between the predispositions to animality and personality. It encompasses all our rational capacities having no specific reference

---

[3] Among the scholars in recent years who have argued that a secular account of human
rights is impossible, prominent is Michael Perry, in his *Toward a Theory of Human Rights*.
Though my argument takes a form different from his, I have learned a good deal from his
discussion.

[4] On occasion I will speak of the theorist as grounding rights, when what I always mean,
strictly speaking, is the theorist *revealing* the ground of the rights in question.

[5] Cambridge: Cambridge University Press, 1999.

to morality. Put most generally, humanity is the capacity to set ends through reason," as contrasted with acting on the basis of impulse, addiction, and the like (118–19).

This capacity, the capacity to set ends through reason, has two sides, the technical and the pragmatic. The technical side "includes our conscious, rational capacities to manipulate things as means to our arbitrary ends." The pragmatic side "enables us not only to set ends but to compare the ends we set and organize them into a system." Thereby, it involves "an active sense of my identity and an esteem for myself." And it presupposes freedom of a certain sort, namely, the ability to resist the immediate coercion of desires and impulses. Kant calls the concept of this sort of freedom the "negative" concept of freedom (119).

One would expect Kant to fasten onto personality as that which grounds obligation and rights. Personality, after all, "seems 'higher' than humanity in that it has essential reference to *moral* value, moral responsibility, and the 'positive' concept of freedom, where humanity includes none of these" (120). Wood argues that Kant chose humanity instead. Because it will make no difference to my argument whether Wood is right about this, I will follow in his footsteps without giving his argumentation. If it was personality that Kant had in mind, then the problems surrounding his grounding proposal are even more serious than they are on Wood's interpretation.

Not only did Kant hold that humanity in a human being makes that being worthy of being treated as an end; Wood cites strong evidence for interpreting Kant as holding that this is the only thing about human beings that gives them worth, and that it gives them equal worth (132–33). "The essence of things is not changed by their external relations; and that which, without taking account of such relations, alone constitutes the worth of a human being is that in terms of which he must also be appraised by whoever does it, even by the supreme being."[6] The formula of humanity as an end in itself has to be interpreted as implying, says Wood, "that all the normal (comparative and competitive) measures of people's self-worth—wealth, power, honor, prestige, charm, charisma, even happy relationships with others—are expressions of an utterly false sense of values" (133). "In other words, the worst rational being (in any respect you can possibly name) has the same dignity or absolute worth as the best rational being in that respect (or in any other)" (132).

That last-quoted paraphrase of Kant's doctrine by Wood ironically displays on its face how implausible the doctrine is. The paraphrase contradicts the doctrine it formulates. Wood speaks of "the worst rational

---

[6] Kant, *Groundwork*, Academy 439. Translation by Mary J. McGregor in McGregor, *Immanuel Kant: Practical Philosophy* (Cambridge: Cambridge University Press, 1996), p. 88.

being" and of "the best rational being," thereby implying that rational beings do differ in worth.

It is possible to hold—in my view not only possible but correct—that though human beings can be compared with respect to, say, wealth, such comparison has nothing whatsoever to do with their worth, their excellence. The wealth of a human being contributes nothing to the worth of that human being, any more than, say, being born in January. It is not something to praise a human being for. So too, having light-colored skin does not contribute to a human being's worth. One can compare human beings with respect to how light their skin is. But color of skin is not a worth-imparting feature of human beings.

Now consider the property of human beings that is at the center of Kant's attention, namely, the capacity for rational agency. Some people have this capacity to a greater degree than others; and those who have it in the same degree exercise it better and worse. Rational nature, says Wood, "comes in degrees. People have varying amounts of technical skill, pragmatic intelligence, or moral wisdom. Their actions exhibit various rational successes and failures. Even their rational capacities tend to develop as they mature and may be impaired in various ways by injury, disease, or old age" (121). Wood then observes that "being an end in itself cannot come in degrees, since a categorical imperative or practical law either has an objective ground or it does not. Kant's position therefore has to be that anything possessing the capacity to set ends and act according to reason is an end in itself, however well or badly it may exercise the capacity."

But if possessing the capacity for rational action gives worth to a human being, how can it be that possessing that capacity to a greater degree does not give a human being greater worth? And how can it be that exercising that capacity better does not also give a human being greater worth? It would remain to consider whether the respect that grounds rights is entirely determined by whether or not one has the capacity at all, not by how much of the capacity one has or by how well one exercises it. But if having the capacity is a good thing, then having more of it is better than having less of it, and exercising it well is better than exercising it poorly. I fail to see why those differences would not impart corresponding differences in worth to the persons who possess and exercise the capacity.

In particular, different exercises of the capacity differ in their moral worth. Kant agreed. How, then, could he not take the next step of holding that these differences in the worth of various *exercises* of the capacity impart differential worth to the *agents themselves*? Wood sees the issue and puts it like this: if the good will is the only unqualified good, as Kant says it is, "how can Kant regard a person with a bad will as the equal of the person with a good will?" (133).

The solution Wood attributes to Kant, and which he himself finds satisfactory, is based mainly on some things Kant says about moral humility. Moral humility requires that one compare one's moral status not to that of others but only to the demands of the moral law. How close one comes to measuring up to the moral law determines one's degree of what Kant calls *inner worth*. Hence, says Wood, though "the *inner* worth of a person, measured solely by comparison to the moral law, may be greater or less according to one's virtue in fulfilling the law one gives oneself, . . . the worth of a person never varies in comparison to others, since the good and the bad alike possess the dignity of humanity" (135).

I find this of no help. The moral worth of a person is an absolute matter, says Kant, not relative. I may be morally better than all my fellows; but that does not tell me what my moral worth is. To determine that, I must determine how I measure up against the moral law, not how I measure up against my fellows. It might just be that though I am the best, relative to them, nonetheless I am, absolutely speaking, a wretched sinner.

At this point Wood introduces the phrase "the law one gives oneself." Yes, it is true, in a way, that on Kant's view one gives the moral law to oneself; but the form and content of the law that one rational being gives himself is exactly the same as that which any other rational being gives himself, and necessarily so. Thus our situation is not that I can measure myself up against the law I gave myself, that you can measure yourself up against the law you gave yourself, and so forth—and that is the end of the matter. Because the moral law I gave myself that I measure myself up against is identical with the law you gave yourself that you measure yourself up against, once I have determined how I measure up against that law, I can glance across to see how you measure up and compare. Given the propensity of humankind to self-deception, there are epistemological barriers to making these comparisons accurately; humility may require doing very little of it. But it can be done; there is an objective fact of the matter that is not totally inaccessible to us.

So it is not true, on Kant's view, that "the worth of a person never varies in comparison to others." It is true that "the good and the bad alike possess the dignity of humanity." But that dignity is the worth of the capacity for rational agency. That capacity comes in different degrees, and is exercised better and worse—judged absolutely.

What Kant should have said is what he does say in the following passage: "I cannot deny respect even to a vicious man; I cannot withdraw the respect that belongs to him in his quality as a human being, even though by his deeds he makes himself unworthy of it."[7] Kant imagines himself having made an absolute moral judgment: the man is vicious. Others are less vicious, more virtuous, better than he is with respect to absolute moral worth. It is not just that their *actions* are morally better, judged absolutely; *they themselves* are morally better. There are vicious *human beings* and there are virtuous *human beings,* and the former are less excellent morally than the latter—judged by reference to the objective moral law. But that does not speak to the vicious man's "quality as a human being." With respect to his humanity, the vicious man is the equal of the virtuous man; both deserve respect with regard to their humanity, equal respect. What counts for the grounding of human rights is one's sheer capacity for rational action, not how much of that capacity one possesses nor how well one exercises that capacity. That is what Kant should have said.

WHY KANT'S PROPOSAL DOES NOT WORK

We are ready for the question: are natural human rights grounded in the capacity for rational agency? There are two basic questions to be considered. Do all and only human beings (among earthlings) possess that capacity? And does possessing that capacity give one a worth that, on the one hand, is greater than the worth of any animal and, on the other hand, is sufficient to account for what we recognize to be natural human rights? I will interweave my treatment of these two questions.

Some human beings do not possess the capacity. One can possess the capacity at a certain time without exercising it at that time; one may be asleep, under general anesthesia, in a temporary coma, in a trance, under hynosis, and so forth. But some human beings not only are not exercising the capacity; they do not *have* it—infants and those suffering from dementia, for example.

Allen Wood takes note of the problem and introduces what he has to say on the matter by highlighting the fact that Kant almost always says that we must treat *humanity* in persons as an end, when what one would expect him to say is that we must treat *persons* as ends *on the ground of* their humanity. What is the import of this way of speaking? Was it Kant's view that it is the abstract entity *humanity* that we must respect rather than concrete human beings? Wood thinks not. "Rational nature is precisely what makes you a person, so that respecting it *in* you is precisely what it means to respect *you*" (144). It is not humanity as such that we

---

[7] Quoted from the *Metaphysics of Morals* (Academy 6: 463), *Kant's Ethical Thought*, in Wood, p. 134.

must respect but humanity *in* someone; and respecting humanity *in* someone is the same as respecting that person *on the ground of* her humanity. They come to the same thing, respecting humanity in someone and respecting someone on the ground of her humanity.

Wood then goes on to argue, however, that it was a mistake on Kant's part to hold "that to respect humanity is always to respect it *in the person* of some being who has it" (143). For this leaves Kant with nothing to say about infants who do not yet have humanity and about adults who have lost it or never acquired it. Because there is no humanity in them to respect, it follows from Kant's view that these human beings do not merit respect. But it would be absurd, says Wood, to suggest that Kant's principle has "nothing to say about how we should treat such people. For we surely would dishonor rational nature if we did not cherish its development in children or failed to strive for its recovery in men and women who have temporarily lost it" (144). Kant has to be corrected. We cannot say that human dignity requires that one *actually possess* the capacity for rational agency; a weaker relation of the human being to the capacity will have to be found than that of possession.

Begin with those suffering from Alzheimer's disease, those in a permanent coma, the severely brain-injured, perhaps some of those in Nazi death camps. How can we get these human beings within the circle of human dignity? Well, though these human beings do not now possess and never again will possess the capacity for rational agency, they did once possess it. So let us thin out the relation that a being must have to the capacity for rational agency. It is not necessary that a being actually possess that capacity; it is sufficient if the being did once possess the capacity. Perhaps the dignity that grounds human rights supervenes on the following property: *being a being that does or did possess the capacity for rational agency*. Both those who now have the capacity and those who once had it, but now do not, have that property.

Infants, however, do not have this new complex property; they neither do possess nor did possess that capacity. Not even the thinned out relation gets them within the circle of human dignity. What is true of most of them, however, is that they are beings such that, if they reach a certain maturity, their maturation will include possessing the capacity. That is also true of those who do not now possess but did once possess the capacity: their maturation includes possessing the capacity. So may it be that the dignity that grounds human rights supervenes on the following property: *being a being such that, if it matures, its maturation includes possessing the capacity for rational agency?*

There are several reasons for concluding that it does not. The most decisive reason is that there are still some human beings who fall outside the circle of dignity. The maturation of some human beings does not include acquiring the capacity for rational agency; they were born with severe mental impairment and never acquire the capacity.

Second, the property we have now arrived at is not very impressive; how much in the way of rights can it ground? It was *possession* of the capacity for rational agency that Kant had in mind when he penned his hymns of praise to the incomparable dignity of humanity. Most human beings have been far less impressed with the worth of possessing that capacity than Kant was. If one had called to the attention of the Nazis that the Jews they were about to gas possessed the capacity for rational agency, they would have said, "So what?" But let that pass; concede, for the sake of the argument, that Kant was right in his claim that possessing that capacity gives to the being who possesses it great worth. The property we have arrived at is not that one, however, but this other one: *being a being such that, if it matures, its maturation includes possessing the capacity for rational agency.* That property is much less impressive than the property of actually possessing the capacity. Would Kant pen hymns of praise to this property?

Third, the evidence points to the conclusion that certain non-human animals also possess the capacity for rational agency. It is clear that Kant thought otherwise. But recall his description of the capacity for rational agency. It is the capacity "to manipulate things as means to . . . arbitrary ends" and the capacity "to compare the ends we set and organize them into a system." In his fine book, *Dependent Rational Animals*,[8] Alasdair Mac-Intyre assembles compelling evidence for the conclusion that Kant was just mistaken in denying this capacity to animals. Certain higher mammals such as dolphins do possess that capacity.

And fourth, if some individual non-human animals are in fact capable of rational agency, then those animals will possess a much more impressive property than that thinned-out one that we wound up with. They will have the property of *actually possessing* the capacity for rational agency. And if that is not sufficiently unsettling, conjoin that capacity for rational agency with some other capacities that a good number of the higher animals do undoubtedly possess, that of feeling pain and that of being attached to their young. The property of possessing those three capacities together is surely a more impressive property than that thinned-out property that we arrived at—and which is still not the possession of all human beings.

Is there any way of avoiding these problems? Not so far as I can see. It is possible to cobble together a property possessed by all human beings that makes reference to the capacity for rational agency. Here is an example: *belonging to a species such that maturation of its properly formed members*

[8] Chicago and La Salle, Ill., Open Court Press, 1999.

includes possessing the capacity for rational agency. But it is not a very impressive property, hardly capable of grounding the rights that we recognize as human rights. And it is a property that some of the higher animals apparently also possess.

If there were no overlap between the highest degree of this capacity that any non-human animal possesses and the lowest degree that a human being can possess without being malformed, then we could carve out a distinction between what we might call *animal* rational agency and *human* rational agency. But the assumption of no such overlap is dubious. And it will still be the case that the property some non-human animals have of actually possessing animal rational agency is more impressive than that property that seriously impaired human beings have, of belonging to a species whose mature properly formed members possess human rational agency.

Let us review the steps in the argument. Kant was impressed with the worth of possessing the capacity for rational agency; always treat any being who possesses that capacity as an end, be it a human being or whatever. A question occurred to us that Kant himself did not raise: what about those human beings who once possessed the capacity but do not now possess it and never will again—relics of possessing the capacity, as it were? Perhaps the worth of the capacity also gives some worth to the beings who stand to it in this relation—less worth, one supposes, than that of those who actually possess the capacity, but still some worth. Then another question occurred to us: what about those immature beings who have never possessed the capacity but whose maturation includes possessing it? May the worth of the capacity also give some worth to beings who stand to it in that relation—less worth than that of those who actually possess the capacity, but still quite a bit? If so, then any being of that sort, be it human or whatever, also merits some respect—though whether enough to ground human rights is a good question. Then we noticed that some human beings are still left out.

I observed that it is possible to find some relation to the capacity for rational agency that these and all other human beings possess. But why stop there in our enumeration of thinned-out relations to the capacity? What about those entities that, though never themselves capable of rational agency, are nonetheless *prized* by someone in the exercise of that capacity, such as a cause to which some rational being gave his life, a building that some rational being lovingly constructed, an animal, a tree, a flower that some rational being loved? Does not the worth of the capacity for rational agency also give some worth to beings that stand to it in this relation—not as much worth as that of those who exercised the capacity in their prizing of these things, but still quite a bit? What rationale is there for saying "no" to this question?

The fatal flaw in Kant's capacities approach to human dignity is now clear. If we insist that the capacity for rational agency gives worth to all and only those who stand to the capacity in the relation of actually possessing it, then it is not *human* rights that are grounded but the rights of those who possess the capacity. But if we try to get all human beings within the circle of dignity by finding some relation to the capacity that all of them possess, then four things happen. The resultant relation is unimpressive; it imparts very little worth to the beings that stand in the relation. Second, the relation appears ever more cobbled together, having no other rationale than to achieve the pre-ordained goal of finding a relation to the capacity that all and only human beings have; why draw the lines this way? Third, there is good reason to believe that some of the higher non-human animals stand to the capacity in that relation. And fourth, the actual possession by some higher animals of various capacities, including that of rational agency, would seem to give them more worth than the worth a being has on account of standing to the capacity of rational agency in that attenuated, thinned-out relation.

I submit that the problem confronting Kant's version of the capacities approach confronts every other version of the capacities approach as well. Whatever capacity one selects, it will turn out that some human beings do not possess the capacity. There is no way around the problems that that fact poses.

Dworkin's Attempt at Grounding Human Rights

Attempts to identify something in human beings that gives them a dignity adequate for grounding human rights need not take the form of a capacities approach; Ronald Dworkin's attempt does not take that form. Dworkin does little to develop his proposal, so I do not spend much time on it; but it is instructive to have it before us.

Almost all of us accept, says Dworkin, "as the inarticulate assumption behind much of our experience and conviction, that human life in all its forms is *sacred*." For some of us this sacredness of human life "is a matter of religious faith; for others, of secular but deep philosophical belief."[9] That is not because the religious and the secular offer different grounds for believing the same thing; it is because "there is a secular as well as a religious interpretation of the idea that human life is sacred."[10] Dworkin proceeds to offer a secular interpretation of the conviction.

[9] Ronald Dworkin, "Life Is Sacred. That's the Easy Part," *New York Times Magazine*, May 16, 1993, p. 36.

[10] Ronald Dworkin, *Life's Dominion: An Argument about Abortion, Euthanasia, and Individual Freedom* (New York: Knopf, 1993), p. 195.

"The nerve of the sacred," he says, "lies in the value we attach to a process or enterprise or project rather than to its results considered independently from how they were produced" (78). That is to say, the sacredness of something resides not in that entity itself but in that entity considered in the light of how it came about. In the case of human beings, one must distinguish two aspects of this genesis. First, every human being is "the highest product of natural creation. . . . [T]he idea that human beings are special among natural creations is offered to explain why it is horrible that even a single human individual life should be extinguished" (82). Second, "each developed human being is the product not just of natural creation, but also of the kind of deliberative human creative force that we honor in honoring art" (82). "The idea that each individual human life is inviolable is therefore rooted . . . in two combined and intersecting bases of the sacred: natural *and* human creation" (83).

> The life of a single human organism commands respect and protection, then, no matter in what form or shape, because of the complex creative investment it represents and because of our wonder at the . . . processes that produce new lives from old ones, at the processes of nation and community and language through which a human being will come to absorb and continue hundreds of cultures and forms of life and value, and, finally, when mental life has begun and flourishes, at the process of internal personal creation and judgment by which a person will make and remake himself, a mysterious, inescapable process in which we each participate, and which is therefore the most powerful and inevitable source of empathy and communion we have with every other creation who faces the same frightening challenge. The horror we feel in the willful destruction of a human life reflects our shared inarticulate sense of the intrinsic importance of each of these dimensions of investment. (84)

Though not a capacities account of human dignity, Dworkin's account falls prey to the same difficulties that beset capacities accounts. From the passage quoted it is clear that Dworkin, like Kant, has his eye on mature properly formed human beings; such beings are creative masterpieces of natural creation and self-creation. But what about a human being who was severely impaired mentally from birth? Dworkin's words lead one to think that he regards such human beings as also sacred. But are they creative masterpieces? Certainly, they are not masterpieces of self-creation. Are they nonetheless masterpieces of natural creation—greater, say, than roaring lions, soaring eagles, affectionate chimpanzees, or playful dolphins?

Gewirth's Attempt at Grounding

Let me turn, finally, to a capacities approach that is not dignity-based—just the reverse of Dworkin's approach—namely, that of Alan Gewirth. Gewirth is like Kant in attempting to ground human rights in the capacity for rational agency; his approach differs from Kant's in that the worth of the capacity plays no role in his argument. The fact that Gewirth's proposal has stirred up a good deal of interest among philosophers, and that it is almost unique in not being a dignity-based approach, is sufficient reason for seeing what it is and discerning why it too does not work.

Gewirth published a number of different statements of his proposal, the later statements taking account of objections raised to earlier ones. I base my discussion on one of his last statements, that to be found in the introduction and first chapter of his 1982 collection, *Human Rights: Essays on Justification and Applications*.[11] Gewirth calls his argument *dialectically necessary*, in contrast to *assertoric*. What he means is that "the argument has established not that persons have rights *tout court* but rather that all agents logically must claim or at least accept that they have certain rights" (54).

Let us have the argument before us in its entirety.

First, every agent holds that the purposes for which he acts are good on whatever criterion (not necessarily a moral one) enters into his purposes. Second, every actual or prospective agent logically must therefore hold or accept that freedom and well-being are necessary goods for him because they are the necessary conditions of his acting for any of his purposes; hence, he holds that he *must* have them. Third, he logically must therefore hold or accept that he has rights to freedom and well-being; for, if he were to deny this, he would have to accept that other persons may remove or interfere with his freedom and well-being, so that he *may not* have them; but this would contradict his belief that he *must* have them. Fourth, the sufficient reason on the basis of which each agent must claim these rights is that he is a prospective purposive agent, so that he logically must accept the conclusion that all prospective purposive agents, equally and as such, have rights to freedom and well-being. (20)

Unless "act" is defined in such a way that the first premise of the argument is analytically true, I doubt that

---

[11] Chicago: University of Chicago Press.

(1) Every agent [always] holds that the purposes for which he
acts are good.

Those engaged in addictive or compulsive behavior seem to me not to
fit the description. But rather than contesting the point, let me move on
to the second premise:

(2) Every actual or prospective agent logically must hold or
accept that freedom and well-being are necessary goods for
him because they are the necessary conditions of his acting
for any of his purposes; hence, he holds that he *must* have
them.

Let me paraphrase what I take Gewirth to be saying. If I seek to bring
about X, then I regard X as good; and if I regard Y as a necessary condition of my bringing about X, then I must also regard Y as good. Now for
any purposive action whatsoever, freedom and well-being are necessary
conditions of my bringing about what I seek to bring about. So I must
regard freedom and well-being as "necessary goods" for me.

The claim, that I must regard as good anything that I judge to be a
necessary condition of bringing about some end that I regard as good,
is true only if what is meant is that I must regard it as *instrumentally*
good for bringing about that end.[12] I may regard that condition, considered by itself, as a distinct evil—something that I must unfortunately put
up with.

Freedom, says Gewirth, "consists in controlling one's behavior by one's
unforced choice while having knowledge of relevant circumstances," and
well-being "consists in having the other general abilities and conditions
required for agency" (47). What then does he mean when he says that
freedom and well-being, so understood, are "the necessary conditions
of his acting for any of his purposes"? Does he mean that I am to
run through each and every one of my purposes and ask, for each, what
is necessary by way of freedom and well-being for achieving that purpose?
Or does he mean that I am to ask what is necessary by way of freedom
and well-being for performing any purposive action at all?

The freedom and well-being yielded by the former strategy would
not only be extremely expansive; there is no plausibility whatsoever in
supposing that we have a right to whatever freedom and well-being is
necessary for doing whatever we purpose to do. That would give the
person intent on murder the right to freedom to murder. What Gewirth

---

[12] I am using "instrumentally" here to cover not only causes but logical and physical
conditions.

has to mean is the freedom and well-being necessary for performing any purposive act at all. Some textual evidence can be offered in support of this interpretation. Referring to the freedom that he wishes to argue we have a right to, Gewirth says that "it must be kept in mind that [this] freedom is a necessary condition of action. A distinction must . . . be drawn between freedoms that are essential for action in general and those that pertain to particular actions whose performance or nonperformance does not affect the general necessary conditions of action" (17–18).

So what is necessary, by way of freedom, for performing any purposive action at all? I would say, exceedingly little. There is, says Gewirth, "a general human right to freedom because freedom is a necessary condition of human purposive action. The freedom in question consists in controlling one's behavior by one's unforced choice while having knowledge of relevant circumstances. . . . This freedom . . . includes the negative freedom of not being interfered with by other persons" (15). I assume that by an "unforced" choice Gewirth means a choice made in the absence of coercion. But coercion does not prevent purposive action; it simply attaches a price to one or more of the options. The martyrs acted purposively even though they were subjected to coercion. The clause about knowledge of relevant circumstances is likewise questionable. Whether or not it is correct to include some such clause in one's definition of "freedom," lack of such knowledge does not prevent purposive action. Last, by the phrase "controlling one's behavior," I assume Gewirth means controlling one's *bodily* actions. But consider the paraplegic: he is capable of engaging in purposive action. We have all had the experience of forming the intention to think about something, and then enacting that intention. Short of taking your life or putting you asleep, into a coma, or into a stupor, there is, so far as I can see, nothing I can do to make purposive action impossible for you. As long as you are alert, you can decide to focus your attention on something. The freedom one needs for performing any purposive action at all is exceedingly little, hardly enough to ground anything approaching the standard schedule of human rights.

Let us move on to the next premise in the argument:

> (3) He must therefore hold or accept that he has rights to freedom and well-being; for if he were to deny this, he would have to accept that other persons may remove or interfere with his freedom and well-being, so that he *may not* have them; but this would contradict his belief that he *must* have them.

Let me go beyond what Gewirth actually says to lay out how I think he must have been thinking.[13] We are to imagine a person who, in his reflections on the necessary conditions of understanding himself as acting purposively, is at the point of having concluded that a bit of freedom and a bit of well-being are necessary if he is to perform any purposive action at all; we are to suppose, further, that he holds that these are goods. Now suppose this person holds that he nonetheless does not have a right to those goods. Should someone deprive him of them, they would not be wronging him. Correlatively, they would not be violating their obligations; they are morally permitted to do that. Gewirth now offers him the following argument. If he holds that what he is aiming at is good, then he must hold that he is morally permitted to aim at it. And if he sees that he must enjoy the goods of freedom and well-being in order to achieve what he is aiming at, then he must hold that he is morally permitted to enjoy those goods of freedom and well-being.[14] But if he is morally permitted to enjoy those goods, then his fellows are not morally permitted to deprive him of them; they are obligated to refrain from doing so. In short, he must hold that he has a right to their refraining.

The argument is fallacious. Recall from our discussion of Hohfeld in chapter 11 the distinction between being morally permitted to do something and having the claim-right to be free from interference in doing

---

[13] Gewirth fleshes out the argument in the following passage:

> The argument may be summed up by saying that if any agent denies that he has rights to freedom and well-being, he can be shown to contradict himself. For, as we have seen, he must accept (1) "My freedom and well-being are necessary goods." Hence, the agent must also accept (2) "I, as an actual or prospective agent, must have freedom and well-being," and hence also (3) "All other persons must at least refrain from removing or interfering with my freedom and well-being." For if other persons remove or interfere with these then he will not have what he has said he must have. Now suppose the agent denies (4) "I have rights to freedom and well-being." Then he must also deny (5) "All other persons ought at least to refrain from removing or interfering with my freedom and well-being." By denying (5) he must accept (6) "It is not the case that all other persons ought at least to refrain from removing or interfering with my freedom and well-being," and hence he must also accept (7) "Other persons may (are permitted to) remove or interfere with my freedom and well-being." But (7) contradicts (3). Since, as we have seen, every agent must accept (3), he cannot consistently accept (7). Since (7) is entailed by the denial of (4), "I have rights to freedom and well-being," it follows that any agent who denies that he has rights to freedom and well-being contradicts himself. (50–51)

See also pp. 23 and 49–50.

[14] The introduction of moral permission at this point is where I go beyond what Gewirth actually says.

it. I may be morally permitted to do something while at the same time others are morally permitted to try to stop me from doing it. Now suppose I regard what I am trying to do as a good thing to do. And let us concede to Gewirth that if I regard it as a good thing to do, then I also regard it as morally permitted for me to do. Suppose further that I cannot do it unless my fellows grant me the freedom to do it. It does not follow that they are obligated to give me that freedom and that I have a claim-right to their doing so. If the person we are imagining does think this, he is reasoning fallaciously.

The last step in the argument is this:

> (4) The sufficient reason on the basis of which each agent
> must claim these rights is that he is a prospective purposive
> agent, so that he logically must accept the conclusion that all
> prospective purposive agents, equally and as such, have rights
> to freedom and well-being.

Once again, the argument, at least as it stands, is fallacious. The premises are these: first, I am logically compelled, by reflection on the fact that I am a purposive agent, to think of myself as having a right to freedom and well-being; and second, there is nothing in this line of thought peculiar to me. The conclusion one would expect Gewirth to draw is that I am compelled to think that others are compelled to think in the same way I am about the implications of their being rational agents. But that is not the conclusion he draws. Instead, he says that I am compelled to think that all of us, myself included, *do in fact* have rights to freedom and well-being.

A great deal of the discussion in the philosophical literature about Gewirth's argument has focused on this last step. As it stands, the conclusion does not follow from the premises. Suppose it does not follow from the fact that I am logically compelled to think a certain way that that way of thinking is correct. Why would it follow from the fact that other people are also logically compelled to think that way? What does bringing other people into the picture add? The question that most commentators have dwelt on is whether additional premises can be supplied to turn this last part of the overall argument into a sound argument. If everything in the argument up to this point were cogent, we would have to delve into those discussions. But because it is not, we do not have to.

Let me note, in conclusion, that even if Gewirth's argument worked, it would ground not human rights but only the rights of those human beings who are capable of rational agency. Though not a dignity argument, Gewirth's argument shares with Kant's dignity argument the same fundamental flaw: at best it grounds the rights of a certain subset of human beings, not of human beings generally.[15]

THE OPTIONS BEFORE US

My topic in this chapter has been whether a secular grounding of human rights is possible. Most secular attempts at grounding are dignity-based approaches; and most of these, in turn, locate human dignity in certain capacities. We have found reason to believe that all of these are bound to fail. Dworkin's approach, though dignity-based, does not locate dignity in capacities. But it too fails, for essentially the same reason that capacities approaches fail. In the following chapter I suggest a secular grounding that is, to the best of my knowledge, not to be found in the literature. Like Dworkin's proposal, it is a dignity-based approach that does not ground dignity in capacities. It will prove no more successful, however, than any of the other secular dignity approaches.

Allan Gewirth's account of human rights is the only secular grounding attempt of which I am aware that is not a dignity-based account; it is a capacities approach that is not dignity-based. We have seen that it too fails.

We are left, then, with the following four options.

(i) We can continue to hold that there are natural rights inherent to a worth possessed by all human beings, and that an articulate secular account of the properties or relationships on which that worth supervenes is highly desirable; we can then live in the hope that some day such a secular grounding will turn up.

(ii) We can continue to hold that there are natural rights inherent to a worth possessed by all human beings, and offer a theistic grounding of such rights, that is, an account of the relationship on which worth supervenes that makes essential reference to God.

(iii) We can give up on the existence of inherent natural human rights, insist that there are nonetheless inherent natural person rights or animal rights, and attempt to articulate a grounding of those.

(iv) We can deny that there are any inherent natural rights whatsoever, while nonetheless insisting on the importance of the so-

[15] Gewirth takes note of the problem and discusses it briefly on pp. 54–55. His solution is that "generic rights must be proportional to the degree to which [human beings] have the abilities of agency" (55). I think he means "have or will have the abilities of agency." He does not consider what this implies for the rights of those who do not and never will have the abilities of agency.

cial practice of according every human being certain rights. When asked to justify our insistence on the importance of this practice, we will not appeal to the worth of human beings, because we believe there is no such worth relevant to rights, but to consequentialist considerations of one sort and another. This is the option Rorty has chosen.

An option that is not available is holding that there are natural rights inherent to a worth possessed by all human beings, but that this worth has no ground, no properties or relationships on which it supervenes. That makes no sense. Worth cannot just float free; always there has to be something that gives the entity such worth as it has, some property, achievement, or relationship on which its worth supervenes.

In the next chapter I offer a theistic grounding of natural inherent human rights. I will not argue, against those who choose the third or fourth of the above options, that there are such rights. For I know of no other argument for this position than one that employs those very theistic premises that I will use in my grounding proposal.

Chapter Sixteen

A THEISTIC GROUNDING OF HUMAN RIGHTS

An Initial Interpretation of *Imago Dei*

The most common suggestion for a theistic grounding of human rights is that such rights are grounded in our being in the image of God. The biblical text appears to lend support to this idea. Recall from our discussion in chapter 3 the passage in Genesis that reads:

> Whoever sheds the blood of a man,
>   by a human shall that person's blood be shed;
> for in his own image
>   God made humankind. (9:6)

All by itself, the suggestion that human rights are grounded in the image of God is void for vagueness, because there is probably no topic in Christian theology that has provoked more indecisive speculation and fruitless controversy than what constitutes the image of God. The origin of the idea is the first chapter of Genesis:

> 26. Then God said, "Let us make humankind in our image, according to our likeness; and let them have dominion over the fish of the sea, and over the birds of the air, and over the cattle, and over all the wild animals of the earth, and over every creeping thing that creeps upon the earth.
> 27. So God created humankind in his image,
>   in the image of God he created them; .
>   male and female he created them.

The passage is both provocative and cryptic, that blend accounting for the centuries of speculation and controversy over what it means.

Given the controversies, how shall we proceed? I propose that we stay away from the theological controversies and look instead at the text that has given rise to the controversies. I think we can arrive at a reliably grounded conclusion as to what the biblical writers meant by the image of God. Our conclusions may well be inadequate for the purposes of theologians; but they will suffice for our purpose of considering whether the *imago dei* can ground human rights.

When confronted with a passage whose thought is obscure because it is not clear what one or more of the words means, one has essentially two strategies available for trying to determine what the writer was saying: one can try to find, in the linguistic culture from which the passage emerged, other occurrences of the same words in which it is clear what they mean, or one can consider the passage in the context of the larger text within which it is located. Naturally, these two strategies can be combined.

One of the suggestions coming from those who have adopted the former strategy in recent years is that *likeness* and *image* must be distinguished. The idea in the background, so it is said, is that of a statue being set up in some public place for the purpose of representing the ruler to the public in his absence. The writer of Genesis is saying that God created human beings in his likeness in order that they might serve as his image within creation. They serve as his image by exercising dominion over the animals.

I agree that this interpretation is possible, though it would be more plausible if verse 27 read "as his image" rather than "in his image." But for our purposes it does not represent a significant departure from the traditional interpretation, which did not distinguish between likeness and image and which held that the writer, in speaking of *likeness* and *image,* was saying something about the character of human beings, not about the purpose for which they were placed in creation. All the questions raised on the traditional interpretation by the pair "in our image" and "according to our likeness" are still raised on the new interpretation by "according to our likeness." Furthermore, both interpretations agree that the clause "let them have dominion" makes reference to the purpose for which human beings were created. The entire disagreement is over whether "in our image" should be interpreted as referring to that purpose or whether it goes instead with "according to our likeness." Because the new interpretation does not differ from the traditional one in any way relevant to our purposes, let me follow the traditional interpretation and equate "image" with "likeness"; those who prefer the new interpretation can easily adapt what I say.

What can we learn from the literary context of the passage? A well-known characteristic of the literature of the Hebrew Bible/Old Testament is its extended use of literary parallelism; over and over we find pairs of lines in which the second line rephrases the thought of the first in somewhat different words, expands on it, adds specificity, and so forth. With this in mind, one immediately notices two parallelisms in the passage:

> Let us make humankind in our image, according to our likeness;
>   and let them have dominion.

and

God created humankind in his image,
male and female he created them.

Karl Barth is famous for taking the latter parallelism as his clue.[1] Construing the second line as an interpretation of the first, Barth argued, with characteristic intellectual and rhetorical brio, that to be created in the image of God is to be created male and female, this being intended by the writer as a way of making the general point that human beings are created to exist in I-Thou relationships with each other and with God.[2] In speaking of the image of God, the biblical witness, says Barth, "makes no reference to the peculiar intellectual and moral talents and possibilities of man, to his reason and its determination and exercise" (185). To understand the passage we must ask what is the "prototype according to which man was created? . . . It is the relationship and differentiation between the I and the Thou in God Himself. Man is created by God in correspondence with this relationship and differentiation in God Himself: created as a Thou that can be addressed by God but also as an I responsible to God; in the relationship of man and woman in which man is a Thou to his fellow and therefore himself an I in responsibility to this claim" (198).

This is an exceedingly strained interpretation. Mammals in general are created male and female; so why would citing the fact that human beings are gendered be a way of making the point that human beings are created to exist in I-Thou relationships with each other and with God, thereby mirroring the relationships among the members of the Trinity?

Barth's response, as I understand it, is to bite the bullet and hold that just as the I-Thou relationship that we find among human beings mirrors a relationship within the Trinity, so too the male-female relationship that we find among the animals dimly mirrors the I-Thou relationship that we find among human beings—and within the Trinity. All gendered species of animals are in the image of God. Though Barth does not explicitly say this, it seems to me the clear implication of the following passage: "It is not in something which distinguishes him from the beasts, but in that which formally he has in common with them, viz., that God has created him male and female, that he is this being in differentiation and relationship, and therefore in natural fellowship with God" (185).

This response highlights the fundamental flaw in Barth's interpretation. Only if we hold that all gendered species of animals bear the image of God can Barth's interpretation be saved from the charge that it is a

---

[1] The parallelism occurs again in Genesis 5:1–2, though this time with "likeness" rather than "image": "When God created humankind, he made them in the likeness of God. Male and female he created them."

[2] Barth's discussion is to be found in his *Church Dogmatics* III/I, pp. 183–206.

strained construal of the text. But no biblical writer suggests that non-human beings bear the image of God. And as for our own interest in grounding natural human rights, if all gendered species of animals bear the image of God, then *imago dei* cannot serve to ground *human* rights. On the other hand, if existing in genuine I-Thou relationships did constitute the image of God, then those human beings suffering from Alzheimer's disease would no longer bear the image of God.

Let us then take the first rather than the second parallelism as our interpretive clue. Taking the second line as giving specificity to the thought of the first, some writers have concluded that to be created in the image of God just is to be given dominion over the animals. This interpretation of the first parallelism cannot be dismissed as impossible. But before we settle on it as the *best* interpretation, let us take a more expansive view of relevant context. Consider the following passage from Psalm 8:

> When I look at your heavens, the work of your fingers,
>   the moon and the stars that you have established;
> what are human beings that you are mindful of them,
>   mortals that you care for them?
>
> Yet you have made them a little lower than God,
>   and crowned them with glory and honor.
> You have given them dominion over the works of your hands;
>   you have put all things under their feet,
> all sheep and oxen,
>   and also the beasts of the field,
> the birds of the air, and the fish of the sea,
>   whatever passes along the paths of the sea. (verses 5–8)

Though the psalmist does not speak of the image of God, the structure of the passage is strikingly like that of Genesis. When he considers the heavens, the psalmist is struck by how comparatively insignificant human beings seem to be. The question crosses his mind: why would God be mindful of such insignificant creatures as these? But then he reminds himself that God has made human beings just a bit lower than God (or than divinities or angels) in the cosmic rank of beings and has given them dominion over the works of God's hand. God created humankind with a uniquely exalted status: in the image of God, as a likeness of God, just a bit lower than God. Being created with that exalted status is intimately connected with being given dominion over the animals.

What is the connection? Is the thought that humankind's exalted status *consists* of being given dominion—that speaking of being created in the image of God and of being just a bit lower than God in the cosmic rank of beings is simply a way of saying that humankind was given dominion? I doubt it. In both passages there is a suggestion of sequence and purpose: first God did this, then God did that, and God did this in order to do that. The two actions of *making* and of *giving dominion* (*letting have dominion*) strike me, at least, as too different in character to make it plausible that by "making in God's image" the writer just means, *giving* (*letting have*) *dominion*. I think it much more likely that his idea was that to be capable of receiving and exercising the blessing or mandate of dominion, one must be a very lofty sort of creature—just a bit lower than God, made in the image and likeness of God. So the writer first characterizes the loftiness of humankind, and then goes on to declare that God, having made these lofty creatures, proceeded to give them dominion.[3] God made them as God did with the end in view of giving them dominion after God had made them.

What the text thus interpreted entitles us to say is that the image of God consists of resembling God with respect (at least) to whatever be the capacities necessary for receiving and exercising the blessing or mandate of dominion. More capacities than those may be included. Other biblical statements concerning the purpose God had in mind for human beings speak in different and more expansive ways than Genesis does; to exercise those other purposes, other capacities are required. Whether those others were understood as included within the image of God remains unclear. We can reliably infer, though, that the image includes at least the capacities necessary for having dominion. We can debate what those capacities are; but if the image is understood as I have suggested, our speculations are given quite definite boundaries, more definite than many theologians have acknowledged.

The interpretation I have been suggesting is supported by an interesting passage from the non-canonical Book of Ben Sira, 17:3ff. The passage opens with the same structure as Genesis 1 and Psalm 8: first the writer characterizes humankind as having exalted status, in this case, that of being made in God's image; then he goes on to say that God gave human beings dominion. What is particularly interesting about the passage is that, unlike Genesis and Psalms, the writer does not stop there but goes on to mention some of the capacities comprising the exalted status.

> He made them according to his own image,
>   and put the fear of him upon all flesh;
>   and [gave them] to have dominion over beasts and birds;

---

[3] I think it is an open question whether exercising dominion is mandated or whether it is permitted as part of a blessing—thus whether the rhetorical force is imperative, "Have dominion," or optative, "May you have dominion." I am myself inclined toward the latter interpretation.

discrimination and tongue and eyes,
    ears and heart he gave them for them to think.
He filled them with knowledge of understanding
    and showed them good and evil . . .
    he bestowed knowledge upon them,
    and allotted to them the law of life.

In *God, Locke, and Equality,* Jeremy Waldron makes an important point that has application here.[4] To think of a certain set of human capacities as those necessary for receiving and exercising the blessing or mandate of dominion is to have a rationale for grouping those capacities together. We must not expect that if we remove from consideration the blessing or mandate, and just look at human capacities all by themselves, we will discern any such rationale. Why group these together? Why not only some of these? Why not others as well? As Platonists never tire of remarking, everything resembles God in some respect and to some degree. So if we are talking about likeness to God, why draw a line *here?*

The blessing or mandate gives a rationale for doing what the psalmist, the writer of Genesis, and the writer of the Book of Ben Sira do, namely, single out these from among all the resemblances to God and give the set a special name, *image of God, likeness of God.* A good deal of the futility of traditional discussions about the image of God has its source right here: rather than allowing the blessing or mandate to shape one's understanding of the image, theologians have set the blessing or mandate off to the side and speculated and argued about which resemblances to God ought to be included within the *imago dei.* That proves hopeless.

I dare say no argument has to be offered for the thesis that being in the image of God (as I have explained it) gives great worth to those creatures who bear the image. The psalmist can scarcely contain himself about this worth: it places those beings who possess this image just a bit below God in the cosmic rank of beings.

A RELATED SORT OF DIGNITY

Before we consider whether the image of God, so understood, can ground natural human rights, let us take note of an alternative grounding idea that is right in front of us. Might it be that human rights are grounded in the relation of human beings to God of having been given the blessing or mandate of dominion—not in resembling God with respect to the capacities presupposed by this relationship, but in the rela-

---

[4] Cambridge: Cambridge University Press, 2002. See esp. chap. 3.

tionship itself? This suggestion does not contradict the first. It is possible that each of these relationships, bearing the image and being given dominion, is capable of grounding human rights. But it is worth considering this new idea in its own right. Surely, God's bestowing the blessing or mandate of dominion on some creatures does give to those creatures a great and unique dignity.

This suggestion for the grounding of human rights is essentially that which Locke employed in the *Second Treatise of Government.* Locke does not speak of the blessing or mandate of dominion. He speaks about God sending human beings into the world to be about God's business. But otherwise the idea is the same. In chapter II, sec. 6, of the *Second Treatise,* Locke says that in the state of nature there is a law of nature that

> teaches all mankind, who will but consult it, that being all *equal and independent,* no one ought to harm another in his life, health, liberty, or possessions: for men being all the workmanship of one omnipotent, and infinitely wise maker; all the servants of one sovereign master, sent into the world by his order, and about his business, they are his property, whose workmanship they are, made to last during his, not one another's pleasure: and being furnished with like faculties, sharing all in one community of nature, there cannot be supposed any such *subordination* among us, that may authorize us to destroy one another, as if we were made for one another's uses, as the inferior ranks of creatures are for ours.

Can Image of God or God-Given Mandate Ground Natural Human Rights?

The question now before us is whether either the image of God or the divine mandate or blessing can ground natural human rights. I take it that no non-human animals possess the *imago dei;* none of them has the full set of capacities required for receiving and exercising the blessing or mandate of dominion. None of them would be praised by the psalmist as being, in its constitution, just a bit lower than gods or angels. Some animals may engage in behavior rather like the more primitive forms of exercising dominion; but they do not genuinely exercise dominion. They lack the requisite capacities. Hence they do not have the dignity of being a bearer of the *imago dei.* And because none of them is capable of exercising the mandate or blessing, none of them is a recipient of it. The biblical writers never suggest otherwise; God gave the blessing or mandate only to human beings.

Nonetheless, neither of these bases of dignity can ground natural human rights. They fall prey to the objections that I lodged in the preceding chapter against capacities approaches in general. It is true that neither consists of capacities *tout court.* The image of God, on the interpretation proposed, consists of *resembling God with respect* to possessing the capacities necessary for exercising dominion. And being a recipient of the dominion mandate or blessing presupposes the capacities rather than being identical with them. But a good many human beings do not have the capacities necessary for exercising dominion. Those who are severely impaired mentally from birth never had them; Alzheimer's patients no longer possess them. Such human beings neither resemble God with respect to possessing those capacities nor can they implement the divine mandate or blessing by employing those capacities. They possess neither the dignity of bearing the image of God, as I have thus far interpreted it, nor the dignity of being recipients of the divine mandate.

A Better Interpretation of *Imago Dei*

Most members of the Christian tradition would find the implication that I have just now highlighted unacceptable. There is a long history of interpretation that holds that humankind lost the image of God when Adam fell. But to the best of my knowledge, no one has held that some human beings possess the image and some do not. That seems bizarre. Is there any way of revising or modifying the suggested interpretation so that it no longer has that consequence?

Well, the Alzheimer's patient, for example, is not just relatively unusual among human beings. There is something wrong with her that medical science in the future may be able to prevent, something unnatural. She is malformed in such a way as to be profoundly malfunctioning. So too for the human being who is severely impaired mentally, and the human being who is in a deep coma. There is something wrong with them, something unnatural. In their case too there is a malformation causing a profound malfunction.

I do not propose developing a theory of human nature here, and certainly not a theory of natures in general. There is a great deal of professed skepticism nowadays about the very idea of human nature. But so far as I can tell, almost everyone works with the idea of there being something wrong with certain human beings—not the idea of the human being *doing* something wrong, but the idea of *there being* something wrong. Almost everybody works with the idea of certain human beings exhibiting some malformation, and the idea of their malfunctioning on that account—not the idea of being unusual in some respect, but the idea of being malformed. Seven-foot-tall human beings are unusual, far more unusual than human beings suffering from dementia. But there is nothing wrong with most of them; they are not suffering from some malformation. Human nature has not gone awry in their case. There is not and will not be any medical research project to prevent or cure seven-footedness.

Insofar as we work with these ideas, we are working with the idea of human nature. The idea of an organism malfunctioning on account of some malformation requires the idea of that organism having a nature; and an organism has a nature if there is a distinction between its being properly formed in some respect and being malformed in that respect. As I suggested above, fundamental to medical science—cosmetic medical science excepted—is this idea of human nature.

I suggest that what we need for an adequate account of *imago dei* is this idea of human nature. The biblical writers, when they said that human beings were created in the image of God in order to exercise dominion, were not ignorant of the fact that some human beings lack the capacities necessary for exercising dominion. Neither were they implying that those human beings do not bear the image of God. Those human beings still have human nature. And that nature is such that the mature and properly formed possessors of that nature resemble God with respect to their capacities for exercising dominion. To bear the image of God is to have that sort of nature. Non-human animals have a nature, but not that sort. Something may have gone awry with human nature in one's own case, so that one lacks those capacities; but one does not, on that account, lack human nature.

Once Again, Image of God and Grounding Natural Human Rights

Does this understanding of the image of God suffice to ground natural human rights? One of the reasons that our initial construal of the image of God, call it the *capacities-resemblance* construal, did not suffice to ground natural human rights is that some human beings do not bear the image of God, thus construed. The *nature-resemblance* construal that I have just now proposed avoids this objection; all human beings bear the image of God when image is thus construed. And it is reasonable to suppose that no non-human animals bear it. So whether the nature-resemblance construal of the image of God suffices to ground natural human rights depends entirely, so far as I can see, on whether each of those beings who bear the image is, on that account, of sufficient worth to ground what are widely recognized as examples of natural human rights.

I mentioned in the preceding chapter that I would myself present a proposal for secular grounding that is distinctly different from any of those considered in the preceding chapter. The idea is now right in front of us. Suppose that from the nature-resemblance construal of *imago dei* one drops the component of resembling God, keeping just the idea of human nature. Does human nature, as I have all too briefly explained it, suffice to ground natural human rights?

Consider any of those malformed and malfunctioning human beings that I have regularly cited as examples: Alzheimer's patients, those in a deep coma, those severely impaired mentally, and so forth. Does the fact that no matter how seriously awry human nature may have gone in their cases, they nonetheless possess human nature, give them a worth sufficient to account for their having rights, including human rights?

I doubt that it gives them such a worth. Suppose that my neighbor to the north owns a Mercedes-Benz that I admire enormously; what a truly excellent automobile. And suppose that my neighbor to the south owns another example of the very same model, but that he can not get his car to run. Mechanics tell him that the engine is beyond repair; if he wants the auto to run, he has to replace the engine.

How much praise and admiration does this second car merit? What gestures of respect are appropriate? If its owner cannot afford to replace the engine, should he nonetheless safeguard the automobile in his garage on the ground that, though something is seriously awry in this case, the design plan for this model is truly admirable? Would I think he had done something quite awful if, in frustration, he just disposed of the thing? I do not think so.

So far as I can see, it is no different for human beings. Yes, a human being in whom human nature is functioning properly is of great worth, truly admirable. But why would one think that a being in whom human nature is seriously malfunctioning is still of great worth just because it has that nature? If its worth is entirely grounded in its possessing human nature, why is it not disposable? The ancient pagan philosophers who thought in terms of human nature regarded such beings as disposable. They may have been wrong about that; they may have been imperceptive to the worth that human nature, all by itself, gives to those who possess it. But to me, at least, it is not at all evident that they were in that way imperceptive.

Now suppose one combines the idea of human nature with the idea of resemblance to God in the way in which those ideas are combined in the nature-resemblance construal of image of God. To possess the image of God is to possess a nature such that properly formed possessors of that nature resemble God with respect to their capacities for exercising dominion. Does that change things?

I do not see that it does. I think the notion of an ideal automobile makes no sense. But suppose it did. Suppose there were Platonic Forms, and that among them was The Ideal Automobile. And suppose that the properly functioning Mercedes that my neighbor to the north owns resembles that ideal very closely. Does the fact that my other neighbor's Mercedes is of the same model as the one that resembles the ideal so closely give it a special worth that otherwise it would not have? Not that I can see.

But does not the fact that the biblical writers suggest that bearing the image of God gives those who bear it an exalted place in the cosmic scale of beings militate against this conclusion? I think not. When the advertising brochure for that particular model of the Mercedes-Benz that my neighbors own describes this model, one must not understand what it says as a generalization concerning each and every example of the model; on that interpretation, what it says is patently false. It is describing properly formed and properly functioning examples of the model. So too, when some field guide to birds describes, say, the golden plover, it is not making generalizations about each and every example of the species; it is describing properly formed and properly functioning examples of the species. It is not describing each and every golden plover but The Golden Plover. So too for the biblical writers. They were not offering generalizations concerning each and every human being; they were describing The Human Being. They had their eye on properly formed and properly functioning human beings.

The conclusion to which we are led is the following. If we interpret the image of God along capacity-resemblance lines, then while those who bear the image do have a truly exalted status in the cosmic scale of beings, not all human beings possess the image. If we more plausibly interpret image of God along nature-resemblance lines, then while all human beings possess the image, possessing it does not, as such, give its bearers a very exalted status; among those who possess the image will be human beings who are seriously lacking in capacities on account of human nature being malformed in their case. The image of God is not adequate, all by itself, for grounding natural human rights.

THE LOCATION OF BESTOWED WORTH IN A TAXONOMY OF WORTH

What we need, for a theistic grounding of natural human rights, is some worth-imparting relation of human beings to God that does not in any way involve a reference to human capacities. I will argue that being loved by God is such a relation; being loved by God gives a human being great worth. And if God loves equally and permanently each and every creature who bears the *imago dei*, then the relational property of being loved by God is what we have been looking for. Bearing that property gives to each human being who bears it the worth in which natural human rights inhere.[5]

Being loved by God is an example of what I shall call *bestowed* worth. So let me begin articulating my proposal for a theistic grounding of human rights by explaining the notion of bestowed worth that I will be employing, and distinguishing it from others kinds of worth. Let me do so by first locating bestowed worth within a taxonomy of different kinds of worth.

When we ask why something has worth or excellence, there are two very different sorts of questions that we might have in mind. We might be asking for what I shall call an *aspectual* explanation of its worth or we might be asking for what I shall call a *philosophical* explanation. Begin with the former.

In asking you why something has the worth it does have, I might be asking you to identify some aspect of the thing that gives it its worth, some aspect on which its worth supervenes.[6] If I hear you praise some food and I then ask, "What's good about it?" that is what I would be asking you to do, identify some aspect of the food that gives it its worth.

One type of answer you might give me is that it is good because it is healthy. It is instrumentally good, good for its effects on the body. Health may in turn be an instrumental good; but at some point, obviously, we have to arrive at something non-instrumentally good that the food contributes to bringing about if it is to be instrumentally good.

Perhaps the food is oatmeal porridge. You say that its goodness supervenes on its being healthy. Your answer invites a further question. What accounts for its being healthy—that is, what accounts *causally* for its being healthy? What makes it good for the body? You might answer that it contains a lot of fiber, very little fat, and it lowers cholesterol. Your answer highlights aspects of the food that account causally for its being good for the body, that last being the aspect on which its goodness supervenes. If the oatmeal is non-instrumentally good because it is healthy, and if its containing a lot of fiber contributes causally to its being healthy, then its containing a lot of fiber is in turn instrumentally good.

Now presumably not everything about fiber contributes to health; it is some aspect of it that does. If so, then in principle we can identify some

---

[5] This is also the view defended by Michael Perry in *Toward a Theory of Human Rights*.

[6] When I speak of aspects of things, I have in mind not some property they possess but *their possession of the property*, and not some action they perform but *their performance of the action*. Aspects of things are thus not universals but abstract particulars. They are *cases* of universals. The medieval philosophers called them *qualia*; a good many philosophers in recent years have called them *tropes*. Aristotle identified them as *things present in things*. Thus the relation that I called *aspect of* is the same as what Aristotle called *present in*. In English, we typically refer to aspects of things with gerundives: "his being hungry," for example.

aspect of the fiber that is instrumentally good, this aspect accounting for the instrumental goodness of the fiber, the instrumental goodness of the fiber accounting in turn for the instrumental goodness of the oatmeal. At some point this chain of instrumentally good aspects has to stop. Its stopping point will be some aspect whose instrumental goodness is *basic*.

Change the example. Suppose the food is not oatmeal porridge but lemon grass soup. Again, the food is good. In this case it is not instrumentally good, however: it does not prolong life, it does not keep one awake, it does not give one energy, nothing of the sort. Its flavor is what makes it good; its goodness supervenes on its having this flavor, not on its bringing about certain effects.

But is not its flavor instrumentally good, some readers will ask—good for bringing about pleasurable gustatory experiences? And is it not therefore a mere variant on the preceding example? The soup is good for bringing about pleasurable gustatory experiences; its goodness supervenes on its bringing about such experiences. And its flavor is one of the things that accounts causally for its doing that.

Maybe so; I will not argue the point. For the purposes of my example, however, let us agree that the soup's goodness is not instrumental; the soup is just good, period. One's pleasurable gustatory experience on tasting it is not what makes it good; savoring it and finding that one likes it is instead our way of gaining acquaintance with its non-instrumental goodness.[7]

We can now ask two questions. We can ask what accounts, causally, for the soup's having the flavor it does have. And we can ask, what is good about its flavor? Let us consider the latter question. Flavors themselves have aspects. And when I ask what is good about the soup's flavor, I am assuming that there is some aspect of the soup's flavor that is itself good and that the goodness of that aspect contributes to making the soup's flavor good. Perhaps what is good about the flavor is its being definitely but delicately lemony. Being definitely but delicately lemony is of non-instrumental worth and contributes that worth to the worth of the flavor, and thereby in turn to the worth of the soup.

---

[7] "Instrumental worth" is a standard piece of terminology in the philosophical literature. There are two quite different phenomena that it is used to refer to. What one might mean by attributing instrumental worth to something is that it causes something of worth. Alternatively, one might have in mind the structure of human action. Some things we choose to bring about because we think there is a chance that bringing them about will cause something else that we want to happen; we choose it as means to a chosen end. Sometimes what is meant by attributing instrumental worth to something is that it has the role of means in the structure of human action. I think that my not signaling this distinction in the text above will not produce confusion; signaling it would only add complication.

We can press the same question yet again, now about the aspect of the flavor that we have identified: what is good about the flavor's being definitely but delicately lemony? Perhaps we can answer the question by identifying some aspect of the lemony aspect of the flavor; perhaps not. In any case, this sequence of questions and answers has to end somewhere, not because we do not know enough, but because of the ontological structure of the situation. The food is non-instrumentally good on account of the non-instrumental goodness of that aspect of the food that is its flavor. Its flavor is non-instrumentally good on account of the non-instrumental goodness of that aspect of the flavor that is its being definitely but delicately lemony. At some point we are confronted with some aspect that is non-instrumentally good but not on account of the non-instrumental worth contributed to it by some aspect that it has; it is non-instrumentally good, period. Let us say, in this case too, that such an entity has *basic* worth—basic *non-instrumental* worth, of course. If, by contrast, some entity has non-instrumental worth on account of the non-instrumental worth contributed to it by some one of its aspects, then it has *non-basic aspectual* worth.

Among the aspects of entities that give them non-instrumental worth is their standing in some relation to something other than an aspect of themselves, some Aristotelian substance. Let us say that such worth is *bestowed* worth. The worth of many objects, for example, is grounded in their being relics of some famous or holy person. I say more about this shortly.

Now for the fundamentally different sort of question one might have in mind when one asks why something has the worth it does have. Suppose that you and I are both of a philosophical bent of mind. We realize that once we have gotten down to the soup's flavor being definitely but delicately lemony, we are down to something whose non-instrumental worth is basic. The aspect-of structure does not go down any farther, or at least appears not to do so. Fully recognizing this, I nonetheless ask, why is the flavor's being definitely but delicately lemony *good?* By no means is it the case that all aspects of things are non-instrumentally good. How do you explain the fact that *this* aspect is good, this *basic* aspect? How do you explain the fact that non-instrumental goodness is attached to it, supervenes on it? This "why" question cannot be answered by probing inside the entity to locate explanatory aspects.

It is at this point that general philosophical accounts of excellence enter the picture. One such account is the Platonist account. There is an entity whose non-instrumental excellence is originary, unaccountable. Plato thought that that entity was The Good Itself; Christians in the Platonist tradition have held that it is God. Everything whose worth is basic and non-instrumental has the worth it does have on account of standing in some relation to the originary good. The worth of all such things is derivative, derived from the originary good by standing to it in that relation.

The Platonist holds that the relation that transfers worth is resemblance or participation. The flavor's being definitely but delicately lemony is good because it stands to God or The Good in the relation of resembling or participating in it. The idea is not that the soup's being definitely but delicately lemony itself possesses an aspect, namely, its resembling or participating in The Good, this aspect being non-instrumentally good and contributing that goodness to the flavor. If that were how it was, the soup would have *bestowed* worth, the goodness of the soup's being definitely but delicately lemony would not be *basic*, and rather than giving a philosophical account of why goodness supervenes on the soup's lemony flavor, we would simply have added one more aspect to the entity. The idea is rather that its resemblance to God or The Good is what accounts for goodness being attached to the lemony aspect of the soup's flavor.

A feature worth noting of the Platonist account of basic non-instrumental goodness is that though the basic non-instrumental goodness of everything other than God or The Good is ontologically derivative rather than original, nonetheless the goodness of such entities belongs to them *intrinsically*. That is to say: they could not exist and fail to stand to God or The Good in the relation of resemblance or participation, and thus could not fail to have the basic non-instrumental goodness that they do have—assuming that God or The Good exists necessarily. The flavor's being definitely but delicately lemony could not fail to be good.

Presently, the most popular philosophical account of goodness in general is the desire-satisfaction account. It provides an illuminating contrast to the Platonist account. Consider the account in its simplest and crudest form. Instances of desire-satisfaction play the explanatory role in the scheme that The Good plays in Plato's scheme and that God plays in Christian Platonism. Their goodness is originary, non-derivative, unaccountable. Of course, whereas God or The Good is one, instances of desire-satisfaction are multiple.

Though instances of desire-satisfaction are the sole entities whose goodness is originary, they are not the only things of worth. Whatever contributes causally to the occurrence of desire-satisfaction has instrumental worth. And whatever is the object of a satisfied desire is likewise of worth. On the Platonist scheme, what accounts for the basic worth of the soup's flavor is its standing to The Good in the relation of resembling or participating in it; on the desire-satisfaction scheme, what accounts for the basic worth of the soup's flavor is its standing to some desire in the relation of satisfying it.

The soup's flavor might have existed without standing in that relation to desire. In that case, it either would have had no worth or would have been of purely instrumental worth. Hence in contrast to the Platonist account, the basic non-instrumental worth of entities is not intrinsic to them.

Bestowed Worth

Having distinguished different types of accounts of worth, and bestowed aspectual worth from other types of worth, some of them easily confused with it, let me now say something more about bestowed worth itself.

In our lives in the everyday we are surrounded by example of bestowed worth—*humanly* bestowed worth. Before we address the lofty matters on our agenda, let us look at some of those everyday examples. Mount Vernon is on the National Registry of Historic Buildings of the United States. Though it is a rather good house, it is by no means the finest of old Virginia plantation houses. Yet most of those other finer houses are not on the registry. The reason Mount Vernon is on the registry is that it was George Washington's house. It is a relic of Washington, as are a good many of the items in the house. Most relics of most U.S. citizens do not find their way onto the National Registry, nor into display cases in museums of national history. The difference is that Washington was a hero of the nation; most of us are not. If some foreigner, knowing nothing about U.S. history, asks in some perplexity why Mount Vernon is treated as of great worth when there are other old Virginia plantation houses of considerably greater architectural merit that are not, we do not dispute his judgment of architectural merit but point out that this was the house of George Washington, the founder of the country. "Oh," says the foreigner, "that explains it." The non-bestowed worth of the house, such as it is, is irrelevant.

A good deal of the worth that we attach to paintings in the modern world is worth as relics. Rembrandt is one of the gods in the pantheon of art. So our scholars and curators work assiduously to discover which paintings came from his hand and which, though they may for all the world look like a Rembrandt, were never touched by his hand. The Rembrandt-like paintings that he did not paint are consigned to the vaults of our museums, no matter what their aesthetic merit; the true Rembrandts, even the "clunkers," are given honored place on our museum walls. In the modern world we treat paintings the way relics of saints were treated in the days of Christendom.

I must not leave the impression that we treasure only the relics of such exalted persons as George Washington, Rembrandt van Rijn, and St. Jerome. Many of us treasure the relics of deceased parents and grandparents, children, friends. To explain to someone why we treasure these objects, we do not point to non-relational aspects of the object that give it worth. We explain that it is a relic of someone we loved; thereby we point to a relational aspect of the object that gives it bestowed worth. We may not use the word "relic"; but that is the idea.

Can we pinpoint the sort of value that a relic has? I think we can. Relics have the value of being such that by treasuring the relic, we honor the person of whom it is the relic. It is a very distinct kind of value, scarcely recognized in the philosophical literature but acknowledged by almost all of us in the living of our lives in the everyday.

A quite different sort of bestowed worth is that which a person acquires by being appointed to some worthy position—the queen in a monarchy appointing someone as her ambassador, for example. Gestures of respect for this person that previously would have been inappropriate are now appropriate; and whereas previously he might have been everyone's friend, now he is the object of envy. As we saw earlier, it was this sort of worth that Locke proposed as the ground of human rights. Human rights, said Locke, are grounded in the worth of being "sent into the world by [God's] order, and about his business." Our argument against Locke's proposal was not that being thus commissioned by God does not bestow worth; it was rather that there are a good many human beings who cannot be about God's business.

I observed that the worth of a relic is the worth of being such that treasuring the relic counts as honoring the person of whom it is the relic. The worth of the relic is just that counting-as sort of worth. Its worth is purely instrumental to the worth of the person—or, more precisely, purely instrumental to honoring the worth of the person . Not so for the worth one acquires by being appointed to some worthy position. There are, of course, situations in which treating the ambassador in certain ways counts as honoring the queen whose ambassador he is, and situations in which treating the ambassador in other ways counts as demeaning the queen. But the worth someone acquires by being appointed ambassador goes beyond that instrumental counting-as worth. The person who is ambassador merits gestures of respect even when the situation is not such that showing respect for the ambassador counts as showing respect for the queen.

Let us move on now to love. Recall the distinction we made, when discussing Augustine, between love as attraction, love as attachment, and love as benevolence. In love as attraction, the lover is attracted by the person loved, drawn to the thing loved, by the worth of some aspect of the person or thing: the blend of beauty and compassion, the flickering heaven-filling splendor of the aurora borealis, and so forth. The love

gives rise to desire for engagement with the thing loved; the lover antici-
pates that his well-being will be enhanced by that engagement.

In its relation to worth of the object, love as attachment is different.
Sometimes attachment is grounded in recognition of the non-bestowed
worth of some aspect of the thing loved; often it is not. The stuffed animal that my friend is showing me is ugly, so ugly that it would be hard to
find a stuffed animal more ugly. It wins the sweepstakes for ugliness. Yet
his child—call him Nathan—loves it. Nathan may himself recognize that
his animal would win no beauty contest among stuffed animals; he may
acknowledge that lots of others are "nicer." But this is the one he loves,
not any of those. This is the one he is attached to; this is the one he is
bonded with.

Love as benevolence is different again. When one is attached to something whose well-being one can enhance, the attachment is almost always
accompanied by benevolence. And sometimes benevolence is evoked by
love as attraction. One believes that the attractiveness of the person loved
will be preserved or enhanced by one's benevolence. But whether benevolence is ever, all by itself, grounded in recognition of the worth of some
aspects of the thing loved, seems doubtful to me.

Love as attraction recognizes and is drawn to worth; it does not, as
such, enhance worth. You are strongly attracted to the music of George
Crumb. How does that add to the worth of the music? Depending on
what I think of your musical taste, I may resolve, given your love of
Crumb's music, to start listening to it. But your attraction to it adds nothing to its worth.

Love as benevolence obviously does enhance worth, at least if it is successful. But the enhancement does not consist simply in the person's
being an object of benevolence; it consists in some alteration in her or
her life that the lover causes. Her life is going better because she now
has adequate food. But having adequate food would make her life better
no matter how that came about, whether by benevolence or in some
other way. Being an object of benevolence is not, as such, an enhancement of worth.

In short, if love bestows worth, it has to be love as attachment that does
this. But does it? Does attachment do this? Well, change the example
that we used above. Rather than supposing that the queen appoints
someone as her ambassador, let us suppose that she befriends someone
in her realm, becomes attached to her. This quite clearly bestows a certain worth on the one befriended. She is now honored and envied in
ways that she was not before. The source of the envy may be the tangible
favors that the queen bestows on her friend. But the queen may not
bestow any such favors. Nonetheless, others will be envious; they regard
the mere status of being a friend of the queen as enviable.

It may well be that situations arise in which honoring the queen's friend counts as honoring the queen, and situations in which demeaning the queen's friend counts as demeaning the queen. But the envy of others will not be confined to envying her for having that curious sort of instrumental worth; they are likely to be relieved that they themselves do not have that sort of worth. The worth bestowed by the queen's friendship is not like the worth bestowed on some artifact by its being a relic of some important person; it is like that bestowed by her choice of someone as ambassador.

From these reflections I conclude that if God loves a human being with the love of attachment, that love bestows great worth on that human being; other creatures, if they knew about that love, would be envious. And I conclude that if God loves, in the mode of attachment, each and every human being equally and permanently, then natural human rights inhere in the worth bestowed on human beings by that love. Natural human rights are what respect for that worth requires.

What Has Not Been Argued

My argument has been hypothetical. I have articulated a theistic grounding of human rights, arguing that if God loves, in the mode of attachment, each and every human being equally and permanently, then natural human rights are grounded in that love; they inhere in the bestowed worth that supervenes on being thus loved. I have not argued that God does in fact so love every creature who bears the *imago dei*. I have argued that a grounding of natural human rights is available to the person who holds the theistic convictions indicated. I have not argued for those theistic convictions themselves. The reader will have discerned, however, that I do in fact hold those convictions.

It is especially at this point in our discussion that we are confronted with what I called, in the Preface, the *Anselmian* character of present-day analytic philosophy. I described it like this:

> Seldom anymore does the analytic philosopher assume that
> he is obligated *qua* philosopher to rationally ground what he
> says in certitudes. . . . The philosopher, approaching the
> practice of philosophy from his life in the everyday, finds
> himself believing many things, both large and small. Perhaps
> he finds himself believing in physicalism. He then regards the
> challenge facing him as a philosopher not to be that of dis-
> carding all those convictions unless he can rationally ground
> them in certitudes; the challenge facing him is that of work-
> ing out the nature and implications of his physicalist convic-

tions in various areas of thought, doing so in such a way as to cope not only with the complications that arise in his own mind but with the objections lodged against his line of thought by others. In principle these objections might prove so powerful that he gives up his physicalism.

In place of the old foundationalist picture, the picture of the academic enterprise now being taken for granted by philosophers in the analytic tradition is what I call *dialogic pluralism.*

As I indicated in the Preface, I myself engage in the practice of philosophy as a Christian. That remained in the background for large stretches of my discussion; here, in our discussion of natural human rights, it has come into the foreground.

The following should be added: if one believes that there are natural inherent human rights, then the fact that the secularist cannot account for those rights, whereas the theist who holds the convictions about God's love that I have delineated can do so, is an argument for theism (of that sort). Not a foundationalist argument, but an argument nonetheless. I believe that there are natural human rights. Human beings, all of them, are irreducibly precious.

BACK TO THE NARRATIVE

In the narrative of those who see the idea of natural rights as born of individualistic and atomistic modes of thought and being at home only in such company, alien on that account to Christianity, the UN Universal Declaration of Human Rights was the final folly, the price paid for the sins of our fathers. My narrative has been the opposite. Not only inherent natural rights but inherent natural *human* rights were implicitly recognized in the moral vision of the writers of the Hebrew and Christian Scriptures, as they were by the Church Fathers; in the writings of the canon lawyers of the twelfth century they were finally not only recognized but given explicit conceptualization.

The general recognition of such rights remained an exceedingly slow and halting process, however, until, quite surprisingly, it burst forth after the horrors of World War II in the UN Declaration. That same moral vision of Scripture in which inherent natural human rights first gained recognition can now be used as a resource for articulating a grounding of such rights. The resources of other religions can be employed as well, those of Judaism, obviously, perhaps those of Islam. But it seems unlikely that any secular attempt at grounding will be successful. In my final chapter I reflect briefly on what this means for our life together.

Chapter Seventeen

APPLICATIONS AND IMPLICATIONS

FIVE TOPICS OCCUPY our attention in this penultimate chapter. In developing my account of rights, I have focused exclusively on persons and human beings. Rather often, however, I have reminded the reader that social entities such as groups and organizations also have rights. It is time to consider how our account applies to the rights of such entities.[1] Second, we must consider the implications of our theory for the question of whether or not additional sorts of entities have rights. Third, in the course of my discussion I have remarked that not only should one not treat persons and human beings with under-respect; one should not treat anything whatsoever as though it had less worth than it does have. It is time to consider the status of that principle. Fourth, I complete the argument of chapter 12 by showing why the account of the nature of obligation that my theory yields is to be preferred to social requirement accounts. And last, I pick up a topic that has been hovering in the wings for a long time now: how do duties of charity fit into the account I have developed? Our discussion of each of these topics must be brief and sketchy; I do no more than give an indication of the main lineaments of an adequate treatment.

THE AGENCY OF SOCIAL ENTITIES

A right, so I have argued, is a legitimate claim to some good in the life or subsequent history of the right-bearer. The good in question is always, at bottom, the good of being treated a certain way. So a (two-party) right against someone is a legitimate claim against that person to their doing or refraining from doing something with respect to oneself. Rights are normative social relationships.

---

[1] I think that such entities as universities, banks, and states are more naturally called *institutions* than *organizations*. But in the writings of sociologists one finds the word "institution" used in quite a different way—in such expressions as "the institution of the family." I do not include *the family* (whatever that may be) among what I call *social entities*. So I will call universities, banks, states, and the like *organizations*. I do wish to include particular families among social entities; they are distinct examples of what I call *groups*.

What accounts for the fact that one has a right against someone to their treating one a certain way is that failure on their part to do so would be for them to treat one in a way that does not fit one's worth. It would fit only something of less worth. Violating an entity's rights may or may not impair the worth of that entity, may or may not *degrade* it. What it necessarily does is *demean* it. Hitler's snub of Jesse Owens in the 1936 Olympics demeaned him.

It follows from the account I have developed that the concept of rights applies only to entities that have or had lives. The concept of rights interrelates entities, on the one hand, with their lives and histories, on the other, by appealing to the fact that sometimes to deprive an entity of a life- or history-good is to treat that entity itself as if it were of less worth than it is.

But social entities are not alive; they are not living organisms. Hence there is no such thing as a state or event in the life of such an entity—so it would appear. But if there is no such thing as a state or event in its life, then there is no such thing as a good in its life. And if there is no such thing as a good in its life, then my general account of rights does not hold for the rights of social entities. Something has to give.

The way out is to do what I announced in chapter 6 that I would eventually do, namely, expand the ordinary concept of life in a certain way. To see how and where that expansion must take place, we must first get clear on some aspects of the ontology of social entities.

I assume that there are such entities. I am well aware of the fact that philosophers of a nominalist cast of mind contest that assumption. They would concede that in our life in the everyday we talk as if there were such entities; we talk as if we refer to them, talk as if we predicate things about them, and the like. But they would insist that, strictly speaking, there are no such entities; when we appear to be talking about them we are really talking about something else. Here is not the place to defend my assumption against the nominalist skeptic. I will be content if the nominalist concedes that, in the points I make, I am getting at something that is indeed the case, though not getting at them in the way the nominalist would want to get at them.

Bank of America recently decided to close its branch nearest to where I live; it sent around a letter announcing this and giving its reasons for doing so. At roughly the same time, Yale University announced that it had decided to change its scholarship program so that, for students coming from poor families, those families would no longer have to make any contribution to the room, board, and tuition of the student; it too made a public statement in which it announced this change in policy and gave its reasons. The point can be generalized: social entities are capable of agency; they have the capacity to do things. In particular they have the capacity to do things for reasons; they are capable of rational agency.[2]

Their agency is accomplished in a curious way, however. The only way a social entity can act is by way of human persons doing certain things; they cannot act on their own. Their agency is always ontologically dependent on the agency of human persons; it is never basic.

The structure of this agency-dependence is different for organizations from what it is for groups. Organizations are incapable of causal agency; their agency is confined to "count-agency." That is to say, the only sort of action they can perform is that which occurs when someone or something performs some action that *counts as* the organization doing something.[3] The only way Bank of America can decide to close its branch office for certain reasons is by someone or something performing some action that *counts as* the bank's deciding to close its branch office for such and such reasons. More specifically, though there may be a chain of such doings, if we follow the chain to its end we will always arrive at some action that some human *person* brought about *causally*. The president of the bank causally brings about his signature on a sheet of paper; that counts as his doing something that in turn counts as the bank's deciding to close its branch office. It follows that, if we set aside those cases in which one action by an institution counts as another action by an institution, the agency of institutions is always *counted-as* agency, never *counting-as* agency.

In my book *Divine Discourse*, I called the phenomenon of one agent's doing something that *counts as* another agent's doing something *double agency*. The agents I had in mind were persons, for example, an ambassador's saying something that counts as his head of state issuing a certain declaration. The double agency that organizations present to us is differ-

---

[2] An especially interesting example of the difficulties faced by those who deny that "the personification of the state" has any ontological basis but who still find it indispensable to ascribe rights and duties to the state is chapter 9 of E. H. Carr's *The Twenty Years' Crisis: 1919–1939* (San Francisco: HarperCollins, 1964). "To deny personality to the state," he says, "is just as absurd as to assert it. The personality of the state is not a fact whose truth or falsehood is a matter for argument. . . . It is a necessary fiction or hypothesis—an indispensable tool devised by the human mind for dealing with the structure of a developed society. . . . Political development necessitated the fiction of the corporate responsibility of the state" (148–49). Carr offers no theory of fiction to explain how it is that the ascription of duties and rights to fictional entities can play the role outside of fiction, in law and ordinary thought, that his account requires.

[3] If we are thinking in terms of J. L. Austin's categories of locutionary, illocutionary, and perlocutionary acts, then, given that institutions and organizations are capable of performing illocutionary acts, they are also capable of performing perlocutionary acts. And Austin thinks of perlocutionary acts as causally generated. This, then, would be an exception to what is said above.

ent in that, though one member of the duality is always (ultimately) a person, the other member is not.

Groups are different from institutions in that they are capable of causal agency. No doubt sometimes when we appear to attribute some action to a group, what we are really doing is attributing that action to some or all members of the group. "The group shouted its approval," we say. What we mean is that member A shouted his approval, member B shouted her approval, and so forth. This is not true for all cases, however, of appearing to attribute some action to a group; sometimes we mean to do what we appear to be doing, namely, attribute the action to the group as such. Suppose that the members of some street gang come upon an object too heavy for any one of them to lift by himself but that they together lift and proceed to use as a battering ram to break down doors. Member A of the gang did not lift the object, member B did not lift the object, and so forth; the *group* lifted it.

To summarize: groups and organizations are capable of agency, in particular, of *rational* agency. Mudslides do things. But mudslides are not capable of rational agency, not capable of doing something for a reason. More specifically yet: groups and organizations are capable of acting and prizing for the reason that the prospective action is thought to be good, just, or obligatory.

Without now filling in all the intervening steps, I conclude that social entities can be accountable for honoring and violating rights; they are, for that reason, subject to moral appraisal. We all take this for granted in our lives in the everyday. We take for granted that states can and do wrong people, that business corporations can and do, that colleges and universities can and do, that gangs can and do. We take for granted that one people (nation) can wrong another by driving it from its homeland, depriving it of its own state, refusing to let its members use their native tongue. Within the realm of justice, groups and organizations function as agents; they can and do wrong people.

Consider the story that a historian might tell of Yale University in the twentieth century. Such a story would be fundamentally different from, say, a story of Lake Michigan in the twentieth century. In a story of Lake Michigan, the only agency attributed to the lake would be causal agency; the lake is incapable of any other sort of agency. In the historian's story of Yale, he would tell of what Yale did by way of counted-as agency. He would tell of the speech actions Yale performed, that is, the illocutionary actions it performed, and of its reasons for performing the ones it did. And subtly or not so subtly he would submit those actions to moral evaluation. He would treat Yale as a moral agent. Until the 1950s, Yale denied admission to almost all applicants that it suspected of being Jewish, while trying to avoid stating in public that that was what it was doing.[4] Those actions were good or bad, just or unjust, right or wrong. The point is that social entities are strikingly like human persons in that they function as agents in the order of justice.

What we have not yet shown, however, is that they themselves have rights, that they can be wronged, that they can function as patients in the order of justice. That is what we assumed all along, however. So let us turn to that.

An Expanded Concept of Life

Given the theory of rights that I have developed, the central issue to be considered here is whether social entities have lives. Human persons are living organisms capable of rational agency. Social entities confront us with the curious phenomenon of entities capable of rational agency that are not living organisms. Shall we say that such entities do not have lives, on the ground that they are not living organisms? Or shall we say that they do have lives, on the ground that they are capable of rational moral agency? If we say they do not have lives, we will have to go back through the preceding chapters and revise them to take account of the fact that the goods to which some entities have rights are not life-goods.

The issue is an issue of how to speak, not of the facts of the matter. That does not imply that the choice is arbitrary. To speak one way is to highlight one set of similarities and differences; to speak the other way is to highlight a different set of similarities and differences.

Let us take a step back to gain a wider perspective. An ineradicable component in my account of rights is the claim that God has rights. That claim, in conjunction with the claim that the goods to which one has rights are goods in one's life or history, implies that God has a life. I think most of us would say that if God does exist and is as the Hebrew and Christian Scriptures represent God as being, and as the main Christian theological tradition represents God as being, then God does have a life, on the ordinary concept of *life*—this in spite of the fact that God is not a living organism and, on the view of many of the main theologians, is outside time. Boethius, for example, famously defined eternity as "the simultaneously whole and perfect possession of interminable life"; and he attributed eternity, thus understood, to God. Aquinas, among many others, accepted this definition (*S. Th.* I, q. 10). In short, there is a long

---

[4] The story is told excellently in Dan A. Oren, *Joining the Club: A History of Jews and Yale* (New Haven: Yale University Press, 2000). Oren's book is full of examples of the attribution of rational agency to Yale University.

tradition of using the term "life" to cover more than biological life, more than the life of organisms.

It is not clear to me whether those who traditionally used the word "life" in this expanded sense thought the capacity for rational agency was sufficient for ascribing life to something. Possibly, they thought that to have a life, an entity must be a center of consciousness if it is not an organism, and of course social entities are not centers of consciousness.

So shall we or shall we not say that social entities have lives? Shall we speak of the life of the Jewish people, the life of Yale University, and the like? In fact, we all do rather often speak this way. It could be argued that in doing so we are using the ordinary concept of *life* metaphorically, not literally. Be that as it may, I propose using the term so that it covers social entities. Thereby we highlight the affinity of social entities to rational agents that are living organisms and downplay their affinity to things like mountains and valleys that they resemble in not being alive.

So let it be agreed that social entities have lives. Are there also goods and evils in their lives? Is there such a thing as the well-being of organizations and groups? If not, then even though they have lives, they do not have rights. In our lives in the everyday we all do talk as if there are goods and evils in the lives of social entities. We speak of certain developments as good or bad for the university, we speak of tribes and indigenous nations as flourishing or not flourishing. I conclude that our account of rights holds, as it stands, for the rights of social entities.

How Social Entities Acquire Rights

What remains is to say a bit about the way in which social entities acquire rights. Begin with the rights involved in voluntary organizations. Suppose that the local chess club has the right to levy annual dues on its members, that the officers of the club have the right to determine whether or not such a levy will be imposed and, if so, its size, and that every member has the right to an equal share in any proceeds generated by activities that the club sponsors. The first two of these are permission-rights coupled with freedom claim-rights, the last is a benefit claim-right. The first is a right of the organization, the latter two are rights of individuals. All three are standing rights. There are no specific rights, and no correlative specific obligations, until the club actually does impose a levy by way of its officers actually deciding that one shall be imposed, and until the club actually does sponsor activities that generate proceeds. Until then, there are no other rights than the standing rights. These standing rights, in each case, have been socially conferred; they are not natural rights. How did that conferral take place?

It took place by the members of the club taking onto themselves the obligations correlative to these rights: the obligation to allow the club to levy annual dues, the obligation to allow the officers to determine those dues, and the obligation to share the proceeds of club-sponsored activities equally with fellow members. The members may have taken these obligations onto themselves by making an informal agreement with each other. Alternatively, they may have gone to the trouble of setting up an organization with by-laws that, among other things, specified the rights mentioned. By becoming a member, one then agrees, tacitly or explicitly, to live up to the by-laws.

With whom did a new member make that agreement? With both the organization and its members. If one fails to live up to the obligations one has taken onto oneself in becoming a member, one wrongs both the organization and one's fellow members. Both have a right against one to one's living up to the obligations one has taken onto oneself.

In short, voluntary organizations acquire rights by social conferral; and the conferral is accomplished, at bottom, by members of the organization generating in themselves the obligation to do so-and-so. They do this by performing the speech-act of promising or agreeing to do that. The rights are, at bottom, speech-generated rights. My analysis is essentially an elaboration of John Locke's analysis of how rights get conferred onto and within voluntary organizations.

Not all organizations are voluntary organizations of members; banks and universities are not. Rights are not socially conferred on them by the promises, pledges, or agreements of their members. They are conferred on them by legislation or social practice, the latter being the functional equivalent of legislation. The state issues a body of banking legislation, that legislation consisting, at bottom, of mandates and promises that the state issues to various individual and social parties within the state. It is those mandates and promises that confer rights on the bank; they generate the rights of the bank.

It should be noted that a good many of the rights of organizations generated by mandates issued by the state are only third-party quasi-rights. The state issues a well-formed mandate to various parties to treat banks in certain ways. Thereby the state generates in itself a right against those parties to their treating banks thus; it generates in those parties an obligation toward the state to treat banks thus; and it generates in banks a third-party quasi-right to be treated thus by those parties. Not all rights of organizations that are generated by the state are third-party quasi-rights, however; the state can promise Bank of America to do something.

The Place of Other Entities in the Order
of Rights and Obligations

Because works of art, for example, have no lives, either in the strict or the extended sense of "a life," they have no rights. At most they have third-party quasi-rights. Someone may have a right against me to my treating some work of art a certain way; but then it is that person who has the right against me, not the work of art. Nonetheless, if works of art have worth, we have obligations toward them. If that worth is purely instrumental to the worth of human lives, then it comes to nothing more than whatever be the worth of the life-states and life-events that the works bring about; and our obligations toward the works of art are, accordingly, entirely absorbed into whatever be our obligations toward human beings and their lives. Whether one judges that works of art do or do not have non-instrumental worth will depend, in good measure, on one's account of aesthetic value. The points just made for works of art also hold, *mutatis mutandis*, for other human artifacts and for such entities as swamps, streams, or mountains.

If the worth of such entities is indeed not purely instrumental to divine and human flourishing, then here at this point obligations outrun rights. There will be ways that I am obligated to treat such entities even though they have no rights against me to my treating them that way; I do not wrong them if I fail to treat them as I ought to treat them. Duties without correlative rights. The principle of correlatives that I announced already in the Introduction remains in force, however. That principle was this: if Y belongs to the sort of entity that can have rights, then X has a right against Y to Y's doing A if and only if Y has an obligation toward X to do A.[5]

The situation for at least some animals and plants is different. Because all animals and plants have lives, and because there are goods and evils in the lives of at least some of them, the structure of our account leads us to say that they have rights—assuming that their worth is not purely instrumental to human life-goods. Anyone who holds, as I am inclined to hold, that non-instrumental worth is determined ultimately by some relation that things bear to the supremely excellent being, God, will be attracted to the view that the worth of living things (and of the natural world generally) is not purely instrumental to human life-goods. If so, then not only can animals be treated lovingly, affectionately, thought-

---

[5] Though our duties toward inanimate objects that do not have rights against us is not an exception to our principle of correlatives, it is an exception to the strong Hohfeld thesis discussed in chapter 11.

fully, cruelly, brutally, reverentially, wantonly, and so forth; they can be treated justly and unjustly. Arguing the point would require not only delving into the precise way in which the worth of natural entities is related to God, but also engaging the recent literature on animal rights. Space prevents our doing that.

Most adherents of one or another of the Abrahamic religions will want to say something more about the rights of animals and plants. They will want to say that God has issued injunctions to you and me concerning our treatment of the animals and plants, and of the natural world generally. The natural world thus has third-party quasi-rights to how it is treated. You and I have obligations toward God as to how we treat the natural world, correlative to those obligations being God's rights against us to how we treat the natural world; thereby the natural world has third-party quasi-rights to how it is treated by us.

Though plants may participate as patients in the realm of justice, obviously they do not participate as agents. They are incapable of moral agency, that is, incapable of acting and prizing under the aspect of the good, the just, and the obligatory. Hence they cannot be accountable for either honoring or violating rights. They can injure people but they cannot wrong them. If animals are likewise incapable of moral agency, as I think they are, then they too cannot participate as agents in the realm of justice.

If animals have rights, then they can be wronged. The role that being wronged plays in their lives is only a pale imitation, however, of the role it plays in the lives of persons. If animals cannot prize under the aspect of the good, the just, and the obligatory, then they cannot apprehend that they have been wronged—injured, yes, but not wronged. And so they cannot be angry in response to believing that they have been wronged. Further, they cannot perform the (illocutionary) action of claiming their rights; you and I must do that on their behalf.

THE UR-PRINCIPLE

From our discussion of rights there emerged a fundamental principle of action: one should never treat persons or human beings as if they had less worth than they do have; one should never treat them with under-respect, never demean them. Once this principle is formulated and held up for attention, it occurs to us that it is but an application of the more general principle that one should never treat *anything whatsoever* as of less worth than it is. All along we have tacitly been employing, as an application of that general principle in addition to the one just mentioned about persons and human beings, that one should never treat life- and history-goods as of less worth than they are.

Now recall a passage from chapter 6: "Good things, even things that excel in goodness, are all about us. There are excellent sunsets, excellent baseball games, excellent philosophy papers, excellent prayers, excellent meals, excellent automobiles, excellent musical works, excellent mutual investment funds, excellent specimens of the dachshund, excellent specimens of the white oak." Add the assumption that though the worth of some of these entities may be entirely instrumental to the worth of human lives and histories, that is not true for all of them; some have worth that is not instrumental to that or anything else. Then the application of the fundamental principle of action, that one should never treat anything as of less worth than it is, goes well beyond persons, human beings, and their life- and history-goods. Whatever be the worth, say, of an ostrich, one should not treat it as if it had less worth than it does have. If it has non-instrumental worth, one should treat it accordingly.

What is the force of the "should" in the *Ur*-principle that one should never treat anything as of less worth than it is? Start with its force in the case of persons and human beings. I should never treat Harriet as befits someone of less worth than her worth. The force of the "should" is the force of obligation—full-cognition (objective) obligation, let us recall, not culpability (subjective) obligation. I am obligated not to treat Harriet as if she had less worth than she does have. If I do treat her as of less worth, then I have failed in my obligation toward her and she has been deprived of a right by me. Assuming my failure is not traceable to non-culpable ignorance on my part, I am guilty, culpable, blameworthy.

I see no reason to suppose that the force of the "should" changes when we move from application of the *Ur*-principle to persons and human beings to application of the principle to animals, plants, works of art, wetlands, life-goods, history-goods, and the like. Why would it change? In each case the principle says exactly the same thing: one should not treat something as if it had less worth than it does have.

Inherent in the concept of obligation is the idea of requiredness: if one is obligated to do something, then it is not just a good thing to do but it is required of one that one do it. A theory of obligation must give an adequate account of that requiredness. I suggest that the requiredness constitutive of obligation is what respect for worth requires.[6] If respect for your worth requires that I treat you in such-and-such a way, then I have an obligation toward you to treat you that way.

---

[6] I thus disagree with G.E.M. Anscombe's thesis, in her well-known essay "Modern Moral Philosophy" (*Philosophy* 33 [1958]), that the concept of obligation is intrinsically connected with the idea of someone issuing legislation.

And in general, for anything whatsoever, one is *obligated* not to treat it as of less worth than it is. The *Ur*-principle that emerged from our discussion is a principle of obligation. It is, in fact, the *fundamental* principle of obligation. The fundamental principle, be it noted once again, of *full-cognition* obligation. If one non-culpably believes that something is of less worth than it is, then, if one treats it in accord with what one believes to be its worth, one is not blameworthy even though one fails in one's (full-cognition) obligation and wrongs it.

The *Ur*-principle that we are never to treat anything as of less worth than it is must be understood as having the status of a universal generalization over specific obligations. I am not to treat A as of less worth than it is, you are not to treat B as of less worth than it is, and so forth, for all persons and all entities. If we were to understand the *Ur*-principle not as a universal generalization over specific obligations, these being grounded in what due respect for the worth of A, B, C, and so forth requires, but as a principle ontologically prior in the moral realm to specific obligations, with those being derived from that prior principle by the application of the principle to the case at hand, then not only would we owe ourselves and our readers an explanation of where that principle comes from, but at the end of the day we would have slid out of the inherent rights conception of justice into the right order conception.

Though the "should" of the *Ur*-principle does not change its sense or force depending on the sort of entity to which it is applied, there is good reason for singling out for special attention the application of the principle to persons and human beings, and for calling the obligations that pertain to such entities *moral* obligations. *Moral* obligations will be those *toward* a person or human being, *moral* rights will be those *of* a person or human being.[7] The reason for singling out moral obligations and rights from obligations and rights generally is, of course, the fact that persons and human beings have a worth far superior to that of anything else.

In my analysis of commands and promises in chapter 12, I appealed to the existence of *standing* rights and *standing* obligations—standing *moral* rights and standing *moral* obligations. Commanding someone to do X generates in him a moral obligation to do X only if one has a standing (permission) right to command an action of this sort of such a person in such a situation. If one does have such a right, then, for such commands of that sort as one may issue to such persons in such situations, one also has a standing (claim) right to their obedience, and they have a standing obligation to render obedience. This appeal to standing moral rights and obligations became directly relevant when we analyzed and appraised the divine command theory of obligation.

---

[7] On this usage, social entities have moral obligations but not moral rights.

In chapter 12 I did not offer an account of standing rights and obligations; I simply appealed to their existence in the course of my argument. It is now clear how, on my theory, they are to be accounted for. Standing rights and obligations are natural rights and obligations; and rights and obligations, in general, are constituted of what respect for worth requires.

WHY SOCIAL REQUIREMENT ACCOUNTS OF OBLIGATION DO NOT WORK

Suppose we call the account of the nature of obligation that I have just now offered the *respect* account. I know of only one other account of the nature of obligation that, to my mind, has any plausibility, namely, the theistic version of the *social requirement* type of account.

In chapter 12 I mentioned that those who embrace a social requirement account of obligation would find my main argument against the divine command theory misguided. The reason they would find it misguided is that their account of the nature of obligation leads them to understand the workings of commands and promises differently from how I understand them; I was tacitly employing the respect account in my understanding of their workings.

My main argument in chapter 12 was the one mentioned just above: though valid commands create in their addressees the moral obligation to do the thing commanded when previously that was not obligatory, such creation cannot occur *ex nihilo*. It can occur only in the context of moral rights and obligations already there—*standing* moral rights and *standing* moral obligations. Social requirement accounts of obligation purport to offer an *ex nihilo* account of the generation of moral obligations. In a situation where previously there were no moral obligations, and thus also no moral rights, now, if a person of a certain sort performs an action of a certain sort, a moral obligation comes into being.

Prominent among the actions cited by social requirement theorists as bringing moral obligations into existence are the issuing of valid commands—but only if the commands and the commander have certain excellences. The social requirement theorist shares my view that all valid commands generate obligations. But he insists that the obligations they generate as such are not *moral* obligations but *pre*-moral *linguistic* obligations.[8] Only when the commands and the commander possess the appropriate excellences do the commands generate *moral* obligations. But those excellences are then sufficient for the commands to generate

---

[8] Adams, *Finite and Infinite Goods*, 243–44 and 266–67.

moral obligations; there need be no standing moral obligations and
standing moral rights.

Now that we have the respect account of the nature of obligation before us, I can complete the argument of chapter 12 by showing why social
requirement accounts of the nature of moral obligation are untenable.
I will take as "canonical" Robert Adams's articulation and defense of
the social requirement theory, in chapters 10 and 11 of his *Finite and
Infinite Goods*.

Those who favor the respect account of the nature of obligation and
those who favor a social requirement account agree that at the heart of
the concept of obligation is a concept of requiredness. The core of the
disagreement between these two accounts lies in how they understand
that requiredness. Social requirement theorists say the requiredness consists of *someone requiring* the action. Within the realm of good things that
I could do, what differentiates those that are obligatory for me from
those that are not is that some suitably excellent agent requires the former of me in a suitably excellent way; their being obligatory *consists in*
their being required of me by that agent in that way. "According to social
theories of the nature of obligation," says Adams, "having an obligation
to do something consists in being required (in a certain way, under certain circumstances or conditions), by another person or a group of persons, to do it" (242).

It is important to be clear on what is meant by someone *requiring* some
action of me. What is meant is that I am placed under pressure by that
person to do it. Perhaps he threatens to blame me should I not do it,
and actually does blame me if I do not do it. Perhaps he threatens to
inflict punishment on me should I not do it, and actually does inflict
punishment on me if I go ahead and do not do it. Or if I am attached
or attracted to him, perhaps he makes clear to me that I would disappoint
him if I do not do it. The term "require," used in this context, has to
be shorn of every suggestion of something's being required *because* it is
obligatory, or *as* obligatory. The idea is that something is obligatory because it is required, not the other way around. Because "require" is sometimes used as a near-synonym of "obligatory," I shall rather often avoid
the term and speak instead of *pressuring* or of *applying pressure*. In his
defense of the social requirement theory, in *Finite and Infinite Goods*,
Adams every now and then also uses the term "pressure" in this way.

My own pre-theoretical intuition is that someone's requiring something of me is just a different phenomenon from its being obligatory for
me to do it. That intuition is supported by the theory articulated in the
preceding pages. Human beings have worth. Respect for their worth requires that they be treated in certain ways. Those ways of being treated
are what they have a right to. Correlative to those rights are obligations.

Hence obligations are also grounded in what respect for worth requires. Nowhere in this line of thought is anything said about somebody requiring something of someone. I regard the difficulties faced by social requirement accounts of obligation as indirect confirmation of this line of thought and of the intuition that it supports.

As with any attempt to develop an account of the nature of obligation, one enters the project of developing a social requirement account with reflective judgments as to which sorts of things are obligatory and which are not. In the course of developing one's account one might be led to alter those initial judgments a bit; but if one enters the project unwilling to make, or incapable of making, any judgments whatsoever as to what is obligatory and what is not, one cannot proceed.[9]

The great challenge facing the social requirement theorist is to locate, for each person, the relevant requirer and the relevant modes of requiring. The minimum criterion for the acceptability of any proposal on this score is that, for any person X, the proposed person or group require of X in the relevant way all and only what is obligatory for X. The theory has to do more than satisfy that minimum criterion, however. The fact that the requirings of some requirer satisfy this minimum criterion might be due, in principle, to the fact that the requirer discerns what is antecedently obligatory for X and resolves to require all and only that of X. So the theorist must somehow show us that something's being obligatory for X *just is* for it to be required of X in this way by this requirer—with the consequence that it is impossible for this requirer to discern what is antecedently obligatory for X, because nothing is antecedently obligatory.[10]

---

[9] Cf. ibid., 246.

[10] John Stuart Mill is sometimes cited as a social requirement theorist; I think it not at all clear that he was. The relevant passage is the following:

> We do not call anything wrong unless we mean to imply that a person ought to be punished in some way or other for doing it—if not by law, by the opinion of his fellow creatures; if not by opinion, by the reproaches of his own conscience. . . . It is a part of the notion of duty in every one of its forms that a person may rightfully be compelled to fulfil it. Duty is a thing which may be exacted from a person, as one exacts a debt. . . .
> There are other things, which we wish that people should do, which we like or admire them for doing, perhaps dislike or despise them for not doing, but yet admit that they are not bound to do; it is not a case of moral obligation, we do not blame them, that is, we do not think that they are proper objects of punishment. (*Utilitarianism*, chapter 5; pp. 47–48 in Hackett edition, Chicago, 1979)

Note what Mill says: a person "may rightfully be compelled" to fulfill his duty, he "ought to be punished in some way" if he does not do it; those who do not do what they are obligated to do are "proper objects of punishment." Mill does not say that what *makes* something obligatory for one is that someone or other pressures one to do it. What he suggests instead is that its being obligatory makes pressure *appropriate, proper, obligatory.* Everything Mill says could be accepted by someone who rejects all social requirement accounts.

It takes no more than brief reflection to see that no human person or group of persons fills the bill for any of us. For each of us there is nobody who pressures us to do only what is obligatory, and no person or group of persons who pressures us to do all that is obligatory. An obvious way to reduce the seriousness of this problem is to declare that only certain modes of pressuring are constitutive of obligation. Most social require-ment theorists declare or assume *commanding* to be, if not the only rele-vant mode of pressuring, certainly the most important. This reduces the seriousness of the problem but does not eliminate it. Though for some of us there may be nobody who commands us to do anything that is not obligatory, each of us is such that there is no person or group of persons who commands that we do everything that is obligatory.

Before we move on, let me call attention to a problem for the social requirement theorist of a less general sort. Sometimes it would be *wrong* to pressure a person to do what is obligatory. Elizabeth ought indeed to do so-and-so. But Elizabeth is psychologically fragile, so much so that it would be wrong for anyone to put any sort of pressure on her to do what she ought to do. Acts of pressuring people to do things are them-selves subject to moral evaluation; and the example makes clear that the moral quality of one's act of pressuring someone to do something may diverge from the moral quality of the act that one pressures them to do. The former may be morally impermissible, while the latter is morally obligatory. The social-requirement theorist has no special difficulty in handling cases in which the *wrong* kind of pressure is applied to get someone to do what we recognize to be obligatory; he will appeal to the existence of some social requirement against applying pressure of that sort. Cases of the sort I have described—cases in which it is wrong to apply *any* pressure on a person to do what she ought to do—are a chal-lenge for him.

The person attracted to the idea that the requirement that is ingredi-ent within obligation consists of *someone requiring* the action in question has two options at this point. He can take the counterfactual route. He can figure out what excellences someone would have to have, and what excellences his requirings would have to have, for his requirings to be constitutive of obligation; and he can then propose that some act is oblig-atory for X if and only if, should an idealized person of that sort exist, that idealized person would pressure X in the relevant way to perform that act. The alternative is the theistic route. One can try to show that God does in fact pressure us to do all and only what is obligatory—and that the excellences of God and of his ways of pressuring us are such that God's pressuring us to do something *makes* it obligatory. The ancestry of theistic requirement theories goes back at least to John Locke's *Essay Concerning Human Understanding*.[11]

Robert Adams, in *Finite and Infinite Goods*, rejects the counterfactual option, for reasons that seem cogent to me, and develops a theistic version of the social requirement account. Let me not rehearse his reasons for rejecting the counterfactual option but turn, instead, to the theistic requirement account.[12]

In the course of his discussion of social requirement theories in general, Adams enunciates a number of criteria for an acceptable account of the nature of obligation. Among the most important are that an account of obligation must be compatible with the fact that there are things that would be good to do but are not obligatory, and must allow for the possibility of supererogatory actions, actions that are better than any that are obligatory, and even for the possibility of some action being the morally best thing to do and yet not obligatory.

> There are things that would be good to do that we don't have to do. I think there are even things it would be best to do (indeed, morally best to do) that we don't have to do; actions that are better than we have to do are *supererogatory*. It is controversial whether any action is supererogatory in this sense, but supererogation is at least conceptually possible. Someone who says something would be morally best but one isn't morally *required* to do it may be making a substantive ethical mistake, but surely need not be manifesting a deficiency of linguistic understanding or an aberration of linguistic usage. This is one way in which the concept of the obligatory marks off a potentially smaller territory than that of the good. (232)

I share with Adams the conviction that the criteria enunciated are conditions for the acceptability of a proposed account of the nature of obligation. My argument will be that a theistic requirement account cannot be developed in such a way as to meet the criteria.

Adams holds that the mode of requirement constitutive of obligation is commanding; God's commanding that something be done is what makes it obligatory. His reason for preferring a divine command theory to the divine will theory favored by some theorists is that the latter eliminates the possibility of acts of supererogation: "The important possibility

---

[11] See *Essay Concerning Human Understanding* I, iii, 12–13, and II, xxviii. 8. In my *John Locke and the Ethics of Belief* (Cambridge: Cambridge University Press, 1996), I called Locke's theory of obligation a divine command theory. I now think that it is instead a divine requirement theory.

[12] His reasons for rejecting the counterfactual option are to be found on p. 246.

for theistic ethics here is the possibility of supererogation. It should be possible for God to decide not to require us to do everything that God would prefer that we do, thus leaving some of the preferred actions supererogatory rather than required. It is controversial within theistic religious traditions whether God in fact has left anything supererogatory; but I think it is no virtue in a theistic metaethics to rule out supererogation as impossible by the very nature of obligation" (260).

But let us recall that requiring something of some person is to be understood throughout as bringing pressure to bear upon that person to do that thing. After noting that Locke appears to limit God's modes of bringing pressure to bear upon us to God's attaching sanctions to certain actions, Adams observes that "I can hardly claim that this is wholly wrongheaded, inasmuch as my underlying social theory of obligation . . . makes the possibility of someone being offended, and the appropriateness of sanctions, in the event of nonfulfillment, a central feature of the nature of obligation." Adams goes on to say, however, that he himself "would particularly stress reasons for compliance that arise from a social bond or relationship with God. As in the case of human social bonds, the force of these reasons depends on the value of the relationship, which theistic devotion will rate very high indeed. If God is our creator, if God loves us, if God gives us all the good that we enjoy, those are clearly reasons to prize God's friendship" (252).

This all seems to me correct. But if so, then surely our relationship to God pressures us to do not just what God commands but anything that God wills. If I prize God's friendship, then, if I come to believe that not doing X would disappoint God, I will feel pressured to do it whether or not God commanded it. Whether I would disobey God by not doing X will have relatively little significance for me; the important question is whether my not doing X would disappoint God. Or perhaps not even that is the important question. If there are things that would please God if I did them but not disappoint God if I did not, then the important question for the person who prizes God's friendship is whether, by doing X, he would please God. God and his relationship to God will pressure him to do whatever he believes will please God, and to avoid doing anything that would disappoint God. But if being thus pressured by God and one's relationship to God is constitutive of the obligatory, then obviously supererogatory actions are impossible. The actions that our initial intuitions told us to be supererogatory prove, on this account, to be one and all obligatory.

Adams observes, in retrospect, that he has "stressed the connection of moral obligation with the possibility of *guilt*, and the connection of guilt with rupture or straining of valued relationships. It is obvious that in theistic traditions guilt has been powerfully connected with rupture or straining of our relationship with God. A divine command theory of the nature of obligation facilitates the understanding of moral guilt as involving offense against a person" (257). But I submit that a divine command theory married to a social requirement theory is a very problematic union. What rationale is there for singling out commands from all the other ways that God and our relationship to God put us under pressure to do things, and declaring that it is commands, and not any of those other modes of pressure, that are constitutive of obligation? I see no such rationale, nor does Adams offer any. He himself remarks that the demand constitutive of obligation "need not take the form of an explicit command or legislation; it may be an expectation more subtly communicated" (246).

Another problem comes to light when we look at the theistic requirement theory from a somewhat different angle. Suppose that I pressure one of my children to practice piano for an hour. I view practicing piano as a good in his life, he thinks it is an evil; so I apply pressure. If he is a very sensitive child, my making clear to him that he will disappoint me if he does not practice will suffice. But if he is like most children, that will not do the trick; some sanction is required. So I tell him that if he does not practice for an hour, he will not be allowed to play with his friends.

Do I, by applying either of these forms of pressure, make practicing piano morally obligatory for him? Not so far as I can see. Given my own view of how commands work, as opposed to how the social requirement theorists think they work, I would have made it morally obligatory had I *commanded* him to practice piano. But if all I do is apply pressure in one or the other of the two ways mentioned, I do not make it morally obligatory. I simply alter the prospective balance of life-goods and life-evils in my child's life, doing so in such a way that he himself now thinks the balance has been significantly altered. I was always of the view that practicing piano would be a good in his life; he thought it was an evil. But now I apply pressure by packaging together practicing piano with the life-good of his not disappointing me, or with the life-good of his playing with his friends. That package proves attractive to him; but it does not make practicing piano morally obligatory. Nothing changes if yet more life-goods are packaged together with practicing piano. The package becomes ever more admirable and attractive; but practicing piano does not become obligatory somewhere along the line. The rabbit of moral obligation cannot be pulled out of a hat that contains nothing but life-goods.

I fail to see that the situation is any different when it is God and our relationship to God that put us under pressure to do certain things. The good act of my helping the blind person across the street now comes bundled together with the life-good of my pleasing God by helping her. That puts me under great pressure to do this good deed; helping her is now bundled together with the great life-good of pleasing God. But how does that make it morally obligatory that I help her? Why does attaching to this good deed a life-good that I find supremely attractive and motivating make the good deed morally obligatory? God has excellences in abundance that I, a parent trying to get my child to practice piano, lack. Does that change things? How?

Adams remarks in one place that "close kin to the views that would collapse the notion of the morally obligatory into that of the morally best are those that would collapse it into the notion of what we have most reason (from a moral point of view) to do" (238). His reaction to such views is that "there is a large difference between doing something irrational and doing something morally wrong. . . . The concept of moral obligation is not there just to tell us about balances of moral reasons, but rather to express something more urgent" (238). I submit that when we look closely at what goes on when someone pressures someone to do something, we see that it consists entirely of introducing additional life-goods as reasons to act a certain way.

Might it be that Adams was mistaken on this last point? As the theist sees things, there is no greater life-good than pleasing God. Not only is this life-good greater than any other; it *trumps* all others, in the sense that no matter how many other life-goods one might bring about by doing what does not please God, the good of pleasing God outweighs all of those together. It is true that one does not make something obligatory merely by piling on reasons for doing it; to get obligation, something of a different order has to be introduced. But pleasing God is of a different order. Though it is one life-good among others, it stands out from all others in that it trumps all others. That trumping function is the new thing that brings forth obligations out of life-goods. Is this what Adams should have said?

Well, it is true that this is a life-good that trumps all others. But if it is the supreme worth of doing what pleases God that makes an action obligatory, then we are confronted once again with the first problem: supererogatory actions have become impossible. In short, the theistic requirement theorist is confronted by the following dilemma: to leave room for supererogatory actions he has to pay the price of arbitrarily declaring that only some of the ways in which our relation to God places pressure upon us are constitutive of obligation; to avoid such arbitrariness he has to pay the price of leaving no room for supererogatory actions.

I have said nothing thus far about the excellences that God must possess if God's requiring something of us is to be constitutive of obligation. An obvious excellence is that God must love us, must seek our well-being; the requirements of a malevolent divinity would not be constitutive of obligations. Another is that God's love must be just; the requirements of an unjust deity would not be constitutive of obligation. If God's love took the form of classical utilitarianism, seeking to maximize the overall quantity of well-being with no consideration for whose well-being it was, God's love would yield injustice and God's requirements would not be constitutive of obligation.

So far as I can see, however, the theistic requirement theory leaves its adherent with no way of specifying justice as among the requisite excellences of God. By virtue of the principle of correlatives, if God treats us justly by honoring our rights, then God treats us as God ought to treat us. But the theistic requirement theorist views obligation as constituted of the appropriately excellent requirements of an appropriately excellent God, and views rights and justice as the correlatives of those obligations. It is not open to him to say that justice is among the excellences of God. Adams recognizes the problem, and says that the theistic requirement theorist will have to employ what he calls a "thin theory" of justice (254). What that thin theory might be, he does not say.

A closely related problem for the theistic requirement account is the following. Judaism, Christianity, and Islam present God as promising and covenanting with human beings, thereby taking onto himself obligations toward those to whom God made the promise and those with whom God made the covenant. An implication of the theistic requirement account is, presumably, that God's taking an obligation onto himself is constituted of God's applying pressure to himself to do the thing promised. I submit that this is untenable.

If there were tendencies within God not to keep his promises, one could, I suppose, imagine God applying pressure to himself to do the thing promised. God might resolve to feel regret should he not do the thing promised, might authorize you and me to complain, and so forth. But there are no such tendencies in God. An unspoken assumption of social requirement theories is that obligations are for those who lack what Kant called a "holy will." Therein lies the point of pressuring people to do things; absent the pressure, they would be less likely to do them. But God's will is a "holy will." The theistic requirement account of the nature of obligation cannot give a plausible rendering of God's taking obligations onto himself by making covenants with human beings and by promising them to do certain things.

Have Duties Rather than Rights Become Basic?

Let us return to what I called the *Ur*-principle: one should never treat anything whatsoever as of less worth than it is. If this is indeed the *Ur*-principle of our theory, does it not follow, when all is said and done, that we have grounded rights in duties? Is that not the ironic upshot of the fact that the fundamental principle of action is a principle of obligation?

That is not the upshot. It appears to be the upshot only because the *Ur*-principle states things from the side of the agent; the principle is a principle of action. Given the fact that we have obligations toward things that do not have rights, obligations are indeed more *general* than rights. But neither from that nor from anything else does it follow that rights have been grounded in obligations.

Consider anything that has a life. For such an entity there is the phenomenon of some person or social entity depriving it of some life-good and thereby treating it with under-respect. Whenever that happens, the person or social entity so acting violates its obligations, and the entity so acted on is deprived of its rights. The two are correlatives of each other; neither grounds the other. Both are grounded in the worth of the entity and in what that worth requires by way of action and restraint from action on the part of persons and social entities.

Here is another objection. Let it be conceded that the *Ur*-principle does not ground rights in duties. But is the principle not an indication of the fact that rights have played a disappearing role in our discussion? For all my talk about rights, is it not an implication of my account that there is no need to talk about rights, that everything that is to be said about rights can be said in the language of obligation?

Not at all. If X has violated his obligation toward Y to treat him in a certain way, then it follows that Y has been deprived of his right against X to be treated that way. But the fact that the former implies the latter does not mean that, in stating the former, one has already stated everything that one states in stating the latter. Recall the analogy offered in the Introduction: if a triangle is equilateral, then necessarily it is also equiangular. But to say that the triangle is equiangular is not to state what has already been stated by saying that it is equilateral.

In the Introduction I defended the thesis that the moral order has two distinct dimensions, the agent-dimension and the patient- or recipient-dimension. Though intimately connected, these are distinct dimensions. My being wronged by you is not the same as your being guilty of failing in your obligations toward me. Absolution, if there is such a thing, may rid you of your guilt; it leaves me in exactly the same moral condition that I was in before your absolution took place. I was wronged and I remain wronged. In using the language of rights, we bring to speech the patient- or recipient-dimension of the moral order. In using the language of obligation, we bring to speech the agent-dimension. We cannot bring to speech the recipient-dimension if we have only the language of obligation available to us.

DUTIES OF CHARITY

It appears that our theory commits us to denying the existence of duties of charity, paradigmatic of such duties being the duty to forgive. A malefactor does not have a right against his victim to being forgiven by the victim. The victim would not wrong the malefactor if, instead of forgiving him, he subjected him to anger, blame, and appropriate hard treatment. It appears to follow that there can be no duty to forgive and, more generally, no duties of charity—a duty of charity being a duty to treat someone a certain way when that person does not have a right against one to one's treating him that way. Conversely, if there are duties of charity, our principle of correlatives must be qualified if not rejected— so it would seem.

The apostle Peter was disturbed by the open-endedness of the instruction to forgive that Jesus had issued to his disciples. So one day he posed to Jesus the *reductio ad absurdum* question, "Lord, if another member of the church sins against me, how often should I forgive him? As many as seven times?" Jesus first gave a hyperbolic answer: "not seven times but . . . seventy-seven times." Then he told the parable about the king who, out of mercy, forgave the large debt owed him by one of his servants who, in turn, mercilessly refused to forgive the much smaller debt owed him by one of his fellow servants. Hearing about this, the king summoned the former servant and said to him, " 'You wicked slave! I forgave you all that debt because you pleaded with me. Should you not have had mercy on your fellow slave, as I had mercy on you?' And in anger his lord handed him over to be tortured until he would pay his entire debt." The lesson Jesus draws is this: "So my heavenly Father will also do to every one of you, if you do not forgive your brother or sister from your heart."[13]

There are various ways of interpreting the force of Jesus' instruction to forgive. That last sentence, all by itself, makes it sound as if he is giving prudential advice on how to please God. But notice that Jesus does not call the unforgiving servant imprudent, he calls him *wicked*; and notice that the point of the whole passage is that we are to imitate God in forgiving. A more plausible interpretation is that Jesus is commending an ideal. Yet more plausible, to my mind, is that he is commanding his disciples to forgive, and thereby generating in them the obligation to do so. In Luke 6:37–38, Jesus also speaks about forgiveness; and here the language is unmistakably the language of commanding. "Do not judge," he says, "do not condemn," "forgive." Forgiving the wrongdoer is a duty. But how

---

[13] The parable occurs in Matthew 18: 21–35. The language about torture must surely also be understood as hyperbolic.

can it be a duty of the disciples to forgive those who wrong them when the wrongdoers have no right against their victims to be forgiven?

The solution to the puzzle is right in front of us. The duty to forgive, when one has such a duty, is a third-party duty. When someone validly commands me to forgive someone who has wronged me, it is not the malefactor but the one issuing the command who has a right against me to my forgiving the malefactor; correspondingly, my duty to forgive is not a duty toward the malefactor but a duty toward the one who validly commanded me to forgive. Neither before nor after the command does the malefactor have a right against me to my forgiveness; neither before nor after do I have a duty toward him to forgive him. On the assumption that Jesus was speaking on behalf of God, it is toward God that his disciples have a duty to forgive those who wrong them, not toward those who wrong them. And it is God who has a right against them, not the malefactors, to their forgiving the malefactors. I suggest that duties of charity in general are third-party duties. Our principle of correlatives remains unscathed. Moral obligations do not outrun rights.[14]

---

[14] Matthew H. Kramer, in "Rights without Trimmings," offers some suggestions as to how a secularist might understand duties of charity. "If we suppose that there is indeed a general duty of charitableness, there are numerous candidates for the role of holding the correlative right. People who belong to the major faiths can attribute the right to God, whereas humanists can attribute it to our overall species. Someone less prone to flights of fancy can ascribe the right to each person's community, broadly or narrowly defined. No matter where exactly we locate the right, we certainly can locate it *somewhere* without strain." In Kramer et al., *A Debate over Rights*, p. 25, n. 11. I leave it to the reader to decide whether it really is as easy as Kramer suggests it is for the humanist to find a holder for the right correlative to a *general* duty of charitableness.

CONCLUDING REFLECTIONS

Our Moral Subculture of Rights

A moral subculture of rights has emerged in the West and elsewhere over the past two millennia. I call it a *sub*-culture because rights constitute only a part of our moral culture as a whole; most of us do not think about morality solely in terms of rights, and most of us do not act as we do only because justice requires it.

Not everybody in the modern world accepts and employs our subculture of rights. Classical utilitarians do not; one's choice of what to do is to be guided solely by estimates of life-goods to be achieved. Those Christians who are agapists do not; we are always and only to act out of gratuitous benevolence and generosity. And from the following passages it is easy to infer what Karl Marx thought about rights: "None of the so-called rights of man goes beyond egoistic man, man as he is in civil society, namely, an individual withdrawn behind his private interests and whims and separated from the community."[1] "Freedom is the right to do and perform what does not harm others. . . . The freedom in question is that of a man treated as an isolated monad and withdrawn into himself. . . . The right of man to property is the right to enjoy his possessions and dispose of the same arbitrarily, without regard for other men, independently from society, the right of selfishness."[2]

The most dramatic expression of our moral subculture of rights has been the emergence of the human rights movement over the past fifty years; not far behind was the emergence in the eighteenth century of liberal democracy on a foundation of natural rights. These are only two among many highlights, however: the gain over the last century in women's rights, in children's rights, in the rights of labor—these are all signal achievements, as was the American civil rights movement and the movement to give Jews their rightful place in the American academy.

Let me pull together some of the main themes of our discussion by briefly describing what I regard as the heart of our moral subculture of rights. A right, so I have insisted, is a normative social relation-

---

[1] "The Jewish Question," in David McLellan, *Karl Marx: Selected Writings* (Oxford: Oxford University Press, 1977), p. 54.

[2] Ibid., p. 53.

ship; specifically, a right is a legitimate claim to the good of being treated a certain way by persons and by those social entities capable of rational action.

If we come across some operative law or social practice according to which someone is to be treated a certain way regardless of the life-goods that might be achieved by not treating her thus, then she has a *right* to the good of being so treated—a legal right, or a social-practice right. For her to have a right to the good of being so treated is for that good to trump other goods; having a right to that good carries peremptory force with respect to all those goods to which no one has a right.

Moral rights are like the rights enshrined in law and social practice in that they have trumping force; they are peremptory. But if that were the end of the matter, we would not yet have a *moral* subculture of rights. On account of having available to us a *moral* subculture of rights, we can ask, about some legislation or social practice that confers rights, not only whether it brings about such-and-such life-goods but whether its conferral of rights honors the rights of members of society; sometimes it is even possible to argue that the rights of the members of society *require* the legislation or practice. So too, when someone violates the law or practice, we can ask not only what life-goods were achieved or lost by this violation but whether someone's rights were thereby dishonored; was the violation, for example, a breach of one's right not to have one's trust betrayed?

In all such cases, we are appealing to a framework of justice that lies behind or above the rights conferred by legislation or social practice; we are appealing to a system of rights by reference to which those laws and social practices that confer rights can themselves be evaluated and by reference to which our departures from those laws and practices can be evaluated. Such rights are *natural* rights.

Natural rights, so I have argued, are grounded in the worth of entities. A person has a right to my treating her a certain way just in case my failure to do so would amount to treating her with under-respect. It is at this point that *being wronged* enters the picture. To treat someone with under-respect is to wrong her. It is not just to fail to grant trumping force to some good to which she has a right. It is to wrong her. To wrong her is to alter her moral condition as patient, or recipient, in the moral order. The conceptuality and language of natural rights enables us to bring to thought and speech the patient dimension of the moral order; therein lie their indispensable importance.

Someone might suggest that natural rights, so understood, are so different from legally and socially conferred rights that it is misleading to call both of them "rights." I think not. Natural rights resemble legally and socially conferred rights in that they have peremptory force. What a natural right adds to peremptory force is the fact that to dishonor a natural right is to wrong someone; it is on account of that "addition" that we are able to employ natural rights for an appraisal of what transpires in society, including, then, an appraisal of the presence or absence of laws and social practices conferring rights. That "addition" makes natural rights highly distinctive. Yet natural rights are like legally and socially conferred rights not only in that they are peremptory but in that they all fit the ancient formula: a person's rights are what is due him or her.

Defending Our Moral Subculture of Rights

I observed in the Introduction that our moral subculture of rights is commonly charged with expressing and abetting an ethos of possessive individualism; the passages just quoted from Marx are a good example of the charge. It is said that the language of rights and, in particular, the language of natural rights is a language made to order for the person preoccupied with his own possessions and entitlements. The conceptuality and terminology of natural rights emerged, so the story goes, from individualistic frames of thought and has no home outside such frames of thought. To combat the malign social influence of possessive individualism we must renounce this part of our moral culture. We should be talking about care and responsibility, not about rights.

Another line of attack comes from the opposite quarter. Rights-talk is charged with being used by social visionaries as a cloak for promoting their impossible ideals. The great social reform movements of the last century were all rights-based movements. If the social visionary can get us to believe that everybody has a right, say, to work that is fulfilling and well rewarded, then he has already achieved a significant rhetorical victory.

Our analysis of rights gives us the material for cogent answers to both charges. Start with the latter. A right is a legitimate claim to the good of being treated a certain way; but many are the good and desirable ways of being treated that we do not have a right to. Those life- and history-goods to which one has a right are only a subset of one's life- and history-goods generally. The third part of my discussion was devoted to offering an account of why it is that one has a right to the good of certain ways of being treated and not to others.

Our answer to the first charge took a more complex form, part systematic, part historical. If rights are legitimate claims to the good of being treated a certain way, then not only do I come into your presence bearing rights against you to how you treat me, but you come into my presence bearing rights against me to how I treat you. The situation is entirely symmetrical. Rights and the recognition of rights, including natural rights, has nothing to do with possessive individualism.

But how then do we account for the fact that the conceptuality and language of rights have acquired the reputation of expressing and abetting possessive individualism? My answer goes as follows. Distinguish between your having a right against me to my treating you a certain way and my *honoring* that right by treating you that way. So too, distinguish between my having a right against you to your treating me a certain way and my *claiming* that right by insisting that I be so treated. An ethos of possessive individualism distorts our ways of dealing with rights—not the rights themselves but our ways of dealing with them. Instead of being as sensitive to your rights as I am to my own, I stridently claim my own rights and ride rough-shod over yours. All moral language is susceptible to distortion: the language of love, the language of duty, the language of virtue—and the language of rights.

An ethos of possessive individualism employs the language of rights for its own purposes. But for the origin of the ethos we have to look elsewhere: to modern capitalism, to that understanding of liberal democracy that says that the governing idea of such a polity is that everyone is to be ensured equal freedom to act as he or she sees fit. And deeper: to the dark side of the human self, to the flaws that afflict all of us and always have, to our inveterate inclinations to pride and to self-preoccupation and to hardening our hearts to the plight of the other. We twist the culture of rights to our malign impulses.

ORIGINS OF THE SUBCULTURE

We all now take for granted our moral subculture of rights. We are oblivious to how extraordinary it is, how extraordinary it is that we would recognize human rights and person rights. We human beings are by nature tribalists. The fact that someone is a species-mate of mine is of no significance, nor is the fact that this species-mate of mine can think and feel and act as I do. It is the members of my tribe, my in-group, who are of worth and hence have rights.

What, then, accounts for the emergence of our moral subculture of rights? My argument has been that it has its origins not in fourteenth-century nominalism or seventeenth century political individualism but in the Hebrew and Christian Scriptures. The writers of the Hebrew and Christian Scriptures did not explicitly conceptualize natural rights; explicit conceptualization had to await the canon lawyers of the twelfth century. They did, however, *recognize* what you and I call "natural rights." They assumed that God, on account of God's worth, has a natural right to our praise and obedience.[3] They held that we human beings have violated that natural right of God; we have wronged God. They speak of God as angry on that account. But they go on to say that God is a forgiving God; God forgives those who have wronged God.

The recognition in the Hebrew Bible/Old Testament of *God's* natural rights is more firm than is the recognition of the natural rights of human beings. But the material for the recognition of the latter is present there, in the affirmation of human worth. In the New Testament this material begins to be regularly employed. Jesus says that we are to forgive those who wrong us just as God forgives those who wrong God; and he says that God treats us as he does because we are of worth.

An obvious question is whether our moral subculture of rights not only belongs to our Judaic and Christian heritage but has philosophical origins as well. I argued that it does not. Almost all of the ancient philosophers did their ethical thinking within the framework of eudaimonism. Our moral subculture of rights did not emerge, and could not have emerged, from eudaimonism. That I am to treat you a certain way because your worth requires it does not enter the purview of the eudaimonist. Only a moral framework that, in its account of practical reason, takes cognizance not only of the worth of life-states and life-events but of the worth of persons and human beings can yield an account of rights. Eudaimonism, along with utilitarianism and Christian agapism, fails that requirement.

An additional point is the following: the focus of the eudaimonist is entirely on action; how to live one's life well is the question that shapes all eudaimonist thought. From among candidates for ends in themselves in our structure of action we are each to make that selection that holds the greatest promise of making one's own life well lived. Insofar as the "passivity" of *being treated* a certain way is seen as having significance, that significance lies entirely in whether or not being so treated contributes instrumentally to living one's life well. That one might be *wronged* in being so treated does not enter the thought of the eudaimonist.

Our Narrative Raises an Unsettling Question

Our analysis and archeology of natural rights answers the charge that the idea of natural rights is inextricable from an ethos of possessive individualism. But the archeology raises an unsettling question of its own. Suppose the secularization thesis is true, that modernization leads to secularization. Suppose, in particular, that the framework of

---

[3] Psalm 96:8: "Ascribe to the Lord the glory due his name."

religious conviction that gave birth to our moral subculture of rights is destined, under conditions of modernity, to erode and be replaced by a variety of secular outlooks. What must we then expect to happen to that subculture?

Our moral subculture of rights has been contested by utilitarians and Marxists who deny the existence of natural rights. In the West, until now, they have usually lost that contest. Most of us acknowledge the existence of natural rights, most of us deplore the violation of natural human rights, and those of us who are theorists often cite, as an objection to utilitarianism and Marxism, that they cannot account for natural rights. But suppose the religious framework that gave rise to our moral subculture of rights gradually erodes. What must we then expect to happen to our moral subculture of rights if it is indeed, as I have argued, part of our religious heritage? What must we expect to happen given our human propensity to tribalism?

In principle some secular perspective could step into the breach, take the place of the eroded religious framework, and everything would remain substantially the same. The only secular framework that holds any promise in this regard is the Kantian framework, which holds that the dignity that grounds natural rights supervenes on our capacity to engage in rational action. I myself, were I developing the Kantian framework, would say that it supervenes on our capacity to act under the aspect (*ratio*) of the good, the just, and the obligatory.

I judge that the capacity for rational action does give considerable worth to those who possess it; the capacity for acting under the aspect of the good, the just, and the obligatory seems to me to give even greater worth. But a good many human beings do not possess these capacities and never will; Alzheimer's patients come immediately to mind, along with those human beings who are so impaired mentally that they are incapable of rational action. So once again our question: suppose that the religious heritage that gave birth to our moral subculture of rights erodes. Must we then expect that those human beings who lack the capacities mentioned, who cannot function as persons, will be endangered? Must we expect that our treatment of them will sooner or later be determined entirely by what best serves the life-goods of the rest of us, not by their right against us to our treating them in certain ways? I think we must.

Were the Kantian framework to replace our religious heritage—a most unlikely prospect!—I think we must expect a further unsettling consequence. The capacity for rational action comes in degrees; and among those who possess the capacity to the same degree, some exercise it better, some worse. If one holds that that capacity gives to those who possess it worth, then I think it would be utterly arbitrary not to hold that those who have more of the capacity and exercise it better are, so far forth, of greater worth, and those who have less of the capacity and/or exercise it worse are, so far forth, of lesser worth. So in a society founded on Kantian principles, where it is widely held that nothing else than rationality determines worth, I think we must expect that the less rational among us will be systematically demeaned. The fact that they are somewhat rational will imply that certain things should never be done to them; but beyond that, the spoils will go to the bright.

Richard Rorty, as we saw in chapter 14 thinks there is no reason to expect any erosion of our rights culture to take place even should our religious heritage be rejected, not even if no satisfactory philosophical framework turns up to take its place. He concedes my argument that our moral subculture of rights was bequeathed us as part of our religious heritage; the present-day secularist is living on inherited capital. But he thinks that that heritage always was confused and mistaken about what it was handing on to us. It claimed that it was handing on to us the recognition of *natural* rights, including the recognition of *natural human* rights. In fact, it was handing on to us no more than various social practices of rights-conferral. In one of the most infamous of Rorty's rather many infamous passages, he says that "when the secret police come, when the torturers violate the innocent, there is nothing to be said to them of the form 'There is something within you which you are betraying. Though you embody the practices of a totalitarian society which will endure forever, there is something beyond those practices which condemns you.' "[4] The clear implication is that there are no natural rights, hence no natural human rights.

Rorty's thought is that though our social practice of human rights emerged from the cradle of Judaism and Christianity, it is now so deeply entrenched into our lives that it can leave its cradle behind and stand on its own feet. Sufficient now for its preservation is

> the sort of long, sad, sentimental story which begins "Because this is what it is like to be in her situation—to be far from home, among strangers," or "Because she might become your daughter-in-law," or "Because her mother would grieve for her." Such stories, repeated and varied over the centuries, have induced us, the rich, safe, powerful people, to tolerate, and even to cherish, powerless people—people whose appearance or habits or beliefs at first seemed an insult to our own moral identity, our sense of the limits of permissible human variation.[5]

---

[4] *Consequences of Pragmatism* (Minneapolis: University of Minnesota Press, 1982), xlii.
[5] Rorty, "Human Rights, Rationality, and Sentimentality," pp. 133–34.

There is something indubitably correct about what Rorty says here. I have never met a human being in whom outrage over actual injustice was stirred up by philosophical essays or even, to any significant degree, by newspaper reports. Far more effective is seeing the faces and hearing the voices of the victims, whether live, on film, or in imaginative literature. *Uncle Tom's Cabin*, full of sentimentality, was far more effective in diminishing the violation of persons in the nineteenth century than was Kant's *Groundwork of the Metaphysic of Morals*.

But two questions come to mind. First, why does Rorty think it important to maintain and expand our social practice of conferring human rights on people? Clearly, he thinks it is important. But why? Obviously, not because in so doing we honor people's natural rights. And Rorty knows well that it is impossible to defend the practice on purely utilitarian grounds. So I suppose he would defend it on the ground that the practice gives expression to our moral sentiment of sympathy, and that that is all the defense it needs. Sympathy both motivates our adherence to the practice and is the rationale for it.

Let me forgo saying anything directly about the latter claim and address myself to the former. The Serbian soldiers were in the presence of the faces and voices of the Bosnian women whom they raped and killed; the Nazi guards were in the presence of the faces and voices of their Jewish victims; the atrocities narrated before the South African Truth and Reconciliation Commission were often face-to-face atrocities.[6] Yet sympathy was not evoked. Rorty talks of sympathy as if it were some insulated part of the self doing its work independently of "reason," executing an end-run around belief and conviction. Sympathy is not like that, not even if we take it to be what the eighteenth-century Scots writers called a "moral sentiment" rather than an emotion. The biblical writers who spoke of the "hardening of the heart" were more perceptive. In Jesus' parable, the priest, the Levite, and the Samaritan all saw the mugged man lying in the ditch along the road between Jericho and Jerusalem; only the Samaritan was "moved with pity."[7]

If a man believes that there is something about the woman in his clutches that makes her unworthy of better treatment, perhaps even makes her deserve everything he is doing to her, seeing her face and hearing her voice will ordinarily evoke no sympathy in him whatsoever. He is more likely to take pleasure in hearing her scream or to be enraged because she isn't taking what she's got coming to her. The affective side of the self cannot, all by itself, expand or even sustain human rights

---

[6] See Antjie Krog's *Country of My Skull: Guilt, Sorrow, and the Limits of Forgiveness in the New South Africa* (New York: Three Rivers, 2000).

[7] Luke 10:30–37.

culture. Conviction must also be engaged—conviction of the right sort, of course, conviction that this human being has great worth.

It is not hard, not hard at all, to come to see some among one's fellow human beings as having little if any worth. All one has to do is focus on their flaws. And flaws there will be; the misanthrope has lots to go on. It is also not hard, not hard at all, to manipulate someone into seeing some among his fellow human beings as having little if any worth; all you have to do is demean them, make them seem loathsome, by bringing their real or invented flaws into the light of public exposure and calling them lice, cockroaches, animals, scum, filth, dirt.

Our Judaic and Christian heritage neither denies nor overlooks the flaws of humankind; some strands in the heritage appear even to revel in them. But in the face of all the empirical evidence, it nonetheless declares that all of us have great and equal worth: the worth of being made in the image of God and of being loved redemptively by God. It adds that God holds us accountable for how we treat each other—and for how we treat God. It is this framework of conviction that gave rise to our moral subculture of rights. If this framework erodes, I think we must expect that our moral subculture of rights will also eventually erode and that we will slide back into our tribalisms.

Not only does the Kantian framework have the flaws already noted; I think it highly dubious that it could ever have the power over imagination and action that the religious framework has. It is one thing to treat with under-respect someone whose worth is that of being capable of rational action; it is something of quite a different order to treat God with under-respect. To wrong God is to wrong someone of vastly greater worth than that rational human being. Wronging comes in degrees; the greater the worth of the wronged, the worse the wronging.

Our moral subculture of rights is as frail as it is remarkable. If the secularization thesis proves true, we must expect that that subculture will have been a brief shining episode in the odyssey of human beings on earth.

A melancholy conclusion to our long, winding discussion—melancholy, that is, if one believes the secularization thesis, or if one lives in that part of the world, Western Europe, for which the thesis seems true. I do not believe the thesis.

GENERAL INDEX

Adams, Robert, 146–47, 231, 235–36,
    256n11, 277–81, 374–81
agape, Nygren's account of, 98–105
Alston, William P., x
Ambrose of Milan, 62
Anaxagoras, 174n41
Annas, Julia, 149n4, 151n5, 152n6, 152–55,
    163–65, 167n32
Anscombe, G.E.M., 371n6
Anselm, xi
Anselmian philosophy, xi, 360–61
apatheia, 158–59, 195
Aquinas, 13–14, 38–41, 178–79, 366
Arendt, Hannah, 189n13
Aristotle, 14, 135, 140, 149n2, 150, 151,
    154, 169–70, 171n38, 178
Arius, 152
Augustine, 144, 160n17, 162, 172,
    180–206, 209, 219–22
Austin, John, 364n2

Baier, Annette, 2
Barth, Karl, 344–45
Basil of Caesarea, 62
benevolence, 99–100
Boethius, 366
Bonaventure, 45n5, 47n6
boosting principle, 305–9
Bowlin, John, 39, 162n23, 167n32,
    171n38, 177
Brett, Annabel S., 58n22
Brewer, Tal, 102n6
Brown, Peter, 201
Brueggemann, Walter, 67, 77–78, 83n20
Burnaby, John, 198n13
Byers, Sarah C., 160n17

capacities approach to grounding human
    rights. *See* human rights
Carr, E. H., 364n2
Chrysostom, John, 60–62, 93
Church Fathers, 59–64
Cicero, 162
claim-rights, 25, 138, *See* also Hohfeld,
    W. W.; rights

Clarke, Samuel, 273–74
Clarke objection, the, 273–74
commands, analysis of, 268–71
compassion, in Augustine, 212, 192–200;
    in eudaimonism, 212–18
Cooper, John, 149n3, 170nn36, 37
corrective justice. *See* rectifying justice
counter-narrative, 53–64
counter-testimony, Israel's, 86
covenant, God's with Israel, 89
Cover, Robert, 51
Cuneo, Terence, xiv, 273n4
Cupit, Geoffrey, 259n12

desire, relation to enjoyment, 185–88
dialogic pluralism, xi
dikaios, translation of, 110–13
dikaiosunē, translation of, 110–13
Diognes Laertius, 157n11, 158n12, 161,
    162n21, 164, 165n28, 174
divine command theory of obligation.
    See obligations
divine fiat account of obligation.
    See obligations
Dole, Andrew, xii
Donahue, Charles, Jr., 58–59
Douglas, Mary, 90n25
duties. *See* obligations
Dworkin, Ronald, 16, 291n3, 333–34

Eberle, Chris, xiv, 135n1, 288n2
eirenéism, 225–26
emotion, Stoic theory of, 159–61
enjoyment, explanation of, 185–88;
    Augustine's doctrine of, 182–84
Enlightenment, contribution to recogni-
    tion of natural rights, 50–52
Epictetus, 215
eros, Nygren's account of, 99
eudaimonism, 149–79, 210, 214–18;
    Augustine's break with, 194–204;
    explanation of, 149–54, 219–22

Feinberg, Joel, 15n13, 254–55
Finnis, John, 227

INDEX OF SCRIPTURAL REFERENCES